T0275564

Immunological Bioinformatics

◯◉◉ Computational Molecular Biology

Sorin Istrail, Pavel Pevzner, and Michael Waterman, editors

Computational molecular biology is a new discipline, bringing together computational, statistical, experimental, and technological methods, which is energizing and dramatically accelerating the discovery of new technologies and tools for molecular biology. The MIT Press Series on Computational Molecular Biology is intended to provide a unique and effective venue for the rapid publication of monographs, textbooks, edited collections, reference works, and lecture notes of the highest quality.

Computational Molecular Biology: An Algorithmic Approach
Pavel A. Pevzner, 2000

Computational Methods for Modeling Biochemical Networks
James M. Bower and Hamid Bolouri, editors, 2001

Current Topics in Computational Molecular Biology
Tao Jiang, Ying Xu, and Michael Q. Zhang, editors, 2002

Gene Regulation and Metabolism: Postgenomic Computation Approaches
Julio Collado-Vides, editor, 2002

Microarrays for an Integrative Genomics
Isaac S. Kohane, Alvin Kho, and Atul J. Butte, 2002

Kernel Methods in Computational Biology
Bernhard Schölkopf, Koji Tsuda and Jean-Philippe Vert, editors, 2004

An Introduction to Bioinformatics Algorithms
Neil C. Jones and Pavel A. Pevzner, 2004

Immunological Bioinformatics
Ole Lund, Morten Nielsen, Claus Lundegaard, Can Keşmir and Søren Brunak, 2005

Ontologies for Bioinformatics
Kenneth Baclawski and Tianhua Niu, 2005

Immunological Bioinformatics

Ole Lund
Morten Nielsen
Claus Lundegaard
Can Keşmir
Søren Brunak

The MIT Press
Cambridge, Massachusetts
London, England

© 2005 Massachusetts Institute of Technology

All rights reserved. No part of this book may be reproduced in any form by any electronic or mechanical means (including photocopying, recording, or information storage and retrieval) without permission in writing from the publisher.

This book was set in Lucida by the authors.

Library of Congress Cataloging-in-Publication Data

Immunological bioinformatics / Ole Lund .. [et al.].
    p. cm. — (Computational molecular biology)
Includes bibliographical references and index.
ISBN 978-0-262-12280-1 (hc alk. paper), 978-0-262-55112-0 (pb)
1. Immunoinformatics. 2. Molecular biology—Computer simulation.
3. Immunology—Mathematical models. 4. Neural networks (Computer science). 5. Machine learning. 6. Bioinformatics. I. Lund, Ole. II. Series.
QR182.2.I46I465   2005
571.9'6'0285—dc22   2005042806

Contents

Preface   ix

1   **Immune Systems and Systems Biology**   **1**
    1.1   Innate and Adaptive Immunity in Vertebrates   10
    1.2   Antigen Processing and Presentation   11
    1.3   Individualized Immune Reactivity   14

2   **Contemporary Challenges to the Immune System**   **17**
    2.1   Infectious Diseases in the New Millennium   17
    2.2   Major Killers in the World   17
    2.3   Childhood Diseases   21
    2.4   Clustering of Infectious Disease Organisms   22
    2.5   Biodefense Targets   24
    2.6   Cancer   30
    2.7   Allergy   31
    2.8   Autoimmune Diseases   32

3   **Sequence Analysis in Immunology**   **35**
    3.1   Sequence Analysis   35
    3.2   Alignments   36
    3.3   Multiple Alignments   52
    3.4   DNA Alignments   54
    3.5   Molecular Evolution and Phylogeny   55
    3.6   Viral Evolution and Escape: Sequence Variation   57
    3.7   Prediction of Functional Features of Biological Sequences   61

4   **Methods Applied in Immunological Bioinformatics**   **69**
    4.1   Simple Motifs, Motifs and Matrices   69
    4.2   Information Carried by Immunogenic Sequences   72
    4.3   Sequence Weighting Methods   75
    4.4   Pseudocount Correction Methods   77

4.5   Weight on Pseudocount Correction   79
4.6   Position Specific Weighting   79
4.7   Gibbs Sampling   80
4.8   Hidden Markov Models   84
4.9   Artificial Neural Networks   91
4.10   Performance Measures for Prediction Methods   99
4.11   Clustering and Generation of Representative Sets   102

5 DNA Microarrays in Immunology   **103**
5.1   DNA Microarray Analysis   103
5.2   Clustering   106
5.3   Immunological Applications   108

6 Prediction of Cytotoxic T Cell (MHC Class I) Epitopes   **111**
6.1   Background and Historical Overview of Methods for Peptide MHC Binding Prediction   112
6.2   MHC Class I Epitope Binding Prediction Trained on Small Data Sets   114
6.3   Prediction of CTL Epitopes by Neural Network Methods   120
6.4   Summary of the Prediction Approach   133

7 Antigen Processing in the MHC Class I Pathway   **135**
7.1   The Proteasome   135
7.2   Evolution of the Immunosubunits   137
7.3   Specificity of the (Immuno)Proteasome   139
7.4   Predicting Proteasome Specificity   143
7.5   Comparison of Proteasomal Prediction Performance   147
7.6   Escape from Proteasomal Cleavage   149
7.7   Post-Proteasomal Processing of Epitopes   150
7.8   Predicting the Specificity of TAP   153
7.9   Proteasome and TAP Evolution   154

8 Prediction of Helper T Cell (MHC Class II) Epitopes   **157**
8.1   Prediction Methods   158
8.2   The Gibbs Sampler Method   159
8.3   Further Improvements of the Approach   172

9 Processing of MHC Class II Epitopes   **175**
9.1   Enzymes Involved in Generating MHC Class II Ligands   176
9.2   Selective Loading of Peptides to MHC Class II Molecules 179
9.3   Phylogenetic Analysis of the Lysosomal Proteases   180
9.4   Signs of the Specificities of Lysosomal Proteases on MHC Class II Epitopes   182

9.5   Predicting the Specificity of Lysosomal Enzymes   182

10 B Cell Epitopes   **187**
10.1   Affinity Maturation   188
10.2   Recognition of Antigen by B cells   191
10.3   Neutralizing Antibodies   201

11 Vaccine Design   **203**
11.1   Categories of Vaccines   204
11.2   Polytope Vaccine: Optimizing Plasmid Design   207
11.3   Therapeutic Vaccines   209
11.4   Vaccine Market   213

12 Web-Based Tools for Vaccine Design   **215**
12.1   Databases of MHC Ligands   215
12.2   Prediction Servers   217

13 MHC Polymorphism   **223**
13.1   What Causes MHC Polymorphism?   223
13.2   MHC Supertypes   225

14 Predicting Immunogenicity: An Integrative Approach   **243**
14.1   Combination of MHC and Proteasome Predictions   244
14.2   Independent Contributions from TAP and Proteasome
        Predictions   245
14.3   Combinations of MHC, TAP, and Proteasome Predictions   247
14.4   Validation on HIV Data Set   251
14.5   Perspectives on Data Integration   252

References   **254**

Index   **291**

Preface

The immune responses are extraordinarily complex, involving the dynamic interaction of a wide array of tissues, cells, and molecules. Immunology has traditionally been a qualitative science describing the cellular and molecular components of the immune system and their functions. The traditional approaches are by and large reductionist, avoiding complexity, but providing detailed knowledge of a single event, cell, or molecular entity. The sequencing of the human genome, in concert with emerging genomic and proteomic technologies, changed the way of studying the immune system drastically. The immunologists are now, maybe for the first time, aiming to provide a comprehensive description of the complex immunological processes. Generation of huge amounts of data made it clear that this goal cannot be achieved without using powerful computational approaches.

Wherever cellular life occurs, viruses are also found. The immune systems are evolved to defend the organism against these intruders. Since viruses evade or interfere with specific cellular pathways to escape immune responses, knowledge of viral genome sequences has helped, in some cases, fundamental understanding of host biology. Studying host-virus interactions at the level of single gene effects, however, fails to produce a global systems level understanding. This should now be achievable in the context of complete host and pathogen genome sequences. So again, understanding host-pathogen interactions calls for a close collaboration between microbiology and immunology at the systems-level.

Immunological bioinformatics is the research field that applies informatics techniques to generate a systems-level view of the immune system. The long-term goal of the research is to establish an *in silico* immune system. This may be done in a stepwise fashion where models are developed for the different components of the immune system. These models can be combined and may help to understand diseases, and develop therapies, vaccines, and diagnostic tools for treatment of major killers such as AIDS, malaria, and cancer.

The immune system does not react to entire pathogens but rather to short fragments (epitopes) of proteins from pathogens. A major branch of immuno-

logical bioinformatics is dedicated to identifying these immunogenic regions
in a broad sense. This book reviews the current state of the art of this branch
and other (related) immunological bioinformatics research.

Audience and Prerequisites

The book is aimed at both students and more advanced researchers with diverse backgrounds. We have tried to provide a succinct description of the
main biological concepts and problems for readers with a strong background
in mathematics, statistics, and computer science. Likewise, the book is tailored
to biologists and biochemists who will often know more about the biological
problems than the text explains, but need some help in understanding the new
data-driven algorithms in the context of biological data. It should in principle
provide enough insights while remaining sufficiently simple for the reader to
be able to implement the algorithms described, or adapt them to a particular
problem.

Content and General Outline of the Book

We have tried to write a book that is more or less self-contained. The bioinformatics methods are first explained in an intuitive way, and later we go into
more detail of the mathematics lying behind them. Only chapter 4 is dedicated to a detailed description of the basic methods. A significant portion
of the book is built on material taken from articles we have written over the
years, as well as from tutorials given at several conferences, including the
ISMB (Intelligent Systems for Molecular Biology) conferences, courses given at
the Technical University of Denmark and Utrecht University.

In each chapter we have tried to show the interesting biological insights
gained from the bioinformatics approach. This, we hope demonstrates how
and why bioinformatics can be used to understand the complexity of the immune system.

Chapter 1 provides an introduction to the challenges of understanding the
immune system from a systems biology perspective.

Chapter 2 contains an overview of the contemporary challenges to the immune system.

Chapter 3 shows how sequence analysis (multiple alignments, phylogenic
analysis, function prediction) can be used to address immunological
questions.

Chapter 4 explains the background for basic bioinformatics tools that are used in this book.

Chapter 5 is dedicated to DNA microarray data. We give a short review of the methods used to analyze such data, and using published examples, explain how these methods can be applied to basic and clinical immunology research.

Chapter 6 deals with Major histocompatibility complex (MHC) binding predictions. The rules that govern the binding of peptides to MHC class I molecules are quite well understood and have been used to design computerized prediction tools. In this chapter we give an introduction to the different methods available to predict MHC class I binding (matrices, artificial neural networks, or hidden Markov models), and outline under which circumstances one method is preferred to the others.

Chapter 7 describes the processing of MHC class I epitopes. Only approximately 20% of all short peptides are potential MHC ligands, because during degradation of proteins into smaller fragments many potential ligands are destroyed. Moreover, short peptides are selectively transported to the endoplasmic reticulum, where they can bind new MHC molecules. In this chapter, we present a detailed analysis of the enzymes that generate MHC binders from large proteins and the translocation of these peptides into the endoplasmic reticulum.

Chapter 8 contains a description of methods that can be used to predict binding of peptides to MHC class II molecules. Presentation of peptides by class II molecules is essential for generating an antibody response and activating macrophages to kill intracellular bacteria.

Chapter 9 describes epitope processing in the MHC class II pathway. In this pathway many different proteases break down antigens in lysosomes and endosomes to generate suitable peptides for MHC class II molecules. We review the known specificities of these enzymes, and perform a phylogenetic analysis of lysosomal proteases. The specificities of these enzymes show a great variety. Some are very specific, while others do not have any amino acid preference.

Chapter 10 describes how a B cell response is initiated and matured. We give special emphasis on recognition of antigens by B cells, and the methods to predict B cell epitopes. As B cells can recognize antigens in their native form, we also show how structural information of a protein can be used for the predictions.

Chapter 11 summarizes how different vaccines are designed and how computational methods are used to optimize these vaccines. Since the publication of the complete genome of a pathogenic bacterium in 1995, hundreds of bacterial pathogens have been sequenced and many new projects are currently underway. This development calls for use of advanced bioinformatics to screen for vaccine candidates.

Chapter 12 gives an overview of the bioinformatics tools and databases available on the Internet for immunology.

Chapter 13 focuses on MHC polymorphism. MHC genes are the most polymorphic genes described until now. In this chapter we first review the factors that cause this polymorphism. Then we introduce a new classification schema of MHC molecules based on their specificities and demonstrate how this classification can be used to understand immunological differences among individuals.

Chapter 14 explains how all the methods described in this book can be integrated to identify immunogenic regions in microorganisms, and host genomes.

Acknowledgments

We would like to thank all the people who have provided feedback on early versions of the manuscript, especially Pernille Haste Andersen, Tim Binnewies, Thomas Blicher, Sune Frankild, Anne Mølgaard, Henrik Bjørn Nielsen, Ludo Pagie, Stan Mareé, Anders Gorm Pedersen, and Jens Erik Pontoppidan Larsen, and all the members of the Center for Biological Sequence Analysis, who have been instrumental for this work over the years in many ways. The mathematical models reviewed in this book were developed in collaboration with many theoretical immunologists. Especially, we would like to thank Rob J. de Boer, José Borghans and Søren Buus for many years of collaboration in understanding different aspects of the immune systems.

Immunological Bioinformatics

Chapter 1

Immune Systems and Systems Biology

The major assignment of an immune system is to defend the host against infections, a task which clearly is essential to any organism. While surprisingly many other organismal traits may be linked to individual genes, immune systems have always been viewed as systems, in the sense that their genetic foundation is complex and based on a multitude of proteins in many pathways, which interact with each other to coordinate the defense against infection.

Full-scale computational models for the entire immune system are therefore also not going to be simple, but will rely on integration of many different components. However, many of these components may be much simpler models of how immune systems — step by step — deal with pathogenic organisms.

In the next decade, integrative approaches will form the basis for advanced, quantitative, and qualitative types of systems biology, in which simulation and modeling will be instrumental in understanding the complex dynamics of entire cells and their functional modules at the molecular level. Immune systems are likely to be high on this agenda. A large variety of experimental techniques are rapidly creating a sound scientific basis for systems biology, and many are capable of generating data at the levels of entire cells, tissues, organs, or organisms. The lists of parts of immune systems are getting more and more complete (although several unknown types of components presumably still await discovery), leading to a much more realistic scenario for the new wave of large-scale computational analysis of these systems. This contrasts with the situation a decade ago, when lack of experimental data prevented many data-driven bioinformatics approaches from being created.

Integrative approaches are also key to more conventional functional analysis of single macromolecules. Integrating data from different experimental domains can often lead to functional hypotheses, which in turn lead to much more efficient design and selection of the most relevant experimental assays in specific situations. As new genome-wide and proteome-wide tissue and disease-specific data continue to accumulate in the public domain, the experimental work needed to assign a function to a specific gene product will already have been performed more and more often.

Integrative biology is already an efficient route toward many scientific discoveries and will most likely become the most efficient route in the future. Integrating quantitative, experimental, and computational approaches will bring new knowledge, novel methods, and innovative technologies to engender improved understanding of immune systems and the processes enabling protection against invading pathogens.

Integrative approaches are based on experimental data and are closely linked to data-driven design of experimental strategies. The growth in the quantity of data enhances the role of integrative techniques. In a decade, it is reasonable to assume that

- the complete DNA sequence for any individual will be determinable at very low cost;

- representative high-resolution three-dimensional (3D) structures of all human proteins will become known, as will protein structures from a wide range of other organisms;

- quantitative information on interaction partners (protein, DNA, or other molecules) for most human proteins will be known;

- hundreds of diseases not caused by any one gene will be understood;

- the "individual gene" as a concept for understanding function and phenotype will have been replaced by systemic approaches at the level of dynamic interaction networks;

- models and simulation environments for subcomponents of higher organisms will exist, such as the immune system of an individual;

- the protein content of any tissue can be measured rapidly, including relative and absolute quantification of proteins and their post-translational modifications;

- most approvals of new drugs will require extensive analysis of response signatures and distinguishing the susceptibility of groups of users by computer simulation;

- words such as foldome, interactome, secretome, glycome, phosphopro-teome, regulome, systeome, vaccinome and, abstractome will appear in most standard textbooks.

This list is by no means complete! Rather, it illustrates what has been called the big bang in biology, in which almost every subfield is expanding from its present state, leading to a completely different, information-driven mode in biological and medical research.

In order to defend the organism the immune system must be able to constantly survey it and discriminate self from nonself, and subsequently act based on the result of the discriminatory process, for example by internalizing, killing, and degrading foreign microbes. While attacking the dangerous, i.e., nonself, the immune systems should be nonreactive to components representing self, in order to avoid autoimmune diseases. Both host defense and self/nonself discrimination seem to be achieved within several phyla by quite different mechanisms. However, many links between, for example, vertebrate and invertebrate immune systems have been found [Hoffmann et al., 1999]. The ancestral genes that gave rise to the most important components of the vertebrate immune systems seem to have existed already in invertebrates, although their function is not yet elucidated.

It is a very challenging task to understand how different immune systems function to achieve their goals. For many decades, the main focus of immunological research has been to study the mammalian immune systems (mainly human and mouse) in isolation. This research provides the basis for our understanding of the basic immune response today. However, still almost any experiment raises more questions than answers. The genomic era gives us the opportunity to tackle understanding of the immune system in a completely different way: the *comparative* approach. The comparison of many immune systems helps to put the immune systems of mammals in perspective and can provide remarkable counterpoints to what is already known. The comparative approach will also play an important role in creating immune system models for individuals. The immune systems have been designed for survival of the population, such that any one type of pathogen will not be able to bring down an entire species. Most vaccines are also designed to fight pathogens on a statistical basis, in the sense that they are not equally effective for all individuals in a population. Systems biology approaches addressed to model individual immune systems are likely to change this situation, leading to an optimal interaction between an individualized vaccine and the immune system of the individual.

The evolution of the immune systems has been influenced by several factors relating to pathogen strategies and to host organism life style. The first and probably most important factor is the strong selection pressure induced by the evolving pathogens. To survive and spread, every pathogen has to evade the host immune responses, potentially in novel ways. Any successful evasion puts additional selection pressure on the host to find ways of blocking evasion. Second, the life style of an organism (e.g., its lifetime) shapes its immune system. If an individual is vital to the species, e.g., in species with small progenies where it takes a long time to reach sexual maturity, it is much more beneficial to waste some cells within an organism than to waste the organism itself. That is the situation with warm-blooded vertebrates. Vertebrate immune systems provide rapid, specific, protective immune responses to infectious agents without causing severe destruction of the host itself. In addition, these immune systems can remember the exposure to a pathogen and thus they induce protection for the host and its offspring (via maternal feeding). This is possible by having a large repertoire of cells that can mount an immune response to almost any conceivable pathogen. At any time only a very tiny fraction of these cells are used, and many of them die without ever getting activated. At the other end of the spectrum, species with large progenies may not favor the selection of complex recognition systems requiring very advanced regulation mechanisms.

The diversity of pathogen genomes is enormous. The many genome projects continue to reveal big surprises. Figure 1.1 shows one of the most recent surprises — a genome atlas [Pedersen et al., 2000] of the newly discovered Mimivirus [Raoult et al., 2004] which has a genome size that is more than twice as large as the genomes of the simplest known prokaryotes, the archaeal parasite *Nanoarchaeum equitans* (0.49 Mbp) and the parasitic bacterium *Mycoplasma genitalium* (0.58 Mbp). It is well known that there is no strong (or easy-to-understand) relation between the complexity of higher organisms and the size of their genomes. In contrast, organisms like viruses and bacteria where the genome replication expense is a major selective factor have more compact genomes. In these smaller genomes most of the sequence is normally accounted for in terms of overall functionality, that is encoding protein, RNA or control regions of various kinds, even if the cellular role of individual genes may be unknown.

The Mimivirus described recently by Raoult et al. [2004] is a double stranded DNA virus growing in amoebae. It was isolated from amoebae growing in the water of a cooling tower of a hospital in Bradford, England. Physically, the capsid has a diameter of at last 400 nm — a virion size comparable to that of a small parasitic bacterium. The Mimivirus genome contains 1,262 putative open reading frames, many of which encode central protein-translation components, DNA repair pathways, topoisomerases and a number of protein categories not previously found in viruses. The number of genes is also more than twice as large as the gene content in the smallest known prokaryotes mentioned above.

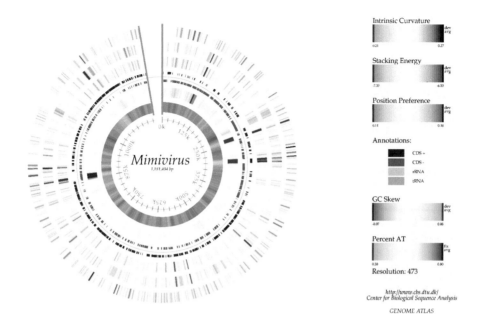

Figure 1.1: Structural atlas of the 1.2 megabase genome of Mimivirus — the currently largest known virus. The genome atlas shows the positions of the putative protein, rRNA and tRNA genes (third and forth circle), local biases in AT content and GC skew (first and second circle), as well as calculated structural features for the DNA double helix, including its intrinsic curvature (outermost circle), stacking energy levels (sixth circle), and nucleosome position preference (fifth circle), along the linear 1.2 Mbp genome. Figure courtesy of David Ussery. See plate 1 for color version.

The genome atlas shown in figure 1.1 indicates the positions of the putative genes (protein and RNA), local biases in nucleotide content, as well as calculated structural features for the DNA double helix, such as its intrinsic curvature and stacking energy levels along the linear 1.2 Mbp genome. From this whole genome view it is clear that several local regions with extreme GC skew may display significant structural properties, and consequently may impact the packing of the chromosome.

The size and highly diverse gene content of the Mimivirus challenge several of the criteria which normally have been used to define what a virus is. A common feature of viruses has been their total dependence on the host translation machinery for protein synthesis [Raoult et al., 2004]. However, the Mimivirus genome contains genes for all key steps of mRNA translation. This impacts the current understanding of viral evolution and may hence also eventually influence the scenarios for the general evolution of immune systems. The Mimivirus may originate from an ancestor which may have had an even more complete ability to synthesize protein, and may thus represent a class of viruses in existence long before the emergence of the three different domains of life. Presently, its genome is larger than at least 20 known cellular organisms from two domains, Archaea and Eubacteria. Most likely even more giant viruses may await discovery.

While all living organisms — and the subsystems responsible for their characteristics — are fundamentally based on genes and transcriptional regulation of gene expression, immune systems are protein-driven, both on the host recognition side, and in terms of the nonself constituents which are being recognized. Any kind of defense depends crucially upon selecting appropriate targets. Proteins are indeed one of the prime targets of the immune system. As carriers of structural and functional information, they are indispensable to all known forms of life. At the same time, their diversity is enormous, making them excellent targets for recognition and discrimination. In fact, one does not have to resort to intact proteins to be confronted with an impressive diversity: using the 20 naturally occurring amino acids, one can generate almost 10^{12} different 9mer peptides. Thus, even relatively short peptides carry sufficient information for accurate discrimination of self from nonself.

Protein-protein interactions and protein-peptide interactions are therefore key to the recognition processes and to the overall functionality of the molecular machines which drive the immune response, e.g., those involved in protein degradation. In terms of modeling and overall systems level understanding, proteome-wide knowledge of protein-protein interaction is therefore essential.

Experimental data on protein-protein interaction were previously a data type that was used more sporadically within bioinformatics as the information resided in scattered form in the scientific literature and not in databases. Due to novel high-throughput techniques interaction data are now produced in larger chunks, and for this reason they are accumulating in public databases and in nonpublic repositories within the commercial sector. Systematic screening of the literature by database teams have also converted in part the bulk of earlier work into data highly useful for modeling and systems analysis.

This makes it possible to produce protein-protein interaction networks, either large-scale, covering thousands of proteins, or more limited, including a small number of specific proteins known to be involved in a given process. Figure 1.2 shows how the amount of data within the largest public protein-protein interaction databases have developed over the last few years. Many of the interaction data sets stem from experiments in nonmammalian organisms, yet these data are extremely useful for modeling networks from the human

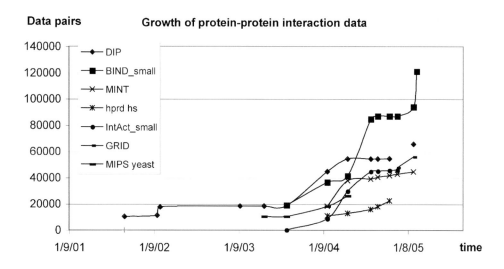

Figure 1.2: Protein-protein interaction data in the largest public databases collecting experimental evidence on the physical association between proteins, either direct pairwise interaction or as complexes. This type of data will for some time presumably not grow exponentially, as is the case for classic data types like nucleotide sequences (GenBank) or protein three-dimensional structures (PDB). The statistics in the figure is based on mere database content and does not take into account data redundancy, different ways of counting binary versus complex interactions, or data for which the underlying protein sequences may be hard to identify in other repositories. In some cases protein-DNA or protein-RNA interaction may also be included. It has been estimated that the protein-protein interaction databases as of 2004 include 3–10% of the actual number of interactions in the human proteome [Bork et al., 2004]. Such estimates are likely to be very rough as it is not presently known how many different proteins are produced from a given gene pool due to alternative pre-mRNA splicing, alternative translation starts, proteolytic degradation, and many other processes which affect the number of interacting protein agents. The human proteome may contain more than 1 million different proteins, which are produced from a genome with a gene pool that is two orders of magnitude lower. Figure courtesy of Olga Rigina.

proteome as a large number of fundamental protein-protein interactions are conserved.

It is not uncomplicated to take advantage of these data as they, like many other types of high-throughput data, are noisy and contain false positives (in addition to false negatives not showing up as direct errors). Part of the error source is purely experimental; another source is represented by data that are wrong in the biological context, where, e.g., two proteins which never are present in vivo at the same time or in the same compartment have been shown to interact, or participate, in the same complex. Irrespective of the organism, protein interactions seem to be organized in topologies with "small world net-work" structures. This means that most proteins have few partners, while only a small number have very many, typically forming a power distribution [Yook et al., 2004]. Obviously, protein interactions display considerable temporal di-versity, where some proteins form highly stable complexes, while others are involved in extremely transient ones. Recently, so-called hub proteins, which interact with many other proteins have been categorized into two categories based on their temporal nature [Han et al., 2004]. *Party* hub proteins and their interactors are expressed close in time, while *date* hub proteins interact with many different proteins at different times. This is, e.g., the case for cell–cycle regulated proteins, where histones will belong to the first category, while a promiscuous cyclin-dependent kinase like CDC28 will belong to the latter cat-egory [de Lichtenberg et al., 2005].

In the context of immune system–related protein-protein interaction net-works it is possible to pull out data from the interaction databases that can link known human immune system players to proteins of unknown function, often via search for orthologs and paralogs in other organisms. As an exam-ple, figure 1.3 shows interaction links found in these databases for Toll–like receptors, which are pattern recognition receptors mediating part of the in-nate immune system, "sensors" of the innate immune system. These receptors are present in plants, invertebrates, and vertebrates and represent a primi-tive host defense mechanism against bacteria, fungi, and viruses [Beutler and Rietschel, 2003]. The figure shows interactions for the interleukin-1 receptor-associated kinase 1 protein, an important adapter in the signaling complex of the Toll/interleukin-1 receptor family. In this case a network with 33 nodes is produced, where several proteins of unknown function display associations with those already known. Such networks, combined with gene expression data and protein compartment data, can obviously be used to form data-driven hypotheses. These hypotheses can be used as quick routes to obtain experi-mental verification since direct, physical interaction is already suggested.

In summary, the optimal way of studying, say, the human immune sys-tem, would be to carry out analysis at several levels including comparative ge-nomics and proteomics, coevolution with pathogens, tissue-specific processes, regulation networks, population dynamics, etc. In other words, contemporary study of immune systems calls for a systems biological approach, where only multidisciplinary work within bioinformatics; genomics; proteomics; cellular, molecular, and clinical immunology; and mathematical modeling can provide efficient answers to many of the basic problems in immunology. In recent years several success stories have demonstrated the necessity of the multidis-ciplinary approach. As a result of these developments, immunological bioin-formatics, the field that this book is about, has emerged and seems to have booming years ahead of it. The aim of this book is to be able to give a flavor

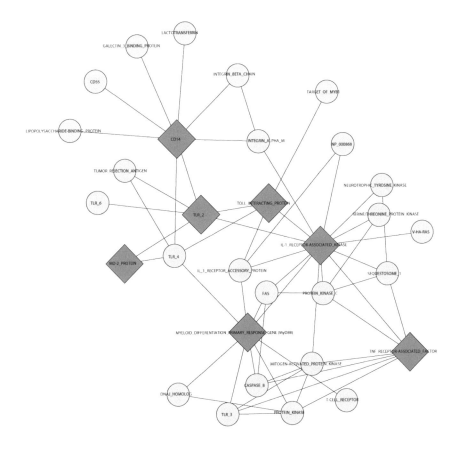

Figure 1.3: Protein-protein interaction network constructed for 33 proteins, which can be linked to interleukin-1 receptor–associated kinase 1 protein (NP_001560) by experimental data extracted from public databases. The network nodes represent proteins, while the edges represent the pairwise physical interactions. All protein-protein interactions given in BIND, DIP and hprd for seven proteins known to be involved in the toll-like receptor MyD88-dependent signaling pathway (as indicated by KEGG, www.genome.jp/kegg/pathway/hsa/hsa04620.html) have been extracted and given here as an interaction network. The seven known proteins are represented by diamond squares, the round circles represent proteins not currently in KEGG as being part of this pathway. Interestingly, the seven known proteins show interactions to many of the same proteins, suggesting that these highly connected proteins might play a role in relation to the pathway. Figure courtesy of Carsten Friis.

of recent developments in this field, together with the necessary background, so that the reader will be able to carry on with practical immunological bioinformatics. The rest of this chapter will give a short overview of the vertebrate immune systems.

1.1   Innate and Adaptive Immunity in Vertebrates

Vertebrate immune systems have two basic branches: innate and adaptive immunity. The former is phylogenetically older and existed in a primitive form in all multicellular organisms, whereas the latter seems to be only 400 million years old and is found only in cartilaginous and bony fish, amphibians, reptiles, birds, and mammals [Thompson, 1995].

Eosinophils, monocytes, macrophages, natural killer cells, Toll–like receptors (TLRs), and a series of soluble mediators, such as the complement system, represent the innate immunity system. On the other hand, adaptive immunity is induced by lymphocytes and can be further divided into two types: humoral immunity, mediated by antibody molecules secreted by B lymphocytes that can neutralize pathogens outside cells; and cellular immunity, mediated by T lymphocytes that eliminate infected cells, and provide help to other immune responses.

The essential difference between innate and the adaptive immunity lies in the means by which they recognize pathogens. The innate immune system distinguishes between *harmful* and *innocuous* according to, e.g., carbohydrate signals [Fearon and Locksley, 1996]. In contrast to this relatively rigid approach, lymphocytes generate a very large repertoire with potential to recognize different and novel antigens. The most efficient defense is obtained when all the components of an immune system "work" together, e.g., the innate immunity may instruct the adaptive immune system on what to respond to [Fearon and Locksley, 1996, Borghans and de Boer, 2002]. Thus, to decide when and how and how much and how long to fight against what seems to be foreign is under the influence of many factors, each induced by a part of the vertebrate host immune system.

The defense against invaders is costly [Moret and Schmid-Hempel, 2000]. Therefore, not surprisingly, any efficient solution found throughout evolution is maintained along very different lines. For example, there are a number of conserved innate defenses between insects and mammalians [Hoffmann et al., 1999], such as TLRs. Thus, in higher vertebrates, the innate immune system is not forgotten; instead it has taken a crucial role of stimulating and orienting the adaptive response. Quite similar organisms have sometimes also chosen to proceed with very different tactics in defending themselves. These differences can be due to different local environments at bottleneck situations during evolution, where the population sizes have been very small.

Diversity is the hallmark of the adaptive immune systems. Both B and T lymphocytes carry specific receptors for antigen recognition, which are assembled from variable (V), diversity (D), and joining (J) gene segments early in lymphocyte development. There are multiple copies of V, D, and J segments, and the recombination of these segments generates a huge repertoire of T and

B cells. The genes responsible for this recombination are called recombination-activating genes, RAG-1 and RAG-2, and their forerunners were inserted into the germ line of early jawed vertebrates by a transposon [Agrawal et al., 1998]. Colonization of an early invertebrate by a transposon represents a fundamental failure of the defense mechanisms of the organism. It is rather ironic that such a failure has been the main reason for evolution of antigen-specific immunity. Having a diverse repertoire gives the basic advantage of being able to mount *different* responses to *different* pathogens. Moreover, the ability to mount a specific response allows organisms to *remember* the pathogens that they have encountered. Thus, the adaptive immune response has become a common characteristic of the higher vertebrates by natural selection.

In addition to defense, vertebrate immune systems face two more important assignments: tolerance to self and homeostasis. The immune system maintains a state of equilibrium, although it is continuously being exposed to self antigens and generating responses to a diverse collection of microbes. To attain this equilibrium, *suppression* is as important as *induction*. Self-reactive lymphocytes are created constantly; however, autoimmune diseases are fortunately a rare phenomenon. After an efficient response to foreign antigens, the immune system returns to a state of rest where the number of immune cells is the same as in the preimmune state. Parallel to obtaining this homeostasis, the repertoire is altered in a way that ensures a protective response to the particular antigen. To create an immune response and to have elevated levels of particular pathogen-specific cells in the postimmune state do not, however, interfere with the host's potential of later mounting immune responses to a large variety of other pathogens.

1.2   Antigen Processing and Presentation

The immune system is one of the best examples of a highly evolved, complex biological system, where functional components are interwoven in many nontrivial ways. The initiation, regulation, and termination of an immune response involve a large number of cells of different types and several stimulatory/inhibitory signals delivered locally and systemically. It is widely accepted that bioinformatics, as part of a systems biology approach, can reveal some answers to the key questions in such complex systems.

Often decisions made during an immune response, e.g., whether or not to respond to a microbial infection, or which type of response to make, are based on the information that is inherent in microbial proteins. These proteins might carry regions that are recognized by B lymphocytes. This recognition can initiate a cascade of processes in the host which results in antibody production against the microbial protein. Similarly, an infected cell can "present" peptides that are generated from the degradation of microbial proteins to immune cells. Indeed, the cellular arm of the immune system, e.g., cytotoxic T lymphocytes, constantly screens cells of the host for such peptides (epitopes) and destroys the cells that present non-self epitopes. In other words, the cellular arm of the immune system sees the world through these peptides.

The presentation of the peptides to the immune cells is done by major histocompatibility complex (MHC) molecules, which have the largest degree of polymorphism among mammalian proteins. Human MHC molecules are called also human leukocyte antigens (HLA). Large parts of immunological bioinformatics research involve predicting which peptides are most likely to be presented by individual MHC molecules, i.e., predict how different hosts perceive their environment. The polymorphism is obviously a means for securing the survival of the population rather than the survival of each and every individual. We will not all be able to fight invading pathogens equally well. These strongly individualized immune responses further complicate the tasks within immunological bioinformatics as predictive methods must be able to handle the diverse genetic background of different groups in the population, and in the longer perspective of each individual.

There are two main pathways to processing and presenting antigens to T lymphocytes. The first (the MHC class I pathway) is used to present endogenous antigens to CD8$^+$ T cells. In order to be presented, a precursor peptide must be generated by the proteasome. This peptide may be trimmed at the N-terminal by other peptidases in the cytosol [Reits et al., 2004]. It must then bind to the transporter associated with antigen processing (TAP) in order to be translocated to the endoplasmic reticulum (ER). Here its N-terminal can again be trimmed by the amino-peptidase associated with antigen processing (ERAAP) while it binds to the MHC class I molecule [Stoltze et al., 2000b]. Thereafter it is transported to the cell surface. Figure 1.4 gives a cartoon representation of the MHC class I pathway.

The majority of the peptides presented on the cell surface originate from selfproteins, and thus are not immunogenic. This is due to negative T cell selection in the thymus, where T cells that recognize selfantigens are destroyed. Only half of the peptides presented are recognized by a T cell [Yewdell et al., 1999]. The most selective step is binding of a peptide to the MHC class I molecule, since only 1 in 200 binds with an affinity strong enough to generate a subsequent immune response [Yewdell et al., 1999]. For comparison the selectivity of TAP binding is reported to be 1 in 7 [Uebel et al., 1997]. This all happens in competition with other peptides, so in order for a peptide to be immunogenic (immunodominant) it must go through the above–described processes more efficiently than other peptides produced in a given cell.

These processing steps are essentially relatively simple examples of "sequence analysis" performed by immune system components, and it is there-

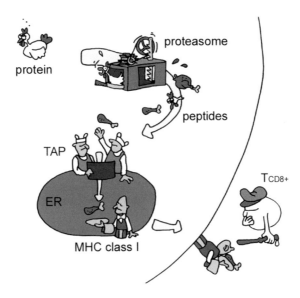

Figure 1.4: The MHC class I pathway. The proteasome cleaves proteins into peptide fragments. These peptides are translocated by the TAP pump over the membrane of the ER. A chaperone known as tapasin stabilizes the MHC class I molecules before peptide binding. The MHC class I molecules are retained in the ER lumen until successful peptide binding occurs. These molecules are subsequently transported to the plasma membrane. Figure courtesy of Eric A.J. Reits. See plate 2 for color version.

fore not surprising that these steps can be modeled quite successfully by bioinformatics approaches. Most of the methods constructed to date have been data-driven in the sense that experimental data related to the processing (fragment cleavage, binding, transport) have been used to produce algorithms reproducing the processing carried out by the immune system. Methods based on first principles, using, e.g., binding templates represented by protein structures (determined by X-ray crystallography or nuclear magnetic resonance) have also been used to generate such algorithms.

The presentation on MHC class II molecules follows a different path [Bryant et al., 2002]: After synthesis and translocation into ER, MHC class II molecules associate with the invariant chain (Ii) and the resulting complex traverses the Golgi complex and accumulates in endosomal compartments. Here Ii is degraded, leaving the MHC class II molecules in the hands of another MHC-like molecule, called HLA-DM in humans. HLA-DM loads MHC class II molecules with the best ligands originating from endocytosed antigens. The peptide MHC class II complexes are subsequently transported to the cell surface for presentation to CD4$^+$ T cells. Figure 1.5 shows the important elements of the MHC

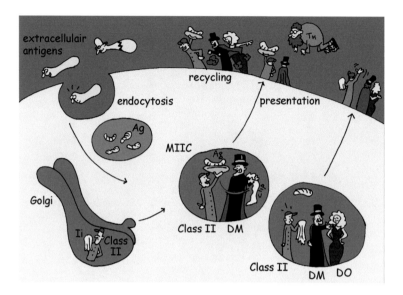

Figure 1.5: The processing steps in the MHC class II pathway. HLA-DO is another MHC class II like molecule expressed mainly in B cells. HLA-DO regulates the function of HLA-DM, but, it is not yet clear when inhibitory and stimulatory effects occur. Figure courtesy of Eric A.J. Reits. See plate 3 for color version.

class II pathway.

Both types of MHC molecules are highly polymorphic, and the specificity of the alleles are often very different. Different individuals will thus typically react to a different set of peptides from a pathogen. As will be explained later (chapters 6 and 8), the specificity of given MHC molecules can be predicted from the amino acid sequence of the pathogen proteins. This can, e.g., be used to select specific epitopes for use in a vaccine, and help to understand the role of the immune system in infectious diseases, autoimmune diseases, and cancers.

1.3   Individualized Immune Reactivity

One would expect that the T cell response — being largely dependent upon MHC-mediated antigen presentation — would be seriously crippled if MHC molecules were very specific and only presented a few peptides. Rather, MHC molecules should have more of a sampling function, i.e., each MHC allele should be able to bind and present many different peptides in order to enable a reasonable representation of the proteins available to the host. However, any sampling function involves some kind of specificity and any degree of specificity has a flip side; those epitopes which are ignored by the MHC would constitute immunological "blind spots." From the point of view of the invader, such blind spots would amount to a constant evolutionary pressure to remove MHC presentable epitopes.

This evolutionary pressure would be persistent and unchanging if there were one, and only one, MHC specificity within the species; and pathogens would eventually succeed in escaping immune control. The immune system has solved this potential problem through MHC polymorphism. In fact, as mentioned above, the MHC is the most polymorphic gene system known. On a population basis, hundreds of alleles have been found for most of the MHC encoding loci (see figure 12.1 for the number of MHC sequences identified until recently). On an individual basis, only one (homozygous) or two (heterozygous) of these alleles are expressed per locus. The number of MHC loci per individual also differs among species. While a heterozygous human would have six MHC class I genes (coded in three loci), e.g., the rhesus macaque can have as many as 22 active MHC class I genes [Daza-Vamenta et al., 2004]. The polymorphism affects the peptide binding specificity of the MHC; one allelic MHC product will recognize one part of the universe of peptides, whereas another allelic MHC product will recognize a different part of this universe. This leads to an individualized immune reactivity. No two individuals will have the same set of immunological "blind spots" and no microorganism could therefore evolve to easily circumvent the immune systems of the entire species. Thus, polymorphism is what allows the MHC to exercise some degree of specificity. From a practical point of view, MHC polymorphism is a huge challenge to any T cell epitope discovery process, underpinning the need for bioinformatical analysis and resources.

Chapter 2

Contemporary Challenges to the Immune System

2.1 Infectious Diseases in the New Millennium

More than 400 microbial agents are associated with disease in healthy adult humans [RAC, 2002]. The number of agents known to be a threat to human and animal health is large and it may not be not feasible (or possible) to develop in a cost-effective manner conventional vaccines against all emerging pathogens: there are only licensed vaccines in the United states for 22 microbial agents [FDA, 2003]. Moreover, since it will take a very long time to estimate the true virulence of these pathogens, the use of complete or partial organisms might not be safe. Immunological bioinformatics can make an important contribution to the rapid design of novel vaccines by identifying the most immunogenic regions on the pathogens. These regions can subsequently be used as candidates for a rational vaccine design.

2.2 Major Killers in the World

It is estimated that 11 million (19%) of the 57 million people who died in the world in 2002 were killed by infectious or parasitic infection [WHO, 2004a]. Table 2.1 shows the major causes of death in the world from infectious diseases.

The three main single infectious diseases are HIV/AIDS, tuberculosis, and Malaria, each of which causes more than 1 million deaths.

2.2.1   AIDS

Acquired immunodeficiency syndrome (AIDS), which is caused by the human immunodeficiency virus (HIV), is now the leading cause of death in young adults worldwide. WHO states that tackling HIV/AIDS is the world's most urgent public health challenge [WHO, 2004b]. More than 20 million people have died from AIDS and an estimated 34 to 46 million others are now infected with the virus. There is as yet no vaccine and no definite cure.

HIV is an enveloped retrovirus that replicates in cells of the immune system. HIV belongs to a group of retroviruses called the lentiviruses[Lever, 2000]. These viruses cause diseases that progress gradually. Often lentivurses persist after an infection and continue to replicate for many years before causing overt signs of disease. HIV-1 and HIV-2 are the only known human lentiviruses.

HIV uses the CD4 protein (often expressed by helper T cells and macrophages) and a chemokine receptor (CCR5 or CXCR4) to infect cells [Pierson and Doms, 2003]. The viral replication occurs only in activated T cells. Primary infection of humans with HIV-1 is associated with an acute mononucleosis-like clinical syndrome which appears approximately 36 weeks following infection [Hansasuta and Rowland-Jones, 2001]. Initially, the concentration of virus in the blood (viremia) can be high, but rapidly diminishes as cytotoxic T cell responses develop. Despite the ongoing immune response HIV infection is not eliminated: HIV establishes a state of persistent infection in which the virus is continually replicating in newly infected cells. The main reason that the infection is not cleared is that HIV can easily generate immune escape mutants: it has a rapid replication rate and a fast mutation rate, which lead to the generation of many variants of HIV in a single infected patient in the course of one day.

The main effect of HIV on the immune system is the loss of $CD4^+$ T cells (for a review see, e.g., Hazenberg et al. [2000]). There are at least two dominant mechanisms for this. First, direct viral killing of infected T cells; and second, killing of infected T cells by cytotoxic lymphocytes that recognize viral peptides. The currently used HAART (highly active antiretroviral therapy) treatment consists of combinations of viral protease inhibitors together with nucleoside analogues and causes a rapid decrease in virus levels and a slower increase in $CD4^+$ T cell counts [Berger et al., 1998]. The treatment usually has severe sideeffects, and many patients cannot continue the treatment for long periods [Laurence, 2004]. Moreover, in the developing world, where HIV/AIDS has its largest burden, HAART is too expensive for use in every HIV-infected individual. Without treatment the concentration of $CD4^+$ T cells (the CD^+ count) decreases gradually, and the body becomes progressively more susceptible to opportunistic infections. Eventually, most HIV-infected individuals develop

AIDS and die; however a small minority remain healthy for many years, with no apparent ill effects of infection. Hopefully, we will be able to learn from these long term nonprogressors how HIV infection can be controlled. If so, it will be possible one day to develop effective vaccines and therapies against HIV.

2.2.2 Tuberculosis

Tuberculosis (TB) is another emerging public health threat. The *Mycobacterium tuberculosis* bacteria (Mtb), the causative agent of TB, is spread from person to person by airborne droplets expelled from the lungs when a person with TB coughs, sneezes, or speaks. Outbreaks may therefore occur in closed settings and under crowded living conditions such as homeless shelters and prisons. It is estimated that onethird of the world's population (1.86 billion people) is infected with Mtb, and 16.2 million people have TB. Approximately 10% of those infected with Mtb develop TB later in life, most of them a few years after infection. Mtb-infected persons can also develop TB if their immune system is impaired, e.g., by HIV infection. In 1995, the year with the highest TB casualty rate to date, nearly 3 million people died worldwide from the disease. Currently, there is only one licensed vaccine against TB in the United States but it is not recommended for use. This vaccine, bacille Calmette-Guérin (BCG), is reportedly highly variable in its efficacy to prevent adult pulmonary TB. It may have a lower efficiency in poor tropical societies where people are more exposed to other mycobacteria in the environment. The protection offered by the vaccine normally lasts until adolescence. The Jordan report, NIAID, 2000 states that "For many reasons, the development of improved anti-TB vaccines has become a necessity for adequate control and elimination of tuberculosis. These reasons include the spread of (multidrug resistant) MDR-TB, the global burden of the TB epidemic, the growing TB/HIV coepidemic in large areas of the world, the enormous practical barriers to controlling TB adequately through administration of what are complicated and costly treatment regimens, inadequate diagnostic methods, and the relative ineffectiveness of the current BCG vaccines."

2.2.3 Malaria

Malaria is a serious and sometimes fatal disease caused by a parasite. Patients with malaria typically become very sick with high fevers, shaking chills, and flulike illness. Four kinds of malaria parasites can infect humans: *Plasmodium falciparum, P. vivax, P. ovale*, and *P. malariae*. Infection with any of the malaria species can make a person feel very ill, but infection with *P. falciparum*, if not promptly treated, may be fatal. Although malaria can be a fatal disease, illness and death from malaria are largely preventable. The World Health Organization estimates that each year 300 to 500 million cases of malaria occur and that more than 1 million people die of malaria, most of them in young children. Since many countries with malaria are already among the poorer nations, the disease maintains a vicious cycle of disease and poverty. Malaria has been eradicated from many developed countries with temperate climates. However, the disease remains a major health problem in many developing countries, in tropical and subtropical parts of the world. An eradication campaign was started in the 1950s, but it failed due to problems, including the resistance of mosquitoes to insecticides used to kill them, the resistance of malaria parasites to drugs used to treat them, and administrative issues. In addition, the eradication campaign never involved most of Africa, where malaria is most common.

Usually, people get malaria by being bitten by an infected female *Anopheles* mosquito. Only *Anopheles* mosquitoes can transmit malaria and they must have been infected by a previous blood meal taken from an infected person. When a mosquito bites, a small amount of blood is taken which contains the microscopic malaria parasites. The parasites grow and mature in the mosquito's gut for a week or more, then travel to the mosquito's salivary glands. When the mosquito next takes a blood meal, these parasites mix with the saliva and are injected into the bite. Once in the blood, the parasites travel to the liver and enter liver cells to grow and multiply. During this incubation period, the infected person has no symptoms. After as little as 8 days or as long as several months, the parasites leave the liver cells and enter red blood cells. Once in the cells, they continue to grow and multiply. After they mature, the infected red blood cells rupture, freeing the parasites to attack and enter other red blood cells. Toxins released when the red cells burst are what cause the typical fever, chills, and flulike malaria symptoms. If a mosquito bites this infected person and ingests certain types of malaria parasites (gametocytes), the cycle of transmission continues.

Because the malaria parasite is found in red blood cells, malaria can also be transmitted through blood transfusion, organ transplant, or the shared use of needles or syringes contaminated with blood. Malaria may also be transmitted from a mother to her fetus before or during delivery (congenital malaria) (This discussion has about malaria has been adopted from http://www.cdc.gov/malaria/faq.htm).

2.3   Childhood Diseases

The term *childhood diseases* normally covers mumps, measles, rubella, chick-enpox, whooping cough, smallpox, diphtheria, tetanus, and polio [DMID, 2004]. These diseases have successfully been controlled in the developed world through vaccines. Over 1 million still die each year from childhood diseases for which vaccines are available. This is mainly due to the vaccines not being available in many underdeveloped countries, and in Russia and the former East Bloc countries where the healthcare systems have deteriorated over the last 15 years.

Even in the developed world challenges still exist [DMID, 2004]:

- Elimination of adverse side effects of vaccines

- Control of childhood diseases in immunologically compromised children

- Development of more easily administered, "child-friendly" vaccines

- Better control of persisting childhood disease threats such as infections caused by rapidly evolving organisms like streptococcus and many microbes causing pneumococcal infection

2.3.1   Respiratory Infections

Infections of the respiratory tract continue to be the leading cause of acute illness worldwide. Upper respiratory infections (URIs) such as the common cold, strep throat, sinusitis, and otitis media (ear infections) are very common, especially in children, but seldom have serious or life-threatening complications. Lower respiratory infections (LRIs) include more serious illnesses such as influenza, bronchitis, pertussis (whooping cough), pneumonia, and tuber-culosis and are the leading contributors to the more than 4 million deaths caused each year by respiratory infections [NIAID, 2002b]. The most common etiological agents of pneumonia are *Streptococcus pneumoniae, Haemophilus influenzae*, and respiratory syncytial virus (RSV) [NIAID, 2002b]. In one study RSV was detected in 36.3% and adenoviruses in 14.3% of cases of acute LRIs [Videla et al., 1998].

2.3.2   Diarrheal Diseases

Another major cause of death is diarrheal diseases which may be caused by a number of pathogens. Even when the most sophisticated methods and diag-nostic reagents are used, more than half of the cases of diarrheal illness cannot be ascribed to a particular agent. Important pathogens include cholera, Shiga

toxin–producing *Escherichia coli* (STEC), enteropathogenic *E. coli* (EPEC), en-
terotoxigenic *E. coli* (ETEC), *Helicobacter pylori*, rotavirus, caliciviruses [Jiang
et al., 2000], *Shigella, Salmonella typhi*, and *Campylobacter* [NIAID, 2002b].

Typhoid fever, which is caused by *Salmonella typhi*, remains a serious public health problem throughout the world, with an estimated 16 to 33 million
cases and 500,000 deaths annually [NIAID, 2002b].

2.4   Clustering of Infectious Disease Organisms

It is difficult to get an overview of the different human pathogens (microorganisms associated with diseases in humans). Figures 2.1 through 2.4 shows the
viruses, bacteria, parasites, and fungi associated with diseases in humans. The
clustering is based on the number of terms in the Swiss-Prot family description
that are identical between the two organisms. The data were extracted from
http://www.cbs.dtu.dk/databases/Dodo.

The pathogens have been selected from appendix B of the Recombinant
DNA Advisory Committee guidelines [RAC, 2002] which includes those biological agents known to infect humans, as well as selected animal agents that may
pose theoretical risks if inoculated into humans. RAC divides pathogens into
four classes.

1. **Risk group 1 (RG1).**   Agents that are not associated with disease in
   healthy adult humans

2. **Risk group 2 (RG2).**   Agents that are associated with human disease
   which is rarely serious and for which preventive or therapeutic interventions are often available

3. **Risk group 3 (RG3).**   Agents that are associated with serious or lethal
   human disease for which preventive or therapeutic interventions may be
   available (high individual risk but low community risk)

4. **Risk group 4 (RG4).**   Agents that are likely to cause serious or lethal
   human disease for which preventive or therapeutic interventions are not
   usually available (high individual risk and high community risk)

In figures 2.1–2.4 names for human pathogens are shown for viruses, bacteria, parasites and fungi. The first column before the pathogen name is the
RAC classification, the second column is the classification of the pathogens
according to the Centers for Disease Control and Prevention (CDC) bioterror
categories A–C, where category A pathogens are considered the worst bioterror
threats [CDC, 2003].

Cause	Deaths (1000)	Percent of total deaths
Infectious and parasitic diseases	10,904	19.1
Tuberculosis	1,566	2.7
STIs excluding HIV	180	0.3
Syphilis	157	0.3
Chlamydia	9	0.0
Gonorrhea	1	0.0
HIV/AIDS	2,777	4.9
Diarrheal diseases	1,798	3.2
Childhood diseases	1,124	2.0
Pertussis	294	0.5
Poliomyelitis	1	0.0
Diphtheria	5	0.0
Measles	611	1.1
Tetanus	214	0.4
Meningitis	173	0.3
Hepatitis B	103	0.2
Hepatitis C	54	0.1
Malaria	1,272	2.2
Tropical diseases	129	0.2
Trypanosomiasis	48	0.1
Chagas' disease	14	0.0
Schistosomiasis	15	0.0
Leishmaniasis	51	0.1
Lymphatic filariasis	0	0.0
Onchocerciasis	0	0.0
Leprosy	6	0.0
Dengue	19	0.0
Japanese encephalitis	14	0.0
Trachoma	0	0.0
Intestinal nematode infections	12	0.0
Ascariasis	3	0.0
Trichuriasis	3	0.0
Hookworm disease	3	0.0
Respiratory infections	3,963	6.9
Lower respiratory infections	3,884	6.8
Upper respiratory infections	75	0.1
Otitis media	4	0.0

Table 2.1: Major causes of death in the world from infectious diseases (2002). The table has been adapted from [WHO, 2004a]. STIs: Sexually transmitted Infections.

The third column before the pathogen name contains a dash if no vaccine is available for the pathogen and a letter indicating the type of vaccine if one is available (A: acellular/adsorbet; C: conjugate; I: inactivated; L: live; P: polysaccharide; R: recombinant; S staphage lysate; T: toxoid). Lower case indicates that the vaccine is released as an investigational new drug (IND)).

2.5 Biodefense Targets

Vaccines have only been made for 14 of the more than 123 agents on the NIAID A-C list. For many of the bacterial agents antibiotic treatment is possible, but may be inefficient if the agent is inhaled [NIAID, 2002a]. The CDC has defined three categories A–C, where category A pathogens are considered to be the worst bioterror threats [CDC, 2003]. Category A agents include *Bacillus anthracis* (anthrax), *Clostridium botulinum* toxin (botulism), *Yersinia pestis* (plague) *Variola major* (smallpox), *Francisella tularensis* (tularemia) and viral hemorrhagic fevers.

Anthrax Even with antibiotic treatment inhalation anthrax is a potentially fatal (40-75% fatality) disease [NIAID, 2002a]. An anthrax vaccine adsorbed (AVA) is licensed in the United States [FDA, 2003]. There are no data to support the efficacy of AVA for pulmonary anthrax in humans, but it has been established that the protective antigen (PA) of *B. anthracis* induces significant protective immunity against inhalation spore challenge in animal models and that PA is the component of AVA responsible for generating such immunity [NIAID, 2000]. Pilot lots of a recombinant PA vaccine are currently being produced [NIAID, 2002a]. The 3D structure of the anthrax toxin has recently been determined. This may be used to discover vaccines or compounds that block the effect of the toxin.

Smallpox Smallpox was eradicated in 1977. The mortality from smallpox infections is approximately 30% [NIAID, 2002a]. The vaccine has serious side effects and is associated with complications which may be life-threatening, especially in persons with an impaired immune system [NIAID, 2002a]. Development of a safer vaccine is therefore a priority. A modified vaccinia Ankara (MVA) vaccine for evaluation in a phase I clinical study is being produced [NIAID, 2002a].

Plague Natural epidemics of plague have been primarily bubonic plague (characterized by enlarged lymph nodes ("swollen glands") that are tender and painful), which is transmitted by fleas from infected rodents. Inhalation of aerosolized bacilli can lead to a pneumonic plague (a form of plague that can spread through the air from person to person; characterized by

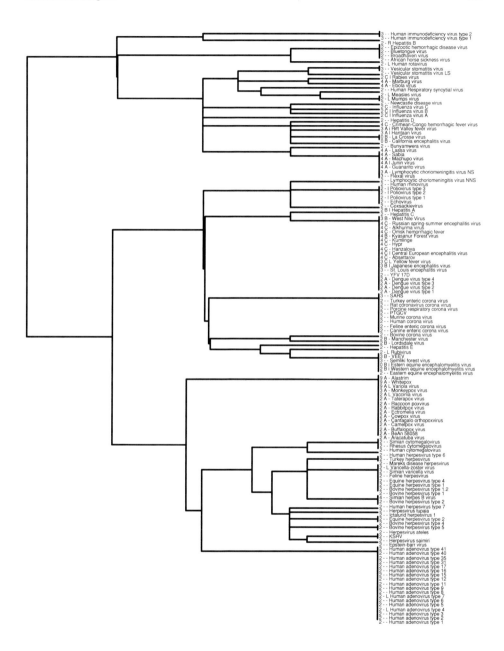

Figure 2.1: Viruses associated with disease in humans.

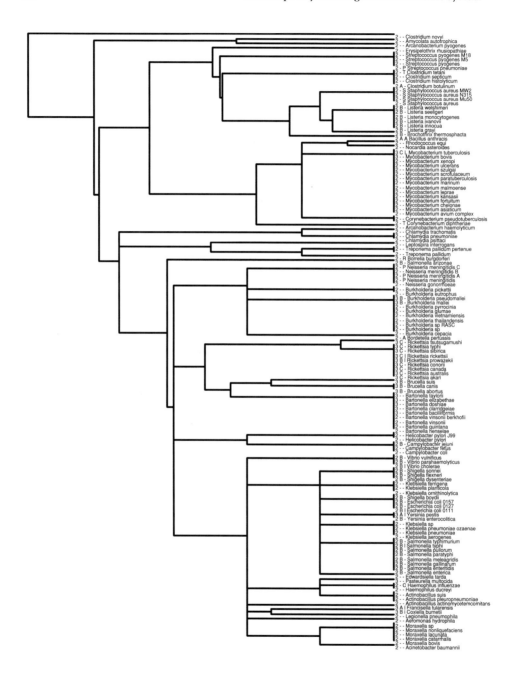

Figure 2.2: Bacteria associated with disease in humans.

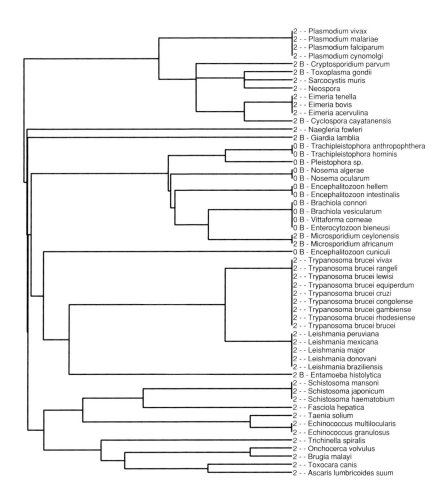

Figure 2.3: Parasites associated with disease in humans.

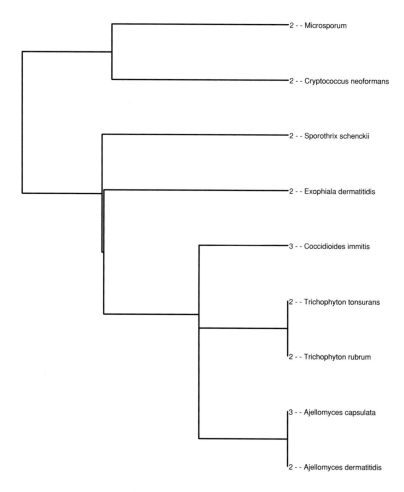

Figure 2.4: Fungi associated with disease in humans.

lung involvement) which untreated has a mortality rate that approaches 100%. Aggressive antibiotic treatment can be effective [NIAID, 2003] No vaccine is currently licensed in the United States. A formalin-killed, whole-cell vaccine (USP) was available until 1999. It could prevent bubonic plague but could not prevent pneumonic plague [NIAID, 2003]. Phase I human trials are planned for candidate vaccines based on the two antigens F1 and V [NIAID, 2003].

Botulism Botulinum toxin is the etiologic agent responsible for the disease botulism, which is characterized by peripheral neuromuscular blockade. Seven antigenic types (A-G) of the toxin exist. All seven toxins cause similar clinical presentation and disease; botulinum toxins A, B, and E are responsible for the vast majority of foodborne botulism cases in the United States. The heavy chain is not toxic, and has been shown to evoke complete protection against the toxin. Sequencing of the *C. botulinum* Hall strain A bacterium genome has been completed.

Tularemia *Francisella tularensis*, which causes tularemia, is a non–spore-forming, facultative intracellular bacterium. If untreated, the disease could lead to respiratory failure. Treatment with antibiotics reduces mortality for naturally acquired cases by 2 to 60%. A live attenuated tularemia vaccine developed by the Department of Defense (DoD) has been administered under an investigational new drug (IND) application to thousands of volunteers [NIAID, 2003]. In vivo studies demonstrate that either CD4 or CD8 T cells can mediate resolution of live vaccine strain (LVS) infections. Antibodies appear to contribute little, if anything, to protective immunity [NIAID, 2002a].

Viral hemorrhagic fevers (VHFs) Viral hemorrhagic fevers encompass a group of similar diseases caused by four types of viruses:

Arenaviruses, associated with Argentine, Bolivian, and Venezuelan hemorrhagic fevers, Lassa fever, and Sabia virus–associated hemorrhagic fever

Bunyaviruses, including Crimean-Congo hemorrhagic fever, Rift Valley fever, and Hantavirus infection

Filoviruses, comprising Ebola and Marburg hemorrhagic fevers

Hemorrhagic flaviviruses, including yellow fever, dengue hemorrhagic fever, West Nile virus, Kyasanur Forest disease, and Omsk hemorrhagic fever.

With very few exceptions (yellow fever), no vaccines or proven treatments exist, and many of the diseases are highly fatal. For Ebola hemorrhagic fever, immunization with an adenoviral (ADV) vector encoding the Ebola glycoprotein (GP) has been shown to protect against disease in cynomolgus macaques. Two tetravalent dengue vaccines will be studied in nonhuman primates in 2003 [NIAID, 2003], and work has been initiated on Marburg and West Nile virus vaccines [NIAID, 2003].

2.6   Cancer

Cancer is one of the three leading causes of death in industrialized countries. Cancers are caused by cells which grow progressively without any regulation. Thus, curing cancer requires destruction of these cells. A possible way of achieving this would be to generate an immune response against these cells (see for a review, e.g., Crittenden et al. [2005]). This implies that the immune system should be able to discriminate tumor cells from healthy cells. The antigenic differentiation in a tumor cell can provide such discriminatory signals. For example, proteins that are crucial in cell cycle regulation, like p53, are going through differentiation in tumor cells. If the differentiated parts of these proteins are presented to T cells on MHC molecules, a T cell response against tumors might be invoked [Marincola et al., 2003, Mocellin et al., 2004]. These *tumor rejection antigens* are usually tumor specific, although they can be shared by tumors of a similar origin. This makes the identification of tumor antigens a very time-consuming process, because for every cancer type new tumor antigens need to be identified.

For over a century researchers have been trying to invoke antitumor immune responses, but, there is still no successful treatment based on immune responses, except for a few types of cancer (see e.g., de Leo [2005]). The main reason is that tumors can escape an immune response in many ways [Mapara and Sykes, 2004]. Tumors are generally genetically unstable, and they can lose their antigens by mutation. Moreover, some tumors lose expression of a particular MHC molecule, totally blocking antigen presentation. These tumors may become susceptible to a natural killer (NK) cell–mediated response Wu and Lanier [2003], but, tumors that lose only one or two MHC molecules may avoid recognition by NK cells.

Recent developments in understanding antigen presentation and the molecules involved in T cell activation together with fast identification of tumor epitopes by bioinformatics tools might allow for new immunotherapeutic strategies.

2.7 Allergy

Allergy belongs to the class of immune responses called hypersensitivity reactions. These are harmful immune responses that produce tissue injury and may cause serious disease. Genetic factors contribute to the development of allergy, but environmental factors may also be important. Allergic reactions are caused by a special class of antibodies called immunoglobulin E (IgE) antibodies [Janeway et al., 2001]. IgE responses are, under normal physiological conditions protective, especially in response to parasitic worms, which are prevalent in less developed countries [Hagel et al., 2004]. In the industrialized countries, however, due to higher standards of hygienic conditions, IgE responses occur almost entirely against allergens. Almost half of the inhabitants of North America and Europe have allergies to one or more common environmental antigens. These allergies are rarely life-threatening, but, they cause much distress and lost time during everyday life.

Allergic reactions occur when allergens cross-link preexisting IgE bound to the mast cells [Gould et al., 2003]. Mast cells line the body surfaces and are very important in signaling local infections to other parts of the immune system. Once activated, they induce inflammatory reactions by secreting several chemical mediators stored in performed vesicles. In allergy, these reactions can cause symptoms that range from itching and burning of the skin to life-threatening systemic anaphylaxis. The severity of the symptoms depends on the dose of antigen and its route of entry. The immediate allergic reaction caused by mast cells is followed by a more sustained inflammation: the late-phase response. This late response involves the recruitment of other effector cells, especially T helper type 2 lymphocytes, eosinophils, and basophils, which contribute significantly to the immunopathology of an allergic response.

For allergies that are not very severe, the best therapy is avoidance of the allergen. This not only avoids the symptoms but also decreases with time the amount of specific IgE in the blood, the main cause of the allergic reactions. Except for avoidance and the use of drugs to treat the symptoms of allergic disease and limit the inflammatory response, two treatments are commonly used in clinical practice [Stokes and Casale, 2004]. The first one is desensitization where the aim is to shift the antibody response from IgE to IgG. IgG antibodies can bind to the allergen and thus prevent it from causing allergic reactions. Patients are injected with escalating doses of allergen, starting with tiny amounts. This injection schedule gradually diverts the IgE-dominated response, driven by T helper 2 cells, to one driven by T helper 1 cells, with the consequent downregulation of IgE production. A potential complication of the desensitization approach is the risk of inducing IgE-mediated allergic responses. The second treatment consists of blocking of the effector pathways, like disabling the recruitment of eosinophils to sites of allergic inflammation.

This can be done by using specific migration molecules that all immune cells have. Finally, a new promise in curing allergy is the use of peptide-based vaccines [Alexander et al., 2002].

2.8   Autoimmune Diseases

One of the most important challenges that vertebrate immune systems face is to discriminate self from nonself. In most cases this discrimination is perfect, but, in some individuals immune reactions against self proteins are induced. The diseases caused by these reactions are called autoimmune reactions [Janeway et al., 2001]. Normally, when an adaptive immune response is generated against a pathogen, the immune response goes on until the pathogen is cleared from the body. When an adaptive immune response develops against self antigens, however, it is usually impossible for immune effector mechanisms to eliminate the antigen completely, because the body goes on generating the proteins that it needs. Therefore, the autoimmune diseases cause chronic inflammatory injury to tissues, which may prove lethal. One exception is type 1 diabetes where the antigen-bearing beta-cells are all destroyed [Mandrup-Poulsen, 2003].

We do not know exactly how these self-reactive immune responses are initiated, but environmental and genetic factors play an important role. The most important environmental factor is the pathogen: there is a strong suspicion that infections can trigger autoimmune disease in genetically susceptible individuals [Prinz, 2004]. This is possible if one or more of the epitopes of the pathogen can cause cross-reactivity with self epitopes. After the clearance of the pathogen, the effector T cells can start recognizing the healthy cells that present the self epitope having mimicry to the pathogenic epitopes, causing autoimmunity. Genetically, susceptibility to autoimmune disease is associated mostly with the MHC genotype. For most of the diseases that show these associations, susceptibility is linked most strongly with MHC class II alleles, but in some cases there are strong associations with particular MHC class I alleles. Most autoimmune diseases strike women more often than men, particularly affecting women of middle age or younger [Janeway et al., 2001].

Autoimmune diseases can be classified into clusters that are typically either organspecific, or systemic. Examples of organ-specific autoimmune diseases are Hashimoto's thyroiditis [Laurent et al., 2004] and Graves' disease [Weetman, 2003], each predominantly affecting the thyroid gland, and type I insulin-dependent diabetes mellitus (IDDM), which

affects the pancreatic islets [Rewers et al., 2004]. Examples of systemic autoimmune disease are systemic lupus erythematosus (SLE) [Alarcon-Riquelme and Prokunina, 2003] and primary Sjögren's syndrome [Rozman et al., 2004], in which tissues as diverse as the skin, kidneys, and brain may all be affected.

For many years immunologists have sought to develop methods for preventing and treating autoimmune diseases by identifying those self antigens that are the target of autoimmune processes [Wraith et al., 1989], and using vaccines based on these antigens to revert the dangerous immune response to a nonharmfull one. However, almost all of these attempts entail risk, and require exact dosage to get any benefit [McDevitt, 2004].

Chapter 3

Sequence Analysis in Immunology

3.1 Sequence Analysis

The concept of protein families is based on the observation that, while there are a huge number of different proteins, most of them can be grouped, on the basis of similarities in their sequences, into a limited number of families. Proteins or protein domains belonging to a particular family generally share functional attributes and are derived from a common ancestor, and will most often be the result of gene duplication events.

It is apparent, when studying protein sequence families, that some regions have been more conserved than others during evolution. These regions are generally important for the function of a protein and/or the maintenance of its three-dimensional structure, or other features related to its localization or modification. By analyzing constant and variable properties of such groups of similar sequences, it is possible to derive a signature for a protein family or domain, which distinguishes its members from other unrelated proteins. Here we mention some examples of such domains that are essential to the immune response.

The immunoglobulin-like (Ig-like) protein domain is a domain of approximately 100 residues with a fold which consists of seven to nine antiparallel β strands. These β strands form a β-sandwich structure, consisting of three or four antiparallel β strands on each side of the barrel, connected by a sulfide bridge. The Ig-like domain is of special importance for the immune system. In addition to immunoglobulin, T cell receptor and MHC molecules carry Ig-like domains, i.e., the main players of the adaptive immune system have all Ig-like domains. This is not a coincidence: the unique structure of this domain allows for maximum flexibility to interact with other molecules. This property makes the Ig-like domain one of the most widespread protein modules in the animal kingdom. This module has been observed in a large group of related proteins that function in cell-cell interactions or in the structural organization and regulation of muscles. The proteins in the Ig-like family consist of one or more of these domains.

Toll-like receptors (TLRs) are a family of pattern recognition receptors that are activated by specific components of microbes and certain host molecules. They constitute the first line of defense against many pathogens and play a crucial role in the function of the innate immune system.

That the field of immunology is almost as big, dispersed, and complicated as all the rest of the biology put together is exemplified by the fact that all the different fields of bioinformatics and sequence analysis are applied to immunological problems. Sequence alignment, structural biology, machine learning and predictive systems, pattern recognition, DNA microarray analysis, and integrative systems biology are all important tools in the research of the different aspects of the immune system and its interaction with pathogens.

3.2   Alignments

Sequence alignment is the oldest but probably the single most important tool in bioinformatics. Being one of the basic techniques within sequence analysis, alignment is, though, far from simple, and the analytic tools (i.e., the computer programs) are still not perfect. Furthermore, the question of which method is optimal in a given situation strongly depends on which question we want the answer to. The most common questions are: How similar (different) are this group of sequences, and which sequences in a database are similar to a specific query sequence. The reasoning behind the questions might, however, be important for the choice of algorithmic solution. Why do we want to know this? Are we searching for the function of a protein/gene, or do we want to obtain an estimate of the evolutionary history of the protein family? Issues like the size of database to search, and available computational resources might also influence our selection of a tool.

3.2.1   Ungapped Pairwise Alignments

From the early days of protein and DNA sequencing it was clear that sequences from highly related species were highly similar, but not necessarily identical. Aligning very closely related sequences is a trivial task and can be done manually (figure 3.1 A). In cases where genes are of different sizes and the similarity

A

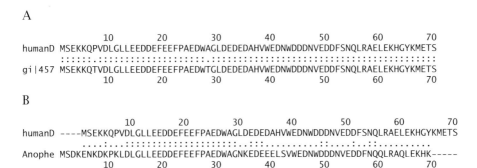

B

Figure 3.1: A) The human proteasomal DSS1 subunit aligned against the zebra fish homolog using the identity matrix. B) The human proteasomal DSS1 subunit aligned to the mosquito homolog.

is less, alignments become more difficult to construct. In such cases it is also of great value to have a graduation of how related sequences are, i.e., a scoring scheme. The simplest scoring is the relative amount of identical entities, also called % identity, or %ID. This simple approach is actually too simple as ,e.g., amino acids share many physical-chemical properties, which means that they can more easily be exchanged than very unrelated amino acids. This means that a scoring system that scores different substitutions differently, a substitution matrix, is a much better approach. The most useful concept has been to estimate how often a given amino acid is exchanged for another in already aligned similar sequences. The most used are the *percentage accepted mutations* (PAM) matrix [Dayhoff et al., 1978] and the *blocks substitution matrix* (BLOSUM) [Henikoff and Henikoff, 1992].Mutations between different types of nucleotides or amino acids is not the only changes that appears in sequences during the evolution. The sequences can also loose or gain sequence entities (deletions or insertions, respectively). This also must affect a similarity score, but for simplicity these complications are left to later sections. The simplest way to calculate an alignment score is to make all the possible overlaps between two sequences, and sum the number of identical amino acids in the two sequences (ungapped alignment, figure 3.1 B).

Sequence alignment is essential to the *comparative immunology* field. The main research line in this field (so far) is to discover origins of the adaptive immune system. Thanks to the homology assessments using sequence alignments with mammalian equivalents of T cell receptors, MHC genes, cytokines, and antibodies, we now know that the adaptive immune system is well developed in the oldest jawed vertebrates, the sharks [Pasquier and Flajnik, 1999]. However, whether or not jawless invertebrates were in possession of such adaptive immunity remains unresolved. The lamprey, which along with its cousin, the hagfish, is the only surviving jawless vertebrate, give immunologists a chance to pinpoint crucial aspects of the origin of the adaptive immune system. So far the search for antibodies, T cell receptors, and genes coding for MHC molecules has failed in these organisms. Recently, however, Pancer et al. [2004] have identified a set of uniquely diverse proteins that are only expressed by lamprey lymphocytes and named them variable lymphocyte receptors (VLRs). The sequence analysis of these proteins has revealed that the VLRs consist of multiple leucine-rich repeat (LRR) modules and an invariant stalk region that is attached to the lymphocyte plasma membrane. The remarkable VLR diversity derives from the variation in sequence and number of the LRR modules. The mature VLRs are thus generated through a process of somatic DNA rearrangement in lymphocytes. These results suggest a novel mechanism that does not involve recombinant-activating genes to generate the large diversity that an adaptive immune system is based upon.

3.2.2 Scoring Matrices

Dayhoff et al. [1978] calculated the original PAM matrices using a database of changes in groups of closely related proteins. From these changes they derived the accepted types of mutations. Each change was entered into a matrix listing all the possible amino acid changes. The relative mutability of different amino acids was also calculated, i.e., how often a given amino acid is changed to any other. The information about the individual kinds of mutations, and about the relative mutability of the amino acids were then combined into one "mutation probability matrix."

The rows and columns of this matrix represent amino acid substitution pairs, i.e., the probability that the amino acid of the column will be replaced by the amino acid of the row after a given evolutionary interval. A matrix with an evolutionary distance of 0 PAMs would have only 1s on the main diagonal and 0s elsewhere. A matrix with an evolutionary distance of 1 PAM would have numbers very close to 1 in the main diagonal and small numbers off the main diagonal. One PAM would correspond to roughly a 1% divergence in a protein (one amino acid replacement per hundred). Assuming that proteins diverge as a result of accumulated, uncorrelated, mutations a mutational probability matrix for a protein sequence that has undergone N percent accepted mutations, a PAM-N matrix, can be derived by multiplying the PAM-1 matrix by itself N times. The result is a whole family of scoring matrices. Dayhoff et al. [1978], imperically, found that for weighting purposes a 250 PAM matrix works well. This evolutionary distance corresponds to 250 substitutions per hundred residues (each residue can change more than once). At this distance

A

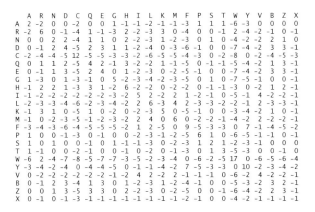

B

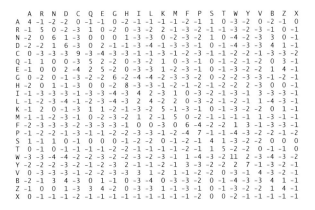

Figure 3.2: Substitution matrices. A) PAM250. B) BLOSUM62.

only one amino acid in five remains unchanged so the percent divergence has increased to roughly 80%. To avoid working with very small numbers the matrices actually used in sequence comparisons is logodds matrices. The odds matrix is constructed by taking the elements of the previous matrix and divide each component by the frequency of the replacement residue. In this way each component now gives the odds of replacing a given amino acid with another specified amino acid. Finally the log of this matrix is used as the weights in the matrix. In this it is now possible to sum up the scores for all positions to obtain the final alignment score. The PAM250 matrix is shown in Figure 3.2.

A

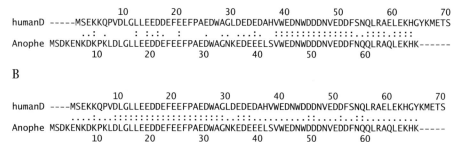

```
                 10        20        30        40        50        60        70
humanD  -----MSEKKQPVDLGLLEEDDEFEEFPAEDWAGLDEDEDAHVWEDNWDDDNVEDDFSNQLRAELEKHGYKMETS
         ..:  .       : :.:.   :      .  .. ....:. ::::::::::::::::::..::::..::::
Anophe  MSDKENKDKPKLDLGLLEEDDEFEEFPAEDWAGNKEDEEELSVWEDNWDDDNVEDDFNQQLRAQLEKHK------
             10        20        30        40        50        60
```

B

```
                 10        20        30        40        50        60        70
humanD  ----MSEKKQPVDLGLLEEDDEFEEFPAEDWAGLDEDEDAHVWEDNWDDDNVEDDFSNQLRAELEKHGYKMETS
        ....:...::::::::::::::::::::::.::::............:......:..:.............
Anophe  MSDKENKDKPKLDLGLLEEDDEFEEFPAEDWAGNKEDEEELSVWEDNWDDDNVEDDFNQQLRAQLEKHK-----
            10        20        30        40        50        60
```

Figure 3.3: (A) The human proteasomal subunit aligned to the mosquito homolog using the
BLOSUM50 matrix. (B) The human proteasomal subunit aligned to the mosquito homolog using
identity scores.

The BLOSUM matrix, described by Henikoff and Henikoff [1992], is another widely used amino acid substitution matrix. To calculate this, only very related blocks of amino acid sequences (conserved blocks) are considered. Originally these were taken from the BLOCKS database of prealigned sequence families [Henikoff and Henikoff, 1991]. Now the blocks are split up further in clusters, each containing the parts of the alignments that are more than X% conserved. The use of these clusters leads to a BLOSUMX matrix. That is, using clusters of down to 50% identities gives a BLOSUM50 matrix, and so forth. For every sequence in each cluster each position is compared to the corresponding position in each sequence in every other cluster. Since it is the *pairwise* number of frequencies that is calculated, the sum of all the substitutions is divided by the number of comparisons. In this way the result is the weighted probability that a given amino acid is exchanged for every other amino acid. In the final matrix, actually, the log ratio of the probability is further scaled so that the BLOSUM50 matrix is in thirds of bits, and the BLOSUM62 matrix is given in half-bits. The BLOSUM62 matrix is shown in figure 3.2.

Since the initial PAM1 matrix is made by very similar sequences, the evolutionary distances between those are very short, and most changes captured will be single base mutations leading to particular types of amino acid substitutions, while substitutions requiring more than one base mutation will be very rare. Even the calculations made to expand this matrix to longer evolution time cannot compensate for this [Gonnet et al., 1992] and therefore the BLOSUM matrices perform better when used for further distance alignment. The matrices are in a format where you can sum up the scores for each match to obtain a total alignment score, and the alignment resulting in the highest score is then the optimal one.

3.2.3   Gap Penalties

Using the BLOSUM50 matrix to align mosquito and human proteasomeal subunits (figure 3.3A) gives a slightly different alignment than just using amino acid identities (figure 3.3B). These two different alignments also reveal that there are two parts of the proteins with a high number of identical amino acids, but without inserting or deleting letters in one of the sequences they cannot be aligned simultaneously. This leads obviously to the necessity of inserting gaps in the alignments.

A gap in one sequence represents an insertion in the other sequence. First, to avoid having gaps all over the alignment these have to be penalized just like unmatching amino acids. This penalty (i.e., the probability that a given amino acid will be deleted in another related sequence) cannot be derived from the database alignments used to create the PAM and BLOSUM matrices, since these are ungapped alignments. Instead, a general gap insertion penalty is determined, usually empirically, and is often lower than the lowest match score. Having only one score for any gap inserted is called a linear gap cost, and will lead to the same total penalty for three single gaps at three different positions in the alignment as having a single stretch of three gaps. This does not make sense biologically, however, since insertions and deletions often involve a longer stretch of DNA in a single event. For this reason two different gap penalties are usually included in the alignment algorithms: one penalty for having a gap at all (gap opening penalty), and another, smaller penalty, for extending already opened gaps. This is called an affine gap penalty and is actually a compromise between the assumption that the insertion, or deletion, is created by one or more events. Furthermore, it is possible to let gaps appended at the ends of the sequences not to have a penalty, since insertions at the ends will have a much greater chance of not disrupting the function of a protein. For a more careful discussion of how to set gap penalties, see Vingron and Waterman [1994].

3.2.4   Alignment by Dynamic Programming

Introducing gaps greatly increases the number of different comparisons between two sequences and in the general case it is impossible to do them all. To compensate for that, several shortcut optimization schemes have been invented. One of the earliest schemes was developed by Needleman and Wunsch [1970] and works for global alignments, i.e., alignments covering all residues in both sequences. As an example, it is here described how to align two very short sequence stretches taken from our previous proteasome alignment. For simplicity, we will use the identity matrix (match=1, mismatch=-1) and a linear gap penalty of -2. Using the Needleman-Wunsch approach

Score matrix

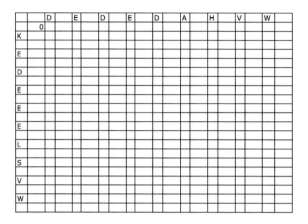

Trace Matrix

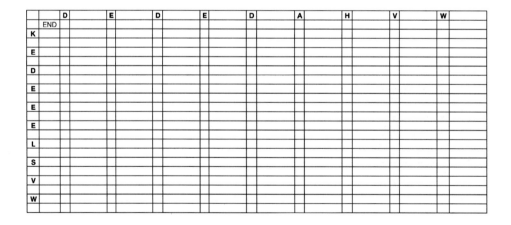

Figure 3.4: Dynamic programming, global alignment. Step 1.

Score matrix

		D		E		D		E		D		A		H		V		W	
	0		-2																
K																			
	-2																			
E																				
D																				
E																				
E																				
E																				
L																				
S																				
V																				
W																				

Trace Matrix

		D		E		D		E		D		A		H		V		W	
	END	-	right																
K	|																			
	up																			
E																				
D																				
E																				
E																				
E																				
L																				
S																				
V																				
W																				

Figure 3.5: Dynamic programming, global alignment. Step 2.

Score matrix

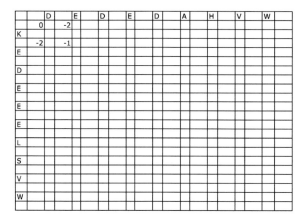

		D		E		D		E		D		A		H		V		W	
		0		-2															
K																			
		-2		-1															
E																			
D																			
E																			
E																			
E																			
L																			
S																			
V																			
W																			

Trace Matrix

		D		E		D		E		D		A		H		V		W	
	END	-	right																
K	|	\																	
	up	diagonal																	
E																			
D																			
E																			
E																			
E																			
L																			
S																			
V																			
W																			

Figure 3.6: Dynamic programming, global alignment. Step 3.

Score matrix

		D	E	D	E	D	A	H	V	W
	0	-2	-4	-6	-8	-10	-12	-14	-16	-18
K										
	-2	-1	-3	-5	-7	-9	-11	-13	-15	-17
E										
	-4	-3	0	-2	-4	-6	-8	-10	-12	-14
D										
	-6	-3	-2	1	-1	-3	-5	-7	-9	-11
E										
	-8	-5	-2	-1	2	0	-2	-4	-6	-8
E										
	-10	-7	-4	-3	0	1	-1	-3	-5	-7
E										
	-12	-9	-6	-5	-2	-1	0	-2	-4	-6
L										
	-14	-11	-8	-7	-4	-3	-2	-1	-3	-5
S										
	-16	-13	-10	-9	-6	-5	-4	-3	-2	-4
V										
	-18	-15	-12	-11	-8	-7	-6	-5	-2	-3
W										
	-20	-17	-14	-13	-10	-9	-8	-7	-4	-1

Trace Matrix

		D		E		D		E		D		A		H		V		W	
	END	-	left	-	left	-	left	-	left	-	left	-	left	-	left	-	left	-	left
K	|	\																	
	up		diagonal	-	left	-	left	-	left	-	left	-	left	-	left	-	left	-	left
E	|		|	\															
	up		up		diagonal		left	-	left	-	left		left	-	left	-	left	-	left
D	|	\	|		|	\													
	up		diagonal		up		diagonal	-	left	-	left		left	-	left	-	left	-	left
E	|		|	\			|	\											
	up		up		diagonal		up		diagonal	-	left		left	-	left	-	left	-	left
E	|		|		|		|		|	\								
	up		up		up		up		up		diagonal		left	-	left	-	left	-	left
E	|		|		|		|		|		|	\						
	up		up		up		up		up		up		diagonal		left	-	left	-	left
L	|		|		|		|		|		|		|	\				
	up		up		up		up		up		up		up		diagonal	-	left	-	left
S	|		|		|		|		|		|		|		|	\			
	up		up		up		up		up		up		up		up		diagonal	-	left
V	|		|		|		|		|		|		|		|	\		\	
	up		up		up		up		up		up		up		up		diagonal		diagonal
W	|		|		|		|		|		|		|		|		|	\	
	up		up		up		up		up		up		up		up		up		diagonal

Figure 3.7: Dynamic programming, global alignment, final matrices (Needleman-Wunsch).

[Needleman and Wunsch, 1970], we first define two identical matrices with the same number of columns as residues in sequence 1 and as many rows as residues in sequence 2 One matrix is used to keep track of the scores and another to keep track of our route (see figures 3.4-3.7).

- **Step 1 (figure 3.4):** In the upper left field of the score matrix is written the score 0. This is the score before having aligned anything. From this field we can move in three directions: Down corresponds to inserting a gap in sequence 1, left to inserting a gap in sequence 2 and diagonal to making a match. Accordingly, a step to the right is -2, a step down is -2, and a diagonal step is $+1$ if the residues are identical, otherwise -1.

- **Step 2 (figure 3.5):** With the limits of the steps, we can easily fill in the first row and the first column of the matrix, since these fields can only be reached from one direction. So in the score matrix we write -2 in field 0,1, since this step corresponds to inserting a gap. In the trace matrix we then write *up* in field 0,1 since this was the direction we were coming from. In field 1,0 we write -2 in the score matrix and *left* in the trace matrix.

- **Step 3 (figure 3.6):** Now we would like to calculate the score of field 1,1. Coming from the left we had -2 in the previous field $(0, 1)$ and will have to add -2 for making a move to the right, inserting a gap in the *other* sequence, resulting in a score of -4. We do likewise if we would come down from field 1,0. We can now also make a diagonal move which means a match between the two first residues. In this example they are not identical and the match will have the score -1. Since we came from 0,0 with the score 0 the match case will result in -1. So we have the possibility to make three different moves resulting in a score of -4, -4, or -1, respectively. We now select the move resulting in the highest score (i.e., -1), and we write this score in field 1,1 in the score matrix. In the trace matrix we write *diagonal* in field 1,1 since this was the type of move made to reach this score.

- **Final steps:** Steps 2 and 3 are repeated until both matrices are filled out (figure 3.7). In the case that two different moves to a field result in the same score, we select the move *coming* from the highest previous score to write in the trace matrix. At any field, we will finally have a score. This score is then the maximal alignment score you can get coming from the upper left diagonal and to the position in the sequences matching that field.

When the matrices are all filled out, the final alignment score is in the lower right corner of the score matrix. In the above example the final alignment score is then −1. The score matrix has now served its purpose and is discarded, and the alignment is reconstructed using the trace matrix. To reconstruct the alignment start in the lower right corner of the final trace matrix (figure 3.7). Following the directions written in the fields, the alignment is now reconstructed backward. Here *diagonal* means a match between the two last residues in each sequence (W match W), and a move diagonal up-left. Next field: *diagonal*, i.e., V match V and a move diagonal up-left. The present field value is now *up*. This means that we introduce a gap in the first sequence to match S in the second sequence and then move one field up in the trace matrix. The rest of the trace is all diagonal, which means no gaps, and the resulting alignment will be

DEDEDAH–VW
KEDEEELSVW

This way to produce an alignment is called dynamic programming, and is still used in major alignment software packages (e.g., the ALIGN tool in the FASTA package uses the Needleman-Wunsch algorithm for global alignments). To illustrate that there *are* differences in the resulting alignments according to which scoring scheme is used, the above alignment using the BLOSUM62 matrix in figure 3.2 and a linear gap penalty of −9 results in the following alignment

DEDEDA–HVW
KEDEEELSVW

So the optimal alignment is only optimal using the chosen substitution scores and gap penalties, and there is no exact way to tell in a particular example if one set of scores gives a more "correct" alignment than another set of scores.

3.2.5 Local Alignments and Database Searches

The global alignment scheme described above is very good for comparing and analyzing the relationship between two selected proteins. Proteins, however, are often comprised of different domains, where each domain may be evolutionarily related to a different set of sequences. Thus when it comes to *searching* for sequences it is more beneficial to only look at the parts of the sequences that actually are related. A search is actually to make pairwise alignment of your query sequence to all the sequences in the database, and order the resulting alignments by the alignment score. For this purpose Smith and Waterman [1981] further developed the dynamic programming approach. The Smith-Waterman algorithm is like Needleman-Wunsch, except that the traces only continue as long as the scores are positive, Whenever a score becomes negative it is set to 0 and the corresponding trace is empty. Using the BLOSUM62 substitution matrix and a linear gap penalty of −9, the score and trace

Score matrix

	D	E	D	E	D	A	H	V	W	
	0	0	0	0	0	0	0	0	0	0
K										
	0	0	1	0	1	0	0	0	0	0
E										
	0	2	5	3	5	3	0	0	0	0
D										
	0	6	4	11	5	11	2	0	0	0
E										
	0	2	11	6	16	7	10	2	0	0
E										
	0	2	7	13	11	18	9	10	1	0
E										
	0	2	7	9	18	13	17	9	8	0
L										
	0	0	0	3	9	14	12	14	10	6
S										
	0	0	0	0	3	9	15	11	12	7
V										
	0	0	0	0	0	0	9	12	15	9
W										
	0	0	0	0	0	0	0	7	9	26

Trace Matrix

	D	E	D	E	D	A	H	V	W	
	END									
K			\		\					
		diagonal			diagonal					
E	\		\		\		\			
		diagonal	diagonal	diagonal	diagonal	diagonal				
D	\		\		\					
		diagonal	diagonal	diagonal	diagonal	diagonal	-	left		
E	\		\		\		\		\		
		diagonal	diagonal	diagonal	diagonal	-	left	diagonal	diagonal	
E	\		\		\		\		\		
		diagonal	diagonal	diagonal	diagonal	diagonal	-	left	diagonal	- left
E	\		\		\		\		\	\	
		diagonal	diagonal	diagonal	diagonal	diagonal	diagonal	diagonal	diagonal	
L			\				\	\	\	\	\
			diagonal	up	diagonal	diagonal	diagonal	diagonal	diagonal	diagonal
S				\		\	\	\	\	\
				diagonal	diagonal	diagonal	diagonal	diagonal	diagonal
V						\	\	\	\
						diagonal	diagonal	diagonal	diagonal
W							\	\	\
							diagonal	diagonal	diagonal

Figure 3.8: Dynamic programming, local alignment, final matrices (Smith-Waterman).

matrices will appear as in Figure 3.8. Now the backtrace of the optimal local alignment starts in the field with the highest score. There might be several equally good alignments, and there are several ways to deal with that, depending on what the goal is. If the two equally good alignments differ in length, one might, e.g., chose the longer. In this example the highest score is 26. This is accidentally again in the lower right corner so the backtrace will begin here. The backtrace will reveal that the local alignment look like this:

```
DEDEDAHVW
EDEEELSVW
```

BLAST The dynamic programming algorithm has the strength that it ensures that the optimal alignment, will always be found, given specific gap penalties and substitution scores. However, even with present-day computerpower this algorithm is far too slow to search the ever-increasing sequence databases of today. For this reason several shortcuts have been made, and one of the most successful is implemented in the widely-used alignment package, BLAST [Altschul et al., 1990, 1997, Altschul and Gish, 1996].

The basic BLAST algorithm consists of 3 steps:

1. **Make a list of words:** A list of neighbor words that have a score of at least T (default 11 for proteins) is made for each n-mer in the query sequence. Per default n=3 for proteins and n=11 for DNA. Any word in the query sequence that scores positive with itself may also be included.

2. **Search the database for the words on the list:** The database is scanned for hits to any of the N words on the list.

3. **Extend hits:** The first version of BLAST extended every hit it found. The newer version requires two nonoverlapping hits within a distance A (default 40) of each other before it extends a hit. The extension is only made until the score has dropped X (default 7) below the best score seen so far. This corresponds to saying this route looks so bad that there is no point in continuing in this direction. The locally optimal alignments are called high-scoring segment pairs (HSPs). If the score of an HSP is above a threshold S_g (default 22 bits) a gapped extension is attempted using dynamic programming. To speed the calculations this phase is only continued until the score falls X_g below the best score seen so far.

3.2.6   Expectation Values

When aligning two sequences it is not clear if a given score is really significant (i.e., might occur by chance by a certain probability). Such a measure can be

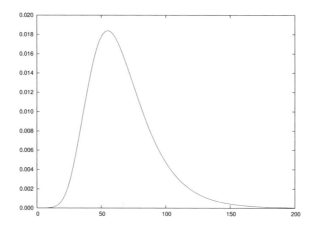

Figure 3.9: Distributions of scores, when aligning a sequence to a database of unrelated sequences.

obtained by aligning a great number of random sequences to the original sequence and from the resulting score distribution calculate the probability that a random sequence would result in a given score. This number is called the expectation-value, or E-value. The random sequences is obtained by shuffling the elements (nucleotides or amino acids) of the original sequence. In this way the score distribution will not be biased by a skewed amino acid distribution of the original sequence.

When searching through databases the question also arises whether a given alignment score confers a relationship between the two aligned regions or not. If we align a sequence to a database of all unrelated sequences and plot the alignment score against how many alignments will have that score we will get a curve like that in figure 3.9. This is called an extreme value distribution. We can from this distribution find out how often a given alignment-score will arise by chance. Thus the E-value is the theoretically expected number of false hits per sequence query, and a lower E-value means a more significant hit. Importantly, the E-value is dependent on the size of the database searched as the chance of getting a false hit rises as the database grows.

Different alignment programs use different approaches to calculate the E-value of a given database hit. FASTA actually makes all possible alignments, and returns a real distribution curve (figure 3.10) and calculates the E-value

```
        opt      E()
< 20     0     0:
  22     0     0:                  one = represents 23 library sequences
  24     0     0:
  26     0     0:
  28     0     3:*
  30     0    16:*
  32     7    64:= *
  34    75   173:====    *
  36   240   354:===========    *
  38   569   586:=======================*
  40  1127   817:===========================================*=============
  42  1379   999:====================================================*================
  44  1277  1102:==========================================================*=========
  46  1183  1122:===========================================================*===
  48   914  1074:======================================================*
  50   733   980:==================================    *
  52   753   862:=====================================  *
  54   661   736:====================================  *
  56   516   615:=======================    *
  58   536   505:====================*==
  60   365   409:================  *
  62   335   328:==============*
  64   273   261:============*
  66   188   206:========*
  68   168   162:=======*
  70   126   127:======*
  72   133    99:====*=
  74    88    77:===*
  76    68    60:==*
  78    56    47:==*
  80    41    36:=*
  82    41    28:=*
  84    34    22:*=
  86    16    17:*
  88    13    13:*          inset = represents 1 library sequences
  90    12    10:*
  92     6     8:*         :====== *
  94     4     6:*         :==== *
  96     3     5:*         :=== *
  98     4     4:*         :===*
 100     2     3:*         :==*
 102     0     2:*         : *
 104     0     2:*         : *
 106     1     1:*         :*
 108     2     1:*         :*=
 110     0     1:*         :*
 112     2     1:*         :*=
 114     0     0:        *
 116     0     0:        *
 118     0     0:        *
>120     0     0:        *
4113207 residues in 11951 sequences
 Expectation_n fit: rho(ln(x))= 5.3517+/-0.00135; mu= -2.1992+/- 0.077;
 mean_var=60.8388+/-13.111, Z-trim: 5  B-trim: 3 in 1/55
 Kolmogorov-Smirnov  statistic: 0.0520 (N=29) at  46
```

Figure 3.10: Distributions of scores, from FASTA alignments of a given sequence to all sequences in a specific database.

making a fit to this curve. BLAST, however, uses a premade empirical curve to assign E-values to each alignment returned from a database search.

PSI-BLAST As described earlier, the scoring matrices used somehow represent the general evolutionary trends for mutations. However, in reality, allowed mutations are very much dependent on, and constrained by their physical context. As an example, it could be possible to insert, delete, or exchange a number of different amino acids in a flexible loop on the surface of a protein and still preserve the overall structure and function of the protein.

```
         A  R  N  D  C  Q  E  G  H  I  L  K  M  F  P  S  T  W  Y  V
 1 I    -2 -4 -5 -5 -2 -4 -4 -5 -5  6  0 -4  0 -2 -4 -4 -2 -4 -3  4
 2 K    -1 -1 -2 -2 -3 -1  3  3 -2 -2 -3  4 -2 -4 -3  1  1 -4 -3  2
 3 E     5 -3 -3 -3  3  1 -2 -3 -3 -3 -2 -2 -4 -3 -1 -2 -4 -3  1
 4 E    -4 -3  2  5 -6  1  5 -4 -3 -6 -6 -2 -5 -6 -4 -2 -3 -6 -5 -5
 5 H    -4  2  1  1 -5  1 -2 -4  9 -5 -2 -3 -4 -4 -5 -3 -4 -5  1 -5
 6 V    -3  0 -4 -5 -4 -4 -2 -3 -5  1 -2  1  0  1 -4 -3  3 -5 -3  5
 7 I     0 -2 -4  1 -4 -2 -4 -4 -5  1  0 -2  0  2 -5  1 -1 -5 -3  4
 8 I    -3  0 -5 -5 -4 -2 -5 -6  1  2  4 -4 -1  0 -5 -2  0 -3  5 -1
 9 Q    -2 -3 -2 -3 -5  4  1  3  5 -5 -3 -3 -4 -2 -4  2 -1 -4  2 -2
10 A     2 -4 -4 -3  2 -3 -1 -4 -2  1 -1 -4 -3 -4  1  2  3 -5 -1  1
11 E    -1  3  1  1 -1  0  1 -4 -3 -1 -3  0  3 -5  4 -1 -3 -6 -3 -1
12 F    -3 -5 -5 -4 -4 -4 -1 -1  1  1 -5  2  5 -1 -4 -4 -3  5  2
13 Y     3 -5 -5 -6  3 -4 -5 -2 -1  0 -4 -5 -3  3 -5 -2 -2 -2  7  1
14 L    -1 -3 -4 -2  1  5  1 -1 -1 -1  1 -3 -3  1 -5 -1 -1 -2  3 -2
15 N    -1 -4  4  1  5 -3 -4  2 -4 -4 -4 -3 -2 -4 -5  2  0 -5  0  0
16 P    -2  4 -4 -4 -5  0 -3  3  2 -5 -4  0 -4 -3  0  1 -2 -1  5 -3
17 D    -3 -2  1  5 -6 -2  2  2 -1 -2 -2 -3 -5 -4 -5 -1  2 -6 -3 -4
```

Figure 3.11: Example of a PSSM.

The corresponding number of allowed substitutions would very probably be much more limited in the core — or in a secondary structure, rich — region of the protein. So if a *general* substitution matrix works well, a matrix representing the *specific* evolutionary trend for a given position in a given protein should work even better. As described by Altschul et al. [1997], this is actually the case.

In the PSI-BLAST approach, first an ordinary BLAST search on the basis of the BLOSUM62 matrix is performed against the database. Second, a position-specific scoring matrix (PSSM) is calculated as described in chapter 4. The matrix is calculated by considering the substitutions observed in pairwise alignments made between the query sequence and the hits that have an expectation value below a selected threshold. Now the calculated matrix (figure 3.11), as a representation of the query sequence, is used to search the database again. So when the alignment score matrix is filled out, we now look in the PSSM for a given position to find the match score between the PSSM and that particular amino acid in the database sequence. For example, if we want to match position 3 in the search sequence, a glutamic acid, to an alanine, the match score is 5. However, if we want to match position 4, also a glutamic acid, to an alanine, the match score is −4. This should illustrate the higher specificity of a PSSM as compared to ordinary substitution matrices.

3.3 Multiple Alignments

When looking at several related sequences, it is often useful and informative to look at all the sequences in one alignment (multiple alignment). The simplest approach is to align all the sequences, one by one, with a single selected "master sequence," and this is what can be obtained by programs like BLAST. However, these programs make only local alignments, and often gaps and in-

A

```
Drosophila_melanogaster    MSAPDKEKEKEKEETNNKSEDLGLLEEDDEFEEFPAEDFRVGDDEEELNVWEDNWDDDNVEDDFSQQLKAHLESKKMET
Anopheles_gambiae          ----------DKENKDKPKLDLGLLEEDDEFEEFPAEDWAGneDEEELSVWEDNWDDDNVEDDFNQQLRAQLEKHK---
Zebrafish                  -----------------QTVDLGLLEEDDEFEEFPAEDWTGLDEDEDAHVWEDNWDDDNVEDDFSNQLRAELE------
HUMAN                      --------------------DLGLLEEDDEFEEFPAEDWAGLDEDEDAHVWEDNWDDDNVEDDFSNQLRAELE------
MOUSE                      --------------------DLGLLEEDDEFEEFPAEDWAGLDEDEDAHVWEDNWDDDNVEDDFSNQLRAELE------
Xenopus_laevis             --------------------DLGLLEEDDEFEEFPTEDWTGFDEDEDTHVWEDNWDDDNVEDDFSNQLRAELE------
Saccharomyces_cerevisiae   ------------------------LEEDDEFEDFPIDTWANGETIkqTNIWEENWDDVEVDDDFTNELKAELDRYKRE--
Neurospora_crassa.         ----DAKSTEPKPEQPVTEKKTAVLEEDDEFEDFPVDDWEAEDTeeAKHLWEESWDDDDTSDDFSAQLKEELK------
```

B

```
Drosophila_melanogaster    ----MSAPDKE----KEKEKEETNNKSEDLGLLEEDDEFEEFPAEDFRVG
Anopheles_gambiae          ----MS--DKEN---KDKPK-------LDLGLLEEDDEFEEFPAEDWAGN
HUMAN                      ----MS----------EKKQ------PVDLGLLEEDDEFEEFPAEDWAGL
MOUSE                      ----MS----------EKKQ------PVDLGLLEEDDEFEEFPAEDWAGL
Zebrafish                  ----MS----------EKKQ------TVDLGLLEEDDEFEEFPAEDWTGL
Xenopus_laevis             ----MSS---------DKKP------PVDLGLLEEDDEFEEFPTEDWTGF
Neurospora_crassa.         ----MASTQPKNDAKSTEPKPEQPVTEKKTAVLEEDDEFEDFPVDDWEAE
Saccharomyces_cerevisiae   MSTDVAAAQAQSKIDLTKKKNE----EINKKSLEEDDEFEDFPIDTWANG
                                  :           :        .   *********:**  : :

Drosophila_melanogaster    ------DDEEELNVWEDNWDDDNVEDDFSQQLKAHLESK--KMET-
Anopheles_gambiae          K-----EDEEELSVWEDNWDDDNVEDDFNQQLRAQLEKH--K----
HUMAN                      ------DEDEDAHVWEDNWDDDNVEDDFSNQLRAELEKHGYKMETS
MOUSE                      ------DEDEDAHVWEDNWDDDNVEDDFSNQLRAELEKHGYKMETS
Zebrafish                  ------DEDEDAHVWEDNWDDDNVEDDFSNQLRAELEKHGYKMETS
Xenopus_laevis             ------DEDEDTHVWEDNWDDDNVEDDFSNQLRAELEKHGYKMETS
Neurospora_crassa.         DTEAAKGNNEAKHLWEESWDDDDTSDDFSAQLKEELKKVEAAKKR-
Saccharomyces_cerevisiae   ETIKS-NAVTQTNIWEENWDDVEVDDDFTNELKAELDRY--KRENQ
                                 :**:.*** :..***. :*: .*.
```

C

```
HUMAN         1    ---------- ---------- ------MSEK KQPVDLGLLE EDDEFEEFPA
MOUSE         1    ---------- ---------- ------MSEK KQPVDLGLLE EDDEFEEFPA
Zebrafish     1    ---------- ---------- ------MSEK KQTVDLGLLE EDDEFEEFPA
Drosophila_m  1    ----MSapDK Ek-------E KEKEET-NNK SE--DLGLLE EDDEFEEFPA
Neurospora_c  1    ----MA--ST QPKNDAKSTE PKPEQpVTEK KTAV----LE EDDEFEDFPV
Xenopus_laev  1    m--------- ---------- -----S-SDK KPPVDLGLLE EDDEFEEFPT
Saccharomyce  1    mstdVA--AA QAQSKIDLTK KKNEEI-NKK S-------LE EDDEFEDFPI
Anopheles_ga  1    ----MS--DK ENKD------ ---------- KPKLDLGLLE EDDEFEEFPA

HUMAN         25   EDWAGLDE-- ----DED-AH VWEDNWDDDN VEDDFSNQLR AELEK----H
MOUSE         25   EDWAGLDE-- ----DED-AH VWEDNWDDDN VEDDFSNQLR AELEK----H
Zebrafish     25   EDWTGLDE-- ----DED-AH VWEDNWDDDN VEDDFSNQLR AELEK----H
Drosophila_m  37   EDFRVGDD-- ----EEE-LN VWEDNWDDDN VEDDFSQQLR AHLES----K
Neurospora_c  41   DDWEAEDtEA AKGNNEA-KH LWEESWDDDD TSDDFSAQLK EELKKveaaK
Xenopus_laev  26   EDWTGFDE-- ----DED-TH VWEDNWDDDN VEDDFSNQLR AELEK----H
Saccharomyce  41   DTWAng--ET IKSNavtqTN IWEENWDDVE VDDDFTNELK AELDR----Y
Anopheles_ga  29   EDWAGNKE-- ----DEEeLS VWEDNWDDDN VEDDFNQQLR AQLEK----H

HUMAN         64   GYKMETS
MOUSE         64   GYKMETS
Zebrafish     64   GYKMETS
Drosophila_m  76   --KMET-
Neurospora_c  90   --Kr---
Xenopus_laev  65   GYKMETS
Saccharomyce  85   --KRENQ
Anopheles_ga  69   --K----
```

Figure 3.12: Multiple alignments of the proteasome DSS1 subunit from different organisms using A) PSI-BLAST, B) ClustalW, and C) DIALIGN. Lower case letters means a part of the sequence that is not significantly aligned.

sertions will be placed differently in the master sequence depending on which
other sequence it is aligned with. Another approach is to align all sequences
pairwise with all other sequences and establish the difference between every
pair. Such a map is called a distance matrix, and from this it is possible to obtain an estimate of which sequences are most related (a cluster), and aligning
those first, and then align all the prealigned clusters against each other. This is
basically what is implemented in the most used multiple alignment program,
ClustalW alias ClustalX [Thompson et al., 1994]. First is calculated a score for
the alignment between each pair of the sequences. These scores are then used
to calculate phylogenetic tree, or a dendrogram, using the clustering method
UPGMA (see Chapter 5). Having calculated the dendrogram, the sequences
are aligned in larger and larger groups. Each of these alignments consists of
aligning 2 alignments, using profile alignments, which are the alignment of 2
groups of already aligned sequences. The method is an extension of the profile
method of Gribskov et al. [1987] for aligning a single sequence with an aligned
group of sequences. With a sequence-to-sequence alignment, a weight matrix
such as BLOSUM62 is used to obtain a score for a particular substitution between the pairs of aligned residues. In profile alignments, however, each of
the two input alignments are treated as a single sequence, but you calculate
the score at aligned positions as the average substitution matrix score of all
the residues in one alignment vs. all those in the other, e.g., if you have 2
alignments with I and J sequences respectively the score at any position is the
average of all the I times J scores of the residues compared separately. Any
gaps that are introduced are placed in all of the sequences of an alignment at
the same position. However, all gaps in the ends of the sequences are free.
This might give some artifacts, especially when sequences of different length
are aligned. Newer multiple alignment algorithms implemented in programs
such as T-Coffee [Notredame et al., 2000] and DIALIGN [Morgenstern, 1999]
handle these problems much better, but the algorithms behind them will not
be described in this book. Figure 3.12 is an example of the differences in the
results, using different alignment algorithms/programs. Note that PSI-BLAST
will only return local alignments, and that the result is based on pairwise alignments to the query sequence, i.e., no clustering has been involved.

3.4 DNA Alignments

Untill now only protein alignments have been described. The basic algorithms
and programs used for DNA alignment, however, are the same as for proteins. DNA alignments are much more difficult since at each position, we can
have one of only four different bases as opposed to one of twenty in peptide
alignments. So we will not have a specific substitution matrix like BLOSUM

or PAM but rather take a step back and use a general substitution score for any match or mismatch but still using affine gap penalties. This makes the probability of any given substitution equally high, and so the significance of the final alignment will be lower. Some nucleotide matrices, however, do have different substitution scores for transitions (Dealing with DNA/RNA sequences from coding regions, however, gives an opportunity to shortcut the alignment by actually aligning the translation products, rather than the actual DNA sequences. This approach has been implemented in most alignment software packages, including FASTA (tfasta [Pearson and Lipman, 1988, Pearson, 1996]) and BLAST (tblast [Altschul et al., 1990, Altschul and Gish, 1996]). In this basic but strong approach, gaps in the aligned DNA sequences will only occur in multiples of triplets. This will, however, not catch examples correctly where frameshifts have actually happened, leading to major changes of larger or smaller parts of the translated protein. For such investigations the programs GenA1 [Hein and Støvlbaek, 1994, 1996] and COMBAT [Pedersen et al., 1998] can be used, but only for pairwise alignments. For multiple alignments an automatic method exists that will translate DNA to peptide, do the multiple alignment using DIALIGN [Morgenstern, 1999], and return the final alignment at the DNA level [Wernersson and Pedersen, 2003]. Multiple DNA alignments are especially useful for investigating the evolution on the molecular level (molecular evolution). With such alignments it is possible to examine exactly which positions in the DNA are more or less likely to undergo mutations that survive and are transferred to the progeny. We can also calculate the chance that a given codon will only allow mutations that will not lead to an amino acid change (silent mutations or synonymous mutations) and compare it to the chance that a substitution leads to an amino acid change (nonsynonymous mutations). This ratio is called dN/dS and an example of such a calculation is given in chapter 7.

3.5   Molecular Evolution and Phylogeny

Phylogenies reveal evolutionary relationships between organisms and specific sequences. In recent years molecular phylogenies have started to play a major role in epidemiological studies of pathogens. These studies provide information about where and when a virulent strain can arise. Not only human pathogens but also viral and bacterial disease-causing agents of livestock are of importance, as such outbreaks can cause great economic loss, as well as increase the chance of a possible cross-species infection. Recent developments of new methods for isolating, amplifying, and sequencing RNA isolated from small samples of blood or tissue have made the molecular phylogeny of pathogens a rapidly expanding research field. Moreover, since many pathogens can mutate at much higher rates than eukaryotes, it is possible to obtain the phylogeny of sequences that diverged only recently.

One interesting application of molecular phylogeny is represented by analysis of the origins of HIV epidemics. Exactly when simian immunodeficiency virus (SIV) was transmitted from nonhuman primates to humans, giving rise to the human immunodeficiency virus (HIV), is still under investigation. Korber et al. [2000] used a phylogenetic analysis of the viral sequences with a known date of sampling to estimate the year of origin for the main group of HIV viruses (HIV-1 M), the principal cause of acquired immunodeficiency syndrome (AIDS). AIDS is caused by two divergent viruses, HIV-1 and HIV-2. HIV-1 is responsible for the global pandemic, while HIV-2 has, until recently, been restricted to West Africa and appears to be less virulent in its effects. SIV viruses related to HIV have been found in many species of nonhuman primates. By analyzing the molecular divergence of the envelope gene, and applying a model which assumes constant mutation rates through time and across lineages, Korber et al. [2000] estimated that the last common ancestor of the HIV-1 M group appeared in 1931 (with a confidence interval of 1916–1941). Using a different molecular clock analysis, where the mutation rate is allowed to change at splitting events, and also when analyzing a different protein, the same estimates were obtained. This approach only identifies when the common ancestor began to diversify; it does not identify the exact time of transmission. Still, given this estimate, one is able to come up with more precise hypotheses about the transmission event.

3.5.1 Phylogenetic Methods

The starting point of any phylogenetic work is a collection of sequences that might be evolutionarily related. Such a set could be extracted from public databases using some of the tools described previously, or it could be data from one's own work. These sequences must now be aligned by the use of multiple alignment software, such as ClustalW. ClustalW also calculates a distance matrix of your sequences, i.e., the relation of each of your sequences to the other sequences in your alignment. A way to visualize the distances in a distance matrix is a tree-like drawing where the distances along the branches correlates with the distances in the distance matrix. Such a drawing is called a phylogenetic tree. One important point about trees is that they are only useful if the described system has been under vertical evolution (i.e., no horizontal gene transfers and recombination), otherwise a simple tree makes no sense. To calculate the grouping and the branch lengths of such a tree, two major approaches are applicable. One approach is optimization methods that will find the tree that gives the optimal fit to the matrix, e.g., the minimal sum of squared errors. Another approach is clustering methods that is related to the optimization methods, but is much faster. The clustering methods, however, do not guarantee the optimal solution.

Two major types of trees exist: rooted and unrooted trees. With rooted trees a common ancestor point is used as the origin of the tree, no matter if this is really scientific sane with the given data. In rooted trees the horizontal distance from the leaves to the origin is directly proportional to the amount of changes. Unrooted trees are used to show relations where no common ancestor is given, and only the evolutionary distance between the leaves can be inferred. In both rooted and unrooted trees, the leaves are grouped in clusters. This grouping depends heavily on the algorithm used. Some algorithms just give one of potentially many, more or less equally probable, outputs. Other approaches actually calculate many different solutions and give the most probable outcome with some indication of how reliable a particular solution is.

As a simple example, we will investigate the phylogenetic relationship between HIV and SIV using a set consisting of 27 different gp120 protein sequences from isolates of HIV-1, HIV-2, chimpanzee SIV, and macaque monkey SIV. The gp120 protein of HIV is crucial for binding of the virus particle to target cells. It is the specific affinity of gp120 for the CD4 protein that targets HIV to those cells of the immune system that express CD4 on their surface (e.g., helper T lymphocytes, monocytes, and macrophages). ClustalW is used to align the sequences (figure 3.13) and, as mentioned earlier, ClustalW also clusters the most related sequences. The information from this clustering can subsequently be used to produce a phylogenetic tree (figure 3.14).

The phylogenetic tree from the analysis (see figure 3.14) shows two separate clusters. One contains SIV from chimpanzee (SIVCZ) together with the HIV-1 sequences, while the other contains SIV from macaque/sooty mangabey together with HIV-2. This indicates that HIV-1 originated from one event where the virus was transmitted from (presumably) chimpanzee to human, while HIV-2 originated from a second, independent event where the virus was transmitted from (presumably) macaque to human.

3.6   Viral Evolution and Escape: Sequence Variation

Coexistence of pathogens with their hosts imposes an evolutionary pressure both for the host immune systems and the pathogens. The coexistence depends on a delicate balance between the replication rate of the pathogen and the clearance rate by the host immune response. Throughout the animal and plant kingdoms we see several quite different strategies developed by the host immune systems to defend themselves against intruders. Similarly, the pathogens have developed an array of immune evasion mechanisms to escape

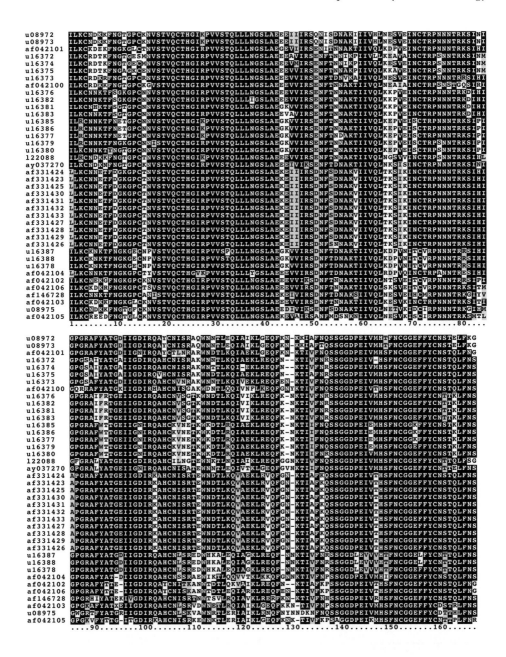

Figure 3.13: ClustalW alignment of 27 HIV/SIV gp120 sequences. The output is modified with the BOXSHADE program.

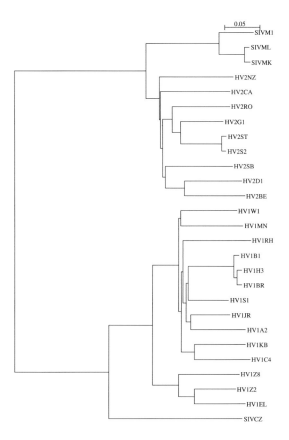

Figure 3.14: A rooted tree of 27 aligned HIV/SIV gp120 sequences. HV1XX=HIV-1 sequences, HV2XX=HIV-2 sequences, SIVMX=SIV (macaque), SIVSX=SIV (sooty mangabey), SIVCZ=SIV (chimpanzee).

their elimination by the host's immune system.

We can divide the immune evasion mechanisms (mainly of viruses) broadly into three categories that allow:

1. avoiding the humoral immune response,

2. interfering with the cellular immune response,

3. disrupting the immune effector functions, e.g., by expressing some cytokines.

The humoral response is impaired whenever the antibody binding sites on a protein (often on the surface) mutate in such a way that binding is no longer possible. Especially neutralizing antibodies, i.e., the antibodies that can block infection of the cells by the pathogen, cause a high selection pressure on the virus to mutate. The most straightforward way of identifying such mutants is via sequence analysis of the pathogenic samples. The first step is to align the sequences to pinpoint which regions of the pathogen are mutating. This may be the region that is under the strongest selection pressure by the antibodies. However, it could also be areas with no constrains. Such alignments demonstrate that the most typical examples of escape from antibody response occur in the influenza virus and HIV. The human body can rapidly mount neutralizing antibodies against the major surface protein of the influenza surface protein, hemagglutinin. The influenza virus evades this humoral response by two mechanisms [Gorman et al., 1992]. First, using point mutations, the viral variants can escape neutralization, but this does not cause severe disease, since there will still be some unaltered epitopes that can be recognized. Second, if RNA segments are exchanged between different strains, the hemagglutinin protein can gain a totally different structure. In such a case, the antibodies made during previous infections are no longer functional and severe pandemics can occur [Claas and Osterhaus, 1998]. Interestingly, the phylogenetic analysis of the hemagglutinin protein shows that the antigenic evolution of the influenza virus is punctuated, i.e., some mutants cause epidemics for almost eight consecutive years, while others last only for two or three years [Smith et al., 2004]. Since the 1960s (when the first sequences were collected) every viral mutant has been able to cause an epidemic for at least two years, after which enough individuals will have acquired immunity to limit the spread significantly (herd immunity).

Similarly, the cytotoxic T lymphocyte (CTL) response can be abrogated whenever peptide binding of MHC molecules or binding of the T cell receptor to the MHC-peptide complex is disturbed. It is relatively difficult to observe such escapes, because they are different for each individual, depending on her or his MHC background. Therefore many CTL escape variants can be circulating in a host population without one becoming the dominant mutant. Only in chronic infections like HIV and hepatitis B is it possible to find these escape mutants in a patient. Again, for HIV we have an extensive amount of data to analyze CTL escape mutants. Using sequence analysis it is possible to see that escape mutations are not spread all over the viral genome, because HIV is not able to tolerate changes equally well in all proteins. HIV has very flexible proteins like the envelope protein, gp160, where up to 35% of the sequence can be different from the wild-type virus [Gaschen et al., 2002]. On the other hand, for some proteins, like capsid protein p24, the surface cannot tolerate point mutations without a severe loss of viral fitness [von Schwedler et al., 2003,

Leslie et al., 2004].

An effective vaccine should be able to target the parts of a pathogenic genome that are quite conserved even under the above-mentioned selection pressures. For example, given that less than a 2% amino acid change can cause a failure in cross-reactive immunity of the influenza vaccine [Korber et al., 2001b], it is obvious that for an HIV vaccine to use the envelope protein would be futile. One approach to deal with such large diversity is to use the consensus or the ancestral virus sequence as a vaccine. Such sequences have the advantage of being central and most similar to circulating strains. Another, safer approach would be to design epitope vaccines, which again requires choosing the most conserved epitopes. But the selection of such epitopes also requires computational analysis that goes beyond what simple sequence comparison techniques can handle, as the binding specificities are influenced by correlations between amino acids present at different peptide positions. A solution to this problem is to use machine learning techniques (see chapter 5).

3.7 Prediction of Functional Features of Biological Sequences

During experimental analysis of the immune system, proteins of unknown function are typically being identified as key players using high-throughput gene expression or proteomics data. The functional assignment of such immune system–related proteins also often requires sequence analysis that goes beyond what can be solved by simple sequence alignment methods. In most genomes no more than 40 to 60% of the proteins can be assigned a functional role based on sequence similarity to proteins with known function. Traditionally, protein function has been related directly to the 3D structure of the protein chain of amino acids, which currently, for an arbitrary sequence, is quite hard (in the general case, impossible) to compute. As the sequence, in a given biochemical context, determines the structure, functional information between two sequences can be transferred by comparing the sequence of amino acids by aligning the two against each other. This method is fast and powerful, but only solves part of the problem: it is still impossible to determine that two quite different sequences encode proteins with essentially the same biochemical function.

Several different methods have been developed which do not rely on direct sequence similarity, but on features which go beyond sequence-wide similarity, such as the gene position in the genome, or integration of local or global protein features. One such method, ProtFun, does not, like sequence alignment, compare any two sequences, but operates in the "feature" space of all sequences. ProtFun is therefore complementary to methods based on alignment and the inherent, position-by-position quantification of similarity between two sequences and their amino acids [Jensen et al., 2002, 2003]. This particular method is still entirely sequence-based and does not require prior knowledge of gene expression, gene fusion, or protein-protein interaction.

For any function assignment method, the ability to correctly predict the functional relationship depends strongly on the function classification scheme used. One would, e.g., not expect that a method based on coregulation of genes will work well for a category like "enzyme," since enzymes and the genes coding for their substrates or substrate transporters often display strong coregulation at the gene and protein levels.

The ProtFun approach to function prediction is based on the fact that a protein is not alone when performing its biological task. It will have to operate using the same cellular machinery for modification and sorting as all the other proteins do. Essential types of post-translational modifications (PTMs) include glycosylation, phosphorylation, and cleavage of N-terminal signal peptides controlling the entry to the secretory pathway, but hundreds of other types of modification exist (a subset of these will be present in any given organism). Many of the PTMs are enabled by local consensus sequence motifs, while others are characterized by more complex patterns of correlation between the amino acids close or far apart in the sequence.

This suggests an alternative approach to function prediction, as one may expect that proteins performing similar functions would share some attributes even though they are not at all related at the global level of amino acid sequence. As several powerful predictive methods for PTMs and localization have been constructed, a function prediction method based on such attributes can be applied to all proteins where the sequence is known.

3.7.1   The ProtFun Method

The ProtFun method integrates (using an artificial neural network approach; see chapter 5 for a general introduction) many individual attribute predictions and calculated sequence statistics (out of many more tested for discriminative value) (see figure 3.15). The integrated method predicts functional categories which can be defined in various ways. The method predicts, e.g., whether a sequence is likely to function as an enzyme, and if so, its category according to the classes defined by the Enzyme Commission. The same scheme can be used to predict any other set of functional classes, including highly specific ones, such as "ligand gated ion channel." It can, for example, be used to identify hormones, growth factors, receptors, and ion channels in the human genome as defined by the Gene Ontology Consortium gene function classification scheme. Obviously, even though such methods produce predictions with false positives and false negatives, they can provide essential clues, e.g., to selecting an assay if the confidence scores are sufficiently high.

The method uses combinations of attributes as input to the neural network for predicting the functional category of a protein. Combinations of attributes can be selected by evaluating their discriminative value for a specific functional category, say proteins involved in transcription or proteins being transporters. Attributes useful for function prediction must not only correlate well with the functional classification scheme, but must also be predictable from the sequence with reasonable accuracy.

Interestingly, the combinations of attributes selected for a given category also implicitly characterize a particular functional class in an entirely new way. This type of method identifies, without any a priori ranking of their importance, the biological features relevant to a particular type of functionality, say attributes which are discriminative for two different categories of ion channels.

The success of the method indicates that (even predicted) PTMs correlate strongly with the functional categories and this fits well with general biological knowledge. For proteins with "regulatory function" one of the most important features turned out to be phosphorylation, consistent with the fact that reversible phosphorylation is a well-known and widely used regulatory mechanism. Glycosylation was also found to be a strong indicator for regulatory proteins. The most important single feature for distinguishing between enzymes and nonenzymes turned out to be predicted protein secondary structure. This also makes sense, as enzymes are known to be overrepresented among all-alpha proteins where the amino acid chain forms an alpha-helix structure, and more rarely are found to be all-β proteins, where the structure is rich in β-sheet.

3.7.2 Individual Sequence Prediction

The ProtFun method can be used to characterize the entire genome, but it is perhaps best suited for obtaining functional hints for individual sequences for later use in assay selection and design. As an example we can take the human prion sequence which is being associated with the Creutzfeldt-Jacob disease. The functionality of this protein, which seems to produce no phenotype when knocked out in mice, was for a long time not fully understood. The ProtFun method predicts (see figure 3.16) with high confidence that the human prion sequence belongs to the transport and binding category, and also that it is very unlikely to be an enzyme. Indeed, prions have now been shown to be able to bind and transport copper, while no catalytic activity has ever been observed. Interestingly, as the prion is a cell surface glycoprotein (expressed by neural cells) it has a distinct pattern of post-translational modification, which most likely contains information which can be exploited by the prediction method

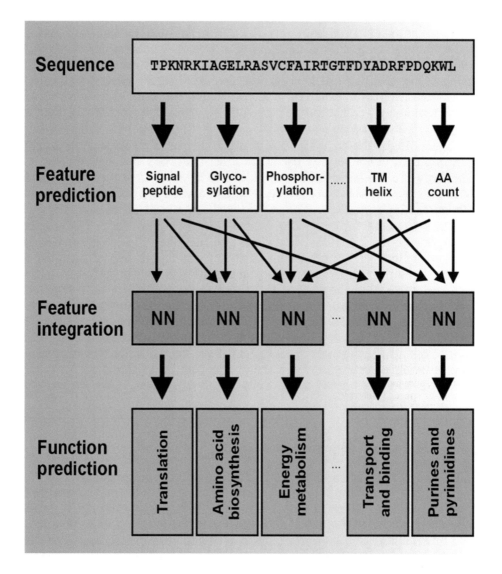

Figure 3.15: The ProtFun neural networks that predict the function of proteins in protein feature space. Each sequence is converted into features and then the networks (NN) integrate these features and provide a prediction for the affinity toward different functional categories. For different categories different protein features will have discriminatory value. During training (using experimentally characterized data) the most discriminative features are determined for each category.

```
######### ProtFun 1.1 predictions ##########

>PRIO_HUMAN

# Functional category                        Prob

  Amino_acid_biosynthesis                     0.020
  Biosynthesis_of_cofactors                   0.032
  Cell_envelope                               0.146
  Cellular_processes                          0.053
  Central_intermediary_metabolism             0.130
  Energy_metabolism                           0.029
  Fatty_acid_metabolism                       0.017
  Purines_and_pyrimidines                     0.528
  Regulatory_functions                        0.013
  Replication_and_transcription               0.020
  Translation                                 0.035
  Transport_and_binding              => 0.831

# Enzyme/nonenzyme                            Prob
  Enzyme                                      0.250
  Nonenzyme                          => 0.750

# Enzyme class                                Prob
  Oxidoreductase (EC 1.-.-.-)                 0.070
  Transferase    (EC 2.-.-.-)                 0.031
  Hydrolase      (EC 3.-.-.-)                 0.057
  Isomerase      (EC 4.-.-.-)                 0.020
  Ligase         (EC 5.-.-.-)                 0.010
  Lyase          (EC 6.-.-.-)                 0.017
```

Figure 3.16: The prediction output from the ProtFun method for the human prion protein, PRIO_HUMAN. The method produces three types of output for functional categories: broad cellular role, enzyme classes, and Gene Ontology categories, only the two first are included here for reasons of space. The number of Gene Ontology categories predicted is growing and is currently around 75. The numerical output can be used, for example, to select an assay, or the order in which different assays should be selected, when confirming experimentally the function of an uncharacterized protein. The ProtFun method is made available at www.cbs.dtu.dk/services.

for functional inference.

The neural network was not transferring functional information just by identifying by sequence similarity from the nearest neighbor in sequence space used to train the system, as the maximal similarity between the prion sequence and the data set used to train and test the ProtFun method was only 14.8% identity at the amino acid level to a proline-arginine-rich repeat protein. Predictions like these are very useful when resolving protein function, because they can be used to generate specific hypotheses and direct laboratory experiments for sequences where no information at all can be obtained by alignment.

3.7.3   Predicting Functional Categories for Systems Biology: the Cell Cycle as an Example

Characterization of the immune system also requires that genes and proteins are grouped into subsystems, where the biochemical task of each protein may be highly different. The ProtFun method can also be used to group sequences in this manner. As an example with relevance for the immune system, we describe here a version of the method that predicts whether a protein is encoded by a periodically transcribed, cell cycle regulated gene, or not. The ability of a cell to replicate itself is one of the most fundamental features of life, and also of disease, most importantly in relation to cancers. The hundreds of genes maintaining the cell cycle work together in a highly robust manner, making it possible for cells to divide under many different growth conditions and other influences from the environment. The robustness is achieved by sophisticated regulation making the periodic gene expression highly stable. The eukaryotic cell cycle is regulated at many levels, from transcription and translation to posttranslational modification and targeted protein degradation. Proteins need not only be produced, but also be removed again when no longer needed. The cell cycle molecular machinery consists of highly diverse proteins, with little sequence similarity.

A key technique being used to elucidate which genes are involved in a given subsystem is the DNA microarray method (see section 5.1). This is also the case for the cell cycle, where gene expression measurements are made during many different time points of the cycle. Unfortunately, many of the "lists" of genes, which have been produced in this way do not agree as much as expected, even if these studies have produced highly valuable information de Lichtenberg et al. [2003, 2004]. Part of the disagreement relates to differences in experimental conditions and procedures, but a large fraction is presumably related to basic noise problems in the DNA microarray technology when measuring the expression level of weakly expressed genes.

The ProtFun function classification technique described above can be used to predict, in feature space, such systems biology related categories de Lichtenberg et al. [2003]. Not all cell cycle related genes are periodic, but many of the key factors enabling the final formation of protein complexes are. The fact that the method with a reasonable high performance is able to separate such two highly diverse categories, demonstrates that many cell cycle proteins indeed display correlations between their features, which are different from those of other proteins. These features include phosphorylation, glycosylation, stability and/or disposition for targeted degradation, as well as localization in the cell.

In relation to the immune system many other sets of proteins creating a given subsystem may also display feature based similarities that can be exploited in a prediction approach like ProtFun. One aim is of course to identify novel components involved, but also to discover whether such biochemically diverse proteins share features which can be used to describe the biology behind their functionality.

Chapter 4

Methods Applied in Immunological Bioinformatics

A large variety of methods are commonly used in the field of immunological bioinformatics. In this chapter many of these techniques are introduced. The first section describes the powerful techniques of weight-matrix construction, including sequence weighting and pseudocount correction. The techniques are introduced using an example of peptide-MHC binding. In the following sections the more advanced methods of Gibbs sampling, ANNs, and hidden Markov models (HMMs) are introduced. The chapter concludes with a section on performance measures for predictive systems and a short section introducing the concepts of representative data set generation.

4.1 Simple Motifs, Motifs and Matrices

In this section, we shall demonstrate how simple but reasonably accurate prediction methods can be derived from a set of training data of very limited size. The examples selected relate to peptide-MHC binding prediction, but could equally well have been related to proteasomal cleavage, TAP binding, or any other problem characterized by simple sequence motifs.

A collection of sequences known to contain a given binding motif can be used to construct a simple, data-driven prediction algorithm. Table 4.1 shows a set of peptide sequences known to bind to the HLA-A*0201 allele.

From the set of data shown in table 4.1, one can construct simple rules defining which peptides will bind to the given HLA molecule with high affinity. From the above example it could, e.g., be concluded that a binding motif must

ALAKAAAAM
ALAKAAAAN
ALAKAAAAV
ALAKAAAAT
ALAKAAAAV
GMNERPILT
GILGFVFTM
TLNAWVKVV
KLNEPVLLL
AVVPFIVSV

Table 4.1: Small set of sequences of peptides known to bind to the HLA-A*0201 molecule.

be of the form

$$X_1[LMIV]_2 X_3 X_4 X_5 X_6 X_7 X_8 [MNTV]_9 \,, \qquad (4.1)$$

where X_i indicates that all amino acids are allowed at position i, and $[LMIV]_2$ indicates that only the specified amino acids L, M, I, and V are allow at position 2. Following this approach, two peptides with T and V at position 9, respectively, will be equally likely to bind. Since V is found more often than T at position 9, one might, however, expect that the latter peptide is more likely to bind. We will later discuss in more detail why positions 2 and 9 are of special importance.

Using a statistical approach, such differences can be included directly in the predictions. Based on a set of sequences, a probability matrix p_{pa} can be constructed, where p_{pa} is the probability of finding amino acid a (a can be any of the 20 amino acids) on position p (p can be 1 to 9 in this example) in the motif. In the above example $p_{9V} = 0.4$ and $p_{9T} = 0.2$. This can be viewed as a statistical model of the binding site. In this model, it is assumed that there are no correlations between the different positions, e.g., that the amino acid present on position 2 does not influence which amino acids are likely to be observed on other positions among binding peptides.

The probability [also called the likelihood p(sequence|model)] of observing a given amino acid sequence $a_1 a_2 \ldots a_p \ldots$ given the model can be calculated by multiplying the probabilities for observing amino acid a_1 on position 1, a_2 on position 2, etc. This product can be written as

$$\prod_p p_{pa} \,. \qquad (4.2)$$

Any given amino acid sequence $a_1 a_2 \ldots a_p \ldots$ may also be observed in a randomly chosen protein. Furthermore, long sequences will be less likely than short ones. The probability p(sequence|background model) of observing the sequence in a random protein, can be written as

$$\prod_p q_a,\tag{4.3}$$

where q_a is the background frequency of amino acid a on position p. The index p has been left out on q_a since it is normally taken to be equal on all positions.

The ratio of these two likelihoods is called the odds ratio O,

$$O = \frac{\prod_p p_{pa}}{\prod_p q_a} = \prod_p \frac{p_{pa}}{q_a} .\tag{4.4}$$

The background amino acid frequencies q_a define a so-called null model. Different null models can be used: the amino acid distribution in a large set of proteins such as the Swiss-Prot database [Bairoch and Apweiler, 2000], a flat distribution (all amino acid frequencies q_a are set to $1/20$), or an amino acid distribution estimated from sequences known not to be binders (negative examples). If the odds ratio is greater than 1, the sequence is more likely given the model than given the background model.

The odds ratio can be used to predict if a peptide is likely to bind. Multiplying many probabilities may, however, result in a very low number that in computers are rounded off to zero (numerical underflow). To avoid this, prediction algorithms normally use logarithms of odds ratios called log-odds ratios.

The score S of a peptide to a motif is thus normally calculated as the sum of the log-odds ratio

$$S = \log_k \left(\prod_p \frac{p_{pa}}{q_a} \right) = \sum_p \log_k \left(\frac{p_{pa}}{q_a} \right) ,\tag{4.5}$$

where p_{pa} as above is the probability of finding amino acid a at position p in the motif, q_a is the background frequency of amino acid a, and $\log_k$ is the logarithm with base k. The scores are often normalized to half bits by multiplying all scores by $2/\log_k(2)$. The logarithm with base 2 of a number x can be calculated using a logarithm with another base n (such as the natural logarithm with base $n = e$ or the logarithm with base $n = 10$) using the simple formula $\log_2(x) = \log_n(x)/\log_n(2)$. In half-bit units, the log-odds score S is then given as

$$S = 2 \sum_p \log_2 \left(\frac{p_{pa}}{q_a} \right) .\tag{4.6}$$

4.2   Information Carried by Immunogenic Sequences

Once the binding motif has been described by a probability matrix p_{pa}, a number of different calculations can be carried out characterizing the motif.

4.2.1   Entropy

The entropy of a random variable is a measure of the uncertainty of the random variable; it is a measure of the amount of information required to describe the random variable [Cover and Thomas, 1991]. The entropy H (also called the Shannon entropy) of an amino acid distribution p is defined as

$$H(p) = -\sum_a p_a \log_2(p_a) , \qquad (4.7)$$

where p_a is the probability of amino acid a. Here the logarithm used has the base of 2 and the unit of the entropy then becomes bits [Shannon, 1948]. The entropy attains its maximal value $\log_2(20) \simeq 4.3$ if all amino acids are equally probable, and becomes zero if only one amino acid is observed at a given position. We here use the definition that $0 \log(0) = 0$. For the data shown in table 4.1 the entropy at position 2 is, e.g., found to be $\simeq 1.36$.

4.2.2   Relative Entropy

The relative entropy can be seen as a distance between two probability distributions, and is used to measure how different an amino acid distribution p is from some background distribution q. The relative entropy is also called the Kullback-Leibler distance D and is defined as

$$D(p\|q) = \sum_a p_a \log_2\left(\frac{p_a}{q_a}\right) . \qquad (4.8)$$

The background distribution is often taken as the distribution of amino acids in proteins in a large database of sequences. Alternatively, q and p can be the distributions of amino acids among sites that are known to have or not have some property. This property could, e.g., be glycosylation, phosphorylation, or MHC binding.

The relative entropy attains its maximal value if only the least probable amino acid according to the background distribution is observed. The relative entropy is non-negative and becomes zero only if $p = q$. It is not a true metric, however, since it is not symmetric ($D(p\|q) \neq D(q\|p)$) and does not satisfy the triangle inequality ($D(p\|q) \not< D(p\|r) + D(r\|q)$) [Cover and Thomas, 1991].

4.2.3 Logo Visualization of Relative Entropy

To visualize the characteristics of binding motifs, the so-called sequence logo technique [Schneider and Stephens, 1990] is often used. The information content at each position in the sequence motif is indicated using the height of a column of letters, representing amino acids or nucleotides. For proteins the information content is normally defined as the relative entropy between the amino acid distribution in the motif, and a background distribution where all amino acids are equally probable. This gives the following relation for the information content:

$$I = \sum_a \log_2 \frac{p_a}{1/20} = \log_2(20) + \sum_a \log_2 p_a \ . \tag{4.9}$$

The information content is a measure of the degree of conservation and has a value between zero (no conservation; all amino acids are equally probable) and $\log_2(20) \simeq 4.3$ (full conservation; only a single amino acid is observed at that position). In the logo plot, the height of each letter within a column is proportional to the frequency p_a of the corresponding amino acid a at that position. When another background distribution is used, the logos are normally called Kullback-Leibler logos, and letters that are less frequent than the background are displayed upside down.

In logo plots, the amino acids are normally colored according to their properties:

- Acidic [DE]: red

- Basic [HKR]: blue

- Hydrophobic [ACFILMPVW]: black

- Neutral [GNQSTY]: green

But other color schemes can be used if relevant in a given context. An example of a logo can be seen in Figure 4.1.

4.2.4 Mutual Information

Another important quantity used for characterizing a motif is the mutual information. This quantity is a measure of correlations between different positions in a motif. The mutual information measure is in general defined as the reduction of the uncertainty due to another random variable and is thus a measure of the amount of information one variable contains about another. Mutual information between two variables is defined as

$$I(A;B) = \sum_a \sum_b p_{ab} \log_2 \left(\frac{p_{ab}}{p_a p_b} \right) , \tag{4.10}$$

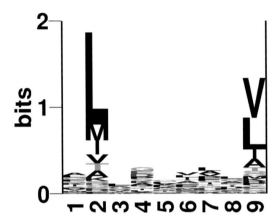

Figure 4.1: Logo showing the bias for peptides binding to the HLA-A*0201 molecule. Positions 2 and 9 have high information content. These are anchor positions that to a high degree determine the binding of a peptide [Rammensee et al., 1999]. See plate 4 for color version.

where p_{ab} is the joint probability mass function (the probability of having amino acid a in the first distribution and amino acid b in the second distribution) and

$$p_a = \sum_b p_{ab} \, , \; p_b = \sum_a p_{ab} \, . \tag{4.11}$$

It can be shown that [Cover and Thomas, 1991],

$$I(A;B) = H(A) - H(A|B) \tag{4.12}$$

where H is the entropy defined in equation(4.7). From this relation, we see that uncorrelated variables have zero mutual information since $H(A|B) = H(A)$ for such variables. The mutual information attains its maximum value, $H(A)$, when the two variables are fully correlated, since $H(A|B) = 0$ in this case. The mutual information is always non-negative. Mutual information can be used to quantify the correlation between different positions in a protein, or in a peptide-binding motif. Mutations in one position in a protein may, e.g., affect which amino acids are found at spatially close positions in the folded protein. Mutual information can be visualized as matrix plots [Gorodkin et al., 1999]. Figure 4.2 gives an example of a mutual information matrix plot for peptides binding to MHC alleles within the A2 supertype. For an explanation of supertypes, see chapter 13.

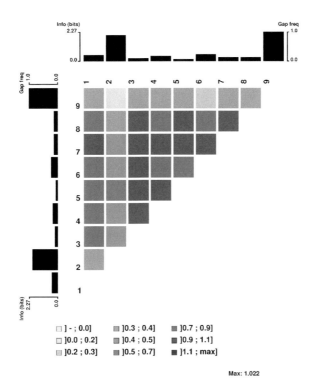

Figure 4.2: Mutual information plot calculated from peptides binding to MHC alleles within the A2 supertype. The plot was made using MatrixPlot [Gorodkin et al., 1999] (http://www.cbs.dtu.dk/services/MatrixPlot/).

4.3   Sequence Weighting Methods

In the following, we will use the logo plots to visualize some problems one often faces when deriving a binding motif characterized by a probability matrix p_{pa} as described in section 4.1.

The values of p_{pa} may be set to the frequencies f_{ab} observed in the alignment. There are, however, some problems with this direct approach. In figure 4.3, a logo representation of the probability matrix calculated from the peptides in table 4.1 is shown. From the plot, it is clear that alanine has a very high probability at all positions in the binding motif. The first 5 sequences in the alignment are very similar, and may reflect a sampling bias, rather than an actual amino acids bias in the binding motif. In such a situation, one would therefore like to downweight identical or almost identical sequences.

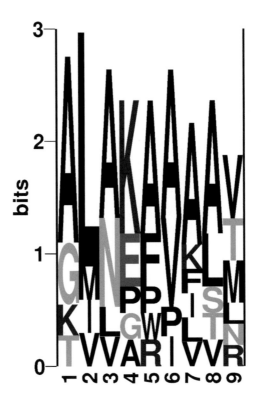

Figure 4.3:   Logo representation of the probability matrix calculated from 10 9mer peptides
known to bind HLA-A*0201.

Different methods can be used to weight sequences. One method is to
cluster sequences using a so-called Hobohm algorithm [Hobohm et al., 1992].
The Hobohm algorithm (version 1) takes an ordered list of sequences as input.
From the top of the list sequences are placed on an accepted list or discarded
depending on whether they are similar (share more than $X\%$ identify to any
member on the accepted list) or not. This procedure is repeated for all sequences in the list. After the Hobohm reduction, the pairwise similarity in the
accept list therefore has a maximum given by the threshold used to generate
it.

This method is also used for the construction of the BLOSUM matrices
normally used by BLAST. The most commonly used clustering threshold is
62%. After the clustering, each peptide k in a cluster is assigned a weight
$w_k = 1/N_c$, where N_c is the number of sequences in the cluster that contains
peptide k. When the amino acid frequencies are calculated, each amino acid in

sequence k is weighted by w_k. In the above example the first 5 peptides will form one cluster, and each of these sequences thus contributes with a weight of $\frac{1}{5}$ to the probability matrix. The frequency of A at position p_1 will then be $p_{1A} = 2/6 = 0.33$ as opposed to $6/10 = 0.6$ found when using the raw sequence counts.

In the Henikoff and Henikoff [1994] sequence weighting scheme, an amino acid a on position p in sequence k contributes a weight $w_{kp} = 1/rs$, where r is the number of *different* amino acids at a given position (column) in the alignment and s the number of occurrences of amino acid a in that column. The weight of a sequence is then assigned as the sum of the weights over all positions in the alignment. The Henikoffs' method is fast as the computation time only increases linearly with the number of sequences. For the Hobohm clustering algorithm, on the other hand, computation time increases as the square of the number of sequences (depending on the similarity between the sequences). Performing the sequence weighting using clustering generally leads to more accurate results, and clustering is the suggested choice of method if the number of sequences is limited and the calculation thus computationally feasible.

Figure 4.4 shows a logo representation of the probability matrix calculated using clustering sequence weighting. From the figure it is apparent that the strong alanine bias in the motif has been removed.

4.4 Pseudocount Correction Methods

Another problem with the direct approach to estimating the probability matrix p_{pa} is that the statistics often will be based on very few sequence examples (in this case 10 sequences). A direct calculation of the probability p_{9I} for observing an isoleucine on position 9 in the alignment, e.g., gives 0. This will in turn mean that all peptides with an isoleucine on position 9 will score minus infinity in equation (4.5), i.e., be predicted not to bind no matter what the rest of the sequence is. This may be too drastic a conclusion based on only 10 sequences. One solution to this problem is to use a pseudocount method, where prior knowledge about the frequency of different amino acids in proteins is used. Two strategies for pseudocount correction will be described here: Equal and BLOSUM correction, respectively. In both cases the pseudocount frequency g_{pa} for amino acid a on position p in the alignment is estimated as described by Altschul et al. [1997],

$$g_{pa} = \sum_b \frac{f_{pb}}{q_b}\, q_{ab} = \sum_b f_{pb}\, q_{a|b}\,. \qquad (4.13)$$

Here, f_{pb} is the observed frequency of amino acid b on position p, q_b is the background frequency of amino acid b, q_{ab} is the frequency by which amino

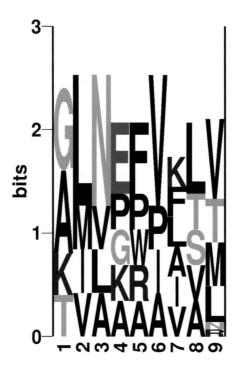

Figure 4.4: Logo representation of the probability matrix calculated from 10 9mer peptides known to bind HLA-A*0201. The probabilities are calculated using the clustering sequence weighting method.

acid a is aligned to amino acid b derived from the BLOSUM substitution matrix, and $q_{a|b}$ is the corresponding conditional probability. The equation shows how the pseudo-count frequency can be calculated. The pseudocount frequency for isoleucine at position 9 in the example in table 4.1 would, e.g., be

$$g_{9I} = \sum_b f_{9b}\, q_{I|b} = 0.3\, q_{I|V} + 0.2\, q_{I|T} \ldots 0.1\, q_{I|L} \simeq 0.09 , \qquad (4.14)$$

where here, for simplicity, we have used the raw count values for f_{9b}. In real applications the sequence-weighted probabilities are normally used. The $q_{a|b}$ values are taken from the BLOSUM62 substitution matrix [Henikoff and Henikoff, 1992].

In the Equal correction, a substitution matrix with identical frequencies for all amino acids (1/20) and all amino acid substitutions (1/400) is applied. In this case $g_{pa} = 1/20$ at all positions for all amino acids.

4.5   Weight on Pseudocount Correction

From estimated pseudocounts, and sequence-weighted observed frequencies, the effective amino acid frequency can be calculated as [Altschul et al., 1997]

$$p_{pa} = \frac{\alpha f_{pa} + \beta g_{pa}}{\alpha + \beta} \ . \tag{4.15}$$

Here f_{pa} is the observed frequency (calculated using sequence weighting), g_{pa} the pseudocount frequency, α the effective sequence number minus 1, and β the weight on the pseudocount correction. When the sequence weighting is performed using clustering, the effective sequence number is equal to the number of clusters. When sequence weighting as described by Henikoff and Henikoff [1992] is applied, the average number of different amino acids in the alignment gives the effective sequence number. If a large number of different sequences are available α will in general also be large and a relative low weight will thus be put on the pseudocount frequencies. If, on the other hand, the number of observed sequences is one, α is zero, and the effective amino acid frequency is reduced to the pseudocount frequency g_{pa}. If we calculate the log-odds score S, for a G, as given by equation (4.5), G gets the score:

$$S_G = \log \frac{g_{pG}}{q_G} = \log \frac{q_{GG}}{q_G q_G} \ , \tag{4.16}$$

where we have used equation (4.13) for g_{pa}. The last log-odds score is the BLOSUM matrix score for $G - G$, and we thus find that the log-odds score for a single sequence reduces to the BLOSUM identical match score values.

Figure 4.5 shows the logo plot of the probability matrix calculated from the sequences in table 4.1, including sequence weighting and pseudocount correction. The figure demonstrates how the pseudocount correction allows for probability estimates for all 20 amino acids at all positions in the motif. Note that I is the fifth most probable amino acid at position 9, even though this amino acid was never observed at the position in the peptide sequences.

4.6   Position Specific Weighting

In many situations prior knowledge about the importance of the different positions in the binding motif exists. Such prior knowledge can with success be included in the search for binding motifs [Lundegaard et al., 2004, Rammensee et al., 1997]. In figure 4.6, we show the results of such a position-specific weighting. The figure displays the probability matrix calculated from the 10 sequences and a matrix calculated from a large set of 485 peptides. It demonstrates how a reasonably accurate motif description can be derived from a very

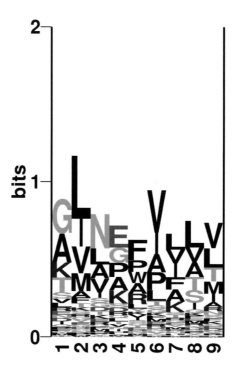

Figure 4.5:   Logo representation of the probability matrix calculated from 10 9mer peptides known to bind HLA-A*0201. The probabilities are calculated using both the methods of sequence weighting and pseudocount correction.

limited set of data, using the techniques of sequence weighting, pseudocount correction, and position-specific weighting.

4.7   Gibbs Sampling

In previous sections, we have described how a weight matrix describing a sequence motif can be calculated from a set of peptides of equal length. This approach is appropriate when dealing with MHC class I binding, where the length of the binding peptides are relatively uniform. MHC class II molecules, on the other hand, can bind peptides of very different length, and the weight-matrix methods described up to now are hence not directly applicable to characterize this type of motif. Here we describe a motif sampler suited to deal with such problems.

The general problem to be solved by the motif sampler is to locate and

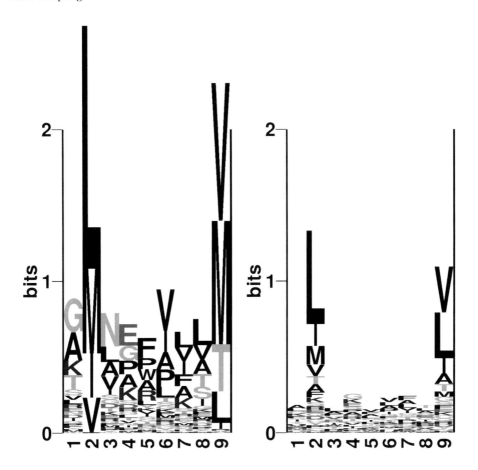

Figure 4.6: Left: Logo representation of the probability matrix calculated from 10 9mer peptides known to bind HLA-A*0201. The probabilities are calculated using the methods of sequence weighting, pseudocount correction, and position-specific weighting. The weight on positions 2 and 9 is 3. Right: Logo representation of the probability matrix calculated from 485 peptides known to bind HLA-A*0201.

characterize a pattern embedded within a set of N amino acids (or DNA) sequences. In situations where the sequence pattern is very subtle and the motif weak, this is a highly complex task, and conventional multiple sequence alignment programs will typically fail. The Gibbs sampling method was first described by Lawrence et al. [1993] and has been used extensively for location of transcription factor binding sites [Thompson et al., 2003] and in the analysis of protein sequences [Lawrence et al., 1993, Neuwald et al., 1995]. The method attempts to find an optimal local alignment of a set of N sequences by means of Metropolis Monte Carlo sampling [Metropolis et al., 1953] of the alignment space. The scoringfunction guiding the Monte Carlo search is defined in terms of fitness (information content) of a log-odds matrix calculated from the alignment.

The algorithm samples possible alignments of the N sequences. For each alignment a log-odds weight matrix is calculated as $\log(p_{pa}/q_a)$, where p_{pa} is the frequency of amino acid a at position p in the alignment and q_a is the background frequency of that amino acid. The values of p_{pa} can be estimated using sequence weighting and pseudocount correction for low counts as described earlier in this chapter.

The fitness (energy) of an alignment is calculated as

$$E = \sum_{p,a} C_{pa} \, \log \frac{p_{pa}}{q_a} \,, \tag{4.17}$$

where C_{pa} is the number of times amino acid a is observed at position p in the alignment, p_{pa} is the pseudocount and sequence weight corrected amino acid frequency of amino acid b and position p in the alignment. Finally, q_a is the background frequency of amino acid a. E is equal to the sum of the relative entropy or the Kullback-Leibler distance [Kullback and Leibler, 1951] in the window.

The set of possible alignments is, even for a small data set, very large. For a set of 50 peptides of length 10, the number of different alignments with a core window of nine amino acids is $2^{50} \simeq 10^{15}$. This number is clearly too large to allow for a sampling of the complete alignment space. Instead, the Metropolis Monte Carlo algorithm is applied [Metropolis et al., 1953] to perform an effective sampling of the alignment space.

Two distinct Monte Carlo moves are implemented in the algorithm: (1) the single sequence move, and (2) the phase shift move. In the single sequence move, the alignment of a sequence is shifted a randomly selected number of positions. In the phase shift move, the window in the alignment is shifted a randomly selected number of residues to the left or right. This latter type of move allows the program to efficiently escape local minima. This may, e.g., occur if the window overlaps the most informative motif, but is not centered on the most informative pattern.

The probability of accepting a move in the Monte Carlo sampling is defined as

$$P = \min(1, e^{dE/T}) \,, \tag{4.18}$$

where dE is difference in (fitness) energy between the end and start configurations and T is a scalar. Note that we seek to maximize the energy function, hence the positive sign for dE in the equation. T is a scalar that is lowered during the calculation. The equation implies that moves that increase E will

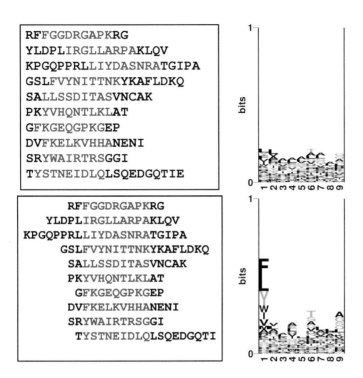

Figure 4.7: Example of an alignment generated by the Gibbs sampler for the DR4(B1*0401) binding motif. The peptides were downloaded from the MHCPEP database [Brusic et al., 1998a]. Top left: Unaligned sequences. Top right: Logo for unaligned sequences. Bottom left: Sequences aligned by Gibbs sampler. Bottom right: Logo for sequences aligned by the Gibbs sampler. Reprinted, with permission, from Nielsen et al. [2004]. See plate 5 for color version.

always be accepted ($dE > 0$). On the other hand, only a fraction given by $e^{dE/T}$ of the moves which decrease E will be accepted. For high values of the scalar T ($T \gg dE$) this probability is close to 1, but as T is lowered during the calculation, the probability of accepting unfavorable moves will be reduced, forcing the system into a state of high fitness (energy). Figure 4.7 shows a set of sequences aligned by their N-terminal (top left) and the corresponding logo (top right). The lower panel shows the alignment by the Gibbs sampler and the corresponding logo. The figure shows how the Gibbs sampler has identified a motif describing the binding to the DR4(B1*0401) allele. For more details on the Gibbs sampler see Chapter 8.

4.8   Hidden Markov Models

The Gibbs sampler and other weight-matrix approaches are well suited to describe sequence motifs of fixed length. For MHC class II, the peptide binding motif is in most situations assumed to be of a fixed length of 9 amino acids. This implies that the scoringfunction for a peptide binding to the MHC complex can be written as a linear sum of 9 terms. In many situations this simple motif description is, however, not valid. In the previous chapter, we described how protein families, e.g, often are characterized by conserved amino acid regions separated by amino acid segments of variable length. In such situations a weight matrix approach is poorly suited to characterize the motif. HMMs, on the other hand, provide a natural framework for describing such interrupted motifs.

In this section, we will give a brief introduction to the HMM framework. First, we describe the general concepts of the HMM framework through a simple example. Next the Viterbi and posterior decoding algorithms for aligning a sequence to a HMM are explained, and finally the use of HMMs in some selected biological problems is described. A detailed introduction to HMMs and their application to sequence analysis problems may be found, e.g., in Durbin et al. [1998] and Baldi and Brunak [2001].

4.8.1   Markov Model, Markov Chain

A Markov model consists of a set of states. Each state is associated with a probability distribution assigning probability values to the set of possible outcomes. A set of transition probabilities for switching between the states is assigned. In a Markov model (or Markov chain) the outcome of an event depends only on the preceding state.

An example of such a model is a B cell epitope model. Regions in the sequence with many hydrophobic residues are less likely to be exposed on the surface of proteins and it is therefore less likely that antibodies can bind to these regions. In this model, we divide positions in a protein in two states: epitopes E and non-epitopes N. We divide the 20 different amino acids in three groups. Hydrophobic [ACFILMPVW] , uncharged polar [GNQSTY] and charged [DEHKR]. This model is displayed in Figure 4.8. Even though this model is highly simplified and does only capture the most simple, of the very complex, features describing the B cell epitopes, it serves the purpose of introducing the important concepts of an HMM.

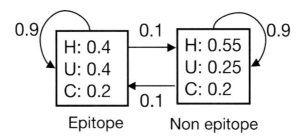

Figure 4.8: B cell epitope model. The model has two states: Epitope E and non epitope N. In each state, three different types of amino acids can be found Hydrophobic (H), uncharged polar (U) and charged (C). The transition probabilities between the two states are given next to the arrows, and the probability of each of the three types of amino acids are given for each of the two states.

4.8.2   What is Hidden?

What is hidden in the HMM? In biology HMMs are most often used to assign a state (epitope or non-epitope in this example) to each residue in a biological sequence (3 types of amino acids in this example). An HMM can, however, also be used to construct artificial sequences based on the probabilities in it. When the model is used in this way, the outcome (often called the emissions) is a sequence like $HHHUHHCH$ .... It is not possible from the observed sequence to establish if the model for each letter was in the epitope state or not. This information is kept hidden by the model.

4.8.3   The Viterbi Algorithm

Even though the list of states used by the HMM to generate the observed sequence is hidden, it is possible to obtain an accurate estimate of the list of states used. If we have an HMM like the one described in figure 4.8, we can use a dynamic programming algorithm like the one described in chapter 3 to align the observed sequence to the model and obtain the path (list of states) that most probably will generate the observations. The dynamic programming algorithm doing the alignment of a sequence to the HMM is called the Viterbi algorithm.

  If the highest probability $P_k(x_i)$ of a path ending in state k with observation x_i is known for all states k, then the highest probability for observation x_{i+1} in state l, can be found as

$$P_l(x_{i+1}) = p_l(x_{i+1}) \max_k(P_k(x_i)a_{kl}) \, , \tag{4.19}$$

where $p_l(x_{i+1})$ is the probability of observation x_{i+1} in state l, and a_{kl} is the transition probability from state k to state l.

By using this relation recursively, one can find the path through the model that most probably will give the observed sequence. To avoid underflow in the computer the algorithm normally will work in log-space and calculate $\log P_l(x_{i+1})$ instead. In log-space the recursive equation becomes a sum, and the numbers remain within a reasonable range.

An example of how the Viterbi algorithm is applied is given in figure 4.9. The figure shows how the optimal path through the HMM of figure 4.8 is calculated for a sequence of $NGSLFWIA$. By translating the sequence into the three states defining hydrophobic, neutral and charged residues, we get $HHHUUUUU$. In the example, we assume that the model is the non-epitope state at the first H, which implies that is $P_E(H_1) = -\infty$. The value for assigning H to the state N is $P_N(H_1) = \log(0.55) = -0.26$. For the next residue, the path must come from the N state. We therefore find, $P_N(H_2) = \log(0.55) + \log(0.9) - 0.26 = -0.57$, and $P_E(H_2) = \log(0.4) + \log(0.1) - 0.26 = -1.66$, since $a_{NN}0.9$, and $a_{NE} = 0.1$. The backtracking arrows are for both the E and the N state placed to the previous N state. For the third residue the path to the N state can come from both the N and the E states. The value $P_N(H_3)$ is therefore found using the relation

$$P_N(H_3) = \log(0.55) + \max\{\log(0.9) - 0.57, \log(0.1) - 1.66\} = -0.88 \quad (4.20)$$

and likewise the value $P_E(H_3)$ is

$$P_E(H_3) = \log(0.4) + \max\{\log(0.1) - 0.57, \log(0.9) - 1.66\} = -1.97 \quad (4.21)$$

In both cases the max function selects the first argument, and the backtracking arrows are therefore for both the E and the N state assigned to the previous N state. This procedure is repeated for all residues in the sequence, and we obtain the result shown in Figure 4.9. With the arrows, it is indicated which state was selected in the $\max_k$ function in each step in the recursive calculation. Repeating the calculation for all residues in the observed sequence, we find that the highest score -4.08 is found in state E. Backtracking through the arrows, we find the optimal path to be $EEENNNNN$ (indicated with solid arrows). Note that the most probable path of the sequence $HHHUUUUU$ would have ended in the state N with a value of -3.48, and the corresponding path would hence have been $NNNNNNN$. Observing a series of uncharged amino acids thus does not necessarily mean that the epitope state was used.

4.8.4   The Forward-Backward Algorithm and Posterior Decoding

Many different paths through an HMM can give rise to the same observed sequence. Where the Viterbi algorithm gives the most probable path through an

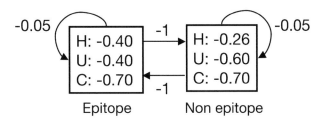

	N	G	S	L	F	W	I	A
	H	H	H	N	N	N	N	N
E	NULL	-1.66	-1.97	-2.28	-2.73	-3.18	-3.63	-4.08
N	-0.26	-0.55	-0.88	-1.53	-2.18	-2.85	-3.48	-4.13
	N	N	N	E	E	E	E	E

Figure 4.9: Alignment of sequence *HHHUUUUU* to the B cell epitope model of figure 4.8. The upper part of the figure shows the log-transformed HMM. The probabilities have been transformed by taking the logarithm with base 10. The model is assumed to start in the non-epitope state at the first *H*. The table in the lower part gives the $\log P_l(x_{i+1})$ values for the different observations in the N (non epitope), and E (epitope) states, respectively. The arrows show the backtracking pointers. The solid arrows give the optimal path, the dotted arrows denote the suboptimal path. The upper two rows in the table give the amino acid and three letter transformed sequence, respectively . The lower row gives the most probable path found using the Viterbi algorithm.

HMM given the observed sequence, the so-called forward algorithm calculates the probability of the observed sequence being aligned to the HMM. This is done by summing over all possible paths generating the observed sequence. The forward algorithm is a dynamic programming algorithm with a recursive formula very similar to the Viterbi equation, replacing the maximization step with a sum [Durbin et al., 1998]. If $f_k(x_{i-1})$ is the probability of observing the sequence up to and including x_{i-1} ending in state k, then the probability of observing the sequence up to and including x_i ending in state l can be found using the recursive formula

$$f_l(x_i) = p_l(x_i) \sum_k f_k(x_{i-1})a_{kl} . \qquad (4.22)$$

Here $p_l(x_i)$ is the probability of observation x_i in state l, and a_{kl} is the transition probability from state k to state l.

Another important algorithm is the posterior decoding or forward-backward algorithm. The algorithm calculates the probability that an observation x_i is aligned to the state k given the observed sequence x. The term "posterior decoding" refers to the fact that the decoding is done *after* the sequence is observed. This probability can formally be written as $P(\pi_i = k|x)$ and can be determined using the so-called forward-backward algorithm [Durbin et al., 1998].

$$P(\pi_i = k|x) = \frac{f_k(i)b_k(i)}{P(x)} .$$ (4.23)

The term $f_k(i)$ is calculated using the forward recursive formula from before,

$$f_k(i) = p_k(x_i) \sum_l f_l(x_{i-1})a_{lk} ,$$ (4.24)

and $b_k(i)$ is calculated using a backward recursive formula,

$$b_k(x_i) = \sum_l a_{kl}p_l(x_{i+1})b_l(i+1) .$$ (4.25)

From these relations, we see why the algorithm is called forward-backward. $f_k(i)$ is the probability of aligning the sequence up to and including x_i with a path ending in state k, and $b_k(i)$ is the probability of aligning the sequence $x_{i+1} \ldots x_N$ to the HMM starting from state k. Finally $P(x)$ is the probability of aligning the observed sequence to the HMM.

One of the most important applications of the forward-backward algorithm is the posterior decoding. Often many paths through the HMM will have probabilities very close to the optimal path found by the Viterbi algorithm. In such situations posterior decoding might be a more adequate algorithm to extract properties of the observed sequence from the model. Posterior decoding gives a list of states that most probably generate the observed sequence using the equation

$$\pi_i^{posterior} = \max_k P(\pi_i = k|x) ,$$ (4.26)

where $P(\pi_i = k|x)$ is the probability of observation x_i being aligned to state π_k given the observed sequence x. Note that posterior decoding is different from the Viterbi decoding since the list of states found by posterior decoding need not be a legitimate path through the HMM.

4.8.5 Higher Order Hidden Markov Models

The central property of the Markov chains described until now is the fact that the probability of an observation only depends on the previous state and that the probability of an observed sequence, X, thus can be written as

$$P(X) = P(x_1)P(x_2|x_1)P(x_3|x_2) \cdots P(x_N|x_{N-1}) \qquad (4.27)$$

where $P(x_i)$ denotes the probability of observing x at position i.

In many situations, this approximation might not be valid since the probability of an observation might depend on more than just the preceding state. However by use of higher order Markov models, such dependences can be captured. In a Markov model of n'th order, the probability of an observation x_i is given by

$$P(x_i) = P(x_i|x_{i-1}, \ldots, x_{i-n}) \qquad (4.28)$$

A second order hidden Markov model describing B cell epitopes may thus consist of two states each with 9 possible observations HH, HU, HC, UH, UU, UC, CH, CU, and CC. By assigning different probability values to for instance the observations HU, UU and CU, the model can capture higher order correlations.

An n'th order Markov model over some alphabet is thus equivalent to a first order Markov chain over an alphabet of n-tuples.

4.8.6   Hidden Markov Models in Immunology

Having introduced the HMM framework through a simple example, we now turn to some relevant biological problems that are well described using HMMs. The first is highly relevant to antigen processing, and describes how an HMM can be designed to characterize the binding of peptides to the human transporter associated with antigen processing (TAP). The second example addresses a more general use of HMMs in characterizing similarities between protein sequences, the so-called profile HMMs.

TAP Transport of the peptides into the endoplasmic reticulum is an essential step in the MHC class I presentation pathway. This task is done by TAP molecules and a detailed description of the function of the TAP molecules is given in chapter 7. The peptides binding to TAP have a rather broad length distribution, and peptides up to a length of 18 amino acids can be translocated [van Endert et al., 1994]. The binding of a peptide to the TAP molecules is to a high degree determined by the first three N-terminal positions and the last C-terminal position in the peptide. Other positions in the peptide determine the binding to a lesser degree. The binding of a peptide to the TAP molecules is thus an example of a problem where the binding motif has variable length, and hence a problem that is well described by a HMM. Figure 4.10 shows an HMM describing peptide TAP binding. The figure highlights the important differences and similarities between a weight matrix and an HMM. If we only

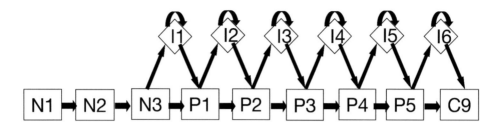

Figure 4.10: HMM for peptide TAP binding. The model can describe binding of peptides of different lengths to the TAP molecules. The binding motif consists of 9 amino acids. The first three N-terminal amino acids, and the last C-terminal amino acids must be part of the binding motif. Each state is associated with a probability distribution of matching one of the 20 amino acids. The arrow between the states indicates the transition probabilities for switching between the states. The amino acid probability distributions for each state are estimated using the techniques of sequence weighting and pseudocount correction (see section 4.4).

consider alignment of 9mer peptides to the HMM, we see that no alignment can go through the insertion states (labeled as I in the figure). In this situation the alignment becomes a simple sum of the amino acid match scores from each of the 9 states N1-N3, P1-P5, and C9, and the HMM is reduced to a simple weight matrix. However, if the peptide is longer than nine amino acids, the path through the HMM must pass some insertion state, and it is clear that such a motif could not have been characterized well by a weight matrix.

Profile Hidden Markov Models Profile HMMs are used to characterize sequence similarities within a family of proteins. As described in chapter 3 a multiple alignment of protein sequences within a protein family can reveal important information about amino acids conservation, mutability, active sites, etc.

A profile HMM provides a natural framework for compiling such information of a multiple alignment. In figure 4.11, we show an example of a profile HMM. The architecture of a profile HMM is very similar to the model for peptide TAP binding. The model is build from a set of match states (P1-P7). These states describe what is conserved among most sequences in the protein family. Some sequences within a family will have amino acid insertions; others will have amino acid deletions with respect to the motif. To allow for such variation in sequence, the profile HMM has insertion and deletion states (labeled as I and D in the figure, respectively). The model can insert amino acids between match states using the insertion state, and a match state can be skipped using the deletion states.

An example of a multiple alignment was given in figure 3.12C. From this type of alignment, one can construct a profile HMM. If we consider positions

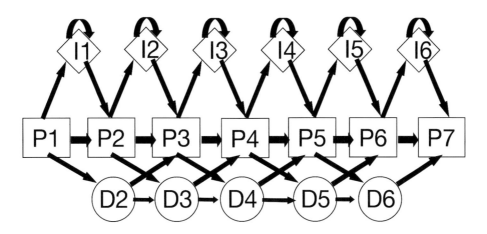

Figure 4.11: Profile HMM with 7 match states. Match states are shown as squares, insertion state as diamonds, and deletion states as circles. Each match and insertion state has an associated probability distribution for matching the 20 different amino acids. Transitions between the different states are indicated by arrows.

in the alignment with less than 40% gaps to be match states, then all other positions are either insertions or deletions. In the example in figure 3.12 *Neurospora crassa* and *Saccharomyces cerevisiae* hence contain an insertion in position 58-64, whereas positions 32-38 in *Saccharomyces cerevisiae*, and positions 35-38 in *Neurospora crassa* are deleted. Note that we count the positions in the alignment, not the positions in the sequence. The figure demonstrates that insertions and deletions are distributed in a highly nonuniform manner in the alignment. Also, it is apparent from the figure that not all positions are equally conserved. The W in position 72 is thus fully conserved in all species, whereas the W in position 53 is more variable. These variations in sequence conservation and in the probabilities for insertions and deletions are naturally described by an HMM, and profile HMMs have indeed been applied successfully to the identification of new and remote homolog members of families with well-characterized protein domains [Sonnhammer et al., 1997, Karplus et al., 1998, Durbin et al., 1998].

4.9   Artificial Neural Networks

As stated earlier the weight-matrix approach is only suitable for prediction of a binding event in situations where the binding specificity can be represented independently at each position in the motif. In many (in fact most) situations this is not the case, and this assumption can only be considered to be an approximation. In the binding of a peptide to the MHC molecule the amino acids might, e.g., compete for the space available in the binding grove. The mutual information in the binding motif will allow for identification of such higher-order sequence correlations. An example of a mutual information calculation for peptides binding to the MHC class I complex is shown in figure 4.2.

Neural networks with a hidden layer are designed to describe sequence patterns with such higher-order correlations. Due to their ability to handle these correlations, hundreds of different applications within bioinformatics have been developed using this technique, and for that reason ANNs have been enjoying a renaissance, not only in biology but also in many other data domains.

Neural networks realize a method of computation that is vastly different from "rule-based techniques" with strict control over the steps in the calculation from data input to output. Conceptually, neural networks, on the other hand, use "influence" rather than control. A neural network consists of a large number of independent computational units that can influence but not control each other's computations. That such a system, which consists of a large number of unintelligent units, in their biological counterparts can be made to exhibit "intelligent" behavior is not directly obvious, but one can with some justification use the central nervous system in support of the idea. However, the ANNs obviously do not to any extent match the computing power and sophistication of biological neural systems.

ANNs are not programmed in the normal sense, but must be influenced by data — trained — to associate patterns with each other.

The neural network algorithm most often used in bioinformatics is similar to the network structure described by Rumelhart et al. [1991]. This network architecture is normally called a standard, feedforward multilayer perceptron. Other neural network architectures have also been used, but will not be described here. The most successful of the more complex networks involves different kinds of feedback, such that the network calculation on a given (often quite short) amino acid sequence segment possibly can depend on sequence patterns present elsewhere in the sequence. When analyzing nucleotide data the applications have typically been used also for long sequence segments, such as the determination of whether a given nucleotide belongs to a protein coding sequence or not. The network can in such a case be trained to take advantage of long-range correlations hundreds of nucleotide positions apart in a sequence.

The presentation of the neural network theory outlined below is based on the paper by Rumelhart et al. [1991], as well as the book by Hertz et al. [1991].

The training algorithm used to produce the final network is a steepest descent method that learns a training set of input-output pairs by adjusting the network weight parameters such that the network for each input will produce a numerical value that is close to the desired target output (either representing disjunct categories, or real values such as peptide binding affinities). The idea with the network is to produce algorithms which can handle sequence correlations, and also classify data in a nonlinear manner, such that small changes in sequence input can produce large changes in output. The hope is that the network then will be able to reproduce what is well-known in biology, namely that many single amino acid substitutions can entirely disrupt a mechanism, e.g., by inhibiting binding.

The feedforward neural network consists of connected computing units. Each unit "observes" the other units' activity through its input connections. To each input connection, the unit attaches a weight, which is a real number that indicates how much influence the input in question is to have on that particular unit. The influence is calculated as the weight multiplied by the activity of the neuron delivering the input. The weight can be negative, so an input can have a negative influence. The neuron sums up all the influence it receives from the other neurons and thereby achieves a measure for the total influence it is subjected to. From this sum the neuron subtracts a threshold value, which will be omitted from the description below, since it can be viewed as a weight from an extra input unit, with a fixed input value of -1. The linear sum of the inputs is then transformed through a nonlinear, sigmoidal function to produce its output. The input layer units does not compute anything, but merely store the network inputs; the information processing in the network takes place in the internal, hidden layer (most often only one layer), and in the output layer. A schematic representation of this type of neural network is shown in figure 4.12.

4.9.1 Predicting Using Neural Networks: Conversion of Input to Output

Formally the calculation in a network with one hidden layer proceeds as follows. Let the indices i, j, and k refer to the output, hidden, and input layers, respectively. The input neurons each receive an input I_k. The input to each of the hidden units is

$$h_j = \sum_k v_{jk} I_k, \tag{4.29}$$

where v_{jk} is the weight on the input k to the hidden unit j. The output from the hidden units is

$$H_j = g(h_j) \tag{4.30}$$

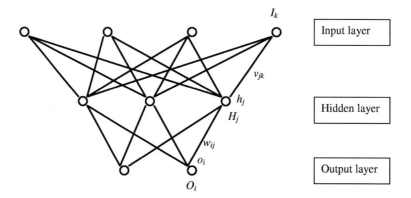

Figure 4.12: Schematic representation of a conventional feedforward neural network used in numerous applications within bioinformatics.

where

$$g(x) = \frac{1}{1 + e^{-x}}$$ (4.31)

is the sigmoidal function most often used. Note that

$$g'(x) = g(x)(1 - g(x)) \,.$$ (4.32)

Each output neuron receives the input

$$o_i = \sum_j w_{ij}H_j \,,$$ (4.33)

where w_{ij} are the weights between the hidden and the output units to produce the final output

$$O_i = g(o_i) \,.$$ (4.34)

Different measures of the error between the network output and the desired target output can be used [Hertz et al., 1991, Bishop, 1995]. The most simple choice is to let the error E be proportional to the sum of the squared difference between the desired output d_i and the output O_i from the last layer of neurons:

$$E = \frac{1}{2} \sum_i (O_i - d_i)^2 \,.$$ (4.35)

4.9.2 Training the Network by Backpropagation

One option is to update the weights by a back-propagation algorithm which is a steepest descent method, where each weight is changed in the opposite direction of the gradient of the error,

$$\Delta w_{ij} = -\varepsilon \frac{\partial E}{\partial w_{ij}} \;\; \text{and} \;\; \Delta v_{jk} = -\varepsilon \frac{\partial E}{\partial v_{jk}} \; . \qquad (4.36)$$

The change of the weights between the hidden and the output layer can be calculated by using

$$\frac{\partial E}{\partial w_{ij}} = \frac{\partial E}{\partial O_i} \frac{\partial O_i}{\partial o_i} \frac{\partial o_i}{\partial w_{ij}} = \delta_i H_j \; , \qquad (4.37)$$

where

$$\delta_i = (O_i - d_i) g'(o_i) \; . \qquad (4.38)$$

To calculate the change of weights between the input and the hidden layer we use the following relations

$$\frac{\partial E}{\partial v_{jk}} = \frac{\partial E}{\partial H_j} \frac{\partial H_j}{\partial v_{jk}} \; , \qquad (4.39)$$

and

$$\frac{\partial E}{\partial H_j} = \sum_i \frac{\partial E}{\partial o_i} \frac{\partial o_i}{\partial H_j} = \sum_i \frac{\partial E}{\partial o_i} w_{ij} \; , \qquad (4.40)$$

and

$$\frac{\partial H_j}{\partial v_{jk}} = \frac{\partial H_j}{\partial h_j} \frac{\partial h_j}{\partial v_{jk}} = g'(h_j) I_k \; , \qquad (4.41)$$

and thus

$$\frac{\partial E}{\partial v_{jk}} = g'(h_j) I_k \sum_i \delta_i w_{ij} \; . \qquad (4.42)$$

In the equations described here the error is backpropagated after each presentation of a training example. This is called online learning. In batch, or offline, learning, the error is summed over all training examples and thereafter backpropagated. However, this method has proven inferior in most cases [Hertz et al., 1991].

In figure 4.13, we give a simple example of how the weights in the neural network are updated using backpropagation. The figure shows two configurations of a neural network with two hidden neurons. The network must be trained to learn the XOR (exclusive or) function. That is the function with the following properties:

$$\begin{aligned} f_{XOR}(0,0) &= f_{XOR}(1,1) = 0 \qquad (4.43) \\ f_{XOR}(1,0) &= f_{XOR}(0,1) = 1 \; . \end{aligned}$$

This type of input-output association is the simplest example displaying higher-order correlation, as the two input properties are not independently

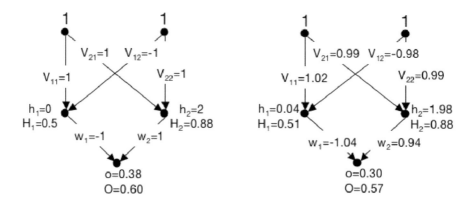

Figure 4.13: Update of weights in a neural network using backpropagation. The figure shows the neural network before updating the weights (left) and the network configuration after one round of backpropagation (right). The learning rate ε in the example is equal to 0.5. Note that this is a large value for ε. Normally the value is of the order 0.05.

linked to the categories. The "1" category is represented by input examples where only one of the two features are allowed to be present — not both features simultaneously. The $(1, 1)$ example from the "0" category is therefore an "exception," and this small data set can therefore not be handled by a linear network without hidden units. The example may seem very simple; still it captures the essence of the sequence properties in many binding sites, where the two features could be charge and side chain volume, respectively. In actual application the number of input features is typically much higher.

In the example shown in figure 4.13, we have for simplicity left out the threshold value normally subtracted from the input to each neuron. The figure shows the neural network before updating the weights and the network configuration after one round of backpropagation. With the example $(1, 1)$, the network output, O, from the network with the initial weights is 0.6. This gives the following relation for δ:

$$\delta = (0.6 - 0)g'(o) = 0.6 \cdot O \cdot (1 - O) = 0.15 , \qquad (4.44)$$

where we have used equation (4.32) for $g'(o)$.

The change of the weights from the hidden layer to the output neuron are updated using equation (4.37):

$$\Delta w_1 = -\varepsilon\, 0.15 \cdot 0.5 = -0.075\varepsilon$$

$$\Delta w_2 \;=\; -\varepsilon\,0.15\cdot 0.88 = -0.13\varepsilon\,. \tag{4.45}$$

The change of the weights in the first layer are updated using equation (4.42)

$$
\begin{aligned}
\Delta v_{11} &= -\varepsilon\, g'(h_1)\cdot 1\cdot \delta\cdot(-1)\\
&= \varepsilon\, H_1\,(1 - H_1)\cdot \delta\\
&= 0.04\varepsilon\\
\Delta v_{21} &= -\varepsilon\, g'(h_1)\cdot 1\cdot \delta\cdot(-1) = 0.04\varepsilon\\
\Delta v_{12} &= -\varepsilon\, g'(h_2)\cdot 1\cdot \delta\cdot 1 = -0.02\varepsilon\\
\Delta v_{22} &= -\varepsilon\, g'(h_2)\cdot 1\cdot \delta\cdot 1 = -0.02\varepsilon\,.
\end{aligned}
\tag{4.46}
$$

Modifying the weights according to these values, we obtain the neural network configuration shown to the right of figure 4.13. The network output from the updated network is 0.57. Note that the error indeed has decreased. When the network is trained on all four patterns of the XOR function during a number of training cycles (including the three threshold weights), the network will in most cases reach an optimal configuration, where the error on all four patterns is practically zero.

Figure 4.14 demonstrates how the XOR function is learned by the neural network. If we construct a neural network without a hidden layer this data set cannot be learned, whereas a network with two hidden neurons learns the four examples perfectly.

When examining the weight configuration of the fully trained network it becomes clear how the data set from the XOR function has been learned by the network. The XOR function can be written as

$$f_{XOR}(x_1, x_2) = (x_1 + x_2) - 2x_1 x_2 = y - z\,, \tag{4.47}$$

where $y = x_1 + x_2$ and $z = 2x_1 x_2$. From this relation, we see that the hidden layer allows the network to linearize the problem into a sum of two terms. The two functions y and z are encoded by the network using the properties of the sigmoid function. If we assume for simplicity that the sigmoid function is replaced by a step function that emits the value 1 if the input value is greater than or equal to the threshold value and zero otherwise, then the y and z functions can be encoded having the weights $v_{ij} = 1$ for all values of i and j and the corresponding threshold values 1 and 2 for the first and second hidden neuron, respectively. With these values for the weights and thresholds, the first hidden neuron will emit a value of 1 if either of the input values are 1, and zero otherwise. The second hidden neuron will emit a value of 1 only if both the input neurons are 1. Setting the weights $w_1 = 1$, and $w_2 = -1$, the network is now able to encode the XOR function.

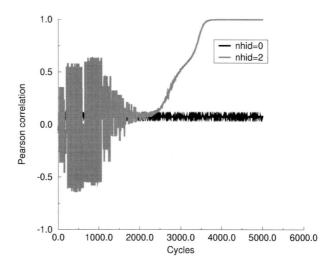

Figure 4.14: Neural network learning curves for nonlinear patterns. The plot shows the Pearson correlation as a function of the number of learning cycles during neural network training. The black curve shows the learning curve for the XOR function for a neural network without hidden neurons, and the gray curve shows the learning curve for the neural network with two hidden neurons.

4.9.3   Sequence Encoding

To feed the neural network with sequence data the amino acids must be transformed into numerical values in the input layer. A large set of different encoding schemes exists. The most conventionally used is the *sparse* or *orthogonal* encoding scheme, where each amino acid is represented as a 20- or 21-bit binary string. Alanine is represented as 10000000000000000000 and cysteine as 01000000000000000000, · · ·, where the last digit is used to represent blank, N- and C-terminal positions in a sequence window, i.e., when a window extends one of the ends of the sequence. Other encoding schemes take advantage of the physical and chemical similarities between the different amino acids. One such encoding scheme is the BLOSUM encoding, where each amino acid is encoded as the 20 BLOSUM matrix values for replacing the amino acid [Nielsen et al., 2003]. A summary of other sequence encoding schemes can be found in [Baldi and Brunak, 2001].

	Predicted positive	Predicted negative	Total
Actual positive	TP	FN	AP
Actual negative	FP	TN	AN
Total	PP	PN	N

Table 4.2: Classification of predictions. TP: true positives (predicted positive, actual positive); TN: true negatives (predicted negative, actual negative); FP: false positives (predicted positive, actual negative); FN: false negatives (predicted negative, actual positive).

4.10 Performance Measures for Prediction Methods

A number of different measures are commonly used to evaluate the performance of predictive algorithms. These measures differ according to whether the performance of a real-valued predictor (e.g., binding affinities) or a classification is to be evaluated.

In almost all cases percentages of correctly predicted examples are not the best indicators of the predictive performance in classification tasks, because the number of positives often is much smaller than the number of negatives in independent test sets. Algorithms that underpredict a lot will therefore appear to have a high success rate, but will not be very useful.

We define a set of performance measures from a set of data with N predicted values p_i and N actual (or target) values a_i. The value p_i is found using a prediction method of choice, and the a_i is the known corresponding target value. By introducing a threshold t_a, the N points can be divided into actual positives A_P (points with actual values a_i greater than t_a) and actual negatives A_N. Similarly, by introducing a threshold for the predicted values t_p, the points can be divided into predicted positives P_P and predicted negatives P_N. These definitions are summarized in table 4.2 and will in the following be used to define a series of different performance measures.

4.10.1 Linear Correlation Coefficient

The linear correlation coefficient, which is also called Pearson's r, or just the correlation coefficient, is the most widely used measure of the association between pairs of values [Press et al., 1992]. It is calculated as

$$ c = \frac{\sum_i (a_i - \overline{a})(p_i - \overline{p})}{\sqrt{\sum_i (a_i - \overline{a})^2}\sqrt{\sum_i (p_i - \overline{p})^2}} , \qquad (4.48) $$

where the overlined letters denote average values. This is one of the best measures of association, but as the name indicates it works best if the actual and predicted values when plotted against each other fall roughly on a line. A value of 1 corresponds to a perfect correlation and a value of -1 to a perfect anticorrelation (when the prediction is high, the actual value is low). A value of 0 corresponds to a random prediction.

4.10.2 Matthews Correlation Coefficient

I f all the predicted and actual values only take one of two values (normally 0 and 1) the linear correlation coefficient reduces to the Matthews correlation coefficient [Matthews, 1975]

$$c = \frac{T_P T_N - F_P F_N}{\sqrt{(T_P + F_N)(T_N + F_P)(T_P + F_P)(T_N + F_N)}} = \frac{T_P T_N - F_P F_N}{\sqrt{A_P A_N P_P P_N}} . \qquad (4.49)$$

As for the Pearson correlation, a value of 1 corresponds to a perfect correlation.

4.10.3 Sensitivity, Specificity

Four commonly used measures are calculated by dividing the true positives and negatives by the actual and predicted positives and negatives [Guggenmoos-Holzmann and van Houwelingen, 2000],

Sensitivity Sensitivity measures the fraction of the actual positives which are correctly predicted: $sens = \frac{TP}{AP}$.

Specificity Specificity denotes the fraction of the actual negatives which are correctly predicted: $spec = \frac{TN}{AN}$

PPV The positive predictive value (PPV) is the fraction of the predicted positives which are correct: $PPV = \frac{TP}{PP}$.

NPV The negative predictive value (NPV) stands for the fraction of the negative predictions which are correct: $NPV = \frac{TN}{PN}$.

4.10.4 Receiver Operator Characteristics Curves

One problem with the above measures (except Pearson's r) is that a threshold t_p must be chosen to distinguish between predicted positives and negatives. When comparing two different prediction methods, one may have a better Matthews correlation coefficient than the other. Alternatively, one may have a higher sensitivity or a higher specificity. Such differences may be due to the choice of thresholds and in that case the two prediction methods may

Rank	Prediction	Actual	TPP	FPP	Area
1	0.1	1	0.33	0	0
2	0.3	0	0.33	0.5	0.17
3	0.35	1	0.66	0.5	0.17
4	0.7	1	1.00	0.5	0.17
5	0.88	0	1.00	1	**0.67**

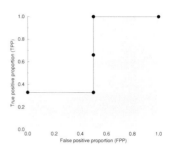

Figure 4.15: Calculation of a ROC curve. The table on the left side of the figure indicates the steps involved in constructing the ROC curve. The pairs of predicted and actual values must first be sorted according to the predicted value. The value in the lower right corner is the A_{ROC} value. In the right panel of the figure is shown the corresponding ROC curve.

be rendered identical if the threshold for one of the methods is adjusted. To avoid such artifacts a nonparametric performance measure such as a receiver operator characteristics (ROC) curve is generally applied.

The ROC curve is constructed by using different values of the threshold t_p to plot the false-positive proportion $FPP = F_P/A_N = F_P/(F_P + T_N)$ on the x-axis against the true positive proportion $TPP = T_P/A_P = T_P/(T_P + F_N)$ on the y-axis [Swets, 1988]. Figure 4.15 shows an example of how to calculate a ROC curve and the area under the curve, A_{ROC}, which is a measure of predictive performance. An A_{ROC} value close to 1 indicates again a very good correlation; a value close to 0 indicates a negative correlation and a value of 0.5, no correlation. A general rule of thumb is that an A_{ROC} value > 0.7 indicates a useful prediction performance, and a value > 0.85 a good prediction. A_{ROC} is indeed a robust measure of predictive performance. Compared with the Matthews correlation coefficient, it has the advantage that it is independent of the choice of t_p. It is still, however, dependent on the choice of a threshold t_a for the actual values. Compared with Pearson's correlation r it has the advantage that it is nonparametric, i.e., that the actual value of the predictions is not used in the calculations, only their ranks. This is an advantage in situations where the predicted and actual values are related by a nonlinear function.

4.11   Clustering and Generation of Representative Sets

When training a bioinformatical prediction method, one very important initial step is to generate representative sets. If the data used to train, for instance, a neural network have many very similar data examples, the network will not be trained in an optimal manner. The reason for this is first of all that the network will focus on learning the data that are repeated and thereby get a lower ability to generalize. The other equally important point is that the performance of the prediction method will be overestimated, since the data in the training and test sets will be very alike.

Generating a representative set from a data set is therefore a very important part of the development of a prediction method. The general idea behind generation of representative sets is to exclude redundant data. In making a representative set one also implicitly makes a clustering since all data points which were removed because of similarity to another data point can be said to define a cluster.

In sequence analysis a number of algorithms exist for selecting a representative subset from a set of data points. This is generally done by keeping only one of two very similar data points. In order to do this a measure for similarity must be defined between two data points. For sequences this can, e.g., be percentage identity, alignment score, or significance of alignment score. Hobohm et al. [1992] have presented two algorithms for making a representative set from a list of data points D.

Hobohm 1 Repeat for all data points on the list D:

  - Add next data point in D to list of nonredundant data points N if it is not similar to any of the elements already on the list.

Hobohm 2 Repeat until all sequences are removed from D:

  - Add the data point S with the largest number of similarities to the non redundant set N.
  - Remove data point S and all sequences similar to S from D.

Before applying the Hobohm 1 algorithm, the data points can be sorted according to some property. This will tend to maximize the average value of this property in the selected set because points higher on the list have less chance of being filtered out. The property can, e.g., be chosen to be the quality of the experimental determination of the data point. The Hobohm 2 algorithm aims at maximizing the size of the selected set by first removing the worst offenders, i.e., those with the largest number of neighbors. Hobohm 1 is faster than Hobohm 2 since it is in most cases not necessary to calculate the similarity between all pairs of data points.

Chapter 5

DNA Microarrays in Immunology

5.1 DNA Microarray Analysis

The study of DNA microarrays has been booming within bioinformatics to such a degree that many now take bioinformatics as a synonym for the analysis of this type of data. However, as explained in chapter 1, DNA microarray data are even more valuable when integrated with other types of data. DNA microarrays are very important for the study of the immune system — in particular the direct interaction between host and pathogen, during and after infection. In the following we will give a short introduction to DNA microarrays. For a more detailed introduction see, e.g., Knudsen [2004] or Quackenbush [2001].

DNA microarrays are used to measure the concentration of different messenger RNAs (mRNAs) in a biological sample. This is for example done by spotting oligonucleotide sequences, known as probes, on a slide (also called a chip), with different sequences spotted on different locations. The mRNA from the biological sample is normally converted to complementary DNA (cDNA) , by reverse transcription, and finally labeled and spotted on a glass slide. If some of the cDNA converted from the sample is complementary in sequence to one of the probes on the slide it will hybridize to it (bind to its complementary part). By marking the cDNA sequences in the sample with a fluorescent dye the concentration can be quantified by a scanner. Two types of chips are often used. The first type is the custom chips, where a robot is used to spot cDNA on glass slides. Normally for one slide two different fluorescent labels are used to distinguish between sample and control. This procedure allows to analyze two samples on the same slide

The second type of array is a prefabricated oligonucleotide chip where the oligonucleotide sequences are synthesized on the chip using photo-lithography. The sample and control are hybridized on two different chips. The most common vendor is Affymetrix. The conventional chips of both types typically cover predefined genes from an entire genome. In the newest versions the entire set of exons from a complete organism is covered. Other, more flexible technologies also exist where the customers themselves can produce custom-made DNA chips. For example, NimbleGen makes DNA microarrays based on micromirror technology (used in data projectors), where the user can define the exact sequences of the probes.

The sample preparation in all cases normally consists of six main steps:

1. Extracting mRNA from sample and control.

2. Converting sample to cDNA or cRNA and labeling with fluorescent.

3. Hybridization of sample to probes on the chip.

4. Washing.

5. Scanning of chip.

6. Image processing of scanned image on computer.

In the Affymetrix technology each gene is covered by several probes . For each gene the chip contains several different 25mer oligonucleotides: $11 - 20$ probes that are perfect matches (PMs) to different regions in the gene, and $11 - 20$ corresponding probes that contain one mismatch (MM) in the 25mer. In the Affymetrix system the signal intensity per probe is calculated as a function of the differences between the intensities between the PMs and the MMs. For additional detail see, e.g., the articles by Li and Wong [2001b,a]. Pairs of PMs and MMs that have large standard deviations from the mean are normally excluded from the calculations. In cDNA chips signal intensities are simply calculated as the difference between the fluorescence level in the spot and the fluorescence level in the surroundings of the spot (i.e., the background).

After the image processing the results are often normalized by adjusting the expression levels relative to a gene or group of genes that are assumed to have a constant expression level between samples [Quackenbush, 2002]. Normally, household genes, which are presumed to be equally expressed under all conditions, or the total amount of mRNA in the sample is used.

For each gene the fold-change (odds ratio) O can be calculated as $O = sample/control$. The odds ratio is normally changed into a log-odds ratio by taking the logarithm $LO = \log(O)$. To establish the significance the experiment must be repeated and the statistical significance can then be established, for example, by using a t-test. If there are more than two different conditions analyses of variance between groups (ANOVA) calculation can be used. This procedure employs the F statistic to test the statistical significance of the differences among the means of two or more random samples from a given population. It can thus be used to establish if a gene has different expression levels under the different conditions tested. ANOVA tests whether the variation of the group averages is significantly greater than the expected variation of the group

$$F = \frac{MSB}{MSE}. \tag{5.1}$$

MSB is calculated as the variance of the means of each group; MSE is calculated as the average of the variances of each group if the groups are of equal size. Remember that the mean μ of N numbers x_i is calculated as $1/N \sum_i x_i$ and the variance is calculated as $1/(N-1) \sum_i (x_i - \mu)$. The F distribution has two parameters: degrees of freedom numerator $d_{fn} = a - 1$ and degrees of freedom denominator $d_{fd} = N - a$, where a is the number of groups and N as above is the total number of data points.

Both the experiment and the control should be repeated. If the experiment and control are not repeated only the most unstable mRNAs will be identified. Since in a single microarray experiment many different mRNA levels are compared, it is important to correct for multiple testing. A number of methods to do this have been developed: Bonferroni, Bonferroni step-down (Holm), Westfall and Young permutation, and Benjamini and Hochberg false discovery rate. The simplest and the most stringent is the Bonferroni correction. All the p-values are corrected by multiplying them with the number of tests which are performed. For an experiment to be significant with $p = .05$ when 1000 different probes are compared, the uncorrected p-value must be smaller than $.05/1000 = .00005$.

5.1.1 Principal Component Analysis

Principal component analysis (PCA) can be used to determine the key variables in a multidimensional data set that can explain most of the variance in the observations. This can be used to analyze and visualize multidimensional data sets. PCA can be applied to DNA microarray data where the experimental conditions are the variables (dimensions), and the gene expression measurements are the observations. This can be used to summarize the ways in which gene responses vary under different conditions, and provide insight into the underlying factors [Raychaudhuri et al., 2000].

5.2   Clustering

If DNA microarray data are available for several different conditions they can be used to define clusters of different genes that behave similarly (up- or down-regulated) in different experiments, i.e., under different experimental conditions or in different mutant strains. Such genes may be part of a common pathway and if one of the genes in a group of coregulated genes is known to be associated with a disease it may indicate that other genes in the group are also associated with that disease. Even if some related genes are missed (false negatives) and unrelated genes are picked up (false positives) the general concept of "guilt by association" seems to work [Quackenbush, 2003, Stuart et al., 2003].

Each gene can be represented by N numbers, i.e., an N-dimensional vector, when N experiments are done. The similarity between different genes can be calculated as a distance in N-dimensional space. The distance between two points x and y in N-dimensional space can be taken to be the Euclidean distance $\sqrt{\sum_i (x_i - y_i)}$. A better measure is the cosine of the angle between the vectors,

$$\cos \alpha = \frac{\sum_i (x_i y_i)}{\sqrt{\sum_i x_i^2} \sqrt{\sum_i y_i^2}}, \tag{5.2}$$

since this measure puts less weight on highly expressed genes. Another good distance measure is the Pearson correlation coefficient. Different algorithms have been used to define clusters. UPGMA (unweighted pair group method using arithmetic averages) [Sokal and Michener, 1958, Durbin et al., 1998], neighbor joining [Saitou and Nei, 1987, Studier and Keppler, 1988] and K-means [MacQueen, 1967] are often-used clustering methods.

5.2.1   UPGMA Method

The UPGMA method is one of the simplest examples of a hierarchical clustering method, i.e., a method where the most similar genes are first grouped together. The algorithm is started by letting all data points define their own cluster. Then pairs of clusters with the shortest distance are combined into one cluster until there is only one cluster.

The distance between two clusters is calculated as the average distance between all data points in the first cluster with all data points in the second cluster. When using UPGMA to draw a tree, all data points are put on a (horizontal) line and the nodes combining clusters are put at a height equal to half the distance between the clusters.

5.2.2   Neighbor-Joining

The neighbor-joining algorithm can be seen as an extension of the UPGMA algorithm. The distance between two points D_{ij} is calculated as $d_{ij} - (r_i + r_j)$ where

$$r_i = \frac{1}{L-2} \sum_k d_{ik}.$$ (5.3)

The distance is calculated in this way because the closest neighbors should not always be joined if they have different average distances to other points in the data set. The description follows that of Durbin et al. [1998].

1. The tree initially consists of all data points as nodes.

2. The pair i, j with the smallest distance D_{ij} is added to the tree as a new node k with branch lengths $d_{ik} = 1/2(d_{ij} + r_i - r_j), d_{jk} = 1/2(d_{ij} - r_i + r_j) = d_{ij} - d_{ik}$, and distances to other data points $d_{km} = 1/2(d_{im} + d_{jm} - d_{ij})$.

3. k replaces i, j in the list of data points.

4. Repeat steps (2) and (3) until there are two data points left which are connected with branch length d_{ij}.

5.2.3   K-Means

The K-means works by dividing the genes into K clusters and is initialized by random assignment of each gene to a cluster. Iteratively the method works by reassigning all genes to their nearest cluster, until convergence or a given number of iterations have been performed. The K-means algorithm differs from the ones described above in that it is not hierarchical. A number of variants of this algorithm exist. A simple version consists of the following

1. Randomly choosing K genes to define centers.

2. All other genes are assigned to that of the K clusters it is closest to.

3. The K centers are redefined as the average of the genes in the cluster.

4. Steps (2) and (3) are repeated.

5.3 Immunological Applications

DNA microarrays may be used to monitor which genes are turned on and off in the host immune system, and in invading pathogens during an infection [Hagmann, 2000]. This may reveal previously unknown alterations of host gene expression during infections with viruses [Tong et al., 2004] or with prions [Xiang et al., 2004]. One advantage is that the sample may not even have to contain the microorganism in question if its effects can be read off from the changed gene expression of the host [Hagmann, 2000].

Microorganisms may try to escape the host immune response by interfering with expression of host immune genes. It has, e.g., been shown by microarray studies that the smallpox virus can modulate the host immune response Rubins et al. [2004]. Helminths may also interfere with the immune system: the eggs of the helminth parasite, *Schistosoma mansoni*, can suppress the ability of the Toll–like receptor ligand-induced activation of immature dendritic cells [Kane et al., 2004]. Cancer cells may also change the expression of cell surface molecules involved in antigen presentation in order to avoid immune surveillance [Suscovich et al., 2004].

The difference between the gene expression in vaccinated and nonvaccinated animals can be elucidated by microarray analysis. Byon et al. [2005] observed significant upregulation of some immune-related genes that are necessary for antiviral defense following vaccination with the viral hemorrhagic septicemia virus glycoprotein. By studying gene expression profiles, they also found significant up- and downregulation of unknown genes upon DNA vaccination. This may be a new basis for establishing the so-called correlates of protection, i.e., markers that predict if a vaccine will work or not. Classically, the level of antibodies has often been used as a correlate of protection, but microarrays may in the future be used to complement or replace it. Moreover, this approach can help us identify other, yet unidentified, players of protection. Similar research can be done by comparing naive and immune animal models. For example, *Helicobacter pylori*-infected mice were characterized by expression of innate host defense markers while immune mice expressed many interferon-gamma response genes and T cell markers [Rahn et al., 2004].

A more medical application is to use microarray data to monitor the clinical status of patients. This may be important for making decisions on when to start or change a treatment. A set of genes that are related to the progression of HIV-1 infection have been identified [Motomura et al., 2004] using microarray technology. Such analysis may be used to understand why different individuals have different disease progression speeds. Gene expression profiles of individual patients may be used to design individualized cancer therapies [Kawakami et al., 2004].

Analysis of gene expression profiles may also be used to distinguish different immune cells. Schiott et al. [2004] used gene expression profiles to show that helper T cell memory populations with or without the CD27 marker are actually functionally different cell populations. Only T cells displaying CD27 require costimulation for T cell receptor triggering.

Chapter 6

Prediction of Cytotoxic T Cell (MHC Class I) Epitopes

Cytotoxic T lymphocytes (CTLs) recognize foreign peptides presented on cells in the body and help to destroy infected or malignant cells. The peptides are presented by the class I major histocompatibility complex (MHC), and the actual binding of the peptide to the MHC molecules is the single most selective event in the antigen presentation process. The process also includes processing (cleavage) of proteins and translocation of peptides from the cytosol into the endoplasmic reticulum (ER). These latter steps, however, only filter out approximately four fifths of all potential 9mer peptides, whereas a particular MHC class I allele only binds 1 in 200 potential peptides [Yewdell and Bennink, 1999].

The class I MHCs (which are also called class I human leukocyte antigens or HLAs in humans) are encoded by 3 different loci on the genome called A, B, and C. Each of the genes is highly polymorphic and for each locus hundreds of different alleles exist. The HLAs are thus highly diverse, and each allele binds a very specific set of peptides. All the different alleles can be divided into at least 9 supertypes, where the alleles within each supertype exhibit roughly the same peptide specificity [Sette and Sidney, 1999, Lund et al., 2004]. The concept of HLA supertypes has great implications for the use of bioinformatical prediction algorithms in the search for novel vaccine candidates. The HLA allele space is very large, and reliable identification of potential epitope candidates would be an immense task if all alleles were to be included in the search. However, many HLA alleles share a large fraction of their peptide binding repertoire, and it is often possible to find promiscuous peptides, which bind to a series of HLA alleles. This allows the search to be limited to a manageable set of alleles. A detailed description of the different HLA supertypes is given in chapter 13.

6.1   Background and Historical Overview of Methods for Peptide MHC Binding Prediction

A number of methods for predicting the binding of peptides to MHC molecules have been developed (reviewed by Schirle et al. [2001]) since the first motif methods were presented [Rothbard and Taylor, 1988, Sette et al., 1989b].

The majority of peptides binding to the HLA complex have a length of eight to ten amino acids. For 9mers, positions 2 and 9 are very important for the binding to most class I HLAs, and these positions are referred to as anchor positions [Rammensee et al., 1999]. For some alleles the binding motifs further have auxiliary anchor positions. Peptides binding to the A*0101 allele thus have positions 2, 3, and 9 as anchors [Kubo et al., 1994, Kondo et al., 1997, Rammensee et al., 1999].

The importance of the anchor positions for peptide binding and the allele-specific amino acid preference at the anchor positions was first described by Falk et al. [1991]. The discovery of such allele-specific motifs led to the development of the first reasonable accurate algorithms [Pamer et al., 1991, Rotzschke et al., 1991]. In these prediction tools, it is assumed that the amino acids at each position along the peptide sequence contribute a given binding energy, which can independently be added up to yield the overall binding energy of the peptide [Parker et al., 1994, Meister et al., 1995, Stryhn et al., 1996]. Similar types of approaches are used by the EpiMatrix method [Schafer et al., 1998], the BIMAS method [Parker et al., 1994], and the SYFPEITHI method [Rammensee et al., 1999]. An example of a peptide binding to an HLA molecule can be seen in figure 6.1.

These methods cannot take into account correlated effects where the binding affinity of a given amino acid at one position is influenced by amino acids at other positions in the peptide. Two adjacent amino acids may, e.g., compete for the space in a pocket in the MHC molecule. Artificial neural networks (ANN) are ideally suited to take such correlations into account.

Several prediction methods have been made publicly available, including weight-matrix methods such as BIMAS [Parker et al., 1994] and SYFPEITHI [Rammensee et al., 1999], weight matrices with optimized position-specific weighting [Yu et al., 2002] and ANNs [Brusic et al., 1994, Adams and Koziol, 1995]. Recently we have developed a comprehensive HLA-peptide binding prediction server including allele-specific weight-matrix predictions for more than 120 HLA alleles, as well as ANNs and weight-matrix predictions for 12 alleles representing 12 distinct HLA supertypes. This NetMHC (NetMHC2.0) server is

A   B

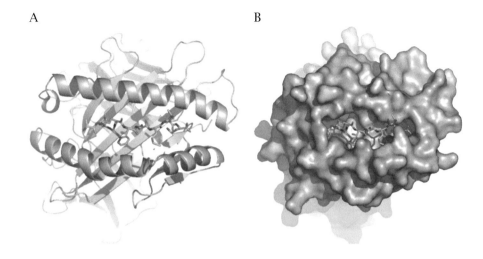

Figure 6.1: Example of peptide binding to MHC class I. (A) Cartoon representation of MHC class I showing that the peptide is binding to a "floor" made by a β-sheet, and restricted on each side by two α-helices. The bound peptide is shown in a sticks representation. B) MHC molecule shown as a molecular surface representation. It can be seen that the binding is closer than it appears from the cartoon model. The figure is based on the PDB (www.rcsb.org/pdb) entry 1q94. Figure courtesy of Anne Mølgaard. See plate 6 for color version.

available at www.cbs.dtu.dk/services/NetMHC. A more comprehensive list of servers can be found in chapter 12.

Detailed predictions of peptide binding have been made by dividing binding affinities into classes of affinity ranges; it has been found that the different classes are associated with different binding sequence motifs [Adams and Koziol, 1995]. Neural networks have also been trained to predict MHC binding using different affinity thresholds [Gulukota et al., 1997]. Mamitsuka trained the transition and emission probabilities of a fully connected hidden Markov model (HMM) using a steepest descent algorithm so as to minimize the differences between the predicted and target probabilities for each peptide [Mamitsuka, 1998].

Other prediction algorithms have been developed to predict not only if a peptide binds but also the actual affinity of the binding [Marshall et al., 1995, Stryhn et al., 1996, Rognan et al., 1999, Doytchinova and Flower, 2001, Buus et al., 2003, Nielsen et al., 2003]. For affinity predictions, ANNs in general outperform the simpler methods [Gulukota et al., 1997, Nielsen et al., 2003], but generally ANNs need a large number of examples in the training [Yu et al., 2002] to achieve accurate predictions.

Buus et al. [2003] have demonstrated that neural networks trained to perform quantitative predictions of peptide MHC binding are superior to conventional classification neural networks trained to predict binding vs. non-binding. Nielsen et al. [2003] have further demonstrated that neural network methods perform significantly better than linear methods in predicting high-affinity peptides.

A central issue in the development of bioinformatical prediction algorithms is the number of training examples needed to achieve reliable predictions. As stated above, ANNs in general need a large number of training data in order to achieve a predictive performance beyond that of the simpler methods. HMMs (or weight matrices), on the other hand, can be trained to a very accurate performance on small data sets by use of the techniques described in chapter 4. Common to both artificial networks and HMMs is that both methods rely on the availability of peptides known to bind a given MHC complex. For many alleles such data are not available or available only in very limited numbers, and for these alleles other approaches have to be taken. The number of MHC-peptide complexes solved by X-ray crystallography is growing. Based on such structural information, an MHC-peptide binding potential can be derived. Such an approach has been taken by Altuvia et al. [1995], Schueler-Furman et al. [2000], Doytchinova and Flower [2001] where peptide binding is predicted by either free energy calculations or threading. In situations where no peptide motif information exists, these energy-based algorithms are highly valuable.

In this chapter, we will demonstrate how bioinformatical methods can be applied to derive prediction methods for HLA-peptide binding. In the first part, we describe how accurate prediction methods can be derived in situations where very limited training data are available. The second part shows how highly reliable prediction methods can be constructed using a combination of many neural networks trained with different sequence encoding schemes.

6.2   MHC Class I Epitope Binding Prediction Trained on Small Data Sets

The highly diverse MHC class I alleles bind very different peptides, and accurate binding prediction methods exist only for alleles where the binding pattern has been deduced from peptide motifs. Predictions in general tend to be more precise when more examples are included in the training [Yu et al., 2002], but experimental data on peptides binding to HLA complexes are published in large numbers for only a few alleles.

It has earlier been shown that a position specific weighted matrix where the weight on selected positions in the matrix describing binding motif is increased performs slightly better for A*0201 predictions than an unweighted matrix [Yu et al., 2002]. A similar result was found in the example for weight-matrix construction in chapter 4, where a weight matrix was constructed from 10 HLA-A*0201 restricted peptide using the technique of sequence weighting, pseudocount correction for low counts, and position-specific weighting. This matrix was shown to share many of the features of a weight matrix trained on close to 500 HLA-A*0201 restricted peptides. It is, however, not clear from these two examples to what extent such a weighting will influence the number of data needed to generate accurate predictors.

In the following section, we will describe a method for predicting which peptides bind to given MHC class I alleles based on scoring matrices with empirical position specific anchor weighting.

6.2.1 Weight-Matrix Training

The selected peptides can be stacked into a multiple alignment and using an ungapped HMM-like approach the log-odds weight matrix was calculated as $log(p_{pa}/q_a)$, where p_{pa} is the frequency of amino acid a at position p in the alignment and q_a the background frequency of that amino acid in the Swiss-Prot database [Henikoff and Henikoff, 1994]. The values for p_{pa} were estimated using the techniques of sequence weighting and pseudocount correction for low counts described in chapter 4 [Altschul et al., 1997, Henikoff and Henikoff, 1992]. A schematic view of the procedure is outlined in figure 6.2. To analyze how the predictive performance of a weight matrix depends on the number of training data, we varied the numbers of peptides included to calculate the weight matrix. For each number of training peptides, 200 data sets were constructed, using the bootstrap procedure [Press et al., 1992], by randomly drawing the chosen number of peptides with replacement from the original data set of peptides.

To visualize the problem one is facing when training a prediction method on limited amounts of data, we generated sequence logos for peptides binding to the A*0201 allele using 10 and 100 peptides, respectively. From the logo constructed using 10 random A*0201 binding peptides (figure 6.3A), it can be seen that the importance of the anchor positions 2 and 9 is not yet visible, while this feature is clearly apparent in the logo based on 100 sequences (figure 6.3B). The amino acid preferences for the hydrophobic amino acids L and L/V at positions 2 and 9, respectively, is, however, present in both logos. Based on the information content visualized with the logos in figure 6.3, a prediction method trained on very little data would very likely benefit by incorporating the prior knowledge about the differential importance of the different positions in the motif. This is naturally done by increasing the relative weight on the anchor positions. The logo of a matrix with position-specific differential weighting at positions 2 and 9 is shown in figure 6.3C.

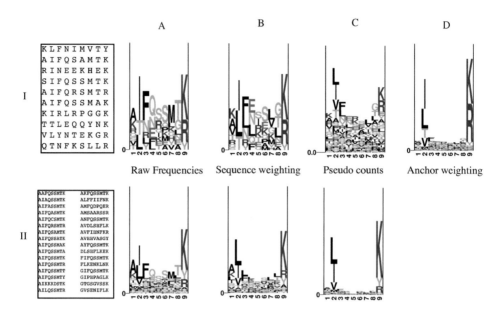

Figure 6.2: Logos showing the distribution of information content after each step in the matrix calculation using few (I) or many (II) A*0301 training peptides. The sequences used for training are shown in the box to the left in each row. The number of peptides in the two examples is 10 and 32, respectively. (A) The distribution of amino acids at each position. (B) After sequence weighting. (C) After low count correction. (D) Extra weight on anchor positions when few peptides are used for training. The logos were calculated as described by Hebsgaard et al. [1996], and visualized using the logo program [Schneider and Stephens, 1990]. Figure reprinted with permission [Lundegaard et al., 2004]. See plate 7 for color version.

Figure 6.4 shows that weight matrix predictions can benefit from such position-specific weighting. A set of weight matrices were generated for the A2 allele A*0201 for a different number of training data. In the work of Yu et al. [2002] all positions in the weight matrix were scaled differently. Here only the weights on the positions 2 and 9 and any addition position assigned as anchor in the SYFPEITHI database [Rammensee et al., 1999], were scaled (biased) by a factor of 5. The different matrices were evaluated on 217 peptides with experimentally determined affinities to the A*0201 allele (K. Lamberth, unpublished). From the figure, it is clear that when using unbiased weight matrices at least 20 training peptides are needed to get a reasonable performance ($A_{ROC} > .8$, Pearsons $r > .5$), and at least 100 training examples to get values comparable to those obtained by publicly available prediction servers. When applying position-specific weighting on the matrices, the performance, on the other hand, is surprisingly high, even for matrices trained with just a

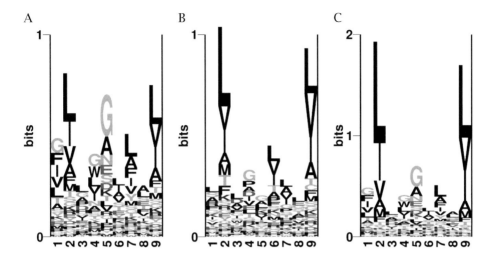

Figure 6.3: Sequence logos generated by 10 (A and C) and 100 (B) randomly chosen A*0201 binding peptides. The logos are constructed using the techniques of sequence weighting and pseudocount correction for low counts. In (C) the method of positionspecific differential weighting of positions 2 and 9 is applied with a weight of 3 [Lundegaard et al., 2004].

handful of peptides. For a number of training peptides of 20, both the public methods and the position-specific weighted matrix reach similar predictive performances.

Figure 6.5 shows that the position-specific weighting approach is also applicable to other HLA alleles The position weighting strategy was applied to train matrices with peptides belonging to the A*0101, A*0301, A*1101, and B*0702 alleles. Note that position 3 is an additional anchor position in the A*0101 allele and that this position thus was also biased for this allele. For each of the 4 alleles, a series of weight matrices were trained by varying the number of training examples. In figure 6.5 it can be seen how the weight matrix predictive performance varies as a function of the number of training examples for each of the 4 alleles. For each allele is shown the performance of an unweighted matrix, a weight matrix with position specific weighting of the anchor positions of the bind motif as assigned in the SYFPEITHI database, and the two public methods of BIMAS [Parker et al., 1994] and SYFPEITHI [Rammensee et al., 1999]. SYFPEITHI predictions were performed using the web server http://syfpeithi.bmi-heidelberg.com, and BIMAS predictions were performed as described at the web server, using matrices downloaded from the website http://bimas.cit.nih.gov/cgi-bin/molbio/hla_coefficient_viewing_page. In all cases reliable predictions were obtainable with matrices trained on as few

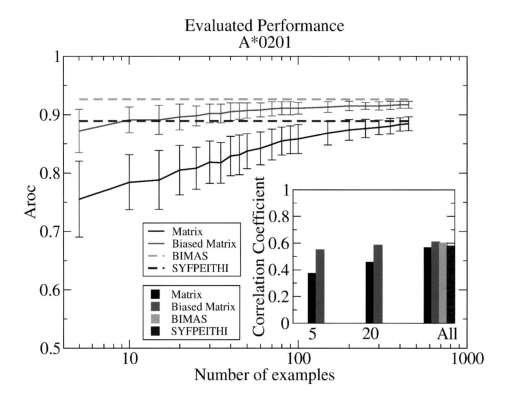

Figure 6.4: Curves of the A_{ROC} value (major graph) and the Pearson correlation coefficient (inserted graph) plotted against the number of training examples randomly selected from the total pool of peptides. Each value is the simple average of 200 independent calculations with the indication of one standard deviation. The matrices were generated and evaluated with peptides binding to the allele A*0201. The score for a given peptide is calculated as the sum of the scores at each position. Training examples were extracted from the databases SYFPEITHI [Rammensee et al., 1999] and MHCPEP [Brusic et al., 1998a]. As evaluation sets, we used peptides for which the affinities for the selected alleles had been measured using the enzyme-linked immunosorbent assay (ELISA) method described by Sylvester-Hvid et al. [2002] (K. Lamberth, unpublished) using a threshold for binders of 500 nM. Predictions were made for the corresponding evaluation set by each of the 200 matrices of each train set size, and the predictive performance was measured in terms of both the linear (Pearson) correlation coefficient between the prediction output and log-transformed measured affinities [Buus et al., 2003] and the area under a receiver operating characteristic (ROC) curve, the A_{ROC} value [Swets, 1988]. The final predictive performance is given as the simple average of the 200 values. Figure reprinted with permission [Lundegaard et al., 2004].

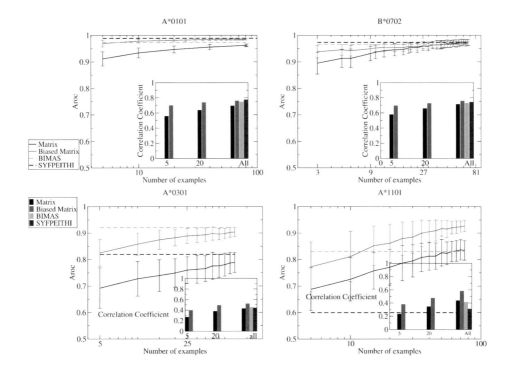

Figure 6.5: Curves of the A_{ROC} value (major graph) and the Pearson correlation coefficient (inserted graph) plotted against the number of training examples randomly selected from the total pool of peptides. Each value is the simple average of 200 independent calculations with the indication of one standard deviation. The matrices were generated and evaluated with peptides binding to the alleles A*0101, A*0301, A*1101, and B*0702. Note that the SYFPEITHI A*1101 predictions were generated using the A03 predictor. Figure reprinted with permission [Lundegaard et al., 2004].

as 5 training examples. For all alleles the performance of the position-specific weighted matrix is comparable to that of the public methods when 20 training examples are available.

Table 6.1 shows the prediction accuracy for predictors for different alleles on severe acute respiratory syndrome (SARS) derived peptides [Sylvester-Hvid et al., 2004] and on peptides from evaluation sets obtained from the MHCBN 3.1 database [Bhasin et al., 2003]. In the evaluation the predictive performance in terms of the A_{ROC} value was calculated for each of the evaluation sets using position-specific weight matrices trained on different numbers of data; an unweighted matrix trained on all available data; and the two public methods, BIMAS and SYFPEITHI.

Allele	Matrix all peptides	Biased matrix 5 peptides	Biased matrix 20 peptides	Biased matrix all peptides	BIMAS	SYFPEITHI
A*0101[1]	1.000	0.992 ± 0.026	1.000 ± 0.002	1.000	1.000	1.000
A*0201[1]	0.925	0.803 ± 0.024	0.830 ± 0.017	0.871	0.907	0.864
A*0101[2]	0.963	0.986 ± 0.011	0.992 ± 0.004	0.997	0.951	0.987
A*0201[2]	0.992	0.973 ± 0.015	0.978 ± 0.006	0.984	0.979	0.970
A*0301[2]	0.912	0.885 ± 0.072	0.873 ± 0.028	0.877	0.857	0.829
A*1101[2]	0.937	0.914 ± 0.038	0.948 ± 0.018	0.968	0.950	0.830[3]
B*0702[2]	0.983	0.972 ± 0.013	0.977 ± 0.009	0.985	0.990	0.990
B*1501[2,4]	0.928	0.932 ± 0.039	N.A.	0.955	0.893	N.A.
B*5801[2,4]	0.892	0.959 ± 0.008	N.A.	0.959	0.994	N.A.

Table 6.1: Evaluation of 200 matrices made by selecting 5 or 20 peptides respectively, by the bootstrap method, or a single matrix generated by all available different peptides from MHCPEP and SYFPEITHI databases. The performance was measured in terms of the A_{ROC} value. Evaluation was performed with peptides extracted from the MHCBN 3.1[1] database, and SARS[2] relevant peptides. [3] Predictions were made using the A03 predictor. [4] The bootstrapping procedure was not used due to the small total number of peptides available. Instead, all possible combinations of the available peptides were used to estimate the standard deviation. Table adapted from Lundegaard et al. [2004].

The analysis confirms that a weight matrix with position specific weighting of the anchor position trained on 20 peptide examples achieves a predictive performance comparable to that of BIMAS and SYFPEITHI. In many cases the performance for a biased matrix trained on only 5 peptide examples is comparable to that of the two public methods.

In summary, we have shown that the empirical knowledge of important anchor positions within the binding motif dramatically reduces the number of peptides needed for reliable predictions. The method leads to predictions with a comparable or higher accuracy than other established prediction servers, even in situations where only very limited data are available for training.

6.3   Prediction of CTL Epitopes by Neural Network Methods

Having described how accurate weight matrix–based methods can be derived when very limited training data are available, we now focus on situations where the training set is large. In such situations neural networks would be the choice of method.

Neural network methods for predicting whether or not a peptide binds MHC molecules have earlier been developed [Brusic et al., 1994, Buus et al., 2003]. In this section we will describe how prediction of MHC I binding peptides may be improved using methods that combine several neural networks, each derived using different sequence encoding schemes.

Brusic et al. use a conventional sparse (orthogonal) encoding of the 20-

amino acid alphabet as well as 6- and 9-letter reduced alphabets [Brusic et al., 1994]. The conventional sparse encoding of the amino acids ignores their chemical similarities. We shall use a combination of several sequence-encoding strategies in order to take these similarities into account explicitly. The different encoding schemes are defined in terms of BLOSUM matrices and hidden Markov models in addition to the conventional sparse encoding. The input to the neural network can consist of a combination of sparse encoding, BLOSUM encoding, and input derived from HMMs. We will show that this can lead to a performance superior to neural networks derived using a single sequence-encoding scheme, especially for the high-affinity binding peptides.

We start by demonstrating that peptides binding to the HLA-A*0204 molecule display signals of higher-order sequence correlations; next we train a series of ANNs using different sequence-encoding schemes, and demonstrate how the combination of many such diverse networks improves the prediction accuracy. In the last part of the section we apply the neural network algorithm to perform a genome-wide search for potential CTL epitopes in the genome of the hepatitis C virus (HCV).

6.3.1   Experimental Data

Two sets of data were used to derive the prediction method. One set was used to train and test the neural networks, and consists of 528 9-mer amino acid peptides for which the binding affinity to the HLA class I molecule A*0204 has been measured by the method described by Buus et al. [1995]. This data set is hereinafter referred to as the Buus data set. The second data set was used to train the HMM. This data set was constructed from sequences downloaded from the SYFPEITHI database [Rammensee et al., 1995]. All sequences from the database were downloaded and clustered into the nine supertypes (A1, A2, A3, A24, B7, B27, B44, B58, and B62) and 3 outlier types (A29, B8, and B46) described by Sette and Sidney [1999]. The sequences in the A2 supertype cluster were aligned manually and trimmed into 211 unique 9-amino acid long peptides. This data set is hereinafter referred to as the Rammensee data set.

6.3.2   Mutual Information

One important difference between linear prediction methods like first-order HMMs and nonlinear prediction methods like neural networks with hidden layers is their capability to integrate higher-order sequence correlations into the prediction score. A measure of the degree of higher-order sequence correlations in a set of aligned amino acid sequences can be obtained by calculating the mutual information matrix. For the case of peptide 9-mers, this is a 9 x

9 matrix where each matrix element is, as described in Chapter 4, calculated
using the formula

$$M_{ij} = \sum_a \sum_b P_{ij}(ab) \log \frac{P_{ij}(ab)}{P_i(a)P_j(b)}. \tag{6.1}$$

In this example the summation is over the 20 letters in the conventional amino
acid alphabet and i, j refer to positions in the peptide. $P_{ij}(ab)$ is the probability of mutually finding the amino acid a at position i and amino acid b
at position j. $P_i(a)$ is the probability of finding amino acid a at position i
irrespective of the content at the other positions, and likewise for $P_j(b)$. A
positive value in the mutual information matrix indicates that prior knowledge of the amino acid content at position i will provide information about
the amino acid content at position j. The statistical reliability of a mutual
information calculation relies crucially on the size of the corresponding data
set. In the mutual information calculation one seeks to estimate 400 amino
acid pair frequencies at each position in the matrix. Such estimates are naturally associated with large uncertainties when dealing with small data sets.
Figure 6.6 shows the mutual information matrix calculated for two different
sets of 9-mer alignments.

The first data set was constructed to obtain the largest possible positive set,
by combining peptides from the Rammensee data set with the peptides from
the Buus data set that were measured to bind MHC (i.e., having a $K_D < 500$
nM). This set contains 313 unique sequences. The second data set was constructed as a negative set by extracting 313 unique random peptides from the
Mycobaterium tuberculosis genome. The mutual information content is calculated using the conventional 20-amino acid alphabet. The figure demonstrates
a signal of mutual information between the seven nonanchor residues positions (1, 3, 4, 5, 6, 7, and 8) in the data set defined by peptides that bind to
the HLA molecule. It is worth remarking that the mutual information content
between any of the two anchor positions (2 and 9) and all other amino acids
is substantially lower than the mutual information content between any two
nonanchor positions.

6.3.3 Combination of More than One Neural Network Prediction

We combine the output from the two networks trained using sparse and BLO-
SUM sequence encoding, respectively, in a simple manner, as a weighted sum
of the two. To select the weight that corresponds to the optimal performance,
we plot the sensitivity/PPV as well as the ROC (relative operating characteristic) curves [Swets, 1988] for a series of weighted sum combinations of the two
network outputs. The sensitivity is defined as the ratio TP/AP. Here TP (true

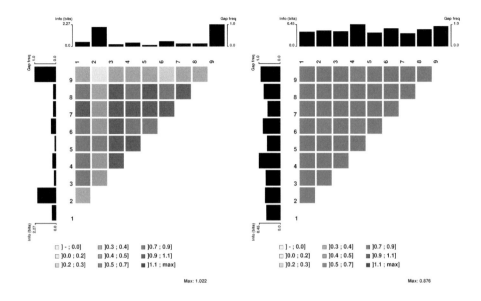

Figure 6.6: Mutual information matrices calculated for two different data sets. The left panel shows the mutual information matrix calculated for a data set consisting of 313 peptides derived from the Rammensee data set combined with binding peptides from the Buus data set (defined as K_D < 500 nM). The right panel shows the mutual information matrix calculated for a set of 313 random peptides extracted from the Mycobaterium tuberculosis genome [Nielsen et al., 2003]. The plot was made using MatrixPlot [Gorodkin et al., 1999] (http://www.cbs.dtu.dk/services/MatrixPlot/).

positives) is the number of data points for which both the predicted score is above a given prediction threshold value and the measured binding affinity is above a given classification threshold value. AP (actual positives) is the total number of data points that have a measured binding affinity above the affinity threshold value. The PPV is defined as the ratio TP/PP. Here PP (predicted positives) is the total number of predictions with scores above the prediction threshold value. The PPV is a measure of the reliability of the prediction method. The ROC curves are closely related to the sensitivity/PPV curves, but with the important difference that one of the axis in the ROC curve is the false-positive proportion FP/AN (actual negatives) and not the true positive-to-predicted positive ratio (the PPV). The area under the ROC curve (A_{ROC}) provides an estimate of the accuracy of the prediction method. A random method will have a value of $A_{ROC} = 0.5$. $A_{ROC} > 0.8$ indicates that the method has moderate accuracy and $A_{ROC} = 1$, that the prediction method is perfect [Swets, 1988]. In a sensitivity/PPV plot, the curve for the perfect method is the one where the area under the curve is unity. The curves are estimated using

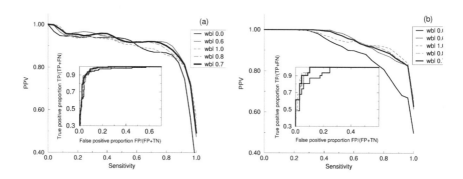

Figure 6.7: (a) Sensitivity/PPV plot calculated using a classification binding affinity of 500 nM for a series of linear combinations of the two neural network methods corresponding to BLOSUM50 and sparse sequence encoding, respectively. The curves were calculated by use of the bootstrap method [Press et al., 1992] using 500 data set realizations. (a) 428 peptides in the test/train data set; (b) 100 peptides in the evaluation set. In the upper graph we determine the optimal performance to be the thick blue curve, corresponding to a combination of the two neural network methods with 70% weight on the BLOSUM50 encoded prediction and 30% weight on the sparse encoded prediction. This set of weights also results in close to optimal performance in the lower graph. Inserts to the graphs show the corresponding ROC curves. Figure adapted from Nielsen et al. [2003].

the bootstrap method [Press et al., 1992]. N data sets were constructed by randomly drawing M data points with replacement from the original data set of M peptides. For each of the N data sets a sensitivity/PPV curve and a ROC curve was calculated and the curves displayed in figure 6.7 are derived from the mean of these N sensitivity/PPV and ROC curve realizations.

In figure 6.7, the sensitivity/PPV curves for the 428 peptides in the train and test set and the 100 peptides in the evaluation set are shown for a measured binding affinity threshold value equal to 0.426, corresponding to a binding affinity of 500 nM. In the inserts to the figures the corresponding ROC curves are shown. From the figure, it is clear that both the sparse and the BLOSUM encoded neural networks have a performance that is inferior to any combination of the two. In figure 6.7(a) the optimal combination is found to have a weight on the BLOSUM encoded network close to 0.7 and a weight on the sparse encoded network close to 0.3. This set of weights for the combination of the two neural network predictions is also, in figure 6.6(b), seen to improve to the prediction accuracy for the 100 peptides in the evaluation set. This is, however, less obvious, due to the small number of binding peptides in the evaluation set. The evaluation set contains 31 peptides with binding affinity stronger than 500 nM.

The Pearson correlation coefficient between the predicted and the measured binding affinities for the sparse encoded, the BLOSUM encoded, and the combined neural network method on the peptides in the train/test set is found to be .849, .887 and .895, respectively. For the peptides in the evaluation set the corresponding values are found to be .866, .926, and .928 respectively.

The neural network training and testing is next repeated using the full data set in a fivefold cross-validation. The combined method, hereinafter referred to as comb-I, is defined using the weights on the BLOSUM and the sparse encoded neural networks, respectively, estimated above.

6.3.4 Integration of Data from the Rammensee Database in the Neural Network Training

In figure 6.8(b), we show the performance of the HMM evaluated on the 528 peptides in the Buus data set. The figure displays a reasonable correlation between the HMM score and the measured binding affinity. This correlation demonstrates that the sequences in the Rammensee data set contain valuable information and that the neural network training could benefit from an integration of the Rammensee sequence data into the training data set. It is, however, not obvious how such an integration should be done. The Rammensee data are binary in nature. They describe that a given peptide does bind to the HLA molecule but not the strength of the binding. The data in the Buus data set, on the other hand, are continuous in that each peptide is associated with a binding affinity. It turns out that a fruitful procedure for integrating the Rammensee data into the neural network training is to use the output scores generated by the HMM as additional input to the neural network. The HMM is trained on the peptides in the Rammensee data set. The model is nine residues long, and the scores used as input to the neural network are the nine scores obtained when aligning a 9-mer peptide to the model. Two neural networks each with 189 input neurons (180 for sequence encoding and 9 to encode the scores from the HMM) are trained in a fivefold manner as described above using the HMM scores combined with the sparse or BLOSUM sequence encoding in the input layer, respectively. In the final combined method, the prediction value is calculated as the simple average with equal weight of the sparse and BLOSUM encoded neural network predictions, respectively.

This method is hereinafter referred to as comb-II and is the one used in the HCV genome predictions described below.

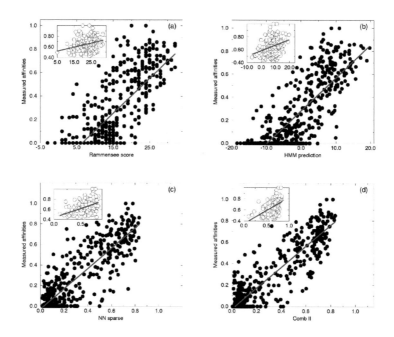

Figure 6.8: Scatterplot of the predicted score vs. the measured binding affinity for the 528 peptides in the Buus data set. The figure shows the performance for four different prediction methods. The insert to each figure shows an enlargement of the part of the plot that corresponds to a binding affinity stronger than 500 nM. (a) Rammensee matrix method, (b) HMM trained on sequences in the Rammensee data set, (c) Neural network trained with sparse sequence encoding, and (d) The comb-II neural network method. The straight-line fit to the data in (c) and (d) have slope and intercept of 0.989, -0.029, and 0.979, -0.027, respectively. Figure reprinted with permission [Nielsen et al., 2003].

6.3.5   Neural Network Methods Compared to HMM Methods and the Matrix Method of Rammensee

In table 6.2, we give the test performance measured in terms of the Pearson correlation coefficient for the 528 peptides in the Buus data set for six different prediction methods: One method is the matrix method of Rammensee et al. [1999]; the second, the HMM trained on the Rammensee data set; and the other four, neural networks methods trained using sparse and BLOSUM sequence encoding, the linear combination of the two, and the linear combination including input from the HMM, respectively. For the matrix method of Rammensee and the HMM, we calculate the Pearson correlation between

Method	Pearson (all)	Pearson (500 nM)	Pearson (50 nM)
Rammensee	0.761 ± 0.016	0.296 ± 0.073	0.066 ± 0.116
HMM	0.804 ± 0.014	0.332 ± 0.061	0.142 ± 0.096
NN_{Sparse}	0.877 ± 0.011	0.438 ± 0.065	0.345 ± 0.090
NN_{Bl50}	0.899 ± 0.010	0.498 ± 0.064	0.382 ± 0.099
Comb-I	0.906 ± 0.009	0.508 ± 0.063	0.392 ± 0.092
Comb-II	0.912 ± 0.009	0.508 ± 0.054	0.420 ± 0.080

Table 6.2: The Pearson correlation coefficient between the predicted score and the measured binding affinity for the 528 peptides in the Buus data set. The six methods in the table are Rammensee: Score matrix method by H. G. Rammensee; HMM: hidden Markov model trained on sequence data in the Rammensee data set; NN_{Sparse}: neural network with sparse sequence encoding; NN_{Bl50}: neural network with BLOSUM50 sequence encoding; Comb-I: combination of neural network trained using sparse and BLOSUM50 sequence encoding, respectively; and Comb-II: combination of neural network trained using sparse, BLOSUM50, and HMM sequence encoding, respectively. The numbers given in the table are calculated using the bootstrap method [Press et al., 1992] with 500 data set realizations. The correlation values are estimated as average values over the 500 data set realizations and the associated standard deviations. Table adapted from Nielsen et al. [2003].

the raw output scores and the logarithmically transformed measured binding affinities even though this might not be what optimally relates the prediction score to the measured binding affinity.

From the results shown, it is clear that the neural network methods all have a higher predictive performance compared to both the method of Rammensee and the HMM. The difference in predictive performance between the neural network and the Rammensee and the HMM methods is most significant for data sets defined by peptides with a binding affinity stronger than 50 nM, thus indicating that the signal of higher-order sequence correlation is most strongly present in peptides that bind strongly to the HLA A2 molecule. The same conclusion can be drawn from the data displayed in figure 6.8. Here the test performance for the 528 peptides is shown as a scatterplot of the prediction score vs. the measured binding affinity for four of the six methods above. Again, it is clear that the neural network methods in general and the combined methods in particular have a higher predictive performance than the Rammensee and the HMM methods. The least-squares straight-line fit to the data shown in figure 6.8 (c) and (d) also validates the quality and accuracy of the neural network predictions. In the two plots the straight line fits have a slope and intercept of 0.989, −0.029 and 0.979, −0.027, respectively, thus demonstrating the strength of the neural network trained on quantitative data in providing a direct relationship between the neural network output and the measured binding affinity.

In figure 6.9, we show the sensitivity/PPV curves calculated for the data

128

Prediction of MHC Class I epitopes

in the 528 peptide set using the four different neural network methods as well as the method of Rammensee and the HMM method. All curves are estimated using the bootstrap method described above. The upper graph shows the sensitivity/PPV curves for the six methods calculated for a classification threshold corresponding to 500 nM, and the lower graph shows the sensitivity/PPV curves for a classification threshold corresponding to 50 nM. In the inserts to the graphs are shown the corresponding ROC curves for the six methods. In the labels to the curves in the inserts, we give the estimated ROC areas [Swets, 1988]. In both graphs, it is clear that the combined neural methods have a performance superior to that of the other four methods. All four neural network methods and in particular the two combined methods have a performance that is substantially higher than that of the Rammensee method. The ranking of the six methods obtained using the ROC area method is identical to the ranking estimated using the Pearson correlation measure given in table 6.2. Using a Student's t-test to compare the mean error of prediction (predicted binding affinity − measured binding affinity) between the comb-II method and the two neural network methods trained with a single sequence encoding, we find that the p-values are less than 10^{-4} and .005 for sparse and BLOSUM sequence encoding, respectively. The individual schemes for ranking the different methods thus all confirm that the combination of several neural network methods trained with different sequence representations has a performance superior to any neural network trained with a single sequence representation. Figure 6.9 further demonstrates that the integration of the data from the Rammensee database in the training of the neural networks, in terms of the HMM input data, increases the reliability of the combined neural network method substantially. For an affinity threshold of 500 nM the plot shows that at a PPV of 0.975 the combined neural network method comb-II has a sensitivity of 0.54, where the combined neural network method comb-I, which does not include HMM data, has a sensitivity of only 0.22. In figure 6.9(a) the largest sensitivity gap between the combined neural method (Comb-II) and the method of Rammensee is found at a PPV equal to 0.7, corresponding to a difference of 0.38 in sensitivity or a difference in the number of true-positive predictions of 29 of a total of the 76 high binding peptides in the data set. In figure 6.9(b) the largest sensitivity gap between the two methods is found at a PPV equal to 0.88, corresponding to a difference of 0.37 in sensitivity or a difference in the number of true-positive predictions of 54 of a total of 144 intermediate binding peptides in the data set.

Both the method of Rammensee and the HMM are linear methods derived from binary affinity data. Neural networks can, on the other hand, both train on data with continuous binding affinities and, if a hidden layer is contained, include higher-order sequence correlations in the output score. To estimate the importance of the ability of the neural network to train on continuous data

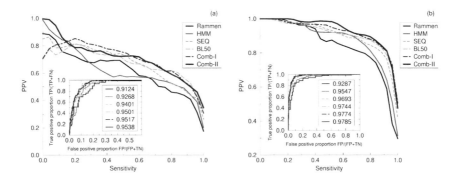

Figure 6.9: Sensitivity/PPV curves calculated from the 528-peptide data set. Six methods are shown in the graphs: Rammensee: matrix method by Rammensee et al. [1999]; HMM: hidden Markov Model trained on data from the Rammensee database; SEQ: neural network with sparse sequence encoding; Bl50: neural network with BLOSUM50 sequence encoding; Comb-I: combination of neural network trained with sparse and BLOSUM50 sequence encoding, respectively; and Comb-II: combination of neural network with sparse, BLOSUM50, and HMM sequence encoding. The upper graph (a) shows the curves for a classification affinity threshold of 50 nM. The lower graph (b) shows the curves corresponding to a classification affinity threshold of 500 nM. The sensitivity/PPV curves were calculated as described in figure 6.8 using 528 data set realizations. In the inserts to the graphs are shown the ROC curves defined in the text. The values given with the labels to each of the curves in the inserts are the area under the ROC curves. Figure adapted from Nielsen et al. [2003].

and the importance of integration of higher-order sequence correlations in the prediction score, we transformed the Buus data set into binary data by assigning peptides with a measured binding affinity stronger than 500 nM an output value of 0.9, and all other peptides a value of 0.1. In a fivefold cross-validation of a neural network using sparse sequence encoding the test performance on the 528 peptides in the Buus data set was found to be 0.838 ± 0.013 and 0.856 ± 0.013 for networks trained without and with a hidden layer, respectively. These numbers should be compared to the 0.877 ± 0.011 obtained for a neural network with a hidden layer trained and tested in a similar manner using continuous affinity data. The result hence confirms the importance of both training the prediction method on data with continuous binding affinities and the ability of the neural network method to integrate higher-order sequence correlation in the prediction score.

6.3.6 HCV Genome Predictions

We use the prediction method (comb-II) to predict the location of potential CTL epitopes in the genome of HCV (GenBank entry: NC 001433). The genome was downloaded from GenBank [Benson et al., 2002].

The HCV genome is relatively small. It contains 9,413 base pairs, and a coding region that translates into 3,002 9-mer peptides. Using the comb-II method to predict the binding affinity for all possible 9-mers in the genome, we find a number of 54 strong binding peptides (affinity stronger than 50 nM) and 177 intermediate binding peptides (affinity stronger than 500 nM). Figure 6.10 shows an atlas representation of the spatial distribution of predicted epitopes for the HCV genome. The atlas shows the location of the annotated proteins, the predicted binding affinity, the location of predicted high and intermediate binding peptides, as well as the estimated amino acid sequence variability mapped onto the DNA sequence of the genome. A detailed analysis of the location of the predicted epitopes in the HCV genome demonstrates that the genome contains regions of high epitope concentration, as well as large regions where epitopes basically are absent. Most striking is the total absence of both strong and intermediate binding peptides in the N-terminal part of the structural E2 (1476-2564) domain of the genome. This domain contains the hypervariable sequence region located in the N-terminal of E2, and one could speculate that the absence of epitopes in the region might be related to viral escape from the host immune system by means of sequence mutations [Cooper et al., 1999]. Further, we observe that epitopes are most abundant in the nonstructural domain NS2 (2565-3407), and in the C-terminal of the structural E2 domain.

6.3.7 Rational Vaccine Design: Identification of Potential CTL Epitopes in the SARS Genome

The use of reliable prediction tools for MHC binding is a critical step in the process of rational vaccine design and development of diagnostic tools. Here we give an example of how prediction of CTL epitopes in combination with high-throughput immunology effectively can guide the identification of CTL epitopes.

The outbreak of the SARS epidemic in 2002–2003 clearly demonstrated how vulnerable humans are to emerging viral diseases. In 7 months the SARS infected more than 8400 persons in over 30 counties worldwide, and caused more than 800 deaths. The rapid spread of the disease and the high mortality rate made the need for rapid development of diagnostic tools and vaccines a matter of the highest priority.

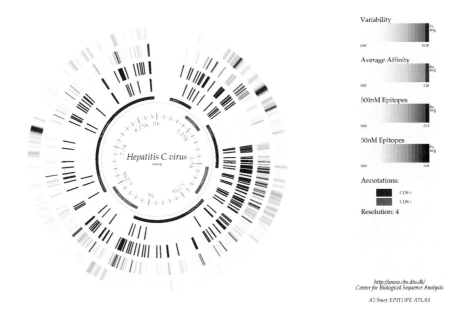

Variability

Average Affinity

500nM Epitopes

50nM Epitopes

Annotations:

CDS

CDS

Resolution: 4

http://www.cbs.dtu.dk/
Center for Biological Sequence Analysis

A2.9mer EPITOPE ATLAS

Figure 6.10: Epitope atlas for the hepatitis C virus. The inner thin (blue) circle shows the location of annotated proteins. the broader circles represent from the center and out: the location of high binding peptides, the location of intermediate binding peptides, the predicted binding affinity value, and the the sequence variability, respectively. The atlas is plotted using the "Genewiz" program of H.H. Staerfeldt. See plate 8 for color version.

At the height of the SARS epidemic in the spring of 2003, we performed a complete genome-wide scan covering all (at that time known) 9 HLA supertypes (covering > 99% of all major human populations). The SARS genome contains close to 10,000 unique 9mer peptides. To identify potential CTL epitopes we applied the method of ANNs and weight matrices. For each HLA supertype, we selected the top 15 candidates for tests in biochemical binding assays. From the 10,000 peptides we thus selected 135 for biochemical validation. The biochemical validation consists of a binding experiment, where the binding affinity between the MHC molecule and the selected peptide is measured in an ELISA experiment [Sylvester-Hvid et al., 2002]. Following this approach, we identified more than 100 potential vaccine candidates, and rapidly identified more than 100 potential SARS CTL epitopes [Sylvester-Hvid et al., 2004]. In figure 6.11, we show a graphical representation of the predicted CTL epitopes

Figure 6.11: Circular epitope map of the linear genome of the SARS coronavirus. From the center outward: indexed RNA, translated regions, observed sequence variation, predicted proteasomal cleavage, predicted A1 epitopes, predicted A*0204 epitopes, predicted A*1101 epitopes, predicted A24 epitopes, predicted B7 epitopes, predicted B27 epitopes, predicted B44 epitopes, predicted B58 epitopes, and predicted B62 epitopes. Figure is a permitted reprint of the cover figure of Tissue Antigens vol. 64 issues 2-4, related to the paper by Sylvester-Hvid et al. [2004]. See plate 9 for color version.

in the SARS genome for the 9 supertypes. Also included in the figure is the sequence variability in the SARS genome and the predicted proteasomal cleavage. At the conclusion of this study, the SARS epidemic had ended and we were unable to get access to patients and test our putative epitopes.

6.4   Summary of the Prediction Approach

When trained on very limited positive examples, matrices and other prediction methods do not contain sufficient information to distinguish between important and less important positions in the binding motif. Empirical knowledge of positions in the motifs that are known to be the most informative can therefore often guide the predictions if the relative weight of these positions is increased. Applying this approach it is possible to obtain reliable predictions of MHC class I binding peptides, even when the allele in question is poorly investigated and few binding examples exist.

When more data are available, ANN methods can be trained to predict MHC-peptide binding with a high reliability. Neural networks can take higher-order sequence correlations into account when predicting peptide-MHC binding. The analysis of the mutual information in peptides that bind HLA-A2 revealed correlations between the amino acids located between the anchor positions. Neural networks with hidden units can take such correlations into account, but simpler methods such as neural networks without hidden units, matrix methods, and first-order HMMs cannot.

Here we have described a method for predicting the binding affinity of peptides to the HLA-A2 molecule which is is a combination of a series of neural networks that as input take a peptide sequence as well as the scores of the sequence to an HMM trained to recognize HLA-A2 binding peptides. The method combines two types of neural networks encoded using a classic orthogonal (sparse) encoding and networks where the peptide sequence is encoded as the BLOSUM50 scores to the 20 different amino acids. It is this ability to integrate higher-order sequence correlations into the prediction score combined with the use of several neural networks derived from different sequence-encoding schemes and the fact that neural networks can be trained on data with continuous binding affinities that allows the neural network method to achieve a high reliability.

The combined approach leads to an improved performance over simpler neural network approaches. We also show that the use of the BLOSUM50 matrix to encode the peptide sequence leads to an increased performance over the classic orthogonal (sparse) encoding. BLOSUM sequence encoding is beneficial for the neural network training, especially in situations where data are limited. BLOSUM encoding helps the neural network to generalize, so that the parameters in the network corresponding to similar and dissimilar amino acids are adjusted simultaneously for each sequence example.

A detailed comparison of the derived ANN method to linear methods such as the matrix method of Rammensee and the first-order HMM has been carried out. The predictive performance was measured in terms of both the Pearson correlation coefficient and sensitivity/PPV and ROC curve plots. For all measures it was demonstrated that the neural network methods in general and the combined neural network method in particular have a predictive performance superior to that of the linear methods.

Alternative ways to make MHC binding predictions when little or no data are available is to use free energy calculations [Rognan et al., 1999] or threading approaches [Altuvia et al., 1995, Schueler-Furman et al., 2000]. These types of methods may be optimal when no peptides are known to bind a given MHC molecule. Also, this approach may give information that is complementary to what can be obtained from the sequence alone and one possible way to improve the predictive accuracy could be to combine predictions based on sequence with predictions based on structure.

As new alleles constantly are being discovered, in humans as well as in animals, it is often important to be able to quickly assign these a general motif of binding peptides, for transplantation purposes or veterinary vaccination programs. Also, for future rational vaccine design, it will be of great value to be able to scan for T cell epitopes as broadly as possible. For this purpose the weight matrix method trained with position-specific weighting gives a major advantage as only very few binders have to be identified to be able to deduce a reliable peptide binding motif.

As an example of the use of bioinformatical prediction tools to guide the process of rational vaccine design, we perform a genome-wide scan for potential CTL epitopes in the genomes of HCV and SARS using the neural network and weight-matrix methods. For the HCV genome the analysis demonstrated that the genome contains regions of high epitope concentration, as well as large regions where epitopes basically are absent. In combination with high-throughput immunology, the genome-wide search for potential CTL epitopes in the SARS genome illustrates how reliable bioinformatical prediction tools can effectively be integrated into the process of vaccine design and diagnostics.

Chapter 7

Antigen Processing in the MHC Class I Pathway

The immune system has to detect even subtle differences in the peptide repertoire presented (by MHC molecules) that might signal an abnormal state. Looking at the evolution of pathogens one can see how critical this peptide sampling process is. As a result of strong selection pressure, many pathogens have
developed complex processes/molecules to inhibit the machinery responsible
for generating these peptides. Also, tumor cells are under strong pressure
to lower antigen presentation, and thus evade immune responses. Many autoimmune diseases are linked to presentation of "unusual self," i.e., the self
peptides that under normal circumstances are not presented and thus not
learned by the immune system as a part of self. Such deviations from the
normal antigen-processing pathways might be sufficient to trigger immune
pathology. Thus, the research concerning the processing of of the presented
peptides has important consequences for vaccine development and the design
of therapeutic strategies to regulate peptide presentation, e.g., for the therapy
of autoimmune diseases or as antitumor therapy. In this chapter we review
how peptides are generated for MHC class I presentation (see figure 7.1).

7.1 The Proteasome

The majority of peptides presented in the context of MHC class I molecules
are generated from the intracellular proteins by the proteasome, an adenosine
triphosphate (ATP) dependent, multisubunit protease. The proteasome plays
the central role in intracellular protein degradation [Kloetzel, 2001, Yewdell
and Bennink, 2001, Stoltze et al., 2000a]. The proteasome is involved both in

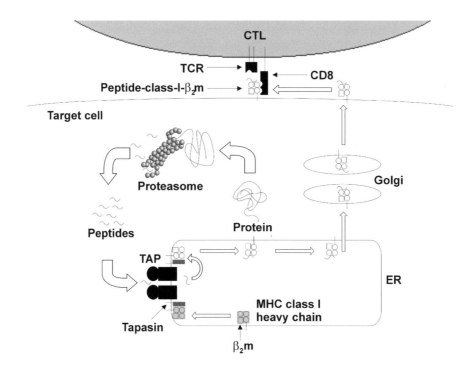

Figure 7.1: Overview of the generation of peptides for MHC class I presentation. A pre-requisite for the induction of a CTL response is the generation of peptides from their precursor polypeptides. The major cytosolic protease associated with the generation of antigenic peptides in particular the C-terminal end of the peptides is the proteasome. The next step is the translo-cation of the peptides from the cytosol to the interior of the endoplasmic reticulum (ER). This transport is facilitated by binding of the peptides to the Transporter associated with Antigen Processing (TAP). Once inside the ER some peptides can bind to to MHC-I. After binding the MHC-I:peptide complex is transported to the surface of the cell, where it may be recognized by CTLs.

the ubiquitin(Ub)-independent and Ub-dependent pathways of protein degra-dation [Rock and Goldberg, 1999]. The eukaryotic proteasome is a complex formed by regulatory units and one cylindrical enzymatic chamber, the 20S proteasome. The 20S proteasome consists of 14 different protein subunits [Groll et al., 1997], of which only three have an active site [Groll et al., 1997, 1999, Tanaka and Kasahara, 1998, Heinemeyer et al., 1997]. The activity of the proteasome in inflammatory sites is altered via induction of the regulatory units and replacement of the constitutive active subunits (β-1[δ,Y], β-2[MC14, LMP9, Z] and β-5[MB1, X]) by their immuno (β-1i[LMP2], β-2i[MECL-1] and β-5i[LMP7]) counterparts [Tanaka and Kasahara, 1998, Groettrup et al., 1996].

Thus two forms of proteasome exist: the "immunoproteasome," which is expressed in cells stimulated by interferon γ (IFN-γ) or tumor necrosis factor α (TNF-α), and in primary and secondary lymphoid organs, and the "constitutive proteasome," which is expressed in healthy normal tissues and in immune-privileged organs like the brain [Noda et al., 2000, Dahlmann et al., 2000, Kuckelkorn et al., 2002]. During an antiviral or antibacterial immune response, immunoproteasomes largely replace constitutive proteasomes [Khan et al., 2001]. This replacement has a positive effect on MHC class I restricted antigen presentation, as has been demonstrated in several systems (see, e.g., [Ehring et al., 1996, van Hall et al., 2000, Morel et al., 2000, Chen et al., 2001, Khan et al., 2001, Sijts et al., 2000, Kuckelkorn et al., 1995, Schultz et al., 2002]). The immunoproteasomes are not absolutely necessary to generate immunogenic epitopes, but immunodominant epitopes are mainly generated by the immunoproteasomes [van Hall et al., 2000].

7.2   Evolution of the Immunosubunits

The first gene duplication giving rise to the general structure of the proteasome in eukaryotes probably occurred prior to the divergence of archaebacteria and eukaryotes [Hughes, 1997, Wollenberg and Swaffield, 2001]. Thereafter, gene duplications occurring prior to the divergence of hagfish and lamprey from jawed vertebrates resulted in immunosubunits [Hughes, 1997].

If we perform a phylogenetic analysis to compare evolutionary traits of different eukaryotic proteasome subunits, we obtain results as shown in figure 7.2. The immunosubunits have accumulated more mutations than the constitutive counterparts, in agreement with an earlier study by Hughes [1997]. There might be two possible explanations for this: (1) the immunosubunit genes reside in a region that has higher mutation rates, i.e., they reside in a mutational "hotspot," or (2) the immunosubunits evolve faster than their constitutive counterparts. To be able to distinguish between these two possibilities, we may calculate the rates of synonymous (ds) and nonsynonymous (dn) nucleotide substitution per site between human and mouse sequences using the method of Yang and Nielsen [2000]. In short, this method involves three steps: (1) counting synonymous and nonsynonymous sites in the two sequences, (2) counting synonymous and nonsynonymous differences between the two sequences, and (3) correcting for multiple substitutions at the same site. The method takes into account two major features of DNA sequence evolution: transition/transversion rate bias and base/codon frequency bias. This property makes it superior to earlier methods to estimate dn/ds ratios.

The rate of nonsynonymous mutation (dn) for all constitutive subunits is approximately 0.4, whereas the immunosubunits can have a dn value of up to

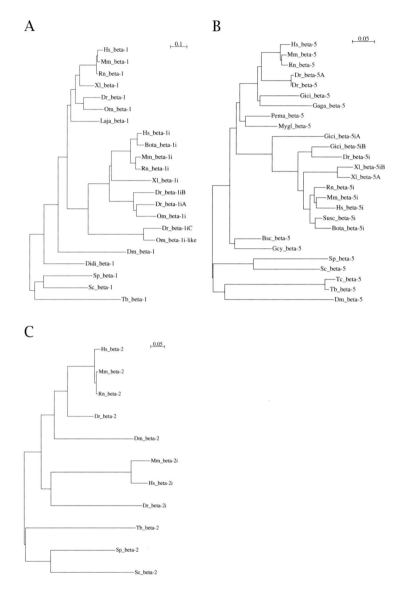

Figure 7.2: Phylogenetic trees of active proteasome subunits. (A) β_{1i} and its constitutive counterpart. (B) β_{5i} and its constitutive counterpart. (C) β_{2i} and its constitutive counterpart. All sequence names containing an "i" are immunosubunits; the others are constitutive subunits. A multiple alignment is made using ClustalW, pairwise distances are calculated using Gonnet series, and the trees are constructed using neighbor-joining. The trees are rooted on nonvertebrate species. Figure reprinted with permission from Kesmir et al. [2003].

subunit	dn	dn/ds	subunit	dn	dn/ds	subunit	dn	dn/ds
α-1	0.287	0.006	β-1	0.400	0.083	β-1i	0.992	0.164
α-2	0.351	0.012	β-2	0.373	0.105	β-2i	0.660	0.138
α-3	0.447	0.011	β-3	0.391	0.048			
α-4	0.406	0.021	β-4	0.257	0.098			
α-5	0.252	0.028	β-5	0.398	0.119	β-5i	0.489	0.186
α-6	0.327	0.090	β-6	0.581	0.106			
α-7	0.362	0.039	β-7	0.432	0.075			
MHC	0.049	1.418						
phosphatase 6	0.359	0.004						

Table 7.1: dn/ds ratio of different proteasome subunits from mice and men. Only the subunits β-1, β-2, and β-5 and their immuno counterparts are active. For comparison, the dn/ds ratio is also calculated for a housekeeping gene, phosphatase subunit 6 (NM_002721 and BC002223), and two MHC class I molecules, HLA-A*02011 (HLA00005) and HLA-A*01011 (HLA00001) from the IMGT/HLA (imgt.cines.fr) [Robinson et al., 2001] database.

1.0 (see table 7.1). Thus, the immunosubunits are indeed coded for in mutational hotspots (i.e., in the MHC class II region). However, all immunosubunits also have higher dn/ds ratios than their constitutive counterparts (see table 7.1), suggesting that the immunosubunits are evolving faster. The subunits that do not have enzymatic activity have lower dn/ds ratios. The immunosubunits are nevertheless not the fastest evolving molecules involved in antigen processing and presentation; MHC molecules evolve even faster ([Tanaka and Nei, 1989, Hughes and Nei, 1988, 1989]; see table 7.1). In summary, this type of phylogenetic analysis points to a functional differentiation between the immunoproteasome and the constitutive proteasome.

7.3   Specificity of the (Immuno)Proteasome

The specificity of the proteasome is often studied by *in vitro* experiments. One example of such an experimental system is the one of Toes et al. [2001], who studied the differences between immunoproteasome and constitutive proteasome specificity. Toes et al. [2001] calculated the frequency distributions of amino acids at cleavage sites and their flanking regions. The cleavage occurs between the P1 and the P1′ position [Berger and Schechter, 1970]. The residues on the left flanking region of the cleavage are called P1, P2, P3, P4, ..., while the right side is referred to as P1′, P2′, ... It has been suggested that the P1 position is the most important position determining cleavage [Altuvia and Margalit, 2000], although the flanking region may also be important [Mo et al., 2000, Beekman et al., 2000, Ossendorp et al., 1996]. One way of analyzing such data is to calculate the information content at the cleavage site and in the region flanking the cleavage site. We use two different information measures. The first one is the Shannon information (as described in section

4.2.1). The second information measure is the Kullback-Leibler information, which identifies by how much the observed distribution differs from the background distribution (see section 4.2.2). In other words this measure corrects the information content for the distribution of amino acids in natural proteins.

The information content for the P1 position in the immunoproteasome digests is much higher than in the constitutive proteasome digests (figure 7.3a,b). In other words, cleavage by the immunoproteasome is restricted to fewer amino acids, whereas the constitutive proteasome is more degenerate, i.e., many different amino acids can be used as potential cleavage sites. Thus, these results suggest that the immunoproteasome is more specific than the constitutive proteasome. Another measure for comparing the specificity of the two forms of the proteasome is the diversity of amino acids present at the P1 position, as defined in terms of the Simpson index. We define the diversity at position i in an alignment as $D(i) = 1/SI(i)$, where $SI(i)$ is the Simpson index, $SI(i) = \sum_{aa} (p_{aa}(i))^2$, and the probabilities satisfy $\sum_{aa} p_{aa}(i) = 1$. This diversity measure yields a value between 1 and 20; the higher the diversity the more degenerate the proteasome (i.e., 20 means that all amino acids are used with equal frequency at a given position, and 1 means that only a single amino acid is found at a given position). The diversity of the P1 position of the immunoproteasome digests is 5.83, and that of the constitutive proteasome is 9.53 (figure 7.3c), again suggesting that the immunoproteasome is more specific.

We can repeat the analysis without taking into account the frequency with which fragments are produced, i.e., we can only look at the observed cleavage sites. The result of the analysis is shown in figure 7.3(d-f). According to the cleavage maps reported in Toes et al. [2001], out of 436 residues in enolase, 55 sites are used by the immunoproteasome only, 73 by the constitutive proteasome only, and 69 by both proteasomes. In other words, the fraction of sites used by the immunoproteasome is $(55 + 69)/436 = 0.28$ and by the constitutive proteasome, $(73 + 69)/436 = 0.33$. The expected value of the overlap then becomes $0.28 \times 0.33 \times 436 = 40$ sites, i.e., the observed overlap is larger than the expected value. The large overlap was also observed in a independent study [Peters et al., 2002]. The 55 sites used exclusively by the immunoproteasome are clearly more specific than the 73 sites used only by the constitutive proteasome as demonstrated by the high information content, and by the low diversity at the P1, P2, and P5′ positions used by the immunoproteasome (see figure 7.3d-f).

In figure 7.3d-f, the Kullback-Leibler information is much lower than the Shannon information for the cleavage sites that are used by both proteasomes. This means that the overlapping sites consist mainly of frequent amino acids that do not carry much information, i.e., the overlapping sites are not very specific. The sites used only by the constitutive proteasome contain hardly

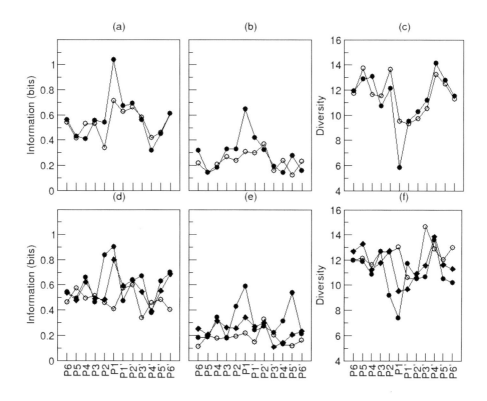

Figure 7.3: Information content and diversity at and around the cleavage sites of the immuno-proteasome (filled circles), and the constitutive proteasome (open circles). In panels (d-f) the observed cleavage sites used only by the immunoproteasome are given by filled circles, while open circles represent sites used only by the constitutive proteasome, and filled diamonds by both. The figure is generated using the frequency data (a-c) and the cleavage maps (d-f) of Toes et al. [2001]. Panels (a) and (d) represent the Shannon information, panels (b) and (e) represent the Kullback-Leibler information, and panels (c) and (f) represent diversity. Cleavage nomenclature according to Berger and Schechter [1970]. Figure adopted from Kesmir et al. [2003].

any motifs, which is indicated by the low information content and the high diversity of amino acid usage. This suggests that the constitutive proteasome uses semispecific and degenerate sequence signals to cleave a protein.

The two proteasomes are also differentiated on the basis of the preferred amino acids at the P1 position. In figure 7.4 the distribution of amino acids at the P1 position is shown. The constitutive proteasome seems to use the acidic amino acids D and E more than one might expect from their distributions in the enolase protein. In the sequence logo of the P1 position of the immunopro-

Figure 7.4: Sequence logo at P1 position of all digested fragments found by Toes et al. [2001]. This sequence logo has been corrected for the fact that some amino acids are found frequently or rarely in the enolase protein, i.e., it is based on Kullback-Leibler information. I-P1 is the P1 position of the immunoproteasome digests, C-P1 stands for the P1 position of the constitutive proteasome digests, and IC-P1 are the P1 positions used by both forms of proteasome. Figure adopted from Kesmir et al. [2003]. See plate 10 for color version.

teasome (figure 7.4), D and E are hardly visible. Thus, the immunoproteasome makes considerably less use of the acidic amino acids than does the constitutive proteasome [Cardozo and Kohanski, 1998, Eleuteri et al., 1997].

Since all these results suggest that the immunoproteasome is a more specific enzyme complex, one would expect the immunoproteasome to use fewer cleavage sites in a given protein. Therefore, it is remarkable that when enolase was degraded with immunoproteasomes and constitutive proteasomes, approximately the same number of cleavage sites were observed (similar results were obtained for degradation of ovalbumin [Cascio et al., 2001]). One reason for this is that the immunoproteasome uses leucine, which is a very abundant amino acid, much more frequently than the constitutive proteasome. Therefore, the immunoproteasome seems to be able to degrade proteins efficiently despite its increased specificity and as a result of this the replacement of the constitutive subunits by immunosubunits does not inhibit cellular growth or viability [Groettrup et al., 2001]. This is important since the cells expressing the immunoproteasome transiently, or for longer periods, need to maintain the necessary housekeeping operations.

7.4   Predicting Proteasome Specificity

Successful prediction of the proteasome cleavage site specificity should be valuable in the design of treatments based on CTL responses. For example, prediction could help in the choice of peptides for use in the treatment of CTL-mediated autoimmune diseases, or in vaccines inducing T cell–mediated immunity. However, the complexity of proteasomal enzymatic specificity makes such predictions difficult.

We will here mention some of the major proteasomal cleavage prediction methods. The first method, FragPredict, was developed by Holzhutter et al. [1999] and is publicly available as a part of MAPPP service (www.mpiib-berlin.mpg.de/MAPPP/), which combines proteasomal cleavage prediction with MHC and TAP binding prediction. FragPredict consists of two algorithms. The first algorithm uses a statistical analysis of cleavage-enhancing and -inhibiting amino acid motifs to predict potential proteasomal cleavage sites [Holzhutter et al., 1999]. The second algorithm, which uses the results of the first algorithm as an input, predicts which fragments are most likely to be generated. This model takes the time-dependent degradation into account based on a kinetic model of the 20S proteasome [Holzhutter and Kloetzel, 2000]. At the moment, FragPredict is the only method that can predict fragments, instead of only possible cleavage sites.

PAProC (www.paproc.de) is a prediction method for cleavages by human as well as wild-type and mutant yeast proteasomes. The influences of different amino acids at different positions are determined by using a stochastic hill-climbing algorithm [Kuttler et al., 2000] based on the experimentally *in vitro* verified cleavage and noncleavage sites [Nussbaum et al., 2001].

Both methods make use of limited *in vitro* data. Moreover, FragPredict is a linear method, and it may not capture the nonlinear features of the specificity of the proteasome. However, another prediction system exists, NetChop [Kesmir et al., 2002], which has two extensions: first, the prediction system is trained on multilayered neural networks using *in vitro* degradation data. This technique is more powerful than PAProC, which uses a one-layered network to predict proteasome cleavage. Second, the approach uses naturally processed MHC class I ligands to predict proteasomal cleavage. Since some of these ligands are generated by immunoproteasomes and some by the constitutive proteasome, such a method should predict the combined specificity of both forms of proteasomes.

The data used to train NetChop stem from two different sources: The first set (MHC ligands) comprises 458 cleavage sites determined by MHC class I ligands of 188 human proteins [Altuvia and Margalit, 2000]. The distribution of amino acid residues around the cleavage site for this data set is shown in logo form in figure 7.5. The MHC ligand region is shown as dotted positions. Note

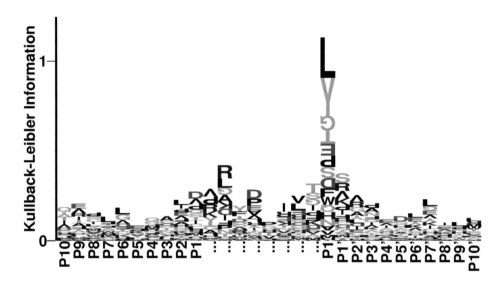

Figure 7.5: Sequence logo of N- and C-terminal cleavage sites for the MHC ligand database (229 unique sites for both terminals); cleavage nomenclature according to Berger and Schechter [1970]. The level of conservation at each position is computed as the Kullback-Leibler information content. The dotted positions correspond to the MHC class I ligand. The information content around the C-terminal is much higher than that around the N-terminal. Note that the P1 position for C-termini is the last position of the MHC class I ligand. Figure reprinted with permission from Kesmir et al. [2002]. See plate 11 for color version.

that the C-terminal cleavage site (i.e., the P1 position; cleavage nomenclature according to Berger and Schechter [1970]) is included in the MHC ligand. In Kullback-Leibler sequence logos amino acid symbols are scaled according to their frequencies of occurrence relative to the background distribution. That is, if an amino acid is overrepresented, it will get a large height. On the other hand, if it is underrepresented, it will also receive a large height, but will be given a negative value so that it can be visualized differently, e.g., as an upside-down letter. If it occurs at nearly the same frequency as the background distribution, it will have a very small height. In generating this logo, the amino acid frequencies within the MHC ligand (excluding the last position) were used to find the background distribution, i.e., the distribution of the amino acids that are not cleaved.

The information content is much higher around the C-terminal than N-terminal, as previously reported by Altuvia and Margalit [2000]. This is probably due to the involvement of other proteolytic processes on generating the N-terminal of MHC class I ligands [Mo et al., 1999, Stoltze et al., 2000b].

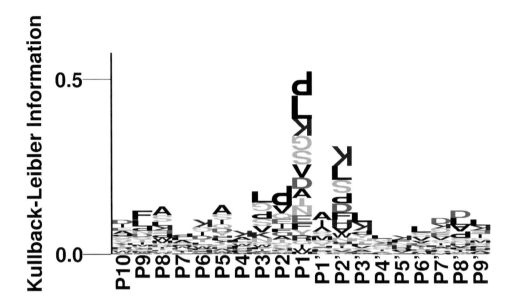

Figure 7.6: Sequence logo generated using *in vitro* data on digestion of enolase and β-casein by human 20S constitutive proteasome. To create this logo, 156 distinct cleavage sites were used. Figure reprinted with permission from Kesmir et al. [2002]. See plate 12 for color version.

The second data set contains *in vitro* degradation data by human 20S constitutive proteasome for two proteins: enolase [Toes et al., 2001], and β-casein [Emmerich et al., 2000]. A sequence logo based on 184 distinct sites from these two proteins is shown in figure 7.6. Here the most significant position is the P1 residue, followed by P2′, P2, and P3. The dominance of the hydrophobic residues (L, V, A) together with the acidic ones (D, E) at these positions is clear, whereas P seems to inhibit cleavage. Comparison of figures 7.5 and 7.6 suggests that the nature of the *in vitro* degradation data is different from MHC class I ligands. This can be due to the involvement of the immunoproteasome in generation of MHC class I ligands. However, a clear conclusion cannot be made here, because the sequence logo displayed in figure 7.5 is indeed a combination of the proteasomal, TAP, and MHC specificities.

Sequence features used for discrimination by the network can be extracted by inspecting the weights of individual neurons. In order to enlarge the analysis of cleavage-promoting and -inhibiting motifs, the weights of a linear network trained on the constitutive proteasome data can be analyzed. In the P1 position large hydrophobic residues (F, L, and polar Y) promote cleavage prediction by the network. Proline at P1 and P2 is strictly cleavage-inhibiting,

Position	Positive effect on cleavage	Negative effect on cleavage
P1	F, L, Y	P, G, T, N, K
P2	Q, Y, V	P, C, D
P3	V	G, Q
P4	P, T	D, K
P2′	H	K, S, R, E, P

Table 7.2:   Cleavage characteristics of human constitutive proteasomes extracted from the analysis of the weights of the artificial neural network. This is a network with one hidden neuron trained on degradation of enolase by human constitutive proteasome and it uses a seven-residue window, giving three residue flanking regions on each site of the cleavage site.

whereas at P4 it is cleavage-promoting, as suggested earlier [Nussbaum et al., 1998, Shimbara et al., 1998]. Glycine seems to be cleavage-inhibiting when present at positions P1 and P3. The P2′ position may have as much influence as P2; charged residues at P2′, e.g., K, R, or E, are cleavage-inhibiting. In the P1′ position both experimental results and theoretical studies suggest a preference for small, β-turn promoting amino acids for cleavage [Kuttler et al., 2000, Altuvia and Margalit, 2000]; however, this could not be detected in the weight logo. For M and W and C, it was not possible to draw any conclusions since these amino acids have a very low frequency in enolase and β-casein. These results are summarized in table 7.2. Interestingly, these characteristics are very similar to the ones suggested earlier for the yeast proteasome [Kuttler et al., 2000].

NetChop was originally trained using sparse coding and consisted of a single neural network (NetChop versions 1.0 and 2.0). Recently, the use of BLO-SUM sequence encoding and hidden Markov model encoding have increased the performance of NetChop significantly [Nielsen et al., 2005]. In the new version of NetChop (NetChop 3.0) a series of neural networks is trained, varying the number of hidden neurons between 2 and 22. The network with the lowest test set error is then selected. The networks are trained in a five-fold cross-validated manner. When applying the networks to predict cleavage sites in an independent data set, the prediction of cleavage of the central amino acid in the sequence window is calculated as the simple average over the five individual neural network predictions. For the combined method using both sparse and BLOSUM encoding in combination with hidden Markov models, the final combined prediction score is taken as the simple average of the two individual predictions. NetChop 3.0 is available at www.cbs.dtu.dk/services/NetChop-2.0.

7.5   Comparison of Proteasomal Prediction Performance

To compare the performance of the three publicly available methods, all the methods above were tested on a set of MHC class I ligands publicly available [Saxova et al., 2003, Nielsen et al., 2005]. In the test the ability of the methods (1) to predict correctly the C-terminal of a ligand and (2) not to predict **major** cleavage sites within the ligand was investigated. N-terminal cleavage analysis was excluded, because the majority of T cell epitopes are trimmed on their N-terminal by other peptidases, e.g., in endoplasmic reticulum [Mo et al., 1999].

The comparison of the predictive performance of FragPredict, PAProC, NetChop 2.0, and NetChop 3.0 is given in figure 7.7. To address the question of whether the difference in predictive performance between different prediction methods is statistically significant, a bootstrap experiment can be performed [Press et al., 1992]. In the bootstrap experiment, a series of N data set replicas is generated by randomly drawing n data points with replacement from the original data set, where n is the size of the original data set. For each data set, the predictive performance of two methods is then evaluated. The p-value for the hypothesis that method M1 performs better than method M2 is then estimated from the simple ratio $(M1 > M2)/N$, where $(M1 > M2)$ is the number of experiments where method M1 outperformed method M2, and N the number of bootstrap replicas. A p-value greater than .95 will indicate that the one method significantly outperforms the other.

Performing the bootstrap experiment comparing the Matthews correlation coefficient values, it was found that the new method (NetChop 3.0) had a performance that is significantly higher than that of NetChop 2.0 ($p < .001$). There are two reasons for the increase in predictive performance. First of all, the network training strategy differs between NetChop 2.0 and NetChop 3.0. In the latter we perform a fivefold cross-validated training, where each network training is stopped when the test set error is minimal. This strategy leads to an ensemble of five networks each with an individual prediction bias. In the training of NetChop 2.0, the fivefold training was performed to estimate optimal parameter settings and the final NetChop 2.0 network is a single network trained on all data using these optimal parameter settings. In a separate experiment it was found that use of network ensemble alone can increase the performance of NetChop 2.0 significantly ($p < .003$). Thus, it is clear that the strategy of generating a network ensemble leads to a higher predictive performance.

The second difference between NetChop 2.0 and NetChop3.0 is the use of different sequence encoding schemes; BLOSUM encoding and the information coming from the hidden Markov model leads to an increase in performance. The gain in sensitivity of NetChop3.0 over that of NetChop 2.0 is 0.07 (0.81-0.74), and is achieved at a constant or slightly increased specificity (0.46 vs.

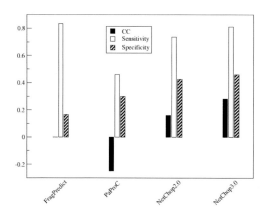

Figure 7.7: Benchmark calculation of cleavage predictions for neural network methods trained on MHC ligand data and evaluated on 231 MHC ligands. The performance values for FragPredict, PAProC, and NetChop2.0 are taken from Saxova et al. [2003]. NetChop3.0 refers to a combination of two neural network ensembles trained using sparse and BLOSUM encoding in combination with the hidden Markov model, respectively. The performance measures are calculated as described in chapter 4. CC is the Matthews correlation coefficient [Nielsen et al., 2005].

0.42 for NetChop 3.0 and NetChop 2.0 methods, respectively). The gain in sensitivity means that the combined neural network method can correctly identify close to 10% more cleavage sites than NetChop 2.0 with no increase in the false-positive rate. The increase in performance is also visible in the correlation coefficient (CC) values: CC is 0.16 for NetChop 2.0 and 0.28 for NetChop 3.0.

A new version of the NetChop20S neural network (based on *in vitro* data only) using the new network training strategy and sequence encoding schemes was also trained [Nielsen et al., 2005]. In figure 7.8, we compare the predictive performance in terms of a ROC curve for the two prediction methods, NetChop20S and NetChop20S-3.0. One important difference between the predictive performance of NetChop20S-3.0 and that of NetChop20S is the large increase in sensitivity (correctly predicted cleavage sites proportion) at low value of the false-positive proportion. At a false-positive rate of 0.1 the sensitivity of NetChop20S method is 0.43, corresponding to a correct identification of only 26 of the 61 cleavage sites. For NetChop20S-3.0 the corresponding sensitivity value is 0.57, and the number of correctly identified cleavage sites is thus 35. Thus the combination of many neural networks trained on different types and combinations of sequence encodings leads to more accurate predic-

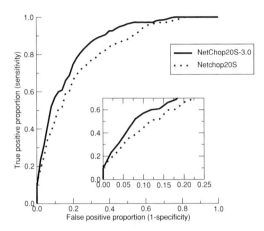

Figure 7.8: ROC curves comparing the predictive performance of the combined NetChop20S-3.0 method and NetChop20S. The curves are calculated using the bootstrap method and are averaged over 1000 bootstrap replicas. The corresponding A_{ROC} values are 0.85 and 0.81 for the combined and NetChop20S methods, respectively. The insert to the graph shows the high-specificity part of the ROC curve in detail. Reprinted with permission from Nielsen et al. [2005].

tion algorithms, i.e., one can obtain an increase in the prediction sensitivity without a loss in the specificity. These results are in agreement with studies showing that the combined approach improves the prediction accuracy of MHC binding (see chapter 6 and [Nielsen et al., 2003]). This new version of NetChop (NetChop 3.0) is available at www.cbs.dtu.dk/services/NetChop-3.0.

7.6   Escape from Proteasomal Cleavage

The CTL response often causes a strong selection pressure on pathogens, forcing these microorganisms to develop different ways to evade the response. These evasions include point mutations or insertions/deletions in the protein sequences that disturb (1) peptide binding of MHC molecules, (2) binding of T cell receptor to peptide-MHC complex, and (3) processing of the peptide. For now we will focus on evasion from proteasomal processing.

Mutations that influence epitope processing are critical, as cases of immune escape due to mutations in an epitope's flanking regions have demonstrated that escape through processing abrogation is of immunological significance [Beekman et al., 2000, Chassin et al., 1999, Goulder et al., 1997]. Cleavage sites generated by the immunoproteasome are sensitive to the surrounding sequence [Niedermann et al., 1999], although no simple cleavage signal is apparent. We took HIV as a model pathogen to study whether it is evolving to prevent cleavage [Yusim et al., 2002]. The majority of HIV CTL escape and cross-reactivity studies focus on the influence of substitutions within an epitope, that would influence only class I HLA and T cell receptor (TCR) interactions by testing of synthetic peptide variants for cross-reactivity in vitro [Cao et al., 1997]. Thus the relative influence of processing escape mutations is not well addressed in the HIV literature.

To analyze the evolution of HIV sequences with respect to proteasomal cleavage, we can use NetChop 2.0 [Yusim et al., 2002]. NetChop 2.0 was used to predict cleavage at every site of each sequence in the alignment. Since we are interested in learning about the tendency of a site to be cleaved at the population level, we considered the distributions of prediction scores obtained for each position from all sequences in the full alignment. The median value of predictions over all sequences obtained for each site in each HIV-1 protein alignment was used to represent the population cleavage prediction score for the site.

The median prediction scores at true C-terminals of experimentally observed HIV epitopes vs. all other remaining sites, and vs. only sites from epitope-lacking regions, were found to be statistically significantly higher using a Mann-Whitney test, for each of the five proteins studied (figure 7.9). NetChop predictions are of course imperfect; a particular site might be misclassified. The highly significant correlation shown in figure 7.9, between C-terminals of identified CTL epitopes and conservation of predicted cleavage sites in an alignment of HIV proteins shows that at the population level (as opposed to just a single strain), NetChop can distinguish classes of positions that are favorable for cleavage, and positions that are embedded in a context that makes cleavage very unlikely. Regional localization of low NetChop scores in areas where there are no defined CTL epitopes suggests that these protein subregions may have reduced epitope processing potential, and that this feature can persist throughout the HIV-1 M group.

7.7 Post-Proteasomal Processing of Epitopes

The C-terminals of CTL epitopes are generated precisely by the proteasome and no further trimming is needed [Cascio et al., 2001]. An exact N-terminal cleavage is, however, less essential since a precursor peptide may be trimmed at the N-terminal by other peptidases in the cytosol [Levy et al., 2002, Reits et al., 2003] and after TAP transport into the ER by peptidases while it binds to the MHC class I molecule [Serwold et al., 2002, York et al., 2002, Saric et al., 2002]. To investigate the extent of N-terminal trimming of CTL epitopes, we

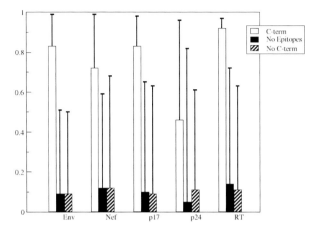

Figure 7.9:   For each protein and for each sequence in the alignment, site-specific prediction scores were computed with NetChop (www.cbs.dtu.dk/Services/NetChop). Then for each site of the alignment the site-specific predictions were calculated as the medians of the predictions from all protein sequences in the alignment. Site-specific predictions were then organized into four groups for each protein: group 1, denoted as "C-term" in the figure, represents the prediction scores at the sites corresponding to known C-terminals of experimentally defined epitopes; group 2, denoted as "No Epitopes," represents the predictions at all sites taken from epitope-lacking regions; and group 3, denoted as "No C-term," refers to the predictions at all sites which do not serve as C-terminals of experimentally observed HIV epitopes. The bars in the figure show the medians of the distributions for each group for each protein. The lines overlapping each bar correspond to the 25th and 75th percentiles of the distributions. Using the nonparametric Mann-Whitney test, the scores for known C-terminal positions, "C-term," were compared to the groups "No Epitope" and "No C-term." For all five proteins the prediction scores at C-terminals of all experimentally observed HIV epitopes were found to be statistically significantly higher than prediction scores in the epitope-poor regions (p24: $p = .002$; Nef: $p = .002$; p17: $p = .002$; RT: $p < .0001$; Env: $p < .0001$) and positions that are not C-terminals of experimental epitopes (p24: $p = .007$; Nef: $p = .001$; p17: $p = .001$; RT: $p < .0001$; Env: $p < .0001$). A different strategy for training NetChop to recognize cleavage sites, based on relative frequency of cleavage events in vitro observed in the enolase and β-casein proteins rather than known epitopes (NetChop-20S), gave a statistically significant difference in the prediction scores between C-terminal positions and epitope-lacking regions for Env ($p = .0012$) and P24 ($p = .0006$), a trend for RT ($p = .08$), but not for p17 ($p = .67$), and Nef ($p = .67$). Figure adopted from Yusim et al. [2002].

used NetChop predictions. In a large set of CTL epitopes (as used to compare different proteasomal prediction methods), we identified the source protein of each epitope and extracted those protein sequences from Swiss-Prot. We estimate the N-terminal extension as the distance from the N-terminal of the epitope to the nearest cleavage site (prediction value > 0.5) at the same side (i.e., we are not normalizing the natural epitope length to define the extension). The output from the neural network is related to the probability of a site being cleaved. The cleavage is however, a stochastic process, and not all potential cleavage sites are used in a given digest [Nussbaum et al., 1998]. To take this stochasticity into account, we estimate the transformation from network output to the probability of being cleaved in a given digest in two steps. The output from the neural network is a score between zero and one, where a value close to one indicates strong preference for cleavage, and visa versa for values close to zero. First, for all residues in the *in vitro* digest data set from Saxova et al. [2003] that are predicted to be preferred cleavage sites (cleavage scores between .8 and 1.0), we calculate the fraction of the residue that were actually cleaved in the digest. We find that in 50% of the cases for the NetChop3.0 predictions and 60% of the cases in NetChop20S-3.0 predictions, a predicted cleavage site is also observed during one digest. In other words, this means that a likely cleavage site will be used by the proteasome only in approximately every second digest. Thus a scaling factor of .5 for the NetChop3.0 and .6 for NetChop20S-3.0 allows us to correctly model the stochastic nature of the proteasome. Second, we use 100 simulated digestions to estimate the average N terminal extension of an epitope. Figure 7.10 shows the N-terminal extension distributions found using the two prediction methods of NetChop3.0 and NetChop20S-3.0 and the above approach to model stochasticity.

Since the NetChop3.0 network is trained on epitope data, and hence might predict a combined specificity of proteasome, TAP and MHC a direct comparison of the two methods is difficult. However, the results given in figure 7.10 suggest that a significant proportion of the epitopes have substantial N-terminal extensions. For the NetChop3.0 method, we find that close to 45% of the epitopes have N-terminal extensions of five amino acids or more, and for the NetChop20S-3.0 method more than 30% of the epitopes have N terminal extensions of three amino acids or more. It is clear that details of these estimates depend strongly on the rescaling used to transform the neural network output into cleavage probabilities. In figure 7.10 we for comparison include a histogram for N-terminal extensions calculated using the raw NetChop3.0 output scores as the cleavage probability. Even with this estimate a substantial fraction of the epitopes have relatively large N terminal extensions. More than 25% have an N terminal extension of 3 amino acids or more. The general conclusion is thus clear: Even though some epitopes would be generated by the proteasome precisely at the N-terminal, the majority of epitopes are generated with a N-terminal extension indicating that N-terminal trimming plays an important role in effective antigen presentation.

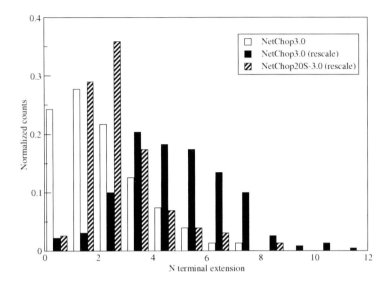

Figure 7.10: Distribution of N-terminal extensions for the 231 epitopes in the Saxová benchmark data set. The N-terminal extension is calculated as the distance to the nearest cleavage site at the N terminal side of the epitope. The stochastic nature of the proteasomal cleavage is estimated from the network output score as described in the text. The filled and dashed bars show the N-terminal extensions predicted using the NetChop3.0 and NetChop20S-3.0 methods, respectively and correcting the predictions for stochasticity. The open bars show the N-terminal extensions predicted using the raw NetChop3.0 output [Nielsen et al., 2005].

7.8 Predicting the Specificity of TAP

Transport of the peptides into the ER is an essential step in the MHC class I presentation pathway. This task is done by TAP molecules that are encoded by the MHC. TAP belongs to the ABC family of ATP-dependent transporters, and comprises two transmembrane chains, TAP1 and TAP2. Different species have different degrees of TAP polymorphism: while there is hardly any functional TAP polymorphism found among humans, the rat has clearly two distinct TAP alleles [Joly and Butcher, 1998].

Peptide and ATP binding result in conformational changes [Reits et al., 2000]. Following an initial peptide binding step (probably very fast), ATP hydrolysis induces pore opening and disrupts peptide binding. The peptide is released from the altered peptide binding site and is translocated through the open pore to the ER. This translocation occurs via simple diffusion. Later the pore closes, and the peptide binding domain returns to the original conformation, completing the translocation cycle.

Peptides that are 8 to16 amino acids long are good substrates for TAP, but 9 to 12 amino acid fragments seem to be the best [Uebel and Tampe, 1999]. The C-terminals of the good substrates are mainly hydrophobic, while acidic amino acids are strongly disfavored. In addition to the C-terminal, the first three residues in the N-terminal seems to be important. In the first two positions basic residues are favored, while the third position can be either a tryptophan or tyrosine. Proline at position 2is the strongest single destabilizing residue found, nearly completely abolishing the binding [Uebel et al., 1997]. The binding motif of the TAP, especially in the C-terminal, resembles closely the binding motifs of many human MHC molecules.

Relatively few methods have been developed to predict the specificity of TAP. Daniel et al. [1998] have developed artificial neural networks using 9mers where TAP binding affinity was determined experimentally. Surprisingly, they found that some MHC alleles have ligands with very low TAP affinities, e.g., HLA-A2. However, it has been shown that TAP ligands can be trimmed in ER before binding to MHC molecules (see above), i.e., a TAP ligand does not need to be 9 amino acids long. Thus, HLA-A2 might easily have precursors of its optimal ligands, which are also good TAP binders.

Recently, Peters et al. [2003a] used a stabilized matrix method to predict TAP affinity of peptides. This method has the advantage of not being bound to only 9mers, but it can also be used for longer peptides. The method assumes that only the first three positions in the N-terminal and the last position at the C-terminal influences the TAP binding. The accuracy of this method is high, and the authors have shown that this method can be used to increase the specificity of MHC binding predictions [Peters et al., 2003a].

With increasing numbers of TAP ligands available on the Internet (e.g., Jen-Pep database,www.jenner.ac.uk [Blythe et al., 2002]), it will likely soon be possible to obtain more accurate TAP predictions.

7.9   Proteasome and TAP Evolution

It has recently been shown that the specificity of human MHC molecules has evolved to fit the specificity of the immunoproteasome [Kesmir et al., 2003]. Thus good MHC ligands also have a high probability to be generated by the proteasome. To add TAP to this evolutionary relation would increase the efficacy of the antigen processing and the presentation even further.

To investigate the footprints of a possible evolutionary fit between TAP and the proteasome specificities, we predict C-terminal cleavage for a set of good TAP ligands. TAP binding peptides were downloaded from the AntiJen database (http://www.jenner.ac.uk/AntiJen/). This database contains a set of close to 350 unique peptides with known TAP binding affinity. Only 63 of these peptides are natural ligands with a "host" protein in the Swiss-Prot database and bind to TAP with an efficient affinity (i.e., affinity < 100,000 nM).

To quantify the similarity between TAP and proteasome specificity, we predict C-terminal cleavage for the above-mentioned TAP ligands. We have shown that our predictor trained on epitope data predicts the C terminal cleavage of epitopes most correctly [Kesmir et al., 2002]. However, these networks might have learned the specificity of the TAP molecule, since TAP binding motifs could be embedded in the epitope data set. Therefore, we use the NetChop20S-3.0 predictor to circumvent a possible bias in the predictions. We predict the average C-terminal cleavage score of these "natural TAP ligands," and compare that to the average cleavage score calculated in the set of natural TAP ligands by shuffling the amino acids in the ligands. For the TAP ligands the average cleavage score is 0.607 ± 0.216, and for the shuffled ligand set the value is 0.427 ± 0.260. The average cleavage score in TAP ligand data set is significantly higher than for the shuffled ligands ($p < .001$ in a Student's t-test for a significantly different means [Press et al., 1992]). Thus, the TAP binding motif, especially the preference of C-terminal, allows for a significantly higher chance of being cleaved by the proteasome. Note that our NetChop20S predictor is trained on the constitutive proteasome specificity. Since the immunoproteasome specificity is much more adapted to TAP specificity [Nielsen et al., 2005], we expect that good TAP ligands be generated by the immunoproteasome more frequently than our estimate here.

The TAP ligand data set we use contains many MHC ligands. Therefore, both analysis presented here might be showing actually the adaptation between MHC molecules and the proteasome. To remove this bias, we predict cleavage of 500.000 9mers selected randomly from proteins in the Swiss-Prot database. In figure 7.11, we plot the average proteasomal cleavage score for each of the 20 amino acids in this large peptide data set by the NetChop20S-3.0 method versus the TAP preference score on the C terminal, which is adapted from a method developed by [Peters et al., 2003a] to predict peptide binding affinity to human TAP molecules. A high proteasomal cleavage score indicates a high chance of cleavage, and a low (negative) TAP score indicates a high chance of TAP transport. The TAP preference score and proteasomal cleavage score is significantly correlated (Kendall's $\tau = -0.44$, $p=0.007$ [Press et al., 1992]). This correlation indicates that the TAP specificity to some degree is adapted so that, the peptides generated by the proteasome are transported efficiently to the ER. While the correlation between the two scores is not perfect, hardly any amino acids are placed in the lower left part of the plot (only K is marginally present in this part of the plot). This part of the plot contains amino acids that are favored by TAP for transport but disfavored by proteasome for

156

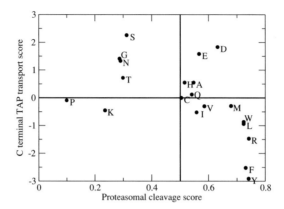

Figure 7.11: Evolutionary relationship between the TAP and proteasome specificities. The average cleavage score (using NetChop20S-3.0) is calculated for a set of 500,000 9mers randomly selected from proteins the in Swiss-Prot database. The C-terminal TAP transport score is adapted from the TAP binding predictor developed by Peters et al. [2003a] and is plotted as a function of the average proteasome cleavage score for each of the 20 amino acids. The lines in the plot give a schematic separation into regions in favor or in disfavor for TAP binding and proteasomal cleavage. Figure reprinted with permission from Nielsen et al. [2005].

cleavage. The lower right part of the plot contains amino acids that favor both proteasomal cleavage and TAP transport, and the upper left corner of the plot amino acids that disfavor both proteasomal cleavage and TAP transport. The amino acids occurring in these two parts of the figure to a large extent overlap with the amino acids preferences earlier identified for the proteasome and TAP [Kesmir et al., 2002, van Endert, 1996]. The cleavage predictor used here is trained on the constitutive proteasome specificity, which has a preference for cleavage after D, E [Kesmir et al., 2003]. This preference is not shared by the immunoproteasome, and one would expect an even stronger correlation between the TAP and proteasomal specificities when the immunoproteasome is considered.

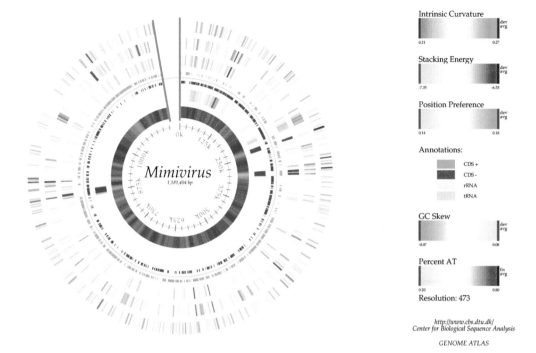

Intrinsic Curvature
dev
avg
0.21   0.27

Stacking Energy
dev
avg
-7.35   -6.53

Position Preference
dev
avg
0.14   0.18

Annotations:

CDS +
CDS -
rRNA
tRNA

GC Skew
dev
avg
-0.07   0.08

Percent AT
fix
avg
0.20   0.80

Resolution: 473

http://www.cbs.dtu.dk/
Center for Biological Sequence Analysis

GENOME ATLAS

Plate 1   Structural atlas of the 1.2 megabase genome of Mimivirus—the currently largest known virus. The genome atlas shows the positions of the putative protein, rRNA and tRNA genes (third and fourth circle), local biases in AT content and GC skew (first and second circle), as well as calculated structural features for the DNA double helix, including its intrinsic curvature (outermost circle), stacking energy levels (sixth circle), and nucleosome position preference (fifth circle), along the linear 1.2 Mbp genome. Figure courtesy of David Ussery. See chapter 1 [figure 1.1].

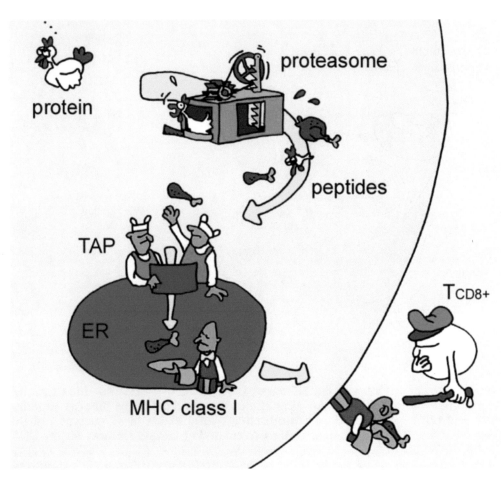

Plate 2 The MHC class I pathway. The proteasome cleaves proteins into peptide fragments. These peptides are translocated by the TAP pump over the membrane of the ER. A chaperone known as tapasin stabilizes the MHC class I molecules before peptide binding. The MHC class I molecules are retained in the ER lumen until successful peptide binding occurs. These molecules are subsequently transported to the plasma membrane. Figure courtesy of Eric A.J. Reits. See chapter 1 [figure 1.4].

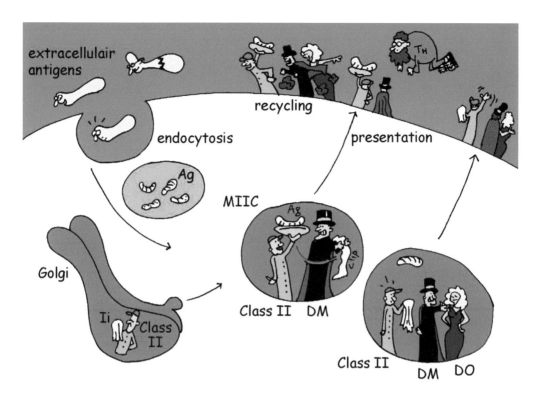

Plate 3 The processing steps in the MHC class II pathway. HLA-DO is another MHC class II-like molecule expressed mainly in B cells. HLA-DO regulates the function of HLA-DM, but it is not yet clear when inhibitory and stimulatory effects occur. Figure courtesy of Eric A.J. Reits. See chapter 1 [figure 1.5].

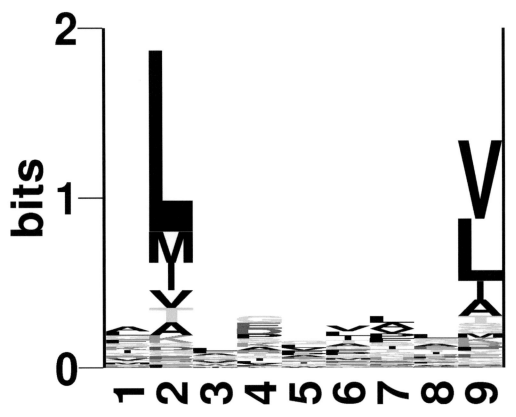

Plate 4 Logo showing the bias for peptides binding to the HLA-A*0201 molecule. Positions 2 and 9 have high information content. These are anchor positions that to a high degree determine the binding of a peptide [Rammensee et al., 1999]. See chapter 4 [figure 4.1].

```
RFFGGDRGAPKRG
YLDPLIRGLLARPAKLQV
KPGQPPRLLIYDASNRATGIPA
GSLFVYNITTNKYKAFLDKQ
SALLSSDITASVNCAK
PKYVHQNTLKLAT
GFKGEQGPKGEP
DVFKELKVHHANENI
SRYWAIRTRSGGI
TYSTNEIDLQLSQEDGQTIE
```

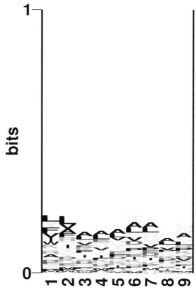

```
             RFFGGDRGAPKRG
          YLDPLIRGLLARPAKLQV
    KPGQPPRLLIYDASNRATGIPA
         GSLFVYNITTNKYKAFLDKQ
           SALLSSDITASVNCAK
           PKYVHQNTLKLAT
            GFKGEQGPKGEP
           DVFKELKVHHANENI
           SRYWAIRTRSGGI
             TYSTNEIDLQLSQEDGQTI
```

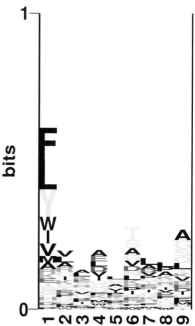

Plate 5 Example of an alignment generated by the Gibbs sampler for the DR4(B1*0401) binding motif. The peptides were downloaded from the MHCPEP database [Brusic et al., 1998a]. Top left: Unaligned sequences. Top right: Logo for unaligned sequences. Bottom left: Sequences aligned by the Gibbs sampler. Bottom right: Logo for sequences aligned by the Gibbs sampler. Adapted from Nielsen et al. [2004]. See chapter 4 [figure 4.7].

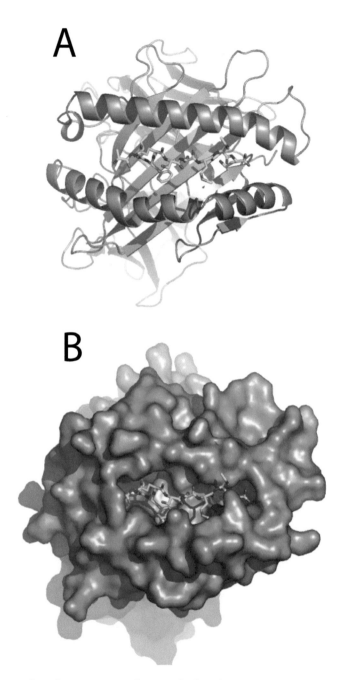

Plate 6 Example of structure of peptide binding to MHC class I. (A) Cartoon representation of MHC class I showing that the peptide is binding on a "floor" made by a β-sheet, and restricted on each side by two α-helices. The bound peptide is shown in a sticks representation. (B) MHC molecule shown in a molecular surface representation. It can be seen that the binding is closer than it appears from the cartoon model. The figure is based on the PDB (www.rcsb.org/pdb) entry 1q94. Figure courtesy of Anne Mølgaard. See chapter 6 [figure 6.1].

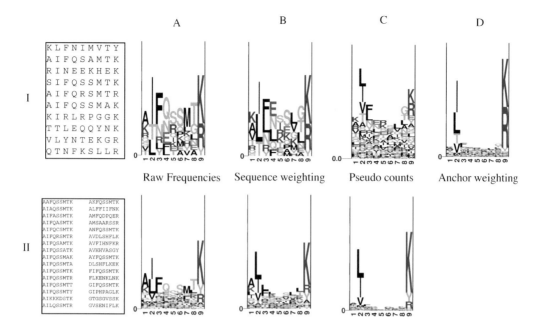

Plate 7 Logos showing the distribution of information content after each step in the matrix calculation using few (I) or many (II) A*0301 training peptides. The sequences used for training are shown in the box to the left in each row. The number of peptides in the two examples is 10 and 32, respectively. (A) The distribution of amino acids at each position. (B) After sequence weighting. (C) After low count correction. (D) Extra weight on anchor positions when few peptides are used for training. The logos were calculated as described by Hebsgaard et al. [1996] and visualized using the logo program [Schneider and Stephens, 1990]. Figure reprinted with permission [Lundegaard et al., 2004]. See chapter 6 [figure 6.2].

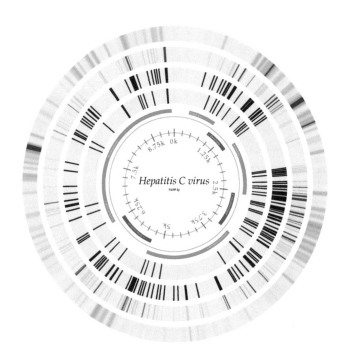
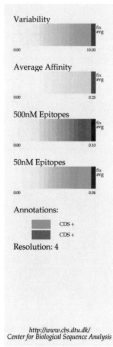

http://www.cbs.dtu.dk/
Center for Biological Sequence Analysis

A2.9mer EPITOPE ATLAS

Plate 8   Epitope atlas for the hepatitis C virus. The inner thin (blue) circle shows the location of annotated proteins, the broader circles represent from the center outward: the location of high binding peptides, the location of intermediate binding peptides, the predicted binding affinity value, and the sequence variability, respectively. The atlas is plotted using the "Genewiz" program of H. H. Staerfelt. See chapter 6 [figure 6.10].

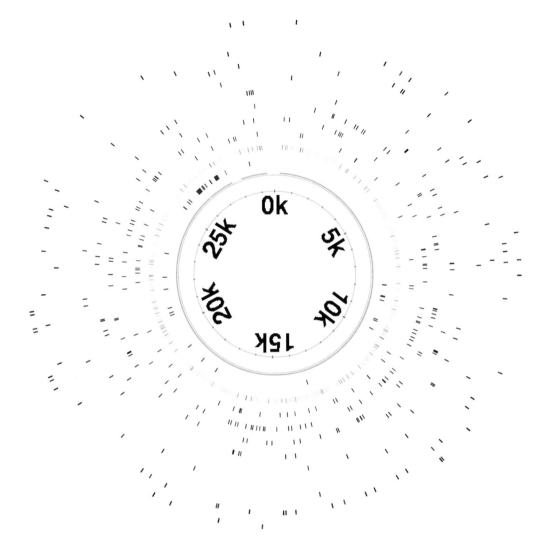

Plate 9 Circular epitope map of the linear genome of the SARS coronavirus. From the center outward: indexed RNA, translated regions, observed sequence variation, predicted proteasomal cleavage, predicted A1 epitopes, predicted A*0204 epitopes, predicted A*1101 epitopes, predicted A24 epitopes, predicted B7 epitopes, predicted B27 epitopes, predicted B44 epitopes, predicted B58 epitopes, predicted B62 epitopes. Figure is a permitted reprint of the cover figure of *Tissue Antigens,* vol. 64 issues 2-4, related to the paper by Sylvester-Hvid et al. [2004]. See chapter 6 [figure 6.11].

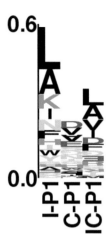

Plate 10 Sequence logo at P1 position of all digested fragments found by Toes et al. [2001]. This sequence logo has been corrected for the fact that some amino acids are found frequently or rarely in the enolase protein, i.e., it is based on Kullback-Leibler information. I-P1 is the P1 position of the immunoproteasome digests, C-P1 stands for the P1 position of the constitutive proteasome digests, and IC-P1 are the P1 positions used by both forms of proteasome. Figure reprinted from Kesmir et al. [2003]. See chapter 7 [figure 7.4].

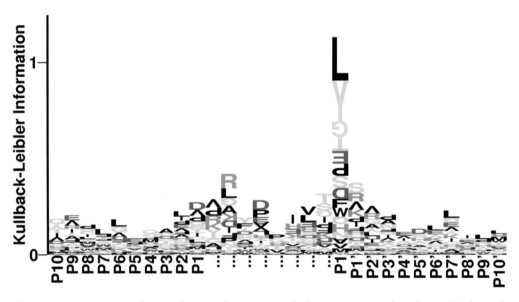

Plate 11 Sequence logo of N- and C-terminal cleavage sites for the MHC ligand database (229 unique sites for both terminals). Cleavage nomenclature according to Berger and Schechter [1970]. The level of conservation at each position is computed as the Kullback-Leibler information content. The dotted positions correspond to the MHC class I ligand. The information content around the C-terminal is much higher than that around the N-terminal. Note that the P1 position for C-terminals is the last position of the MHC class I ligand. Figure reprinted with permission [Kesmir et al., 2002]. See chapter 7 [figure 7.5].

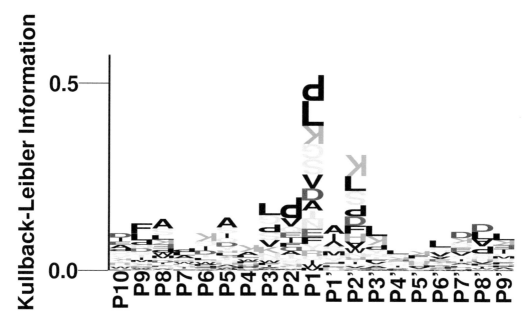

Plate 12 Sequence logo generated using *in vitro* data on digestion of enolase and β casein by human 20S constitutive proteasome. To create this logo, 156 distinct cleavage sites were used. Figure reprinted with permission [Kesmir et al., 2002]. See chapter 7 [figure 7.6].

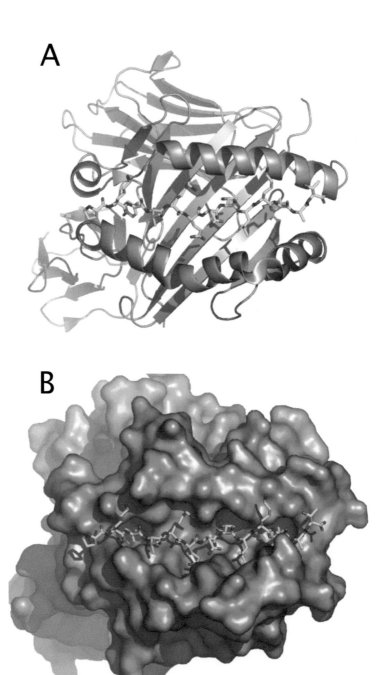

Plate 13 Example of structure of peptide binding to MHC class II. (A) Cartoon representation of MHC class II showing that the overall structure of the complex is similar to MHC class I complexes (see plate 6). The bound peptide is shown in a sticks representation. (B) MHC class II molecule shown in a molecular surface representation. It can be seen that the binding groove is open in the ends in contrast to MHC class I. The figure is based on the PDB (www.rcsb.org/pdb) entry 1j8h. Figure courtesy of Anne Mølgaard. See chapter 8 [figure 8.1].

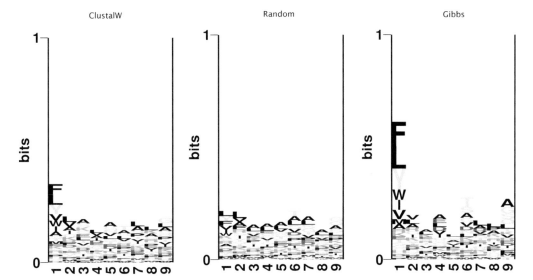

Plate 14 Logos of amino acid frequencies in three distinct alignments of the peptides in the training set. The alignments are generated using the methods of ClustalW, a random placement, and the Gibbs motif sampler, respectively. The height of a column in the logo is proportional to the information content in the sequence motif and the letter height is proportional to amino acid frequency [Schneider and Stephens, 1990]. Figure reprinted with permission [Nielsen et al., 2004]. See chapter 8 [figure 8.5].

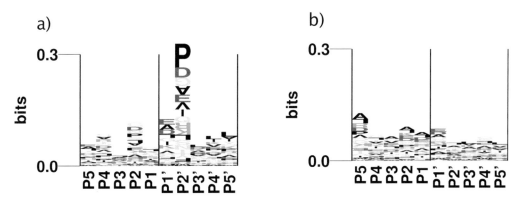

Plate 15 Kullback-Leibler logo displaying the motifs surrounding the (a) N-terminals and (b) C-terminals of HLA class II binding peptides. The end of the epitope is shown by a vertical bar. The letters are shown upside down if they occur less frequently at that position than in Swiss-Prot in general. The data used to make this figure were generated by Gabery and Sjö [2004], Jiang et al. [2005]. See chapter 9 [figure 9.3].

AEP cleavage sites

Non preferred sites

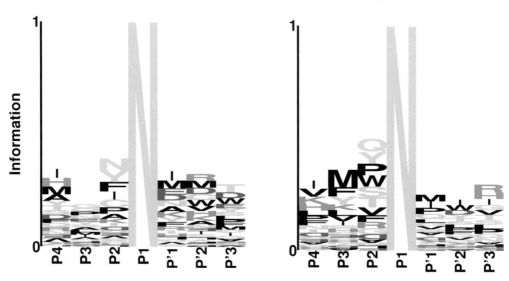

Information

P4 P3 P2 P1 P'1 P'2 P'3

P4 P3 P2 P1 P'1 P'2 P'3

Plate 16 The sequence logo of AEP cleavage sites with their flanking region (left panel) and a similar logo for all the other asparagine residues in the proteins studied (right panel). Part of the data was kindly provided by Dr. Colin Watts, University of Dundee, and the rest was extracted during a literature study. See chapter 9 [figure 9.4].

A

B

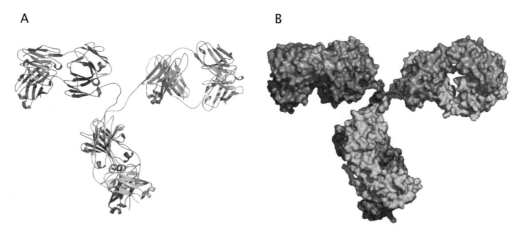

Plate 17 Schematic cartoon (A) and surface (B) representation of an intact antibody (PDB entry 1IGT [Harris et al., 1997]). The light chains are shown in orange, the heavy chains in blue and green. The graphical representations of molecules in this chapter were prepared using PYMOL (www.pymol.org [Liang et al., 2003]. Figure courtesy of Thomas Blicher. See chapter 10 [figure 10.1].

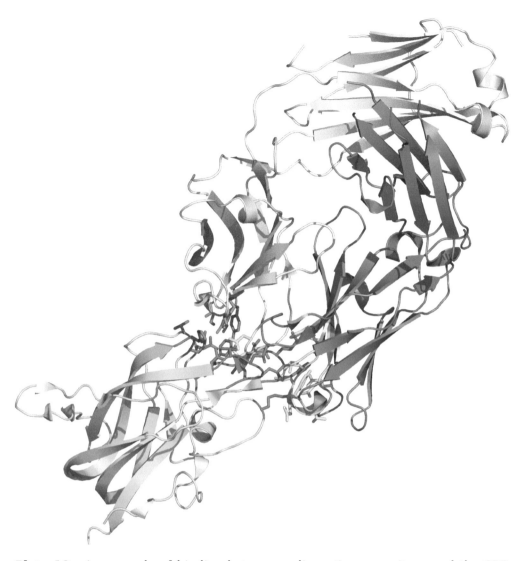

Plate 18 An example of binding between a discontinuous epitope and the CDR regions of a specific antibody: the factor VII protein and a Fab fragment from an inhibitory antibody (PDB code 1IQD [Spiegel et al. 2001]). Factor IV (in cyan) and the inhibitory antibody Fab fragment consisting of a heavy and light chain (in blue and yellow, respectively) is shown. The residues of factor VII involved in the interaction are shown in magenta, whereas the interacting residues in the Fab fragment are shown in green (heavy chain) and orange (light chain). Development of an immune response to infused factor VII is a complication affecting many patients with hemophilia A. Inhibitor antibodies bind antigenic determinants on the factor VII molecule and block its procoagulant activity. Figure courtesy of Pernille Haste Andersen. See chapter 10 [figure 10.3].

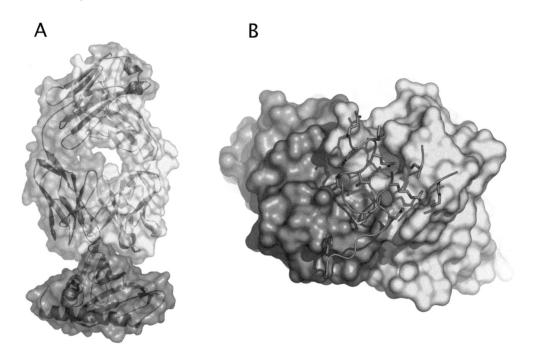

Plate 19 Allergen-Fab complex (PDB entry: 1FSK [Mirza et al., 2000]). (A) Cartoon backbone with transparent space-filling representation. The light chain of the Fab fragment is shown in orange, the heavy chain in yellow. Birch pollen protein (Bet v1), an allergen, is shown in blue. Notice how several loops from each chain of the Fab interact with the allergen. (B) Close-up picture of the Fab-Bet v1 complex. Amino acid residues from several discontinuous strands in Bet v1 (in blue) contribute to the interaction with the antibody. The surface of the Fab is shown in yellow (heavy chain) and orange (light chain). Figure courtesy of Thomas Blicher. See chapter 10 [figure 10.4].

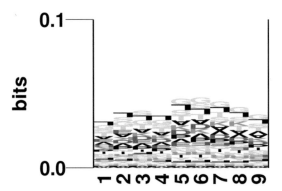

Plate 20 Kullback-Leibler sequence logo of 9-amino acid-long peptides extracted from the data given in table 10.1, where position 5 always corresponds to an epitope region. Notice that hydrophobic amino acids like leucine are appearing upside down, indicating that these amino acids occur less frequently than expected. See chapter 10 [figure 10.5].

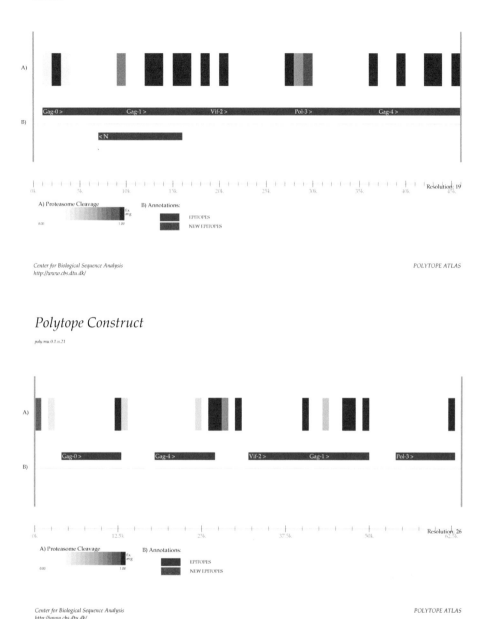

Plate 21 Two configurations of the HIV A2 polytope. The upper panel shows the initial configuration with the epitopes placed head to tail in a random manner. The lower panel shows the optimized polytope construct. In each panel (A) gives the predicted proteasomal cleavage, and (B) gives the epitope sequences (in blue) and the location of new predicted epitopes (in red). The units on the x-axis are arbitrary; 1k corresponds to one amino acid. See chapter 11 [figure 11.1].

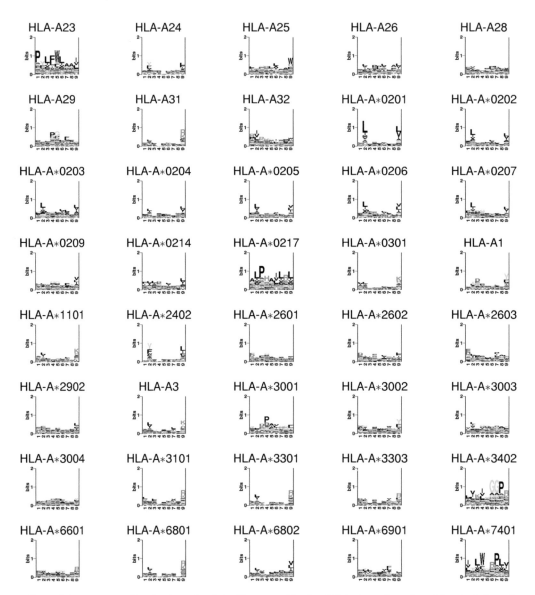

Plate 22 Logos displaying the binding motifs for HLA-A molecules. The height of each column of letters is equal to the information content (in bits) at the given positions in the binding motif. The relative height of each letter within each column is proportional to the frequency of the corresponding amino acid at that position. Figure reprinted from Lund et al. [2004]. See chapter 13 [figure 13.1].

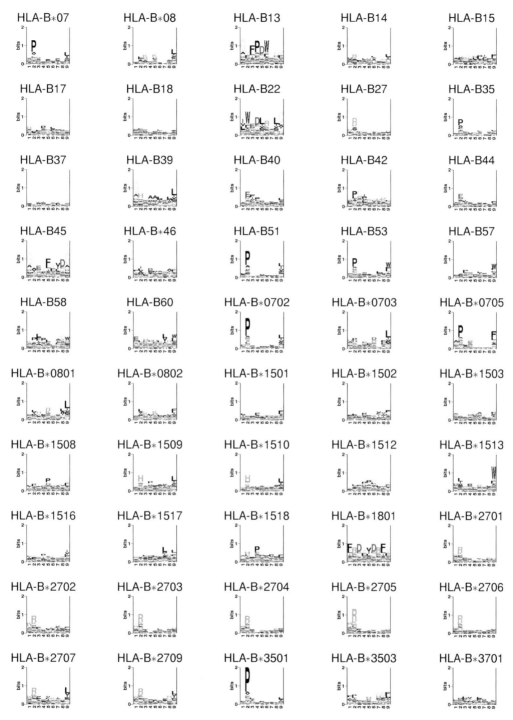

Plate 23 Logos displaying the binding motifs for HLA-B molecules. For details on the logo representation, see plate 22. Figure reprinted from Lund et al. [2004]. See chapter 13 [figure 13.2].

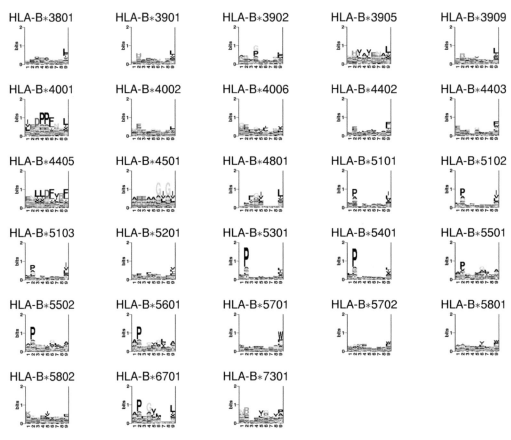

Plate 24 Logos displaying the binding motifs for HLA-B molecules. For details on the logo representation, see plate 22. Figure reprinted from Lund et al. [2004]. See chapter 13 [figure 13.2].

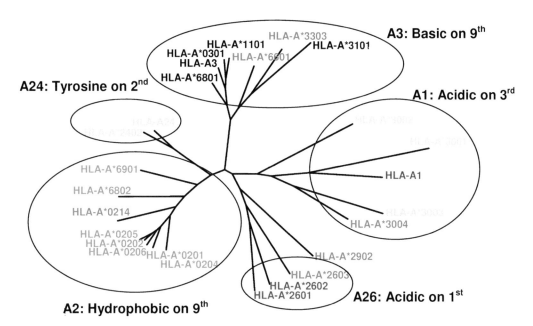

Plate 25 Tree showing clustering of HLA-A specificities. The alleles are colored according to the supertype classification by Sette and Sidney [1999]: A1: red, A2: orange, A3: black, A24: green, A29 and nonclassified alleles: gray. Figure reprinted from Lund et al. [2004]. See chapter 13 [figure 13.3].

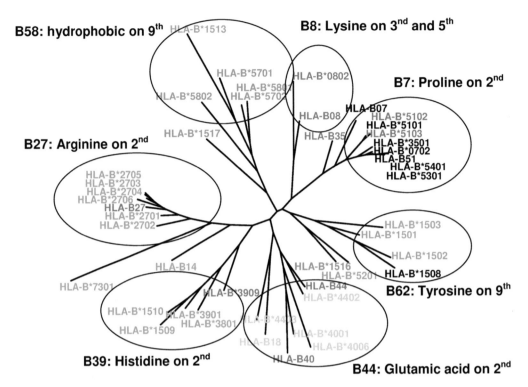

Plate 26 Tree showing clustering of HLA-B specificities. The alleles are colored according to the supertype classification by Sette and Sidney [1999]: B7: black, B27: orange, B44: green, B58: blue, B62: violet, and nonclassified alleles and outliers (B8 and B46): gray. Figure reprinted from Lund et al. [2004]. See chapter 13 [figure 13.4].

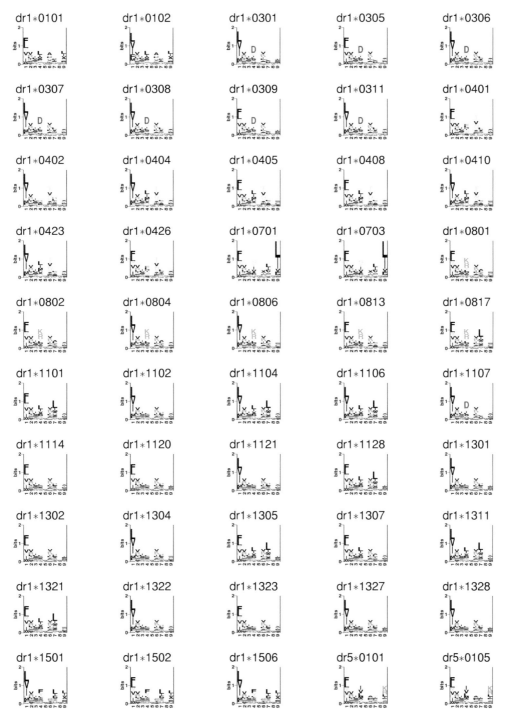

Plate 27 Logos displaying the binding motifs for 50 different HLA class II molecules. For details on the logo representation see plate 22. Figure reprinted from Lund et al. [2004]. See chapter 13 [figure 13.5].

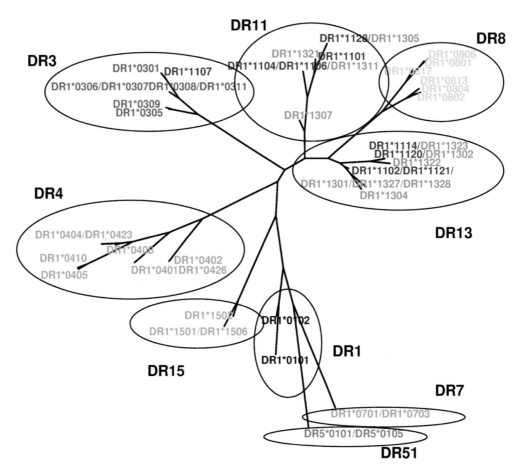

Plate 28 Tree showing the clustering of 50 different HLA class II molecules based on their peptide-binding specificity. The proposed clusters are circled and labeled. Figure reprinted from Lund et al. [2004]. See chapter 13 [figure 13.6].

Chapter 8

Prediction of Helper T Cell (MHC Class II) Epitopes

Only a small fraction of the possible peptides that is generated from proteins of pathogenic organisms actually generate an immune response. The most selective step in antigen presentation is the binding to the MHC molecule [Yewdell and Bennink, 1999]; thus prediction of which peptides that will bind a specific MHC complex constitutes an important step in identifying potential T cell epitopes suitable as vaccine candidates. The specificity of this binding and that of some of the other processes involved in antigen presentation can be predicted from the amino acid sequence, and such predictions can be used to find and select epitopes for use in rational vaccine design and diagnostics. The aim is obviously also to increase the understanding of the role of the immune system in infectious diseases, autoimmune diseases, and cancers.

While MHC class I molecules mainly sample peptides from the cytosol, MHC class II samples peptides derived from endocytosed proteins. Unfolded polypeptides bind MHC class II molecules in the endocytic organelles (reviewed by Castellino et al. [1997]). Peptides presented by MHC class II molecules in turn activate CD4+ helper T lymphocytes (HTLs) to stimulate cellular and humoral immunity against the microorganisms.

Each of the MHC molecules has a different specificity, and the task of deriving MHC prediction algorithms for all alleles is immense. However, many MHC alleles have very similar binding specificities, and it is therefore often possible to find promiscuous peptides, which bind to a series of MHC variants. This has important implications, since it allows for high accuracy predictions for MHC alleles also in situations where the binding motif is poorly characterized [Brusic et al., 2002].

157

A   B

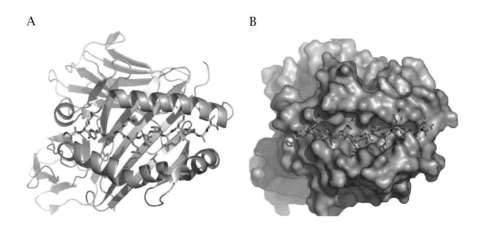

Figure 8.1: Example of structure of peptide binding to MHC class II. (A) Cartoon representation of MHC class II showing that the overall structure of the complex is similar to MHC class I complexes (see figure 6.1). The bound peptide is shown in a sticks-representation. (B) MHC class II molecule shown on a molecular surface representation. It can be seen that the binding groove is open in the ends in contrast to MHC class I. The figure is based on the PDB (www.rcsb.org/pdb) entry 1j8h. Figure Courtesy of Anne Mølgaard. See plate 13 for color version.

As opposed to MHC class I, the binding cleft of MHC class II molecules is open-ended (figure 8.1), and allows the bound peptide to have significant "dangling ends." As a result MHC class II binding peptides have a broad length distribution complicating binding predictions. Thus identification of the correct alignment is a crucial part of identifying the core of an MHC class II binding motif. The MHC class II binding motifs have relatively weak and often degenerate sequence signals. While some alleles like HLA-DRB1*0405 show a strong signal for certain amino acids at the anchor positions, other alleles like HLA-DRB1*0401 allow basically all amino acids at all positions [Rammensee et al., 1999]. In this chapter, we describe how bioinformatics algorithms may be used for predicting MHC class II binding, using the so-called Gibbs motif sampler as an in-depth example.

8.1   Prediction Methods

Most of the work published on MHC class II ligand predictions has focused on the HLA-DR alleles. Only a limited number of HLA-DQ and HLA-DP alleles have been investigated. Godkin et al. [1998] have used eluted peptide sequence data to characterize the binding motif of the HLA-DQ8, and HLA-DQ2 alleles. The HLA-DP molecules have scarcely been studied. Initially, they appeared less important in the immune response than HLA-DR and HLA-DQ molecules, because HLA-DP incompatibility did not seem to contribute to the risk of graft-vs.-host disease. However, it is now known that even a single mismatch can be sufficient to trigger a specific T cell response after bone marrow transfer [Gaschet et al., 1996]. Castelli et al. [2002] use a biochemical binding assay for the HLA-DP4 allele to verify binding of a set of synthetic peptides. From the analysis they were able to characterize the amino acid preferences of the anchor positions.

For the HLA-DR alleles many different methods have been applied to predict peptide-MHC binding, including simple binding motifs, quantitative matrices, hidden Markov models (HMMs), and artificial neural networks (ANNs). For class I these gap- and alignment-free methods can readily be applied since the binding motif is well characterized and most natural peptides that bind MHC class I are of close to equal length [Parker et al., 1994, Brusic et al., 1994, Rammensee et al., 1999, Buus et al., 2003, Nielsen et al., 2003]. However, the situation for MHC class II binding is quite different due to the great variability in the length of natural MHC binding peptides. This length variability makes alignment a crucial part of predicting peptide binding. Quantitative matrices estimated from experimentally derived position-specific binding profiles have given reasonable performance in prediction of MHC class II binding [Sette et al., 1989a, Hammer et al., 1994, Marshall et al., 1995, Sturniolo et al., 1999]. However, such matrices are very costly to derive and more importantly they lack the flexibility of data-driven machine-learning methods to be refined in an iterative manner when more data become available. Brusic et al. [1998b] have described a hybrid method for predicting peptide-MHC class II binding. They handle the alignment problem using an evolutionary algorithm and subsequently apply artificial neural networks to classify peptides as binding or nonbinding.

8.2   The Gibbs Sampler Method

The advanced motif sampler method [Nielsen et al., 2004] is based on the Gibbs sampler method described by Lawrence et al. [1993]. Details of the method are given in chapter 4. The method attempts to find an optimal local alignment of a set of N sequences by means of Monte Carlo Metropolis [Metropolis et al., 1953] sampling of the alignment space. In situations where the sequence pattern is very subtle and the motif is weak, this is a highly complex task, and conventional multiple sequence alignment programs will typically fail. In the following, we describe an implementation of the Gibbs sampler method specialized and optimized to locate and characterize the motif of MHC class I and class II binding. The method applies the techniques of sequence weighting and

pseudocount correction for low counts as well as differential position-specific
weighting and generation of consensus weight matrices to estimate the binding motifs. A web server implementing the essential features of the Gibbs
sampler is available at http://www.cbs.dtu.dk/biotools/EasyGibbs/.

8.2.1 Gibbs Sampling

The algorithm samples possible alignments of a number of sequences, N. For
each alignment a log-odds weight matrix is calculated as $\log(p_{pa}/q_a)$, where
p_{pa} is the frequency of amino acid a at position p in the alignment and q_a is
the background frequency of that amino acid. The values of p_{pa} are estimated
using sequence weighting and pseudocount correction for low counts.

The fitness (energy) of a Gibbs-based alignment is calculated as the
Kullback-Leibler distance [Kullback and Leibler, 1951] between the observed
amino acid distribution in a window and a background distribution,

$$E = \sum_{p,a} C_{pa} \log \frac{p_{pa}}{q_a}, \tag{8.1}$$

where C_{pa} is the occupancy number of amino acid a at position p in the alignment. p_{pa} and q_a are as described above.

The set of possible alignments is, even for a small data set, very large. To allow for an effective sampling of the alignment space the Monte Carlo Metropolis algorithm [Metropolis et al., 1953] is applied. The method implements a
single sequence and a phase shift Monte Carlo move. The probability of accepting a move in the Monte Carlo sampling is defined using the conventional
Monte Carlo Metropolis relation $P = \min(1, e^{dE/T})$, where dE is the difference
in energy between the end and start configurations and T a scalar. Details on
the implementation of the Gibbs sampler and the Monte Carlo moves are given
in chapter 4.

8.2.2 Weight-Matrix Calculation: The Parameters of the Gibbs Sam-
pler

A central part of the motif sampler algorithm is the weight-matrix calculation,
and the Gibbs sampler has a series of free parameters defining how a weight
matrix is calculated from a multiple alignment. The most important parameters are the

- sequence weighting method

- pseudocount correction method

Supertype	N	Allele	N	N_{bind}
A1	92	HLA-A*0101	283	27
A2	626	HLA-A*0204	528	144
A3	228	HLA-A*0301	212	5
B7	201	HLA-B*0702	154	24

Table 8.1: Data for the training and evaluation of the HLA class I binding predictions. The first column gives the supertype names included in the calculation, the second column the number of unique 9mer peptides in the training set, the third column the HLA allele name for the evaluation set data, and the fourth and fifth columns the total number of peptides and the number of binders in the evaluation set, respectively. Binders were determined using a threshold of 500 nM.

- weight on pseudocount correction

- position specific weighting.

The optimal settings of the parameters have to be determined first. This can be done in a large-scale benchmark calculation using data sets where the alignment is not a question. For this purpose HLA class I binding peptides are highly suitable. We know they contain a binding motif, and they are all of nearly equal length so alignment will not be necessary.

Peptides known to bind MHC class I molecules are available from a number of sources (see chapter 12). In this example they were extracted from the databases of SYFPEITHI and MHCPEP [1]. To overcome the alignment issue, only peptides of length 9 were included. The peptides were clustered into the nine HLA supertypes (A1, A2, A3, A24, B7, B27, B44, B58, and B62) as described by Sette and Sidney [1999]. These peptides constitute the training set for the MHC class I binding weight matrices. Data sets of peptides, for which the binding affinity to the MHC complex had been measured as described by Sylvester-Hvid et al. [2002] were available to us for four of the nine supertypes (A1, A2, A3, and B7). These data sets were used to evaluate the prediction accuracy of the corresponding weight matrix. To avoid overtraining, any peptide found in the training set was removed from the evaluation set. In table 8.1, we provide the number of unique peptides in the training set, the number of peptides in the evaluation set, and the corresponding allele names, as well as the number of binding peptides (affinity stronger than 500 nM) for each of the four supertypes.

Two different strategies for sequence weighting were tested: sequence clustering and sequence weighting as described by Henikoff and Henikoff [1994]. For sequence clustering, we used a Hobohm 1-like algorithm [Hobohm

---

[1] SYFPEITHI: http://syfpeithi.bmi-heidelberg.com/, MHCPEP: http://wehih.wehi.edu.au/mhcpep/

et al., 1992] with ungapped alignment and sequence identity of 62% as cluster threshold. After the clustering, each peptide in a cluster is assigned a weight equal to $1/N_c$, where N_c is the cluster size. In the Henikoff and Henikoff sequence weighting scheme an amino acid is assigned a weight $w = 1/rs$, where r is the number of different amino acids at a given position in the alignment and s the number of occurrences of the amino acid. The weight of a sequence is then assigned as the sum of the amino acid weights. The method of Henikoff and Henikoff is fast as the computation time only increases linearly with the number of sequences. For the clustering algorithm, on the other hand, computation time increases as the square of the number of sequences.

Two strategies for pseudocount correction were tested in this work, equal and BLOSUM correction, respectively. In both cases the pseudocount frequency is estimated as described in chapter 4 [Altschul et al., 1997]. For the equal correction, a substitution matrix with identical frequencies for all amino acid substitutions is applied. For BLOSUM correction, a BLOSUM62 [Henikoff and Henikoff, 1992] substitution matrix was applied. The effective amino acid frequency is calculated as a weighted sum of the pseudocount frequency and the observed frequency [Altschul et al., 1997].

In many situations prior knowledge about the importance of the different positions in the binding motif exists. Such prior knowledge can with success be included in the search for binding motifs [Lundegaard et al., 2004]. Details of the sequence weighting methods, the methods for pseudocount correction, their combination into the effective amino acid frequency, and the position-specific weighting are given in chapter 4.

To estimate the significance of a given alignment, the Gibbs sampler compares the information content to a null model. The null model is defined in terms of background amino acid frequencies. Here we use a background estimated from the amino acid distribution in the Swiss-Prot database [Bairoch and Apweiler, 2000].

Now we apply the Gibbs sampler to the MHC class I binding motif problem in order to estimate the optimal setting for the parameters that determine the generation of weight matrices from fixed alignments. For each parameter setting, we estimate weight matrices for the four supertypes, A1, A2, A3, and B7, using the peptides in the training sets, and subsequently evaluate the predictive performance on the corresponding evaluation set. The predictive performance is calculated using both the Pearson correlation between the log-transformed affinities and the weight-matrix predictions [Nielsen et al., 2003], and the nonparametric A_{ROC} measure (the area under the ROC (relative operating characteristics) curve [Swets, 1988]). By applying the same parameter setting to all four data sets, we minimize the risk of overfitting. As a comparison, we evaluate the predictive performance of weight matrices derived using the HMMer package [Eddy, 1998] on the four evaluation sets.

Figure 8.2 shows the prediction accuracy estimated in terms of the Pearson correlation and the A_{ROC} value, respectively, for the two different sequence weighting schemes for a series of pseudocount weights for the four data sets. In all situations, the use of a BLOSUM62 matrix (BLOSUM correction) for estimating the pseudocounts gives better predictive performance than using an identity matrix (equal correction). As a comparison, the prediction accuracy of the weight matrices estimated using HMMer, as well as the prediction accuracy using the SYFPEITHI prediction method, is shown. It is clear that the two sequence weighting schemes have similar predictive performance and that the optimal performance is found for a value of the pseudocount weight close to 50 for the Henikoff and Henikoff sequence weighting and for a value close to 200 for the clustering sequence weighting. Since the sequence-weighting scheme based on sequence clustering has slightly better performance, we will in the following use this sequence-weighting scheme and consequently we set the pseudocount weight to 200. Moreover, from the figure it is clear that the predictive performance of the Gibbs sampler is comparable to that of both HMMer and the SYFPEITHI prediction methods.

As stated previously, prior knowledge regarding the importance of the different positions in the binding motif exists. This is, e.g., the case for the MHC class I binding motif where the binding for most alleles is largely determined by the fitness of the peptide to the binding pockets at positions 2 and 9 in the motif [Lundegaard et al., 2004].

Figure 8.3 shows the predictive performance of the weight matrix for class I binding when such position-specific weighting is included in the motif search. The position-specific weighting scheme is determined as the set of anchor residues defined in the SYFPEITHI database, extended with auxiliary anchors occurring at positions 2 or 9. For the A1 supertype, positions 3 and 9 are specified as anchor positions, whereas positions 2 and 7 are auxiliary anchor positions. This means that positions 2, 3, and 9 are included as positions with high weight in the motif search for this supertype. For the other supertypes of A2, A3, and B7, the motif positions with higher weight are positions 2 and 9.

The results shown in the figure indicate indeed that a position-specific weighting of 2 to 3 gives the highest predictive performance.

8.2.3   MHC Class II Binding

Using the class I adjusted parameters, the Gibbs sampler can be applied to identification of the binding motif of MHC class II molecules from known binding peptides of variable length. First a data set is needed, so again peptides binding to the MHC class II molecule HLA-DR4(B1*0401) were extracted from the SYFPEITHI [Rammensee et al., 1999] and MHCPEP [Brusic et al., 1998a]

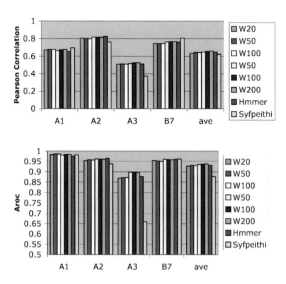

Figure 8.2: Predictive performance of the Gibbs sampler for the two schemes of sequence weighting of Henikoff and Henikoff and sequence clustering, respectively. The figure compares the predictive performance in terms of the Pearson correlation coefficient (upper plot) and A_{ROC} (lower plot) for the four supertypes of A1, A2, A3, and B7, as well as the average of the four. The ROC curves were calculated using a threshold of 500 nM to define binders vs. nonbinders. For the Henikoff and Henikoff sequence-weighting scheme, the performance is given for pseudocount weights of 20, 50, and 100 (the top of the legend box). For clustering performance is shown for pseudocount weights of 50, 100, and 200 (the lower part of the legend box). For each supertype the last two sets of bars give the performance of the HMMer package and the SYFPEITHI website predictor, respectively.

databases. The data set consists of 532 unique peptide sequences. Peptides that do not have hydrophobic residues at the p_1 position in the binding motif were removed [Brusic et al., 1998a], or formulated differently, a peptide is removed if no hydrophobic residues are present in the first $N - L + 1$ positions, where N is the peptide length and L is the motif length. The hydrophobic filter removes 28 peptides. Furthermore, the data set is reduced to remove unnatural peptide sequences with an extreme amino acid content by removing peptides with more than 75% alanine. The final training set has 456 unique peptides. The length distribution in the training set ranges from 9 to 30 residues with the majority of peptides having a length of 13 amino acids.

We now apply the Gibbs sampler to estimate the binding motif and corresponding weight matrix for the HLA-DR4(B1*0401) molecule. We apply the Gibbs sampler with the parameter settings described above. In order to ensure

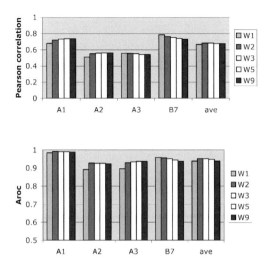

Figure 8.3: Prediction performance of the Gibbs sampler for different position-specific weight values. The upper figure gives the performance in terms of the Pearson correlation and the lower figure the A_{ROC} values for a relative weight of 1, 2, 3, 5, and 9, respectively, on the selected positions. The ROC curves were calculated as described in figure 8.2. The last set of bars in each figure gives the average performance over the four supertypes.

that only hydrophobic residues are present at the p_1 position in the motif, we restrict the single sequence move in the Monte Carlo procedure to only select from the set of hydrophobic amino acids. The scalar T is initialized to 0.15 and lowered to 0.001 in 10 uniform steps. At each value of T, 5000 Monte Carlo moves are performed. The acceptance of a move is determined using the Monte Carlo Metropolis acceptance criteria described in section 8.2.1. The motif length is fixed at 9 amino acids. The alignment space has a very large number of local maxima with close to identical energy. In order to achieve an effective sampling of these local maxima, we repeat 100 MC calculations with different initial configurations. In figure 8.4, we show the predictive performance for the 100 weight-matrix solutions as a function of the Kullback-Leibler distance estimated from the final sequence alignment. The predictive performance is evaluated on a set of 105 peptides described by Geluk et al. [1998] (see below).

The figure demonstrates that the Kullback-Leibler distance correlates with the predictive performance. However, the correlation is not perfect and the optimal solution (highest Kullback-Leibler distance) is not the one with the

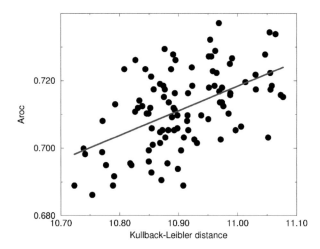

Figure 8.4: Predictive performance as a function of the Kullback-Leibler distance: 100 weight matrices were estimated from distinct Monte Carlo calculations. The different weight matrices were evaluated on the set of 105 peptides described in the text, and the predictive performance in terms of an A_{ROC} value is plotted as a function of the Kullback-Leibler distance. The solid line shows a least-squares straight-line fit. The correlation coefficient is 0.53. Figure reprinted with permission [Nielsen et al., 2004].

optimal predictive performance. Wanting to obtain an effective sampling of the suboptimal solutions, we calculated a consensus weight matrix as the average over the top five highest-scoring weight matrices (the average over 5, 10, and 20 top scoring matrices, gives similar results).

From the SYFPEITHI database the anchor positions in the binding motif are estimated to be located at positions 1, 4, 6, 7, and 9 for this HLA molecule. Anchor positions estimated from the logos of a weight matrix calculated using the Gibbs sampler with equal weights on all positions confirms this weighting scheme at all positions except position 7 (see figure 8.5, right panel). Hence, we use positions 1, 4, 6, and 9 with an increased weight to guide the Gibbs sampling.

As an estimate of how other conventional alignment methods perform on this motif detection problem, we align the sequences in the training set using the ClustalW package [Thompson et al., 1994, Chenna et al., 2003] with a high gap opening penalty to ensure ungapped alignment, since initial experiments showed that this resulted in the best performance. Furthermore, we generate a control by placing the sequences in a random alignment with hydrophobic

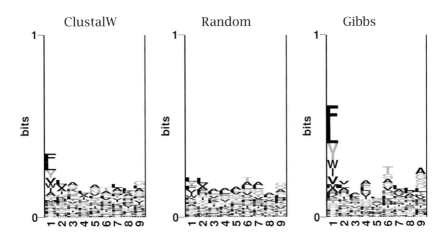

Figure 8.5: Logos of amino acid frequencies in three distinct alignments of the peptides in the training set. The alignments are generated using ClustalW, a random placement, and the Gibbs motif sampler, respectively. The height of a column in the logo is proportional to the information content in the sequence motif and the letter height is proportional to amino acid frequency [Schneider and Stephens, 1990]. Figure reprinted with permission [Nielsen et al., 2004]. See plate 14 for color version.

amino acids at the p_1 position. From the alignments, we estimate the amino acid frequencies in the 9-amino acid long core region and make logos from these frequency estimates (shown in figure 8.5).

Figure 8.5 demonstrates that the identification of the binding motif from the training data is indeed a complex and difficult task. The ability of the Gibbs sampler to detect the subtle sequence motif in a set of peptide sequences is apparent from the figure. ClustalW is, on the other hand, unable to detect any motif except from the strong hydrophobic amino acid preference at position p_1. In figure 8.6, we show a part of the alignment obtained by the Gibbs sampler for the HLA-DR4(B1*0401) binding motif recognition. Figures 8.5 and 8.6 demonstrate how the Gibbs sampler, through the Monte Carlo moves, is able to place the sequences in register and move from an initial random configuration with close to zero information content to a final alignment configuration with high information content describing the peptide binding motif in detail.

8.2.4 Benchmark Calculations

The predictive performance of the Gibbs sampler is benchmarked on 10 data sets and compared to that of the TEPITOPE method [Sturniolo et al., 1999], as well as to the weight matrix derived from the ClustalW alignment.

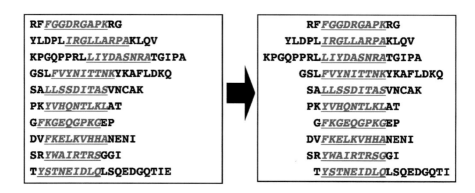

Figure 8.6: An alignment generated by the Gibbs sampler for the DR4(B1*0401) binding motif. In the left panel are shown the unaligned sequences, and in the right panel the aligned sequences. The core motif is shown underlined and in italics. Figure reprinted with permission [Nielsen et al., 2004].

The 10 data sets are the eight data sets described by Raghava (MHCBench, http://www.imtech.res.in/raghava/mhcbench), and two experimental data sets described by Southwood et al. [1998] and Geluk et al. [1998], respectively. The binding of a peptide is calculated as the score of the highest-scoring 9mer subpeptide. We use the nonparametric A_{ROC} measure [Swets, 1988] to compare the accuracy of the different prediction methods. In order to calculate a ROC curve the data set must be classified into binders and nonbinders. For the eight MHCBench data sets, peptides with an associated binding value of zero are assigned to be nonbinding, and all other peptides are binders. For the Southwood and Geluk data sets, an affinity of 1000 nM is taken as threshold for peptide binding [Southwood et al., 1998] (similar results are obtained for threshold values in the range 500–10,000 nM). To reduce the chance of overfitting by evaluating the prediction performance on data points included in the training, we repeat the benchmark calculation on homology-reduced data sets. The homology reduction is performed so that no data point in the evaluation sets has a match in the training set with sequence identity greater than 90% over an alignment length of at least 9 amino acids. Table 8.2 gives a brief description of both the original and the homology-reduced benchmark data sets in terms of the number of peptides and the number of binders, respectively.

In figure 8.7, we show the results of the benchmark calculation. The Gibbs sampled weight matrix has comparable or better predictive performance than that of both TEPITOPE and the ClustalW weight matrix. In all cases

Set	Original		Homology-reduced	
	N	N_{bind}	N	N_{bind}
MHCBench 1	1017	694	496	226
MHCBench 2	673	381	416	161
MHCBench 3A	590	373	334	130
MHCBench 3B	495	279	325	128
MHCBench 4A	646	323	381	111
MHCBench 4B	584	292	375	120
MHCBench 5A	117	70	110	65
MHCBench 5B	85	48	84	47
Southwood	22	16	21	15
Geluk	105	22	99	19

Table 8.2: Description of the MHC class II benchmark (MHCBench) data sets. The first column gives the name of the data set; the second and third columns, the number of peptides and the number of peptides classified as binders for the complete sets; the fourth and fifth columns, the same number for the reduced data sets. For the Southwood and Geluk data sets a threshold of 1000 nM and for the MHCBench data sets a threshold value of 0.5, were used to determine binders.

the ClustalW weight matrix has a performance that is lower than that of the Gibbs sampled matrix. In order to estimate the significance of the difference in performance between the Gibbs sampler and the TEPITOPE methods, a bootstrap experiment was performed [Press et al., 1992]. For each of the data sets, 1000 data sets were generated by extracting N data points with replacement. Here N is the number of data points in the original data set. The performances of both the Gibbs and the TEPITOPE methods are then evaluated on each of the data sets, and the p-value for the hypothesis that the TEPITOPE method performs better than the Gibbs sampler is estimated as the fraction of experiments where TEPITOPE has the better performance of the two. The results of this calculation demonstrate that for five of the ten data sets (the Southwood set, set 1, set 2, set 4A, and set 4B) the Gibbs sampler has a performance that is significantly higher than that of TEPITOPE ($p < 0.05$). Only for one data set (set 5B), does the TEPITOPE method perform better than the Gibbs sampler ($p = 0.96$). For the remaining four data sets the difference in predictive performance is found to be insignificant ($0.05 < p < 0.95$).

The average A_{ROC} values for the Gibbs sampler, the TEPITOPE matrix, and the ClustalW matrix methods are 0.744, 0.702 and 0.667 for the complete data set, and 0.673, 0.630, and 0.599 for the reduced data sets, respectively.

For two of the ten data sets (set 5A and set 5B) the TEPITOPE weight matrix has a higher A_{ROC} value than the Gibbs matrix. For the set 5B this difference is statistically significant ($p = 0.96$). In order to analyze why the Gibbs sampler has poor performance on the two data sets, we estimated the amino acid

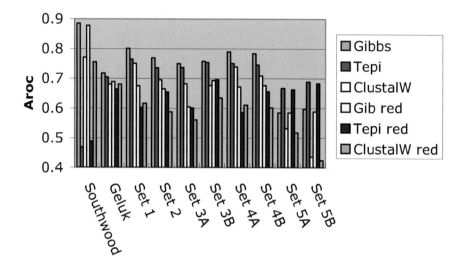

Figure 8.7: Prediction accuracy for the Gibbs sampler, the TEPITOPE, and the ClustalW weight-matrix methods, for the ten benchmark data sets described in the text. For each data set the first three bars give the performance on the complete data sets, and the last three bars the performance on the reduced data sets, respectively. Figure reprinted with permission [Nielsen et al., 2004].

composition in the two sets and compared it to that of the other benchmark sets and the training set. In this analysis, we find that both sets have an extremely high content of cysteine in the subset of peptides that bind MHC. In set 5B, e.g., 45 of the 85 peptides contain at least one cysteine, and 37 of the 45 bind MHC. These numbers stand in contrast to the low cysteine content in the training set. Here, only 47 of the 456 peptide sequences contain cysteine. The TEPITOPE weight matrix has a particular behavior for cysteines in that the score for this amino acid at all positions is zero.

To verify whether the cysteine content could explain the poor behavior of the Gibbs sampler as compared to the TEPITOPE matrix method, we repeated the above benchmark calculation substituting all occurrences of cysteine with alanine in the benchmark data sets. The result of the calculation is shown in Figure 8.8. The Gibbs sampled weight matrix in the cysteine-substituted benchmark calculation also for the reduced data sets has a better or comparable predictive performance compared to that of the TEPITOPE matrix method. Especially, one should note that the performance on the two sets 5A and 5B is comparable for the two methods. Repeating the bootstrap experiment for

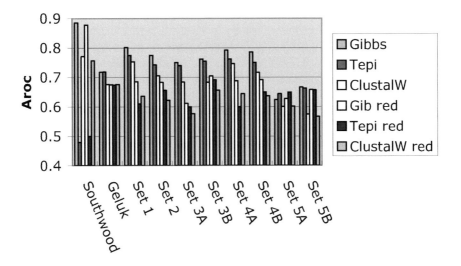

Figure 8.8: Cysteine-substituted benchmark. Prediction accuracy of the Gibbs sampled, the TEPITOPE, and the ClustalW weight-matrix methods for the ten benchmark data sets described in the text. All occurrences of cysteine are replaced with alanine. For each data set the first three columns give the performance on the complete data sets, and the last three columns give the performance on the reduced data sets. Figure reprinted with permission [Nielsen et al., 2004].

the set 5B, applying cysteine substitution, gave a p-value of 0.5. This demonstrates that it indeed was the unusual cysteine content that led to the poor performance of the Gibbs sampler for the two data sets. Similarly, one should note that the performance of the Gibbs sampler for the other eight data sets is similar to that shown in figure 8.5. The average A_{ROC} values for the Gibbs sampled matrix, the TEPITOPE, and the ClustalW weight matrix, respectively, are 0.755, 0.703, and 0.692 for the complete data sets and 0.690, 0.630, and 0.637 for the reduced data sets.

One other striking observation from figures 8.7 and 8.8 is the poor performance of the TEPITOPE method on the Southwood data set. A simple calculation outlines a possible explanation for this poor performance. If one calculates the odds (frequency/background) values for the amino acid composition at the possible p_1 positions in the Southwood data set, one finds that the three amino acids with the highest odds ratios are F, W, and Y. This stands in contrast to the finding in the other data sets where no particular bias is found in the amino acids with the highest odds. The amino acid composition bias at the p_1 position in the Southwood data set originates from the selection bias in the prediction algorithm used to select the peptides for binding assay verification [Southwood et al., 1998]). In the TEPITOPE weight matrix, the p_1 position is modeled in a very crude manner, in that all nonhydrophobic amino acids have a value of -999, and the hydrophobic amino acids have a value of either 0 (F, W, and Y) or 1 (I, L, M, and V). In the Gibbs sampler matrix, this picture is more differentiated. Here the difference in weight matrix score between the common (I, L, M, and V) and the rare amino acids (F, W, and Y) is, on average, 10. The importance of this distinction between the different allowed amino acids becomes clear, if one sets the p_1 weight matrix values for F, Y, and W of the TEPITOPE matrix to 9. Using the modified TEPITOPE matrix the A_{ROC} value is increased to 0.80. The average performance on the other data sets in the benchmark calculation is comparable to that of the original TEPITOPE matrix.

8.3   Further Improvements of the Approach

We have in this chapter shown how the Gibbs sampler method can be applied for detecting the binding motif for MHC class I and class II molecules. The Gibbs sampler method implements the techniques of sequence weighting and pseudocount correction for low counts. These techniques allow the algorithm to handle situations where only very few data points are available and limit the effect of any sequence redundancy in the training data set.

Peptides binding to MHC class II are typically longer than the core motif and correct alignment is key to obtaining good prediction performance. The Gibbs sampler performs well in this task. The optimal Gibbs sampler solution (the one with the highest information content) is not necessarily the optimal predictor, and, as shown, including suboptimal solutions in an ensemble average increases the predictive performance of this method.

Prediction of class II MHC epitopes is a difficult task, and the prediction accuracy of the described method is far from perfect. Moreover, as we demonstrated here, the nature of the test set can influence the performance results drastically. At least two avenues exist where one can expect to achieve higher accuracy. One avenue is the development of more sophisticated prediction methods. For MHC class I a combination of many artificial neural networks with different types of sequence encoding lead to predictors of improved accuracy [Nielsen et al., 2003]. Using the Gibbs sampler as an alignment preprocessing step as described by Brusic et al. [1998b], a similar approach might be beneficial for MHC class II predictions. A second avenue to improved prediction algorithms is the generation of relevant training data. For MHC class I the use of quantitative binding data as opposed to classification data leads to higher accuracy predictors [Buus et al., 2003, Nielsen et al., 2003]. Furthermore, a guided iterative training process where new data points are selected from experimental binding assay verification by the methods like QBC (query by committee) can, in a highly cost- and time-efficient manner, lead to high-accuracy prediction methods [Christensen et al., 2003]. A similar approach might be applied to the MHC class II problem. The weight matrix obtained by the Gibbs sampler or other methods can generate first-generation peptide predictions for verification in binding affinity assays. Subsequently, the QBC method can guide the process of generating informative data that upon exper-imental verification can in turn provide high quality-prediction methods.

Chapter 9

Processing of MHC Class II Epitopes

The degradation of the antigen in the MHC class II pathway is rather different from that in the MHC class I pathway (see figure 9.1). First of all, in the MHC class II pathway mainly the exogenous proteins are presented. Protein intake through endocytosis leads to formation of endosomes, which become increasingly acidic as they progress and eventually fuse with lysosomes. These vesicles contain aspartic and cysteine proteases, which are activated as the acidity increases and thereby degrade the protein into peptides (for a recent review, see Watts [2004]). The protease activity can generate and destroy MHC class II epitopes. The peptides susceptible to destructive processing might survive if they can be loaded to MHC class II molecules early. The MHC class II molecules themselves are quite resistant to proteolysis; therefore the core peptide is completely protected while the rest of the peptide can be trimmed by endosomal endopeptidases hydrolyzing internal amide bonds and exoproteases hydrolyzing one or two amino acids from either the N- or C-terminal [Chapman, 1998]. A type II membrane protein, called the invariant chain (Ii), is associated with newly synthesized MHC class II proteins in the ER. Ii stabilizes MHC molecules and directs transportation to early endosomes. Proteolytic cleavage of Ii is important for the correct peptide loading of MHC class II. A part of Ii, called CLIP (class II associated invariant chain), occupies the peptide binding groove of the MHC class II molecule. Interaction of MHC class II with a MHC class II-like molecule (called HLA-DM in humans), catalyzes the release of CLIP allowing other peptides to bind [Watts, 2004]. In this chapter, we review the specificity of the many proteases playing a role in MHC class II antigen processing and report some results on analyzing the specificity of these enzymes.

175

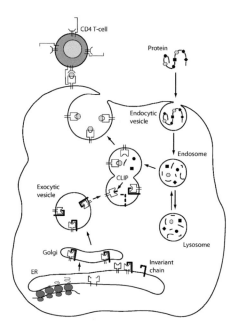

Figure 9.1: The MHC class II presentation pathway. Newly synthesized MHC molecules are stabilized by Invariant chain (Ii) in ER and transported to exocytic vesicles via the trans-Golgi network. Alternatively, the MHC-Ii complex can be transported to the membrane and then rapidly
internalized into endosomes. Mature endosomes/lysosomal containing degradation products
of proteins fuse with exocytic vesicles. Due to high enzymatic activity in the fused vesicles Ii
is degraded, however, the binding groove of MHC molecule remains occupied by CLIP. HLA-DM
(an MHC class II-like molecule, not shown in the figure) regulates the removal of CLIP and allows
peptide binding. The MHC-peptide complex is then transported to the cell membrane. Figure
courtesy of Maite Severins.

9.1   Enzymes Involved in Generating MHC Class II Ligands

Processing of antigens in the MHC class II pathway is achieved by many different peptidases [Watts, 2004]. The principal enzymes and their specificity are
briefly reviewed here; for a more extensive review, see Honey and Rudensky
[2003]. Each enzyme can be quite specific and often these specificities do not
overlap. A key question is the level of redundancy in the system: how large a
part of these specificities are indeed necessary to be able to develop sufficient
helper T cell responses? Is each enzyme responsible on its own for generating
a specific response, or is "generic" protease activity sufficient? Also, we would
like to know how the hierarchy of the epitopes (immunodominant, dominant,
subdominant) is affected by the specificity and distribution of these enzymes.

Name	Protease Family	Expression	Preference
Cathepsin L	C1	B cells, Dendritic cells (DCs), thymocytes	?
Cathepsin S	C1	B cells, DCs, macrophages, epithelial cells	?
Cathepsin B	C1	B cells, DCs, macrophages	–Arg-Arg-|-Xaa
Cathepsin C	C1	Mast cells, B cells	Xaa-Xbb-|-Xcc^a
Cathepsin D	A1	B cells, DCs, macrophages	–Ala-Phe-|-Phe-Ala
Cathepsin E	A1	B cells	Arg-Arg bonds
Cathepsin F	C1	Epithelial cells, macrophages	?
Cathepsin K	C1	Osteoclasts, macrophages	?
Cathepsin H	C1	Monocytes, spermatids	?

^{a} Except when Xaa is Arg or Lys, or when Xbb or Xcc is Pro.

Table 9.1: Major cathepsins involved in antigen processing in lysosomes. The protease family C contains cysteine proteases, while A is aspartic proteases.

At the moment, we have little data available to be able to answer these questions. More information about peptidases is available in the MEROPS database (merops.sanger.ac.uk, [Rawlings et al., 2004]).

9.1.1 Cathepsins

Most mammalian lysosomal cysteine proteases are cathepsins. Cathepsins have been identified as key regulatory enzymes for MHC class II presentation, because they degrade Ii, as well as the antigen [Honey and Rudensky, 2003, Watts, 2004, Ebert et al., 2002]. Table 9.1 gives a summary of different types of cathepsins involved in antigen presentation. Cathepsins, like proteases in general, are divided into four groups according to the identity of the critical residue in their active site. Cysteine-, aspartyl-, serine-, and metalloproteases (cathepsins) have cysteine, aspartate, serine, and metal ions in their active sites, respectively, which serve as nucleophiles during the attack on the carbonyl carbon of the amide bond.

Recent studies have pointed to novel roles for cathepsins. For example, cathepsins C and S regulate the levels of stored proteases in the mast cell secretory granules [Henningsson et al., 2003] and cathepsin L plays a role in cell signaling [Chapman, 2004]. In B lymphoblastoid cells cathepsin B is found in early and late endosomes, but absent from lysosomes, while cathepsins H, S, D, and C are distributed between late endosomes and lysosomes [Lautwein et al., 2004]. This suggests that cathepsin B might be involved in the initial proteolytic attack on a given antigen.

Little is known about how cathepsins, together with other lysosomal proteases, work *in vivo* to generate T cell epitopes. However, *in vitro* analysis with purified cathepsins has recently identified the specificity of some cathepsins. Cezari et al. [2002] found that cathepsin B, a thiol protease, has a broad specificity for peptide bonds, but preferentially cleaves –Arg-Arg-|-Xaa (Xaa any amino acid) bonds in small molecules. Cathepsin C has similar broad specificity, but preferentially cleaves Xaa-Xbb-|-Xcc, except when Xaa is Arg or Lys, or when Xbb or Xcc is Pro [Turk et al., 2001]. Cathepsin H can act as an aminopeptidase as well as an endopeptidase, and has a preference for cleaving after Arg [Dodt and Reichwein, 2003]. Both aspartic proteases, cathepsin D and E, also play a role in intracellular protein degradation, in addition to the generation of antigenic peptides. Cathepsin D has a preference for cleaving after hydrophobic residues, especially –Ala-Phe-|-Phe-Ala [Pimenta et al., 2001]. Cathepsin E was found to have a special preference for Arg-Arg bonds; however, this is only confirmed in neutral pH and it remains doubtful whether or not this preference would be the same in the acidic lysosome environment [Athauda and Takahashi, 2002].

9.1.2   Interferon–Gamma Reducible Lysosomal Thiol Protease (GILT)

In humans, GILT is constitutively present in late endocytic compartments of antigen presenting cells (APCs). GILT belongs to the thioredoxin family, and catalyzes the reduction of disulfide (S-S) bonds in protein substrates [Arunachalam et al., 2000]. To assess the involvement of GILT in MHC class II-restricted presentation of antigenic proteins containing disulfide bonds, Maric et al. [2001] generated a GILT-deficient mouse. In the absence of GILT, presentation of two major lysozyme antigenic epitopes to T cells is partially or completely abrogated. These data provide the first demonstration that the pool of proteolytic enzymes found in the endocytic pathway is not always sufficient to release the full spectrum of peptides for T cells to respond. GILT is likely to have an impact on the array of peptides (especially from proteins containing disulfide bonds, like hen egg lysozyme) constitutively presented on APCs in lymphoid organs.

9.1.3   Alanyl Aminopeptidase N (APN)

APN (or CD13) is a transmembrane ectoenzyme occurring on a wide variety of cells. In contrast to monocytes and granulocytes, lymphocytes of peripheral blood do not express APN. APN can trim the N-terminal of any peptide, although it slows down whenever it encounters a proline [Dong et al., 2000]. Almost all of the lysosomal proteases are not able to further degrade the peptides once they are bound to MHC class II molecules. However, Larsen et al.

[1996] showed that the N-terminal of the peptide could, even while bound to MHC class II molecules, be digested by APN. This can directly effect T cell antigen recognition.

9.1.4   Asparaginyl Endopeptidase (AEP)

AEP is solely responsible for processing of microbial tetanus toxin antigen [Manoury et al., 1998]. AEP seems to be a very specific enzyme: it uses only asparagine as a cleavage site; however 10% of all asparagines in a protein are indeed cleaved [Dando et al., 1999]. AEP might be a very important enzyme in the MHC class II pathway, because some data suggest that other lysosomal proteases can degrade some proteins, e.g., mylein basic protein, only if the initial cleavages are made by AEP [Beck et al., 2001]. Thus, AEP on its own can determine the antigenicity of some proteins. Deficiency in AEP is not lethal: AEP knockout mice were normally born and fertile, although their body weights were significantly reduced [Shirahama-Noda et al., 2003]. The processing of lysosomal proteases (cathepsins B, H, and L) into efficient forms depends fully on AEP, making AEP again a crucial player in the generation of MHC class II epitopes. Plant homologs of mammalian AEP seem to have a similar function, i.e., they degrade proenzymes in storage vesicles.

9.2   Selective Loading of Peptides to MHC Class II Molecules

Since new MHC class II molecules reach endosomal/lysosomal compartments while bound to Ii, epitope presentation is totally dependent on the degradation of Ii. Only after this degradation will the binding groove be able to bind other peptides. Ii degradation occurs in a stepwise manner. The initialization of Ii degradation is done by AEP [Manoury et al., 2003], but might be performed by other proteases as well. The subsequent steps involve cathepsins S and L [Honey and Rudensky, 2003]. Deficiency in cathepsin S or L can reduce the helper T cell repertoire to 30% (first shown by Nakagawa et al. [1998]). This effect is not only due to impairment of the Ii degradation [Honey et al., 2002], but also because of inefficient positive selection, as the MHC class II bound peptide ligand repertoire is severely reduced. After degradation, part of Ii, CLIP, remains bound to the MHC molecule.

Removal of CLIP and peptide loading of MHC class II molecules require yet another accessory molecule, designated HLA-DM in human and H2-M in mouse (for a review see [Kropshofer et al., 1999, Brocke et al., 2002]). HLA-DM is an MHC class II-like molecule which is nonpolymorphic. The binding of HLA-DM to the HLA-DR (one of the three HLA class II loci) molecule enables an open conformational state of the peptide binding groove [Kropshofer et al., 1996].

This open state probably allows for the release of CLIP and leaves the complex of the HLA-DM and MHC class II molecule available for binding other peptides. Only stably binding peptides can bring the groove back to the closed state and stabilize the HLA-DR molecule. In this case HLA-DM dissociates, allowing the HLA-DR-peptide complex to travel to the cell surface and interact with helper T cells. A low-affinity peptide would not be able to achieve dissociation of HLA-DM molecules, and thus may be easily exchanged for a higher-affinity peptide. This reaction follows the rules of Michaelis-Menten kinetics, where HLA-DM acts like a catalyst. Because of this peptide editing property, HLA-DM is an important player in the antigen presentation pathway. The peptide editing can even continue on the cell surface: about 10 % of HLA-DM can be found on the surface of the B cells and dendritic cells [Arndt et al., 2000]. HLA-DM deficient cells cannot perform antigen presentation on MHC class II molecules, because CLIP remains bound to the peptide binding groove.

In the MHC class I pathway, tapasin has a similar role in facilitating peptide loading and selecting the optimal ligands (for a review, see, e.g., [Brocke et al., 2002]). Tapasin and HLA-DM are structurally different and their sole function seems to be the regulation of peptide loading of MHC molecules. These two molecules apparently allow for keeping otherwise instable MHC molecules "in waiting", which might be essential for rapid presentation of peptides from pathogens in infected cells. Several autoepitopes causing autoimmune diseases have been reported to be low-affinity binders of disease-associated MHC class II molecules. It is possible that the real cause of autoimmunity in those cases are mistakes in regulation of tapasin and HLA-DM at the gene and protein level.

As in the MHC class I presentation pathway, the pathogens try to evade CD4[+] T cell responses via blocking presentation on the MHC class II molecules. To our knowledge there are no examples of specific evasion from degradation in lysosomes/endosomes. However, several viruses can downregulate MHC class II expression, degrade HLA-DM molecules, or interfere with the transport of MHC class II complexes (for a review, see Vossen et al. [2002]).

9.3   Phylogenetic Analysis of the Lysosomal Proteases

Classification schemes based on the overall structure of the proteins [Barrett and Rawlings, 2001] assign cathepsins to two families of lysosomal proteases, the S1 family (represented by the serine protease cathepsin G) and the C1 family. Within the C1 family, the aspartyl proteases (cathepsins D and E, also called the A1 subfamily) are thought to have diverged from the cysteine proteases. This division is also clear in the phylogenetic analysis based on human sequences given in figure 9.2. The analysis comprises thirteen cathepsin se-

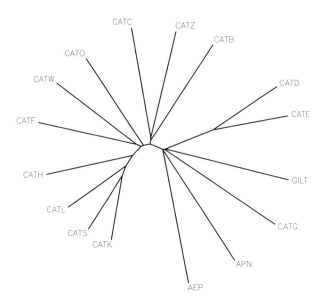

Figure 9.2: Phylogenetic tree of the enzymes involved in generating MHC class II epitopes. Thirteen cathepsin sequences, as well as GILT, AEP, and APN, are included.

quences, and the GILT, AEP, and APN sequences. All the cathepsins except CATG, CATD, and CATE are cysteine proteases. CATE and CATD are aspartyl proteases, and CATG is a serine protease. GILT, AEP, and APN are the proteases described in sections 9.1.2–9.1.4. The cathepsins are placed in three groups: All cysteine proteases form one group, the aspartyl proteases (CATE and CATD) another group, and CATG, GILT, AEP, and APN form isolated groups with branches connected close to the root of the tree, showing that these sequences share no or only have very remote sequence homology.

Although several proteases mentioned in this chapter have been identified in a variety of organisms, little is known about the phylogenetic relationship between these enzymes involved in antigen processing. Using cephalochordate, agnathan, and bony fish cathepsins, together with cathepsin sequences available from other vertebrates, Uinuk-Ool et al. [2003] studied the evolution of the cathepsin family. They found that all cathepsins originate from two very old lineages, the B and the L lineages, which diverged early in the evolution of eukaryotes.

The emergence of the adaptive immune systems seems to have increased dramatically the size of the cathepsin family. Presumably, at first, the phylogenetically oldest cathepsins with broad tissue distribution are used to generate the peptide pool for MHC class II molecules, like cathepsin B and L. Later, several gene duplications resulted in more tissue-specific cathepsins, like cathepsin S, which is found mainly in APCs and thymocytes [Driessen et al., 1999]. Since these enzymes have different specificities, the differentiation in the tissue distribution seems to be an efficient way of presenting different sets of peptides on different cell types.

9.4   Signs of the Specificities of Lysosomal Proteases on MHC Class II Epitopes

The MHC class II compartment hosts several (most yet unknown) regulation systems that balance the creative and destructive proteolytic forces on antigen substrates. The final peptide presented on MHC class II molecules is a result of the combination of all enzymatic specificities summarized above. A logo of a large set of epitopes found the SYFPEITHI database [Rammensee et al., 1999] known to bind HLA class II (706 epitopes from 62 HLA types) demonstrates this (see figure 9.3). In the figure is shown a logo of the N-terminals (left panel) and C-terminals (right panel) of peptides presented by MHC class II. The flanking regions of the epitopes were identified by locating the protein "hosting" the epitope in the Swiss-Prot database [Bairoch and Apweiler, 2000].

Clearly, at the N-terminals the signal is stronger than at C-terminals. Probably the abundance of Pro at position 2 of the epitope shows signs of the cleavage-inhibiting motif of, e.g., ANP. At the C-terminals all enzymes can be acting, reducing the signal/motif to a minimum.

9.5   Predicting the Specificity of Lysosomal Enzymes

Reliable prediction tools on peptidase/protease specificity are not available, because data on substrate specificity of lysosomal enzymes are very limited. One promising approach is 2D gel electrophoresis, in conjunction with tandem mass spectrometry (MS), which can potentially identify and characterize natural enzyme substrates and their products. Bredemeyer et al. [2004] chose the serine protease granzyme (Gzm) B as a test enzyme to evaluate this approach

a)   b)

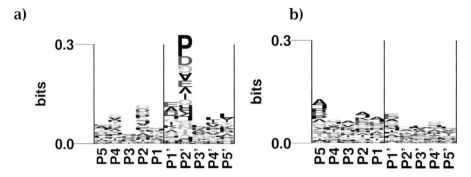

Figure 9.3: Kullback-Leibler logo displaying the motifs surrounding the a) N-terminals and b) C-terminals of HLA class II binding peptides. The end of the epitope is shown by a vertical bar. The letters are shown upside down if they occur less frequently at that position than in Swiss-Prot in general. The data used to make this figure were generated by Gabery and Sjö [2004], Jiang et al. [2005]. See plate 15 for color version.

and detected seven murine proteins as natural ligands of Gzm B. Unfortunately, this proteomic screening method did not detect several known substrates of Gzm B, which demonstrates that the "protease proteomics" will not be the optimal solution for identifying protease substrates.

Here we will review a few initial bioinformatics attempts to predict specificity of these enzymes.

9.5.1 Predicting Specificity of Cysteine Endopeptidases

Using the degradation data available for cathepsins B and L, Lohmuller et al. [2003] developed a method (PEPS) that uses individual rule-based cleavage site scoring matrices. When P4 to P2′ (i.e., three flanking positions left of the cleavage site and two right of the cleavage site) positions were included in these matrices, the performance was optimal, suggesting that the flanking region surrounding the cleavage site of these enzymes is not large. The data sets used to develop the method consist of five proteins for each enzyme, and this obviously limits the performance of the method. Scanning for cathepsin B and L substrates in human and mouse proteome, and comparing those with known substrates, Lohmuller et al. [2003] concluded that the method is not yet useful to predict, e.g., MHC class II ligands. For example, proteomics analysis of cathepsin L-deficient fibroblasts identified seven abundant proteins, which suggests that these proteins are natural substrates of cathepsin L. However, only one of these proteins was predicted by PEPS as a possible substrate for cathepsin L.

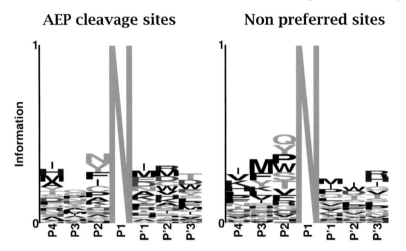

Figure 9.4: The sequence logo of AEP cleavage sites with their flanking region (left panel) and a similar logo for all the other asparagine residues in the proteins studied (right panel). Part of the data was kindly provided by Dr. Colin Watts, University of Dundee, and the rest was extracted during a literature study. See plate 16 for color version.

9.5.2   Predicting Specificity of AEP

At the moment AEP cleavage sites are known in 18 proteins [Manoury et al., 1998, Dando et al., 1999, Beck et al., 2001, Mathieu et al., 2002, Antoniou and Watts, 2002, Sarandeses et al., 2003]. These proteins have 402 asparagine residues, where only 42 are used by AEP as a cleavage site. Three proteins, horse myoglobin, rat tyrosine aminotransferase, and horse ferritin, are resistant to AEP, which gives a total of 27 asparagine residues that are definitely not used by AEP as cleavage sites. A sequence logo of the sites that are cleaved by AEP and the flanking regions of other asparagines (i.e., the ones that are not cleaved) are shown in figure 9.4.

Since AEP can cleave folded proteins efficiently, it was first studied whether or not the cleavage sites that are used by AEP occur on the surface of the proteins. Of 42 cleavage sites, 25 occur in "exposed" regions; however, also 50% of the asparagines that are resistant to AEP cleavage occur in the exposed regions. Thus, being exposed does not seem to be a discriminatory factor for AEP cleavage prediction. There can be two explanations for this. First, this result is based on surface accessibility predictions, which are only 75% accurate. Second, the lysosomes are highly acidic environments, which can cause the unfolding of the protein before coming into contact with AEP.

Another biological process that seems to play a role in AEP cleavage is N-glycosylation. Manoury et al. [1998] report that N-glycosylation can eliminate sites of processing by AEP. There are two main motifs defined for N-glycosylation: the Asn-Xaa-Thr and Asn-Xaa-Ser motifs (Where Xaa is not Pro). The Asn-Xaa-Thr motif was never found among the cleavage sites in this data set. Asn-Xaa-Ser occurs twice, but in both cases N-glycosylation is not predicted according to the NetNGlyc server (www.cbs.dtu.dk/services/NetNGlyc). So N-glycosylation can be used as a filter to predict AEP cleavage sites.

A series of neural networks are trained to predict AEP specificity based on the known AEP cleavages and proteins resistant to AEP cleavage (C. Kesmir & C. Watts, unpublished results). Neural networks have earlier been used to predict the specificity of viral proteinases of SARS and picornaviruses [Blom et al., 1996, Kiemer et al., 2004]. All positions between P4 and P3' are necessary to get better predictions. The effect of neighboring residues on AEP cleavage might depend on each other (e.g., the effect of Ala in P3 is determined also by which amino acid is found at P2'), because a neural network without any hidden neurons, i.e., a linear prediction method, performs very poorly. This suggests that a nonlinear prediction method might be necessary to predict AEP specificity, although having more data might prove that this statement is not valid. Preliminary results suggest that it is possible to develop a method which is able to predict 72% of the AEP cleavage sites, while identifying 90% of the noncleavage sites (i.e., the asparagines that are not used by AEP) correctly (C. Kesmir & C. Watts, unpublished results). This results in a Matthews correlation coefficient of 0.60. If more data become available, the performance of such a predictor will most likely increase.

Chapter 10

B Cell Epitopes

The humoral response is mediated by antibodies (immunoglobulin molecules), which are produced by B lymphocytes. B lymphocytes can bind to antigens by their immunoglobulin receptors. When they become activated, they start to secrete a soluble form of this receptor (antibodies) in large amounts; figure 10.1 shows an example of an antibody molecule. Note the overall Y-shape (or T-shape) of the antibody with the two antigen binding (Fab) fragments shown at the top left and right of the antibody and the constant fragment (Fc) shown below. The linker regions connecting the constant with the variable regions allow great flexibility in the relative orientation of the domains. The highly variable tip of a Fab fragment that can bind to epitopes is called the paratope and is made up of the so-called complementary determining regions (CDRs) in the antibody sequence.

The binding of antibodies to, e.g., a virus, can coat the surface so that it cannot infect cells [Burton et al., 2001]. Viruses or bacteria covered by antibodies are also more easily taken up (phagocytosed) and destroyed by scavenger cells of the immune system such as macrophages. These cells can take up the antigen using their receptors for the constant Fc part of the antibody molecules. Antigens covered by antibodies can also activate the complement system. This can lead to lysis of bacteria and enveloped viruses by the creation of a pore (membrane attack complex) in the membrane. Complement components on the surface of microorganisms can also facilitate phagocytosis, by immune cells with complement receptors.

Contrary to T cells that recognize fragments of proteins bound to MHC molecules, the antibodies recognize a protein in its native form without it being cleaved or bound to molecules such as the MHC molecules. This enables immune responses to extracellular pathogens. Therefore, the antibody response is crucial in the defense against most pathogens. The fact that B cells

A   B

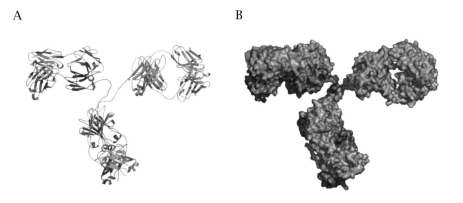

Figure 10.1: Schematic cartoon (A) and surface (B) representation of an intact antibody (PDB entry 1IGT [Harris et al., 1997]). The light chains are shown in orange, the heavy chains in blue and green. The graphical representations of molecules in this chapter were prepared using PYMOL (www.pymol.org, [Liang et al., 2003]). Figure courtesy of Thomas Blicher. See plate 17 for color version.

recognize the folded structure of the antigen makes prediction of B cell epitopes much more difficult than the prediction of T cell epitopes.

In this chapter, we will review germinal center (GC) reactions where the antibody responses go through several rounds of mutation and selection, and we will shortly discuss the mathematical models that are developed to address optimal mutation schema, selection mechanisms, and kinetics of the affinity maturation. Having understood how effective antibody responses are generated, we will then explain the principles behind B cell epitope prediction.

10.1 Affinity Maturation

Early in the primary immune response, the antibodies are of poor quality, i.e., of low affinity. In order to provide long-lasting immunity, antibodies must acquire much higher affinity and should remain in the body in high amounts. This is achieved by a process called "affinity maturation." There are two components which are essential for affinity maturation to take place. First, B cells must generate a high frequency of mutations (hypermutation) to produce large numbers of mutants with different affinities. Second, there has to be a strong mechanism of selection of mutants that encode high-affinity antibodies. GCs are specialized microenvironments in secondary follicles that provide the right conditions for affinity maturation to take place [Berek et al., 1991, MacLennan, 1994, Jacob et al., 1991, Leanderson et al., 1992] (see figure

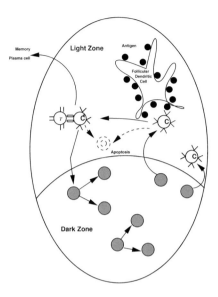

Figure 10.2: Overview of the germinal center reaction. Antigen specific B cells shortly after entering germinal centers down-regulate their B cell receptor (BCR) and undergo rapid cell proliferation in the dark zone (dotted circles). During these cell divisions BCR genes accumulate somatic mutations. After a number of cell divisions, the affinity of the cell is evaluated. The cell changes its phenotype, re-expresses the BCR (circles marked with 'C'), and competes with other B cells to bind the antigen (filled small circles) on follicular dendritic cells (FDCs). If antigen binding is successful, the B cell gets enough survival signal to go and search for a T cell (circles marked with 'T'). The cognate interaction with T cell might ensure selecting only the B cells that are after somatic mutations still unreactive to self [van Eijk et al., 2001]. Failure during antigen binding or interaction with T cell results in apoptosis. The successful cells can (1) differentiate to plasma or memory B cells and leave the germinal center reaction, or (2) recycle back to the dark zone and repeat the proliferation-selection cycle. Adapted from Kesmir and de Boer [1999].

10.2 for an overview of GC reactions).

10.1.1   How are High Affinity Antibodies Generated?

In a GC environment activated B cells switch on a hypermutation mechanism that affects the variable region of the B cell receptor and alters the affinity of the antibodies they encode [Betz et al., 1993, Yelamos et al., 1995, Wiens et al., 1998, Klein et al., 1998, Kelsoe, 1999, Wabl et al., 1999]. The mutation rate is roughly 10^{-3} per base pair per division [Berek and Milstein, 1987], which is six orders of magnitude higher than spontaneous mutations. Mutations are not evenly distributed throughout the variable region of the B cell receptor, but are concentrated in CDRs, which encode the amino acids that make contact with the antigen [Levy et al., 1988]. Transitions are more frequent than transversions, and both strands are hypermutation targets (for a review, see [Jacobs and Bross, 2001]). Analysis of large databases of somatically mutated antibodies reveals that {A,G}G{C,T}{A,T} seems to be a common target for the hypermutation machinery. Especially, AGC and AGT triplets (both coding for serine) are mutating more than other codons [Levy et al., 1988]. The protein necessary for switching on hypermutation in B cells is the activation-induced cytidine deaminase [Muramatsu et al., 2000], although this protein does not seem to be necessary to initiate GC reactions.

With such a high mutation rate, each B cell is expected to produce approximately one mutant per cell division. Somatic mutations are generally of no benefit: in most of the cases they lead to loss of antigen binding. One puzzling feature of affinity maturation is the efficiency by which high-affinity mutants are achieved. Kepler and Perelson [1993b] approached this question from an optimal control perspective and calculated the schema of the hypermutations that would most efficiently generate high-affinity mutants. It is important that a higher-affinity B cell mutant does not mutate again to become a low-affinity mutant. They suggested that if a GC reaction consists of cycles of mutation-free proliferation, followed by mutation and selection, one could overcome the mutational decay of high-affinity mutants. These cycles could occur if the selected mutants instead of leaving GC traverse back to the proliferation area. The model of Kepler and Perelson [1993b] was received with great interest in the immunology community, and to date it has probably been the mathematical model that initiated most experimental studies to prove its conclusions. However, more than a decade of research has not managed to prove that the suggested schema of the hypermutation is the correct *in vivo* scenario.

10.1.2 Competition Among B cells

The antigen is stored in the form of immune complexes on follicular dendritic cells (FDCs). Each new B cell mutant must bind to an antigen in order to avoid apoptosis [Koopman et al., 1997]. This basic fact makes the antigen the main selective agent of a GC reaction. The strong selection in GCs results in an *all-or-none* behavior: GCs either contain hardly any high-affinity cells, or they are almost completely taken over by high-affinity mutants [Radmacher et al., 1998, Berek et al., 1991]. This *all-or-none* behavior implies that *take-over* rates are extremely high; Radmacher et al. [1998] calculated the take over rate of a mutant, having a ten-fold increase in affinity, to be four per day. In the last decade many theoretical models of affinity maturation have been published (e.g., [Kepler and Perelson, 1993a,b, Oprea and Perelson, 1997, Oprea et al.,

2000]). These models, although good at simulating the *average* behavior of
a GC, are poor in explaining the *all-or-none* behavior. The major reason for
this pitfall is the use of affinity-proportional selection mechanisms, where B
cells compete with each other indirectly for available antigen. In addition, the
selection decreases when the affinities of the competing cells increase.

To obtain better insights into the selection mechanisms, a spatial GC model
has been developed in which B cells move, die, divide, and mutate. The for-
malism used was first developed for adhesion-based sorting by Graner and
Glazier [1992] and Glazier and Graner [1993], and was extended to represent
a GC reaction by Kesmir and de Boer [2003]. In this model, B cells compete
with each other for getting enough space (i.e., for getting enough survival signals) on the FDC surface. A spatial affinity-based sorting of the B cells on the
FDC can be obtained if it is assumed that B cells with increased affinity have
an increased cellular adhesion to the FDC presenting antigen. This leads to
a "winner-takes-all" selection because, by the adhesion-based cellular sorting,
only the highest-affinity B cells receive survival signals and are rescued by FDC
[Kesmir and de Boer, 2003].

10.1.3   Role of T Cells in GC Reactions

To initiate a GC reaction, B cells should present antigen effectively to activated
T cells surrounding the follicle; the importance of this cognate interaction is
shown in Garside et al. [1998]. The initial dependence of a GC reaction on T cell
help seems to continue after GCs are established. Following affinity-based selection, GC B cells have to perform efficient cognate interactions with T cells to
increase their survival chance [MacLennan et al., 1997a, Lindhout et al., 1997].
Interference with the cognate interaction between GC T and B cells disturbs
the GC reaction [Linsley et al., 1992, Ronchese et al., 1994, Gray et al., 1994,
Han et al., 1995, MacLennan et al., 1997b].

The role of T cells in GC reactions has been studied in a mathematical
model [Kesmir and de Boer, 1999]. The model suggests that T cells play a
major role at the onset of the GC reaction; later only very few T cells suffice
to keep a GC reaction going. This is because at later stages of the GC reaction
fluctuations in the number of rescued B cells are compensated by their high
proliferation capacity.

10.2   Recognition of Antigen by B cells

Having an understanding of how high-affinity B cells are generated during an
immune response, we will now switch to the antigenic regions recognized by
B cells. B cell epitopes are normally classified into two groups: continuous

and discontinuous epitopes. A continuous epitope, (also called a sequential or linear epitope) is a short peptide fragment in a protein that is recognized by antibodies specific for that protein. A discontinuous epitope is composed of residues that are not adjacent in the primary structure (amino acid sequence), but are brought into proximity by the folding of the polypeptide chain (see figure 10.3 for an example). The classification is not clear-cut as discontinuous epitopes may contain linear stretches of amino acids, and continuous epitopes may show conformational preferences. This is illustrated in figure 10.4, which shows an example of an antibody interacting with a birch pollen protein (an allergen). Even though the central binding site is a loop protruding from the surface, the antibody also interacts with amino acids from other parts of the amino acid chain of the allergen.

The typical protein-antibody complex has the following properties [van Regenmortel, 1996]:

- Contact area of 700-900 Å.

- Amino acids from most CDR regions participate in binding; half of these are aromatic amino acids.

- Discontinuous epitopes are formed by two to five participating regions.

- Binding affinity Ka is typically in the range of 10^{-7} - 10^{-9}M.

- Up to 48 water molecules may be present in the binding interface.

- Binding is enthalpy-driven, not entropy-driven.

- Mutations outside the contact area may influence binding affinity.

Ninety percent of antibodies raised against a protein react with discontinuous fragments (reviewed by van Regenmortel [1996]). This makes B cell epitope prediction a very challenging research field. Predicting continuous epitopes is a simpler problem, and to identify continuous epitopes may be still useful for synthetic vaccines or as diagnostic tools [van Regenmortel and Muller, 1999]. Predicted continuous epitopes may be used to immunize animals to produce antibodies that are cross-reactive with the native protein [van Regenmortel and Pellequer, 1994]. Moreover, continuous epitope predictors can be integrated in prediction of discontinuous epitopes, as the latter epitopes often contain linear stretches [Hopp, 1994].

10.2.1   Prediction of Continuous Epitopes

The first method for predicting antigenic determinants (linear B cell epitopes) was developed by Hopp and Woods [1981, 1983]. The basic assumption of

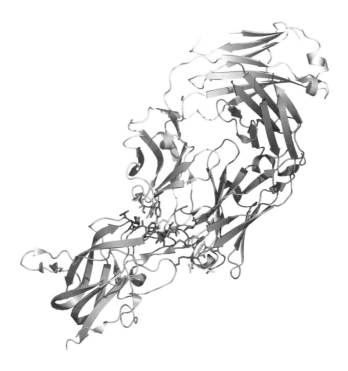

Figure 10.3: An example of binding between a discontinuous epitope and the CDR regions of a specific antibody: the factor VII protein and a Fab fragment from an inhibitory antibody (PDB code 1IQD Spiegel et al. [2001]). Factor IV (in cyan) and the inhibitory antibody Fab fragment, consisting of a heavy and light chain (in blue and yellow, respectively) is shown. The residues of factor VII involved in the interaction are shown in magenta, whereas the interacting residues in the Fab fragment are shown in green (heavy chain) and orange (light chain). Development of an immune response to infused factor VII is a complication affecting many patients with hemophilia A. Inhibitor antibodies bind antigenic determinants on the factor VII molecule and block its procoagulant activity. Figure courtesy of Pernille Haste Andersen. See plate 18 for color version.

this method is that antigenic determinants are found on regions of proteins that have a high degree of exposure to solvent. Therefore, Hopp and Woods [1981] assigned to each amino acid in a sequence its hydrophilicity propensity (according to the hydrophilicity scale generated by Levitt [1976]) and looked at groups of six residues, as this is the normal size of an antigenic determinant. The highest peak in this analysis turned out to be a very good predictor of the antigenicity, yielding no wrong assignments in their 12 protein test set. The second and third peaks resulted in a mixture of correct and wrong predictions, and therefore were less reliable.

A   B

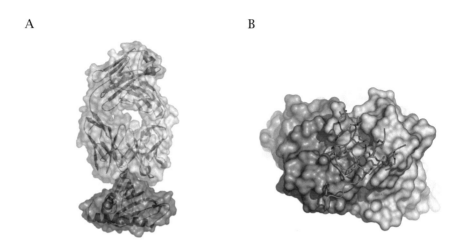

Figure 10.4: Allergen-Fab complex (PDB entry: 1FSK [Mirza et al., 2000]). (A) Cartoon backbone with transparent space- filling representation. The light chain of the Fab fragment is shown in orange, the heavy chain in yellow. Birch pollen protein (Bet v1), an allergen, is shown in blue. Notice how several loops from each chain of the Fab interact with the allergen. (B) Close-up picture of the Fab-Bet v1 complex. Amino acid residues from several discontinuous strands in Bet v1 (in blue) contribute to the interaction with the antibody. The surface of the Fab is shown in yellow (heavy chain) and orange (light chain). Figure courtesy of Thomas Blicher. See plate 19 for color version.

Following these promising results, a number of methods have since been developed with the aim of predicting linear epitopes using a combination of amino acid propensities (like HPLC-derived hydrophilicity, solvent accessibility, flexibility, hydropathy, amino acid residue propensity of being in a certain secondary structure) [Parker et al., 1986, Jameson and Wolf, 1988, Debelle et al., 1992, Maksyutov and Zagrebelnaya, 1993, Alix, 1999, Odorico and Pellequer, 2003]. To test the performance of these methods on predicting continuous and discontinuous epitopes, Pellequer et al. [1993] proposed a benchmark test data set containing 85 continuous epitopes in 14 proteins. Table 10.1 shows this database with epitope annotations. Most data are taken from [Pellequer et al., 1993] and the references therein. An exception is scorpion neurotoxin where the data are taken from Devaux et al. [1993]. All annotations in Pellequer et al. [1993] were checked against the original references. Sequences were downloaded from Swiss-Prot [Bairoch and Apweiler, 2000]. Pellequer et al. [1993] found that the method based on turn propensity (i.e., the propensity of an amino acid to occur within a turn structure) had the highest sensitivity. Seventy percent of the residues predicted to be in epitopes by

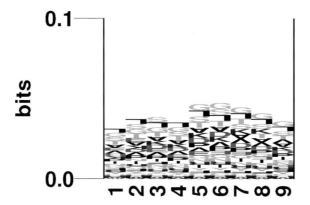

Figure 10.5: Kullback-Leibler sequence logo of 9-amino acid-long peptides extracted from the data given in table 10.1, where position 5 always corresponds to an epitope region. Notice that hydrophobic amino acids like leucine are appearing upside down, indicating that these amino acids occur less frequently than expected. See plate 20 for color version.

this method were actually in epitopes. The sensitivity for methods based on other propensities were in the range of 36 to 61% [Pellequer et al., 1991].

We have further analyzed the epitope regions in the Pellequer data set (table 10.1). Figure 10.5 shows a sequence logo of all positions in epitope regions with their four residue flanking regions on the right and left sides. That is, we made a sequence logo of 9 amino acid-long stretches from this data set, where position 5 is always included in an epitope. Almost all the hydrophobic amino acids are underrepresented, supporting the idea that linear B cell epitopes should occur in hydrophilic regions of the proteins.

Recently, the most extensive study made in predicting linear B cell epitopes was published by Blythe and Flower [2005]. In this study 484 amino acid propensities from the AAindex database (www.genome.ad.jp/, [Kawashima and Kanehisa, 2000]) were used to test how well peaks in single-amino acid scale propensity profiles are (significantly) associated with known linear epitope locations. They used 50 epitope-mapped proteins defined by polyclonal antibodies as a test set, which is the best nonredundant test set currently available. Unfortunately, Blythe and Flower [2005] found that even the predictions based on the most accurate amino acid scales are only marginally better than random, and they suggest using more sophisticated approaches to predict the linear epitopes.

Different ways of measuring the accuracy of epitope predictions have been suggested [van Regenmortel and Pellequer, 1994, Hopp, 1994]. Pellequer

```
   124 CHO sp|P01556|CHTB_VIBCH Cholera enterotoxin, beta chain -Vibrio cholerae
MIKLKFGVFFTVLLSSAYAHGTPQNITDLCAEYHNTQIYTLNDKIFSYTESLAGKREMAIITFKNGAIFQVEVPGSQHIDSQKKAIERMKDTLRIAYLTEAKVEKLCVWN
NKTPHAIAAISMAN
--------------------.......EEEEEEEEEE........EEEEEEEEEE.....EEEEEEEEEEEEEEEE...................EEEEEEE
EEEEEEEE......
   104 CYT sp|P00001|CYC_HUMAN Cytochrome c - Homo sapiens (Human).
GDVEKGKKIFIMKCSQCHTVEKGGKHKTGPNLHGLFGRKTGQAPGYSYTAANKNKGIIWGEDTLMEYLENPKKYIPGTKMIFVGIKKKEERADLIAYLKKATNE
EEEE....EEEEEEEEEEEEE........EEEEEEEEEEE...EEEEEEEEEEEEEEEEE............................
   389 HBV sp|P03138|VMSA_HPBVY Major surface antigen precursor -Hepatitis B
MGQNLSTSNPLGFFPDHQLDPAFRANTANPDWDFNPNKDTWPDANKVGAGAFGLGFTPPHGGLLGWSPQAQGILQTLPANPPPASTNRQSGRQPTPLSPPLRNTHPQAMQ
WNSTTFHQTLQDPRVRGLYFPAGGSSSGTVNPVLTTASPLSSIFSRIGDPALNMENITSGFLGPLLVLQAGFFLLTRILTIPQSLDSWWTSLNFLGGTTVCLGQNSQSPT
SNHSPTSCPPTCPGYRWMCLRRFIIFLFILLLCLIFLLVLLDYQGMLPVCPLIPGSSTTSTGPCRTCMTTAQGTSMYPSCCCTKPSDGNCTCIPIPSSWAFGKFLWEWAS
ARFSWLSLLVPFVQWFVGLSPTVWLSVIWMMWYWGPSLYSILSPFLPLLPIFFCLWVYI
-------------------------------------------------.EEEEEEEEEEEEEEEE.....EEEEEEEEEEEEEE.............EEEEEEEEEE
EEEEEEEE...EEEEEEEEEEEE...............EEEEEEEEEEEEEEE..............EEEEEEEEEEEEEEEeEEEEEEEE.................
...........
   165 HCG sp|P01233|CGHB_HUMAN Choriogonadotropin beta chain - Human
MEMFQGLLLLLLLSMGGTWASKEPLRPRCRPINATLAVEKEGCPVCITVNTTICAGYCPTMTRVLQGVLPALPQVVCNYRDVRFESIRLPGCPRGVNPVVSYAVALSCQC
ALCRRSTTDCGGPKDHPLTCDDPRFQDSSSSKAPPPSLPSPSRLPGPSDTPILPQ
-------------------EEEEEEE.............................EEEEEEEEEEEE...............................
.EEEEEEEEEEEE....EEEEEEEEEEEEEE...EEEEEEEEEEEE
   187 IFB sp|P01574|INB_HUMAN Interferon beta precursor - Human
MTNKCLLQIALLLCFSTTALSMSYNLLGFLQRSSNFQCQKLLWQLNGRLEYCLKDRMNFDIPEEIKQLQQFQKEDAALTIYEMLQNIFAIFRQDSSSTGWNETIVENLLA
NVYHQINHLKTVLEEKLEKEDFTRGKLMSSLHLKRYYGRILHYLKAKEYSHCAWTIVRVEILRNFYFINRLTGYLRN
--------------------.....EEEEEEEEEEEEEEEEE.......................EEEEEEEE...............EEEEEEEEE.......
........EEEEEEEE...EEE
   143 LEG sp|P02238|LGBA_SOYBN Leghemoglobin A (Nodulin 2) - Soybean.
VAFTEKQDALVSSSFEAFKANIPQYSVVFYTSILEKAPAAKDLFSFLANGVDPTNPKLTGHAEKLFALVRDSAGQLKASGTVVADAALGSVHAQKAVTDPQFVVVKEALL
KTIKAAVGDKWSDELSRAWEVAYDELAAAIKKA
..............EEEEEEEEE........................EEEEEEEE.............................EEEEEEE........EEE
EEEEEE.............EEEEEEEEEEEE
   147 LYS sp|P00698|LYC_CHICK Lysozyme C precursor - Chicken
MRSLLILVLCFLPLAALGKVFGRCELAAAMKRHGLDNYRGYSLGNWVCAAKFESNFNTQATNRNTDGSTDYGILQINSRWWCNDGRTPGSRNLCNIPCSALLSSDITASV
NCAKKIVSDGNGMNAWVAWRNRCKGTDVQAWIRGCRL
-------------------....................EEEEEEEEEEEEEEEEEE........EEEEEEEEEEEEEEEEEE..........
   118 MHR sp|P02247|HEMM_THEZO Myohemerythrin (MHR) - Themiste zostericola.
GWEIPEPYVWDESFRVFYEQLDEEHKKIFKGIFDCIRDNSAPNLATLVKVTTNHFTHEEAMMDAAKYSEVVPHKKMHKDFLEKIGGLSAPVDAKNVDYCKEWLVNHIKGT
DFKYKGKL
...EEEEEE....EEEEEE.......EEEE.......EEEE...EEEEEEEEEE......EEEEEE...EEEEEE.....................E
EEEEE...
   153 MYO sp|P02185|MYG_PHYCA Myoglobin - Sperm whale
VLSEGEWQLVLHVWAKVEADVAGHGQDILIRLFKSHPETLEKFDRFKHLKTEAEMKASEDLKKHGVTVLTALGAILKKKGHHEAELKPLAQSHATKHKIPIKYLEFISEA
IIHVLHSRHPGDFGADAQGAMNKALELFRKDIAAKYKELGYQG
EEEEEE....EEEEEEEE.......................EEEEEEEEeEEEEEEE..........................EEEEEE......
..EEEEEEE.EEEEEEE.................EEEEEE..
   185 PIL sp|P04127|PAPA_ECOLI PAP fimbrial major pilin protein - E. coli
MIKSVIAGAVAMAVVSFGVNNAAPTIPQGQGKVTFNGTVVDAPCSISQKSADQSIDFGQLSKSFLEAGGVSKPMDLDIELVNCDITAFKGGNGAKKGTVKLAFTGPIVNG
HSDELDTNGGTGTAIVVQGAGKNVVFDGSEGDANTLKDGENVLHYTAVVKKSSAVGAAVTEGAFSAVANFNLTYQ
---------------------....EEEEEEEE............................EEEEEEEEEEEEE................EEEEEEEEEEEE.
....EEEEEEEEEeeEEEEEEEEEEEE..EEEEEEEEEEEEE
   189 RAS sp|P01112|RASH_HUMAN Transforming protein p21/H-RAS-1 Human
MTEYKLVVVGAGGVGKSALTIQLIQNHFVDEYDPTIEDSYRKQVVIDGETCLLDILDTAGQEEYSAMRDQYMRTGEGFLCVFAINNTKSFEDIHQYREQIKRVKDSDDVP
MVLVGNKCDLAARTVESRQAQDLARSYGIPYIETSAKTRQGVEDAFYTLVREIRQHKLRKLNPPDESGPGCMSCKCVLS
EEEEEEEEEEEEEEE........EEEEEEEEEEEEEEEE.............................EEEEEEEEEEEEE............EEEEEEEEEEEEEEEEE..
.............
   406 REN sp|P00797|RENI_HUMAN Renin precursor,  - Human.
MDGWRRMPRWGLLLLLWGSCTFGLPTDTTTFKRIFLKRMPSIRESLKERGVDMARLGPEWSQPMKRLTLGNTTSSVILTNYMDTQYYGEIGIGTPPQTFKVVFDTGSSNV
WVPSSKCSRLYTACVYHKLFDASDSSSYKHNGTELTLRYSTGTVSGFLSQDIITVGGITVTQMFGEVTEMPALPFMLAEFDGVVGMGFIEQAIGRVTPIFDNIISQGVLK
EDVFSFYYNRDSENSQSLGGQIVLGGSDPQHYEGNFHYINLIKTGVWQIQMKGVSVGSSTLLCEDGCLALVDTGASYISGSTSSIEKLMEALGAKKRLFDYVVKCNEGPT
LPDISFHLGGKEYTLTSADYVFQESYSSKKLCTLAIHAMDIPPPTGPTWALGATFIRKFYTEFDRRNNRIGFALAR
-------------------.....EEEEEEEEEE..EEEEEEEEE.......EEEEEEEEE...................EEEEEEEEE.......EEEEEEEEEE.........
......EEEEEEEE...EEEEEEEEE.........EEEEEEEEE...................EEEEEEEEEEEEEE......EEEEEEEEEEEE.........
....................EEEEEEEEEE.......EEEEEEEEEEEE..EEEEEEEEEE
    85 SCO sp|P01484|SCX2_ANDAU Neurotoxin II precursor - Sahara scorpion
MNYLVMISLALLFVTGVESVKDGYIVDDVNCTYFCGRNAYCNEECTKLKGESGYCQWASPYGNACYCYKLPDHVRTKGPGRCHGR
-------------------eeeEEEEEEEEEE................EEEeeeEEE...--
   158 TMV sp|P03570|COAT_TMV Coat protein - Tobacco mosaic virus.
SYSITTPSQFVFLSSAWADPIELINLCTNALGNQFQTQQARTVVQRQFSEVWKPSPQVTVRFPDSDFKVYRYNAVLDPLVTALLGAFDTRNRIIEVENQANPTTAETLDA
TRRVDDATVAIRSAINNLIVELIRGTGSYNRSSFESSSGLVWTSGPAT
EEEEEEEEEE........EEEEEEEEEEEEEE.EEEEE..............EEEEEEeEEEEEE.......EEEEEEEEEEEEE.............EEEEEEEE
EE............EEEEEEEEEEEEEE..EEEEEEEEEE
```

Table 10.1: Database of fourteen proteins with assigned epitopes from Pellequer et al. [1993]. Dashes (-) were added in the assignment field if the downloaded sequences had a longer N-terminus than the sequences used in the original studies. The first line of each entry contains the length of the sequence, short name, Swiss-Prot ID and mnemotechnic name, description, and source. Next lines contain the sequence followed by the assignment. -: Part of the sequence is not included while determining epitopes, E: epitope, e: overlapping epitopes .: no epitope.

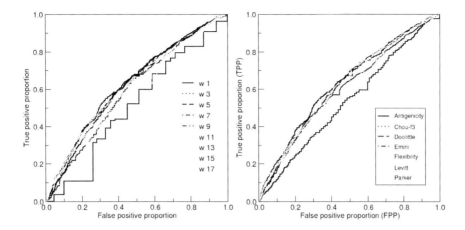

Figure 10.6: Left panel shows ROC curves for epitope predictions using a Doolittle hydrophobicity scale [Kyte and Doolittle, 1982] averaged over different window sizes. The scale has been inverted by multiplying all numbers by -1. ROC curves for linear epitope predictions using different amino acid propensities and a window size of seven is given in the right panel.

suggests using the specificity as a measure of accuracy, while Hopp suggests using the PPV. The former measure will favor methods that make very few (but mainly correct) predictions (underpredict), while the latter will favor methods that make many (large coverage) predictions (and overpredict) (see chapter 4 for definitions of specificity and PPV). Another issue is whether to make the statistics on a per residue or on a per epitope basis. Here we use ROC curves (as explained in chapter 4 and [Swets, 1988]) evaluated on a per residue basis. The Doolittle hydrophobicity scale was used to find the optimal window size. The results given in figure 10.6 (left panel) suggest that a window size of seven is optimal.

In figure 10.6 (right panel) different amino acid propensities are compared using a window size of seven. Different amino acid propensities were used to make predictions: Welling [Welling et al., 1985], Chou-f3 [Chou and Fasman, 1978], Doolittle [Kyte and Doolittle, 1982], Emini [Emini et al., 1985], Levitt [Levitt, 1978], Parker [Parker et al., 1986], Totls [Cornette et al., 1987]; all taken from Pellequer et al. [1991]. The average value of the amino acid propensities in a window according to one of these scales was assigned to the central amino acid in the window.

Pellequer et al. [1991] found in a comparative study that the scales of Emini, Levitt, Chou and Fasman, Parker and Cornette (see above for references) performed marginally better than the others. This is in agreement with figure 10.6, where there is little difference between these scales. The scale of

aa	e	n	LO
A	0.068	0.075	-0.308
C	0.029	0.031	-0.135
D	0.066	0.039	1.558
E	0.055	0.051	0.227
F	0.033	0.052	-1.351
G	0.085	0.066	0.721
H	0.020	0.022	-0.346
I	0.038	0.068	-1.634
K	0.071	0.061	0.439
L	0.080	0.093	-0.422
M	0.016	0.019	-0.380
N	0.041	0.046	-0.357
P	0.058	0.039	1.180
Q	0.044	0.034	0.742
R	0.036	0.043	-0.515
S	0.082	0.066	0.600
T	0.076	0.063	0.553
V	0.054	0.074	-0.948
W	0.008	0.023	-3.001
Y	0.040	0.035	0.359

Table 10.2: Frequencies of different amino acids (aa) in epitopes (e) and nonepitopes (n), and the log-odds ratio (LO) in half-bits (calculated as $2 \log_2 (e/n)$) of the data given in table 10.1.

Parker (HPLC-derived hydrophilicity) performs marginally better than the others. None of these scales are very accurate though, as was found by Blythe and Flower [2005]. In order to find 50% (a true-positive proportion of 0.5) of the epitopes one must accept that more than 28% (a false-positive proportion of 0.28) of the nonepitopes are also predicted to be epitopes.

In order to find the theoretical maximum of the predictions using different amino acid propensities, a new scale is constructed (given in table 10.2) based on the frequencies of the different amino acids in the epitopes, and nonepitopes in our training set. Figure 10.7 shows a comparison between the ROC curves for epitope predictions using the Parker scale and the scale derived from the training set. The two curves are quite similar, i.e., the Parker scale is close to being the optimal amino acid propensity measure for this data set.

In summary, all the attempts reviewed above suggest that there is only a weak correlation between the sequence profiles generated using amino acid propensities and the known location of linear epitopes. The hypothesis that a single amino acid propensity can be used to predict linear B cell epitopes accurately is thus not supported by the available data. Given the complexity

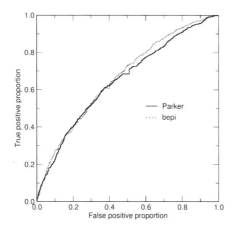

Figure 10.7: ROC curves for epitope predictions using Parker scale [Parker et al., 1986] and a scale derived from the amino acid frequencies of the epitope and nonepitope regions given in table 10.1 (given in table 10.2 and shown as "bepi" in the legend). Both predictions use a window of seven, where the central position in the window is the average of seven amino acid propensities in the window.

of antibody-antigen interactions, this is not a surprising result. Preliminary data suggest that even a nonlinear prediction method such as a neural network does not improve the accuracy of predictions based on single amino acid propensities significantly. The development of more sophisticated methods may be required to predict linear B cell epitopes accurately. One approach would be to use the sequence to predict the (local) structure of the protein, and use this as input to an epitope prediction algorithm. In the next section, we will see how B cell epitopes can be predicted if the structure of the protein is available.

10.2.2   Predicting Discontinuous B Cell Epitopes

A major step forward in understanding the nature of the discontinuous epitopes has been the identification of the antibody-antigen complex structures at high resolution (see figures 10.4 and 10.3 for examples). Antibodies can only bind to amino acids which are exposed on the surface of proteins. The surface of proteins is normally defined as the atoms which are accessible to water. This is computationally found as regions which are accessible to a spherical probe with a 1.4 Å radius. Since antibodies are larger than water molecules it may be sensible to use larger probes for finding antibody binding sites. Novotny et al. [1986] showed that antigenic regions correlated better with regions accessible to contacts with large (10 Å radius) probes than with small (1.4 Å) probes.

Another approach to predict B cell epitopes from protein structures is to calculate a protrusion index (PI) [Thornton et al., 1986], i.e., how much different parts of a protein stick out. To calculate the PI the protein is approximated by an ellipsoid with the same moments of inertia as the real protein. This ellipsoid is then scaled. Residues with a C_α atom which are just inside an ellipsoid that contains $N\%$ of the C_α atoms are assigned a PI value of $N/10$.

Barlow et al. [1986] showed that no surface patches on proteins with the size of an antibody footprint are composed entirely of amino acids which are close to each other in the amino acid sequence. This was shown by placing a sphere on each surface atom in the protein and calculating the fraction of other surface atoms within that sphere which belonged to residues that were local in the amino acid chain. They therefore concluded that all epitopes are to some extent discontinuous.

Different experimental techniques can be used to define conformational epitopes. The best one is of course to solve the structure of an antibody-antigen complex. Since this is very time-consuming it is often useful to make a lower-resolution determination of the epitopes. One method is to do an alanine scan [Cunningham and Wells, 1989, Jin et al., 1992, Zhang et al., 2004], i.e., to replace a residue in the protein by an alanine and see how it affects binding of an antibody. This can then be repeated for other residues in the protein.

Phage-display experiments can also be used in combination with computational methods to search for conformational epitopes. Enshell-Seijffers et al. [2003] used phage display peptide libraries and structural information to predict the binding sites of a monoclonal antibody (mAb) specific for HIV-1 gp120 protein. Scanning a library of 10^9 random peptides, they isolated eleven peptides with a significant binding to this mAb. Their main assumption is that these affinity-selected peptides, due to their specific binding to the mAb of interest, must reflect structural elements of the original epitope. Their algorithm to predict the real epitope of the mAb is based on the assumption that pairs of amino acids which are next to each other in the isolated peptides often correspond to pairs of amino acids which are spatially (but not necessarily sequentially) next to each other on the surface of the antigen. Another possibility would be to try to find peptides that represent conformational epitopes directly by inspection of the surface structure of the antigen. It could be useful to be able to use linear peptides representing conformational epitopes in vaccines to generate antibodies against conformational epitopes on the native protein.

10.3   Neutralizing Antibodies

Depending on where in an antigen a B cell epitope occurs, the consequences of antibody binding differ. For example, if an antibody can efficiently block the receptors mediating infection, the infection rate decreases drastically. Such antibodies are called neutralizing antibodies (nAbs). A number of studies have suggested that the induction of nAb responses is critical for virus elimination and protective immunity [Battegay et al., 1993, Planz et al., 1996, Thomsen et al., 1996, Brundler et al., 1996, Zinkernagel, 1996, Planz et al., 1997, Baldridge et al., 1997]. In infections with cytopathic viruses (viruses that kill cells), nAbs are generated within 6 to 14 days, whereas with some viruses like HIV [Weiss et al., 1985, Robert-Guroff et al., 1985, Moore et al., 1994], HBV [Barnaba et al., 1990], and lymphocytic choriomeningitis virus (LCMV) [Battegay et al., 1993], they are not generated until 50 to 150 days have elapsed. Both LCMV and HBV are noncytopathic viruses.

These observations suggest that there is a correlation between the degree of cytopathic effect and the speed of nAb production. Non-neutralizing antibodies appear very early during LCMV and HBV infections; therefore the delay in the nAb response cannot be explained by reduced antigenic stimulus [Battegay et al., 1993]. However, nAb–producing B cells do become infected in LCMV and HBV infections, most probably because neutralizing surface immunoglobulin might serve as a receptor for the infection [Barnaba et al., 1990, Planz et al., 1996]. The delay may therefore be caused by the elimination of infected B cells by cytotoxic T cells [Barnaba et al., 1990, Battegay et al., 1993, Planz et al., 1996]. Using a simple mathematical model it is shown that CTLs have a twofold effect on the nAb dynamics: Apart from killing infected B cells [Planz et al., 1996], CTLs also suppress the proliferation of the nAb-producing B cells by limiting the antigenic stimulus [Keşmir and de Boer, 1998]. Thus, reducing the proliferation rate of nAb-producing B cells, the production of nAb is delayed in infections with noncytopathic viruses.

To predict which regions of an antigen can induce neutralizing antibodies is one of the ultimate goals of immunological bioinformatics. The mechanism of neutralization is not fully understood. Early studies suggested that virus neutralization was a single-hit mechanism, i.e., that the binding of one antibody to a virus completely neutralized it. This was based on the observation that the infectivity of viruses declined exponentially (first-order decay) after they were mixed with antibodies, with no lag phase as would be expected if two or more antibodies had to bind. The first-order decay is, however, also compatible with an incremental neutralization model where each antibody partly neutralizes the virus [Icenogle et al., 1983].

In a recent review Burton et al. [2001] favor a simple model: In most cases neutralizing antibodies bind to the surface of the virus and interfere with the attachment of the virus to the target cells or the fusion with it and the neutralization is proportional to the number of antibodies bound, no matter where on the surface they bind. Due to their size and flexibility a bound antibody may interfere with virus-cell binding within a relatively large area determined by their reach. For HIV-1, e.g., it has been found that when a fraction f of the antibody binding sites on the gp120 envelope protein is occupied by antibodies, the infectivity relative to when no antibodies are bound is approximately $(1 - f)^3$. The gp120 molecules sit together three and three (in trimers) on the surface of HIV-1 and this finding is thus consistent with a model where the binding of an antibody to one gp120 on the surface of an HIV-1 virion takes out the trimer of gp120 molecules it sits in [Schønning et al., 1999].

Chapter 11

Vaccine Design

Vaccination can broadly be defined as the administration of a substance to a person with the purpose of preventing a disease. This substance is often a killed or weakened microorganism. Vaccination works by creating a type of immune response that enables the memory cells to later respond to a similar organism before it can cause disease. The earliest documented examples of vaccinations are from India and China in the 17th century, where vaccination with powdered scabs from people infected with smallpox was used to protect against the disease. Smallpox used to be a common disease throughout the world and 20 to 30% of infected persons died from the disease. Smallpox was responsible for 8 to 20% of all deaths in several European countries in the 18th century [André, 2003]. The tradition of vaccination may have originated in India in AD 1000 [Plotkin and Orenstein, 1999]. In 1721 Lady Mary Wortley Montagu brought the knowledge of these techniques from Constantinople (now Istanbul) to England. Two to three percent of the smallpox vaccinees, however, died from the vaccination itself so it was an important step forward when Benjamin Jesty and, later, Edward Jenner could show that vaccination with the less dangerous cowpox could protect against infection with smallpox. This experiment inspired the word *vaccination*, which is derived from *vacca*, the Latin word for cow. The vaccination with cowpox (vaccinia) still has serious side effects and leads to the death of 1 in 10,000 vaccinees. It is possible that it was the introduction of the smallpox vaccine that was a significant factor in the population growth and improvement in health seen at that time [André, 2001]. Smallpox was officially declared eradicated by WHO in 1980 and vaccination against smallpox was discontinued.

In 1879 Louis Pasteur showed that chicken cholera weakened by growing it in the laboratory could protect against infection with more virulent strains, and in 1881 he showed in a public experiment at Pouilly-Le-Fort that his anthrax vaccine was efficient in protecting sheep, a goat, and cows. In 1885 Pasteur developed a vaccine against rabies based on a live attenuated virus, and a year later Edmund Salmon and Theobald Smith developed a (heat) killed cholera vaccine. Over the next 20 years killed typhoid and plague vaccines were developed. It was not until 1927 that the next live vaccine was developed: the bacille Calmette-Guérin (BCG vaccine) against tuberculosis.

After the Second World War the ability to make cell cultures, i.e., the ability to grow cells from higher organisms such as vertebrates in the laboratory, made it easier to develop new vaccines, and the number of pathogens for which vaccines can be made have almost doubled. Before that time many vaccines, were grown in chicken embryo cells (from eggs), and even today many vaccines such as the influenza vaccine, are still produced in eggs, but alternatives are being investigated [Mabrouk and Ellis, 2002].

Vaccines have been made for only 34 of the more than 400 known pathogens that are harmful to man. These are listed in table 11.1. Some of the vaccines, however, are not used to their full potential. It is estimated that immunization saves the lives of 3 million children each year, but that 2 million more lives could be saved if existing vaccines were applied on a full-scale worldwide [André, 2003].

11.1   Categories of Vaccines

Vaccines can be broadly classified into three groups [Ellis, 1999]: live, subunit (killed or inactivated), and genetic.

11.1.1   Live Vaccines

Live vaccines are able to replicate in the host but are attenuated (weakened), i.e., they do not cause disease. They are advantageous because they often induce a broad immune response, low doses of vaccine are sufficient, and they induce a *long-lasting* protection [Ellis, 1999, Plotkin and Orenstein, 1999]. However, they may cause adverse reactions and they may be transmitted from person to person. Many different methods of attenuation have been invented [Ellis, 1999, Plotkin and Orenstein, 1999]. The one most frequently used is a passage in cell culture, i.e., growing the pathogen for many generations in the laboratory. This technique has been used to develop live vaccines against polio and tuberculosis (BCG). Other attempts to make attenuated vaccines involve the development of temperature-sensitive mutants which cannot grow at 37° C, or reassortant viruses containing genes from two different viruses. Finally, attenuated vaccines can also be made by deleting genes that are responsible for virulence by recombinant methods.

Organism	Type	Vaccine Type	Year
Variola virus	Virus	Live	1798
Rabies virus	Virus	Inactivated	1885
Salmonella typhi	Bacteria	Live	1896
Vibrio cholerae	Bacteria	Inactivated	1896
Yersinia pestis	Bacteria	Inactivated	1897
Corynebacterium diphtheriae	Bacteria	Toxoid	1923
Bordetella pertussis	Bacteria	Acellular	1926
Clostridium tetani	Bacteria	Toxoid	1927
Mycobacterium tuberculosis	Bacteria	Live	1927
Yellow fever virus	Virus	Live	1935
Influenza virus type A	Virus	Inactivated	1936
Influenza virus type B	Virus	Inactivated	1936
Coxiella burnetii	Bacteria	Inactivated	1938
Rickettsia prowazekii	Bacteria	Inactivated	1938
Rickettsia rickettsii	Bacteria	Inactivated	1938
Central European encephalitis virus	Virus	Inactivated	1939
Poliovirus types 1, 2, and 3	Virus	Inactivated/Live	1962
Measles virus	Virus	Live	1963
Mumps virus	Virus	Live	1967
Rubivirus	Virus	Live	1969
Staphylococcus aureus	Bacteria	Staphage lysate	1976
Streptococcus pneumoniae	Bacteria	Polysaccharide	1977
Human adenovirus types 4 and 7	Virus	Live	1980
Neisseria meningitidis	Bacteria	Polysaccharide	1981
Hepatitis B	Virus	Recombinant	1986
Haemophilus influenzae	Bacteria	Conjugate	1987
Hantaan virus	Virus	Inactivated	1989
Japanese encephalitis virus	Virus	Inactivated	1992
Varicella-zoster virus	Virus	Live	1994
Hepatitis A	Virus	Inactivated	1995
Escherichia coli	Bacteria	Inactivated	1995
Junin virus	Virus	Live	1996
Bacillus anthracis	Bacteria	Adsorbed	1998
Borrelia burgdorferi	Bacteria	Recombinant	1998

Table 11.1: List of diseases for which a vaccine has been made. The table shows the organism name, type (Virus/Bacteria), the vaccine type, and the year the vaccine was invented/licensed. The list have been compiled from FDA [2003], Plotkin and Orenstein [1999], Brooks et al. [2001], Marshall et al. [2003], NIAID [2000], Choi et al. [2003]. The data were extracted from http://www.cbs.dtu.dk/databases/Dodo.

11.1.2 Subunit Vaccines

Subunit vaccines are easier to produce, but they generally induce less CTL response than live vaccines, because viral and bacterial proteins are not produced in the cells of the vaccinated individual. The classic way of making subunit vaccines is to inactivate a whole virus or bacterium by heat or by chemicals. The vaccine may be purified further by selecting one or a few proteins which confer protection. This has been done for the *Bordetella pertussis* vaccine to create a *better-tolerated* vaccine that is free from whole microorganism cells [Romanos et al., 1991].

The hepatitis B virus (HBV) vaccine was originally based on the surface antigen purified from the blood of chronically infected individuals. Due to safety concerns, the HBV vaccine became the first to be produced using recombinant DNA technology [Moss et al., 1984]. It is now produced in bakers' yeast (*Saccharomyces cerevisiae*). Recombinant technologies can also be used to produce viral proteins that self-assemble to viral-like particles (VLPs) with the same size as the native virus. VLP is the basis of a promising new vaccine against human papilloma virus (HPV) [Marshall et al., 2003].

Many bacteria have polysaccharides in their outer membrane and these have been used to make vaccines against *Neisseria meningitidis* and *Streptococcus pneumoniae*. Polysaccharides generate a T cell-independent response and this makes them inefficient in children younger than 2 years old. This obstacle can be overcome by conjugating these polysaccharides to peptides and this principle has been used in vaccines against *Streptococcus pneumoniae* and *Haemophilus influenzae* [Ellis, 1999].

Toxins are responsible for the pathogenesis of many bacteria. For bacteria such as *Bordetella pertussis*, *Clostridium tetani*, and *Corynebacterium diphtheriae*, vaccines based on inactivated toxins (toxoids) have been developed. This has traditionally been done by chemical means but it can now also be done by altering the DNA sequences that are important for encoding toxicity.

11.1.3 Genetic Vaccines

Genetic vaccines are relatively easy to produce, and they can induce a cellular response. One technique to make a genetic vaccine is to inject DNA encoding for a viral or bacterial protein (also called naked DNA) intramuscularly. Some of the muscle cells will then take up this DNA and will begin to produce the encoded protein. The DNA can also be used to coat small gold particles which are then shot into the tissue and hence the cell nuclei. Another strategy is to use recombinant strains of viruses or bacteria as so-called vectors to carry epitopes from other pathogens, and thereby vaccinate against these. Most of the focus within the field of genetic vaccines has been on viruses such as vaccinia, adenovirus, or alphaviruses, and bacteria such as *Salmonella typhi* or *Mycobacterium tuberculosis*.

Genetic vaccines may also be designed to carry one or more epitopes rather than whole proteins. A number of computational methods for identifying specific epitopes have been reviewed in previous chapters. The next chapter will give an overview of web-based services based on these tools. These can be used to design epitope vaccines [Sette and Fikes, 2003], not only for identification of the epitopes but also for selecting combinations of them with desired properties; e.g., in relation to pathogen variation. Ishioka et al. [1999] suggest that epitope-based vaccines are advantageous because they can:

- be more potent,

- be controlled better,

- induce subdominant epitopes (e.g. against tumor antigens where there is tolerance against dominant epitopes),

- target multiple conserved epitopes in rapidly mutating pathogens like HIV and Hepatitis C virus (HCV),

- be designed to break tolerance,

- overcome safety concerns associated with entire organisms or proteins.

Epitope-based vaccines have been shown to confer protection in animal models (see [Snyder et al., 2004] and references in Rodriguez et al. [1998] and Sette and Sidney [1999]).

11.1.4 Passive Immunization

The vaccines described above are examples of active immunizations, where an agent is introduced to create a protective immune response. In passive immunization antibodies are harvested from infected patients or animals and are then used to protect against disease. Passive immunizations are still used in special cases against many pathogens: cytomegalovirus, hepatitis A and B viruses, measles, varicella, rubella, respiratory syncytial virus, rabies, *Clostridium tetani*, varicella-zoster virus, vaccinia, *Clostridium botulinum*, and *Corynebacterium diphtheriae* [Marshall et al., 2003].

11.2 Polytope Vaccine: Optimizing Plasmid Design

A short epitope sequence is often capable of inducing protective immunity against a large and complex pathogen. Including several such immunogenic epitopes in a "polytope" vaccine construct (reviewed by [Suhrbier, 2002]) may induce immunity against multiple antigenic targets, multiple strain variants, or

Sequence	Protein	Position	Name
VLAEAMSQV	Gag	362	Gag0
NTVATLYCV	Gag	80	Gag1
GLADQLIHL	Vif	101	Vif2
ILKEPVHGV	Pol	476	Pol3
SLYNTVATL	Gag	77	Gag4

Table 11.2: The five peptides included in the HIV A2 polytope construct. The first column gives the peptide sequence, the second column the HIV protein the epitope originates from, the third column the epitope position in the protein, and the last column the name of the epitope in the polytope plots (figure 11.1). The five peptides are all known HLA-A2 restricted epitopes [Corbet et al., 2003].

even multiple pathogens. Such an immunization is highly relevant to induce protection against organisms like HIV and Epstein-Barr virus where immune escape is an important issue, or for cancer treatment where immunization with subdominant epitopes might be effective in breaking the tolerance [Suhrbier, 1997, Thomson et al., 1998].

Large efforts have been invested in making a proof-of-concept for the polytope DNA vaccine approach. Ishioka et al. [1999] have shown that protective immunity against HIV and HBV in HLA transgenic mice can be obtained by immunizing with a polytope DNA minigene encoding nine dominant CTL epitopes. Others have obtained similar results for human papilloma virus, HIV, and melanoma [Doan et al., 2005, Woodberry et al., 1999, Mateo et al., 1999]. However, as of today no polytope vaccine has been shown to induce protection in humans. "Computational vaccinology" based on quantitative prediction approaches may help design better polytope vaccines [Flower et al., 2003].

When a polytope is delivered as a DNA vaccine, successful immunization can be obtained only if the epitopes encoded by the polytope are correctly processed and presented. Thus, cleavage by the proteasome in the cytosol, translocation into the ER by the TAP complex, as well as binding to MHC class I should be taken into account in an integrative manner. The design of a polytope can be done in an effective way by modifying the sequential order of the different epitopes, and by inserting specific amino acids that will favor optimal cleavage and transport by the TAP complex, as linkers between the epitopes.

Here we give an example of an optimized HIV polytope. This polytope is constructed from five known HLA-A2 restricted epitopes from different HIV proteins [Corbet et al., 2003]. The epitopes are listed in table 11.2.

For simplicity we focus only on the proteasome cleavage and MHC binding aspects of the antigenic processing and presentation, i.e., we leave out TAP from our analysis here. The quality of the polytope can be evaluated in terms of four measures:

1. The number of poor C-terminal cleavage sites of epitopes (predicted cleavage < 0.9)

2. The number of internal cleavage sites (within epitope cleavages with a prediction larger than the predicted C-terminal cleavage)

3. The number of new epitopes (number of processed and presented epitopes in the fusing regions spanning the epitopes)

4. The length of the linker region inserted between epitopes.

The prediction of proteasomal cleavage and MHC class I binding is done using the methods described in chapters 6 and 7. The polytope is optimized by permutating the order of the epitopes, and by insertion of linker amino acids in between the epitopes. The optimization seeks to minimize the above four terms by use of Monte Carlo Metropolis simulations [Metropolis et al., 1953].

In figure 11.1 a graphical representation of two polytope constructs is shown. The upper figure shows the polytope configuration before optimization, and the lower figure the polytope after antigen processing and presentation have been optimized. In the initial polytope, the epitopes are placed head to tail in random order (figure 11.1, upper panel). This construct has a relatively poor predicted antigenic processing and presentation score: one of the epitopes (Gag-0) has a poor C-terminal cleavage score, three epitopes (Gag-0, Gag-1, and Gag-4) have strong internal cleavage sites (one epitope, Gag-1, has four internal cleavage sites), and one new epitope is predicted in the fusion region spanning two epitopes (Gag-0 and Gag-1). After the polytope optimization (figure 11.1, lower panel) all epitopes have a strong C-terminal cleavage, only one internal cleavage site remains (in Gag-1), and no new epitopes appear in the fusion regions. It thus seems natural to expect that the optimized polytope construct should have a high chance of presenting all five epitopes, and hence a higher chance of inducing immunity. A natural extension of the outlined approach will be to include the TAP transport efficiency in the optimization procedure.

11.3 Therapeutic Vaccines

Vaccines are normally administered to healthy individuals to prevent disease. Nevertheless, there is a growing trend to use vaccines to treat the patients that already have a disease. Efforts are being devoted to developing therapeutic vaccines against tumors, AIDS, allergies, autoimmune diseases, hepatitis B,

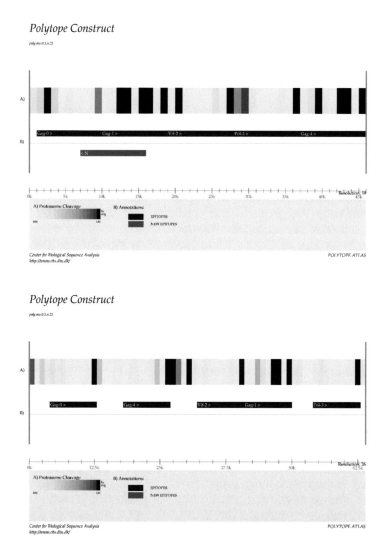

Figure 11.1: Two configurations of the HIV A2 polytope. The upper panel shows the initial configuration with the epitopes placed head to tail in a random manner. The lower panel shows the optimized polytope construct. In each panel (A) gives the predicted proteasomal cleavage, and (B) the epitope sequences (in blue), the location of new predicted epitopes (in red). The units on the x-axis are arbitrary; 1k corresponds to one amino acid. See plate 21 for color version.

tuberculosis, malaria, and, possibly, against the bacteria that cause gastric ulcers. The idea behind a therapeutic vaccine against autoimmune diseases and allergy is to suppress an already existing immunity, while vaccines for cancer and persistent infections aim to boost the existing immunity or induce new immune responses.

11.3.1 Cancer Vaccines

The aim of using a cancer vaccine is to break the tolerance of the immune system against tumors. Therapeutic cancer vaccines can be classified into three groups. The first group consists of polyvalent vaccines that can be composed of whole tumor cells, peptides derived from tumor cells *in vitro*, or heat shock proteins prepared from autologous tumor cells (for a review, see Ragupathi and Livingston [2002]). The second group is tumor-specific antigen–defined vaccines. These vaccines are probably the most difficult ones to develop, as each individual tumor can have a unique collection of antigens. Mutations can easily accumulate in tumor cells due to high proliferation rates. Therefore, the investigators search for antigens with three main characteristics: (1) maximal immunogenicity, (2) wide expression by different tumor types, and (3) maximal tumor specificity, i.e., minimal expression in healthy cells [Mocellin et al., 2004]. The last group of cancer vaccines aim to increase the amount of dendritic cells (DCs) that can initiate a long-lasting T cell response against tumors. Tumor-DC hybrids, or DCs loaded with peptides, whole tumor cells, or tumor RNA, are used as agents in this class of vaccines.

Obviously, not all of these trials are leading to the desired results, but, there are sufficient data to support the notion that therapeutic cancer vaccines can induce antitumor immune responses in humans with cancer (for a review, see [Lewis, 2004]). Antigenic variation is a major problem that therapeutic vaccines against cancer face. The tools from genomics and bioinformatics can provide ways to circumvent these problems. First, one can use sequence analysis (chapter 3) and diversity measures (chapter 4) to identify the most conserved protein regions from a specific tumor with least similarity to other human proteins. Then the polytope approach explained above can be used to generate cancer vaccines from these conserved epitopes specific for tumor cells.

11.3.2 Allergy Vaccines

Immunotherapeutic vaccines against allergies represent an area which has received much attention lately due to the increasing occurrence of allergies in industrialized countries. The traditional approach is to vaccinate with small doses of purified allergen, i.e., induce tolerance. Second-generation vaccines are under development based on recombinant technology. One promising vaccine candidate developed by Niederberger et al. [2004] uses genetically engineered derivatives of Bet v 1 protein, which is the main cause of birch pollen allergy (see figure 10.4 for the structure of this protein). More than 100 million people world-wide are effected by this allergen. Patients having pollen allergy often have large amounts of IgE antibodies specific for Bet v 1 protein. When exposed to pollen, the IgE-Bet v 1 complexes are formed on the surface of mast cells and basophils. This initiates a series of cellular reactions that cause inflammation [Kinet, 1999]. Immunization with the derivatives of Bet v 1 induces a strong IgG antibody response specific for allergen Bet v 1. IgG antibodies do not bind to mast cells and basophils; instead they can efficiently clear the allergen, Bet v 1, before IgE-allergen complexes are formed. This results in a ten-fold reduction in inflammation caused by basophils [Niederberger et al., 2004]. Moreover, IgG antibodies induced by the vaccine are also specific for Bet v 1 cross-reactive allergens, i.e., the vaccine can suppress allergy to related pollens.

It is well established that contact with seasonal allergens induces a strong IgE memory response that causes the symptoms to repeat year after year (see, e.g., [Durham et al., 1997]). Therefore, another desired effect of the therapeutic vaccine against allergies is to reduce this memory response, so that in the coming allergen-rich seasons the patient remains symptom-free even without the repeated vaccination. Niederberger et al. [2004] show that genetically engineered Bet v 1 vaccine can also reduce pollen-specific IgE memory response significantly. In short, this vaccine is a good example of switching a "wrong" immune response to a less harmful one.

11.3.3   Therapeutic Vaccines against Persistent Infections

The effort to develop this group of vaccines has been blooming recently, especially for preventing HIV-related disease progression. Most of the first candidate HIV-1 vaccines were based entirely or partially on envelope proteins to boost neutralizing antibodies (see chapter 10). However, these vaccines have not been successful [Cohen, 2003], because the envelope proteins are the most variable parts of the HIV genome [Gaschen et al., 2002], and because they were composed of monomeric gp120 molecules that induce antibodies that did not bind to trimeric gp120 on the surface of the virions. A number of recent vaccines are also designed to induce strong cell-mediated responses. These include vaccines based on several different viral vectors with or without priming with DNA or a recombinant antigen (see, e.g., [Shiver et al., 2002]).

The huge potential for immune escape by HIV remains the major problem for the HIV vaccines. Escapes from CTL responses are associated with disease progression and high viral loads [Leslie et al., 2004, Friedrich et al., 2004]. While some CTL epitopes escape recognition quickly because they are not functionally constrained, others might need several compensatory mutations. This is because the latter group of epitopes lie in functionally or structurally constrained regions of HIV-1. The p24 capsid protein, e.g., is known to be one of the most conserved proteins of HIV-1 [Novitsky et al., 2002, Leslie et al., 2004, Gaschen et al., 2002]. P24 is part of the Gag protein complex, which controls the assembly of HIV-1 virions and plays a crucial role in the entry to target cells [Gottlinger, 2001, Adamson and Jones, 2004]. P24 contains a stretch of 20 residues, which is conserved across all retroviruses and is essential for viral assembly, maturation, and infectivity [Gamble et al., 1997]. It has been shown that most of the capsid surface cannot tolerate point mutations without a severe loss of viral fitness [von Schwedler et al., 2003, Leslie et al., 2004]. In contrast, the Nef protein is known to be polymorphic, and during acute infection immune responses to Nef are typically replaced by responses to more conserved regions of HIV-1 [Lichterfeld et al., 2004].

11.3.4   Vaccines against Autoimmune Diseases

The biggest success story for therapeutic vaccines was achieved against multiple sclerosis, an autoimmune disease where T cells specific for mylein basic protein (MBP) can cause inflammation of the central nervous system. The vaccine uses copolymer 1 (cop 1), a protein that highly resembles MBP. Cop 1 competes with MBP in binding to MHC class II molecules, but it is not effective in inducing a T cell response (reviewed by [Kipnis and Schwartz, 2002]). On the contrary, cop 1 can induce a suppressor T cell response specific for MBP, and this response helps diminish the symptoms of multiple sclerosis. Inspired by this example, a vaccine based on the same mechanisms is developed for myasthenia gravis [Sela and Mozes, 2004].

11.4   Vaccine Market

The vaccine market has increased fivefold from 1990 to 2000, but with annual sales of 6 billion euros it is still less than 2% of the total pharma market. The major producers are GlaxoSmithKline (GSK), Merck, Aventis Pasteur, Wyeth, and Chiron who have 85% of the market. The main products are hepatitis B, flu, MMR (measles, mumps, and rubella) and DTP (diphtheria, tetanus, pertussis) vaccines which represent more than half the market. Of these 40% are produced in the United States and the rest is evenly split between Europe and the rest of the world [Gréco, 2002]. It currently costs between 200 and 500 million US dollars to bring a new vaccine from the concept stage to market [André, 2002].

Chapter 12

Web-Based Tools for Vaccine Design

In classic immunological research, results could be recorded by pen and paper or in a spreadsheet, but new experimental high-throughput methods such as sequencing, DNA arrays, and proteomics have generated a wealth of data that cannot be efficiently handled and mined by classic approaches. The field of immunological bioinformatics has been growing rapidly in the past years to provide accurate methods for analysis of emerging immunological data. Many of the methods have been made available on the Internet and can be used by experimental researchers without expert knowledge of bioinformatics. This chapter attempts to give an overview of the methods currently available and to point out the strengths and weaknesses of the different methods.

12.1   Databases of MHC Ligands

Several databases of MHC binding peptides now exist on the web (see table 12.1).

SYFPEITHI: The SYFPEITHI database contains information on peptide sequences, anchor positions, MHC specificity, source proteins, source organisms, and references to publications. The database has more than 4000 peptide sequences known to bind MHC class I and class II molecules and is based on previous publications on T cell epitopes and MHC ligands from many species [Rammensee et al., 1999].

MHCPEP: The other major database of peptides that bind MHC is the MHCPEP database [Brusic et al., 1998a]) which comprises over 13.000 peptide sequences known to bind MHC molecules. Entries were compiled from pub-

Name	Principal Investigators	URL	Description
SYFPEITHI	Rammensee	www.syfpeithi.de/	Natural MHC ligands
MHCPEP	Brusic, Harrison	wehih.wehi.edu.au/mhcpep	MHC binding peptides
JenPep	Flower	www.jenner.ac.uk/jenpep2	MHC and TAP ligands, B cell epitopes
MHCBN	Raghava	www.imtech.res.in/raghava/mhcbn	Tools for subunit vaccine design
HLA ligand/motif Database	Hildebrand	hlaligand.ouhsc.edu	Ligand database/prediction
HIV molecular immunology database	Korber	hiv-web.lanl.gov/content/ immunology/	HIV epitopes
EPIMHC	Reinherz	immunax.dfci.harvard.edu/Tools/ db_query_epimhc.html	MHC ligands

Table 12.1: Databases of MHC binding peptides.

lished reports as well as from direct submissions of experimental data. Each entry contains the peptide sequence, its MHC specificity, and, when available, experimental method, observed activity, binding affinity, source protein, anchor positions, and publication references. Unfortunately, the database has, since June 1998, been static. The database can be downloaded as an ASCII file.

JenPep: The JenPep database is a newer database that contains quantitative binding data of peptides to MHC and TAP, as well as B and T cell epitopes [Blythe et al., 2002]. The database contains more than 8000 entries.

MHCBN: MHCBN [Bhasin et al., 2003] is a database of MHC binding and nonbinding peptides containing 17,129 binders, and 2648 nonbinders for more than 400 MHC molecules.

HLA Ligand/Motif Database: This site contains a database that can be searched by defining allele and specificity, amino acid pattern, ligand/motif in sequence of amino acids, author's last name, or advanced search with more criteria [Sathiamurthy et al., 2003].

HIV Molecular Immunology Database: The HIV molecular immunology database is an annotated, searchable collection of HIV-1 cytotoxic and helper T cell epitopes and antibody binding sites. The goal of the database is to provide a comprehensive listing of well-defined HIV-1 epitopes [Korber et al., 2001a].

EPIMHC: An MHC ligand database that can be searched based on sequence, length, class, species, and on whether a ligand is an epitope or not.

NIH has this year started an immune epitope database (IEDB) and analysis program (www2.niaid.nih.gov/Biodefense/Research/resources.htm#immepi) to design, develop, populate, and maintain a publicly accessible, comprehensive immune epitope database containing linear and structural antibody epitopes and T cell epitopes. This database may eventually incorporate most of the data from the above described databases. It will be available at www.immuneepitope.org/.

Name	URL	Description
BIMAS	bimas.dcrt.nih.gov/molbio/hla_bind	Prediction of MHC class I binding using matrices
SYFPEITHI	www.syfpeithi.de/	Prediction of MHC class I and II binding
PREDEPP	bioinfo.md.huji.ac.il/ marg/Teppred/mhc-bind	MHC class I epitope prediction
Epipredict	www.epipredict.de/	Prediction of HLA class II restricted binding
ProPred	www.imtech.res.in/raghava/propred	MHC class II prediction
MHCPred	www.jenner.ac.uk/MHCPred	HLA class I predictions
NetMHC	www.cbs.dtu.dk/services/NetMHC-2.0	Prediction of HLA class I binding using ANNs and HMMs
LpPep	zlab.bu.edu/zhiping/lppep.html	Prediction of HLA-A2 binding
MAPPP	www.mpiib-berlin.mpg.de/ MAPPP/expertquery.html	Registration needed for expert model. Combined open reading frame, MHC binding, and proteasomal cleavage

Table 12.2: Servers for predicting binding of peptides to MHC molecules.

12.2 Prediction Servers

12.2.1 Prediction of MHC Binding

Several peptide-MHC binding prediction servers exist on the web (table 12.2). As indicated in the table some of the web-based methods also allow prediction of binding to MHC class II molecules. Most methods available on the web for predicting MHC-peptide binding are matrix methods. Matrices or hidden Markov models (HMMs) may be derived from a set of ligand sequences as described in chapter 4. In these methods the amino acid on each position in the motif gives an independent contribution to the prediction score. Neural networks can generate more accurate predictions if correlations between positions exist, and if there are enough data to train a neural network properly.

BIMAS: The BIMAS method was developed by Parker et al. [1994]. The method is based on coefficient tables deduced from the published literature. For HLA-A2, peptide binding data were combined together to generate a table containing 180 coefficients (20 amino acids x 9 positions), each of which represents the contribution of one particular amino acid residue at a specified position within the peptide [Parker et al., 1994].

SYFPEITHI: The SYFPEITHI predictions are based on published motifs (pool sequencing, natural ligands) and take into consideration the amino acids in the anchor and auxiliary anchor positions, as well as other frequently occurring amino acids within a binding motif. The score is calculated according to the following rules: Each residue in a certain peptide is given a specific value depending on whether it occurs in an anchor or auxiliary anchor position, or if it is one of the preferred residues. Ideal anchors will be given 10 points, unusual anchors 6 to 8 points, auxiliary anchors 4 to 6 points, and preferred residues 1 to 4 points. Amino acids that are regarded as having a negative effect on the binding ability are given values between -1 and -3 [Rammensee et al., 1995, 1999]. On the SYFPEITHI website predictions can be made for 6 different MHC class II alleles and 21 MHC class I alleles.

PREDEPP: In this method the peptide structure in the MHC groove is used as a template upon which peptide candidates are threaded, and their compatibility to bind is evaluated by statistical pairwise potentials. This method has the advantage that it does not require experimental testing of peptide binding, and can thus be used for alleles where only few data are available [Schueler-Furman et al., 2000].

Epipredict: This server is based on a method that uses synthetic combinatorial peptide libraries to describe peptide-HLA class II interaction in a quantitative way. The binding contribution of every amino acid side chain in an MHC class II ligand is described by allele-specific 2D databases [Jung et al., 2001].

ProPred: The ProPred method [Singh and Raghava, 2001] is based on the matrices published by Sturniolo et al. [1999], and is an implementation and extension of the TEPITOPE program [Hammer, 1995, Raddrizzani and Hammer, 2000].

MHCPred: Prediction of binding to 11 different HLA class I alleles and 3 HLA class II alleles using a 3D quantitative structure-activity relationship method [Guan et al., 2003].

NetMHC: Prediction of HLA class I binding using neural networks and weight matrices [Buus et al., 2003, Nielsen et al., 2003, 2004]. NetMHC includes allele-specific weight-matrix predictions for more than 120 HLA alleles, and artificial neural network (ANN) and weight matrix predictions for 12 alleles representing 12 distinct HLA supertypes. The neural network methods have been trained using quantitative binding data generated by an ELISA assay [Sylvester-Hvid et al., 2002], and predict the binding affinity. They thus differ from methods performing classification only (binding vs. nonbinding according to a threshold).

LpPep: A new method for predicting high affinity MHC-binding peptides based on linear programming [Peters et al., 2003b].

Two well-known prediction methods, TEPITOPE and EpiMatrix [Meister et al., 1995, de Groot et al., 1997] that are not available through the web are listed in table 12.3. TEPITOPE is popular since it allows prediction of peptides of many different class II molecules. Another prediction method, PREDICT, for MHC class I, II, and TAP binding from the Brusic group [Yu et al., 2002] is also not available through the web at the moment.

12.2.2 Prediction of Proteasomal Cleavage Sites

Different methods for predicting proteasomal cleavage sites exist on the web (table 12.4).

Name	URL	Description
TEPITOPE	www.vaccinome.com	PC program for class II predictions can be downloaded
EpiMatrix	epivax.com/epimatrix.html	Commercial epitope prediction
Predict		Prediction of class I, II, and TAP binding

Table 12.3: MHC binding predictions not publicly available on the Internet.

Name	URL	Description
PaProC	paproc.de	A matrix-based method for protasomal cleavage prediction
MAPPP	www.mpiib-berlin.mpg.de/ MAPPP/cleavage.html	Proteolytic fragment predictor
NetChop	www.cbs.dtu.dk/ services/NetChop	A neural–network based protasomal cleavage prediction
	bioinfo.md.huji.ac.il/marg/cleavage/	Matrix score to predict proteasomal cleavage

Table 12.4: Prediction of proteasomal cleavage sites.

PAProC (Prediction algorithm for proteasomal cleavages) is a prediction tool for cleavages by human and yeast proteasomes, based on experimental cleavage data [Kuttler et al., 2000, Nussbaum et al., 2001]. An updated version of the PAProC program based on in vitro immunoproteasome cleavage data [Toes et al., 2001] is also in the making according to the PAProC homepage.

MAPPP comprises two different algorithms. One aims at predicting potential proteasomal cleavage, based on a statistical analysis of cleavage-determining amino acid motifs present around the scissile bond [Holzhutter et al., 1999]. The second algorithm, which uses the results of the cleavage site analysis as an input, provides predictions of major proteolytic fragments [Holzhutter and Kloetzel, 2000].

NetChop [Kesmir et al., 2002] is a method based on neural networks that have been trained on different data sets. The network, which was trained on C-terminal cleavage sites of 1110 publicly available MHC class I ligands, performs best in predicting the boundaries of CTL [Saxova et al., 2003]. The specificity of this network may resemble the specificity of the immunoproteasome. NetChop3.0 is now available [Nielsen et al., 2005].

The parameters of Altuvia and Margalit [2000] analysis are also recently available on the net. Another method based on support vector machines can be found at www.imtech.res.in/raghava/pcleavage.

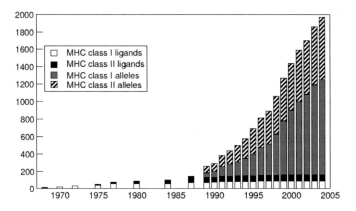

Figure 12.1: The growth in the number of known MHC sequences and MHC ligands. The graph is adopted from the IMGT/HLA database (www.ebi.ac.uk/imgt/hla/). Notice the exponential growth in the number of MHC alleles (sequences) compared to more or less stable levels of known MHC ligands.

12.2.3 Combined Predictions

The MAPPP server (table 12.2) allows the user to make an open reading frame (ORF) search combined with MHC binding and proteasomal cleavage site predictions.

12.2.4 TAP Predictions

The only web-based prediction tool for TAP binding was developed by Bhasin and Raghava [2004] and is based on support vector machines (www.imtech.res.in/raghava/tappred).

12.2.5 MHC Sequence Databases

A number of databases containing sequences of proteins of immunological interest exist on the web (table 12.5).

IMGT/HLA: The HLA sequence database currently contains 1156 MHC class I and 712 class II alleles. There are also 11 TAP molecules and 54 MICA sequences. Figure 12.1 shows the growth of this database in time.

IMGT: IMGT, the international ImMunoGeneTics project, is a collection of databases specializing in immunoglobulins, T cell receptors, and the MHC of all vertebrate species. The IMGT project was established in 1989 by the Université Montpellier II and the CNRS (Montpellier, France) and works in close

Name	URL	Description
IMGT/HLA	www.ebi.ac.uk/imgt/hla/	HLA sequence database
IMGT	imgt.cines.fr/	Sequences of MHC, TCR, and immunoglobulin molecules
ASHI	www.ashi-hla.org	Sequences, gene and haplotype frequencies
MHCDB	www.hgmp.mrc.ac.uk/ Registered/Option/mhcdb.html	Database of MHC sequences

Table 12.5: MHC sequence databases.

Name	URL	Description
Birkbeck College, London	www.cryst.bbk.ac.uk/pps97/assignments/ projects/coadwell/MHCSTFU1.HTM	Structure and function of the MHC proteins
MHC-Peptide interaction database	surya.bic.nus.edu.sg/mpid/	Structural information on MHC peptide interaction
ELF	hiv-web.lanl.gov/content/hiv-db/ ALABAMA/epitope_analyzer.html	Epitope location finder
SYFPEITHI	www.syfpeithi.de/Scripts/ MHCServer.dll/Info.htm	Rammensee's links
CBS	www.cbs.dtu.dk/courses/27485.imm/links.php	CBS links
Web review	www.hiv.lanl.gov/content/hivdb/ REVIEWS/Lund2002.html	Review Lund et al. [2002]

Table 12.6: Sites providing useful information and links related to immunological bioinformatics.

collaboration with the EBI.

ASHI: The American Society for Histocompatibility and Immunogenetics (ASHI) hosts databases of gene and allele frequencies together with other information relevant to vaccine design and the general biology of antigen processing and presentation.

MHCDB: "Registered users only" database of MHC sequences.

12.2.6   Useful Sites

A number of other resources relevant to immunology and vaccine design are listed in table 12.6.

Chapter 13

MHC Polymorphism

As a result of fast evolution (thanks to the short generation time of microorganisms), hosts are under constant selection pressure to invent processes that counteract pathogenic invasion. Since the generation time of the vertebrate host is much longer than that of pathogens, obviously the evolution of the host has a much slower pace. The polymorphism of the MHC molecules is one result of this coevolution between the host and its pathogens. The polymorphism is one of the major reasons why mammalian organisms cannot be eradicated by infections by a single pathogen: Pathogens that escape from presentation by the MHC molecules of one individual may not be able to escape the presentation by another individual carrying a different MHC molecule.

13.1   What Causes MHC Polymorphism?

Although there have been extensive debates over the selection pressures leading to the high polymorphism of MHC molecules, there is still not a widely accepted model for a mechanism (see Apanius et al. [1997] for a detailed review). The common view is that MHC polymorphism arises because of the heterozygote advantage. Different MHC molecules bind different peptides, and thus present different parts of a pathogen to T cells. If a host is heterozygous in its MHC loci, it can thus provide a broader immune response, which in turn would make pathogenic adaptation more difficult. This theory, known as the theory of overdominance or heterozygote advantage [Hughes and Nei, 1988, 1989, 1992], is supported by recent studies on HIV-1 patients. Carrington and O'Brien [2003] have reviewed data showing that the degree of MHC heterozygocity correlates with a delayed onset of progress to AIDS.

There exist a number of mathematical models focusing on the heterozygous advantage as the main reason for MHC polymorphism. Work in the general area of population genetics models suggests that the heterozygous advantage is sufficient to explain the high MHC polymorphism observed in several MHC loci [Maruyama and Nei, 1981, Takahata and Nei, 1990, Hughes and Yeager, 1998]. These models assume that all heterozygous individuals would have the same fitness (higher than the homozygous individuals) irrespective of the MHC molecules that they harbor. This is, however, an unrealistic assumption, as it is now well established that different MHC alleles show different degrees of protection to specific pathogens [van Eden et al., 1980, Klein et al., 1994, Hill et al., 1991]. de Boer et al. [2004] show that when the classic population genetics models are corrected for this unrealistic assumption, it is no longer possible to obtain more than 10 alleles per loci. Thus, the heterozygous advantage alone cannot explain the large MHC polymorphism observed in mammalian (and most vertebrate) populations.

An additional mechanism that could enlarge MHC polymorphism is frequency-dependent selection by host-pathogen coevolution. Since it is a good strategy for pathogens to adapt to the most common MHC alleles in a population, the rare alleles would have a selective advantage. This will in time cause the frequency of rare alleles to increase, and the common alleles will become rare. The dynamic picture arising from this scenario resembles the well known principle of red-queen dynamics from ecology [van Valen, 1973]. The studies of the snail-trematode parasite system support that such a frequency-dependent selection can take place in nature, as in this system the parasite evolves to become most virulent in the dominant host genotype. For humans HIV-1 is an example of a rapidly adapting pathogen to most common MHC alleles in the population [Trachtenberg et al., 2003, Scherer et al., 2004].

The relative role of frequency-dependent selection and heterozygote advantage is discussed extensively in the literature [Lewontin et al., 1978, Aoki, 1980, Hughes and Nei, 1988, 1989]. Recently Borghans et al. [2004] and Beltman et al. [2002] have developed a computer simulation model of coevolving hosts and pathogens to study the relative impact of these two mechanisms. This model shows that 1) the frequency-dependent selection scenario alone can account for the existence of at least 50 alleles per MHC loci, and 2) if the host population size is large enough, the MHC polymorphism does not become too dynamic, i.e., a large set of MHC alleles can persist over many host generations even though host MHC frequencies change continuously.

Many other factors such as MHC-dependent mate selection, geographic and social isolation, and strong selection pressures by severe infections (population "bottlenecks") can influence the degree of MHC polymorphism arising in a population. The chimpanzee species is in this respect very interesting: de Groot et al. [2002] have shown that almost any chimpanzee gene is more polymorphic than human genes, probably because the chimpanzee is an older species. However, the polymorphism of MHC genes seems to be much lower than in humans, possibly due to a strong selection pressure caused by simian immunodeficiency virus (SIV) infection. Even though host-pathogen evolution seems to be sufficient to explain the large MHC polymorphism [Borghans et al., 2004, Beltman et al., 2002], all other factors mentioned here, together with frequency-dependent selection, generate the MHC polymorphism we observe in many vertebrate populations today.

13.2   MHC Supertypes

The previous section reviewed factors that play a role in generating extremely polymorphic MHC genes. This polymorphism, although very essential to protect a population from invasion by pathogens, generates a major drawback for epitope-based vaccines, which otherwise, from many perspectives, are the most promising vaccine candidates (see chapter 11).

Each MHC molecule has a different specificity. If a vaccine needs to contain a unique peptide for each of these molecules it will need to comprise hundreds of peptides. One way to counter this is to select sets of a few HLA molecules that together have a broad distribution in the human population. Gulukota and DeLisi [1996] compiled lists with 3, 4, and 5 alleles which give the maximal coverage of different ethnic groups. One complication they had to deal with is that HLA alleles are in linkage disequilibrium, i.e., the joint probability of an allelic pair may not be equal to the product of their individual frequencies, $(P(a)P(b) \neq P(ab))$. This means that it is not necessarily optimal to choose the alleles with the highest individual frequencies. Moreover, Gulukota and DeLisi [1996] find that populations like the Japanese, Chinese, and Thais can be covered by fewer alleles than the North American black population which turns out to be very diverse. Thus different alleles should be targeted in order to make vaccines for different ethnic groups or geographic regions.

A factor that may reduce the number of epitopes necessary to include in a vaccine is that many of the different HLA molecules are not functionally different, i.e., they have similar specificities. The different HLA molecules have been grouped together in what is called supertypes [Del Guercio et al., 1995, Sidney et al., 1995, Sette and Sidney, 1999]. This means ideally that if a peptide can bind to one allele within a supertype, it can bind to all alleles within that supertype. In practice, however, only some peptides that bind to one allele in a supertype will bind to all alleles within that supertype. A number of different criteria have been used to define these supertypes, including structural similarities, shared peptide binding motifs, identification of cross-reacting peptides, and ability to generate methods that can predict cross-binding peptides [Sidney et al., 1996]. For HLA class I molecules Sette and Sidney [1999] defined nine supertypes (A1, A2, A3, A24, B7, B27, B44, B58, B62) which were reported to cover most of the HLA-A and -B polymorphisms. They argued that the different alleles within each of these supertypes have almost identical peptide-binding specificity. They found that while the frequencies at which the different alleles were found in different ethnic groups were very different, the frequencies of the supertypes were quite constant. Assuming Hardy-Weinberg equilibrium (i.e., infinitely large, random mating populations free from outside evolutionary forces), they found that more than 99.6% of persons in all ethnic groups surveyed possessed at least one allele within at least one of these supertypes. They also showed that the smaller collections of supertypes A2, A3, B7 and A1, A2, A3, B7, A24, and B44 covered in the range of 83.0 to 88.5% and 98.1 to 100.0% of persons in different ethnic groups, respectively. Three alleles, A29, B8, and B46, were found to be outliers with a different binding specificity than any of the supertypes. These may define supertypes themselves when the specificity of more HLA molecules is known.

Some work has also been done to define supertypes of class II molecules. It has been reported that 5 alleles from the DQ locus (DQ1, DQ2, DQ3, DQ4, DQ5) cover 95% of most populations [Gulukota and DeLisi, 1996]. It has also been reported that a number of HLA-DR types share overlapping peptide-binding repertoires [Southwood et al., 1998].

There are recently developed bioinformatical approaches to identification of HLA supertypes [Lund et al., 2004, Reche and Reinhertz, 2004] defining a novel measure for the difference in the specificities of different HLA molecules and using the measure to revise the HLA class I supertypes. In the work of Lund et al. [2004] also MHC supertypes for class II molecules are defined, using published specificities for a number of HLA-DR types. This work will be described in detail below.

13.2.1   A Novel Method to Cluster MHC Binding Specificities

In the first part of this section we will be dealing with how to cluster HLA Class I alleles into supertypes. The basic idea behind the approach is to construct weight matrices of binding peptides as described in chapters 6 and 8, and then use these matrices as a representation of the binding specificity of a given allele. Then all the matrices are compared and clustered by their similarity in the binding space. This is a powerful alternative to clustering based on MHC sequence similarities.

First, a data set of alleles and their binding peptides is needed: The different class I molecules used in this example can be seen in table 13.1. The corresponding HLA ligands were extracted from the SYFPEITHI [Rammensee et al.,

1995, 1999] and MHCPEP [Brusic et al., 1998a] databases. All lines containing amino acid information were treated as sequences and blanks were replaced by X. For each allele, weight matrices were built using a program implementing a Gibbs sampler algorithm that estimates the best scoring 9mer pattern using the Monte Carlo sampling procedure described in chapter 8. In brief, the best scoring pattern is defined in terms of highest relative entropy [Cover and Thomas, 1991] summed over a 9mer alignment. The program samples possible alignments of the sequences in the input file. For each alignment a weight matrix is calculated as $\log(p_{pa}/q_a)$, where p_{pa} is the estimated frequency of amino acid a at position p in the alignment and q_a is the background frequency of amino acid a in SWISS-PROT [Boeckmann et al., 2003]. The values for p_{pa} are estimated using sequence weighting and correction for low counts. Sequence weighting is estimated using sequence clustering [Henikoff and Henikoff, 1994]. The correction for low counts is done using the BLOSUM weighting scheme in a similar way to that used by PSI-BLAST [Altschul et al., 1997].

   In order to define a clustering of HLA molecules, the difference in specificities (the distance) between each pair of HLA molecules is first calculated. The distance d_{ij} between two HLA molecules (i, j) is calculated as the sum over each position in the two motifs of one minus the normalized vector products of the amino acid's frequency vectors [Lyngsø et al., 1999]:

$$d_{ij} = \sum_p (1 - \frac{p_p^i \cdot p_p^j}{|p_p^i||p_p^j|})$$
(13.1)

p_p^i, and p_p^j are the vectors of 20 amino acid frequencies at position p in matrix i and j, respectively; $\cdot$ denotes the vector product and $\|$ the calculation of the Euclidian length of the vector. Dividing all distances by the largest distance d_{ij}^{max} normalizes the distance matrix.

   The distance matrices were used as input to the program neighbor from version 3.5 of the PHYLIP package:
(http://evolution.genetics.washington.edu/phylip.html),
which implements the neighbor joining method of Saitou and Nei [1987]. Default parameters were used. If the lengths of tree branches became negative they were put to zero. To estimate the significance of the neighbor joining clustering, we employed the bootstrap method [Press et al., 1992]. A set of matrices were generated by randomly taking out a column N times with replacement from the original matrix set. Here N is the motif length, which is set to 9 throughout the calculation. Each of the N columns in the matrices contains the scores for having each of the 20 amino acids at that position. A tree for each such matrix set is then calculated. Repeating this experiment 1,000

times, we can estimate a consensus tree, and corresponding branch boots-trap values. The bootstrap values on branches are the fraction of experiments where one given subset of alleles were connected to all the other alleles with only a single branch, i.e., the fraction on the experiments where the alleles in the given subset clustered together. We further can estimate bootstrap values for suboptimal tree constructions and compare the probability of one tree construction to another.

13.2.2 HLA-A and HLA-B

Log-odds weight matrices can be calculated for each allele in the SYFPEITHI database using Gibbs sampling as described above. The resulting matrices can be visualized as sequence logos, and the logos showing the specificities for the HLA-A and HLA-B molecules are listed in figures 13.1 and 13.2. The differences in specificities of the different alleles can be seen on the logos. The logo for A*0201, e.g., shows a preference for hydrophobic amino acids both on positions 2 and 9, while the logo for A*1101 shows that this allele only has a preference for hydrophobic amino acids in position 2, but basic amino acids in position 9.

Table 13.1 lists the classification of HLA class I types into supertypes by Sette and Sidney [1999]. Each of the 150 alleles shown in table 13.1 is either described in the Sette and Sidney paper or appears in the SYFPEITHI database [Rammensee et al., 1999].

Figures 13.3 and 13.4 show clusterings based on the specificities for HLA-A and HLA-B, respectively. For the HLA-A alleles these trees were made only for those alleles where at least five sequences with a length of at least nine amino acids could be found in the SYFPEITHI database, and the HLA-B tree only for alleles where at least 15 peptide sequences were included. This means that not all alleles in table 13.1 are shown in these figures. The names of the alleles in the trees are colored according to the classification of Sette and Sidney [1999], and the unclassified alleles are shown in gray. The trees were constructed using the bootstrap method.

By visual inspection of the simple motifs the results shown in table 13.1 were extracted. Sette and Sidney [1999] explicitly assigned 109 of the alleles to a supertype. We have assigned 23 additional alleles/serotypes to a supertype based on the name and specificity listed in table 13.1, the information in the SYFPEITHI database, the HLA facts book [Marsh et al., 2000], and the logos and trees in figures 13.1 and 13.3. These are marked with an "o" in table 13.1. Some of the supertypes defined by Sette and Sidney [1999] seem to contain alleles with specificities which are quite diverse from the other alleles in the supertype, and in eight cases we changed the assignment given by Sette and

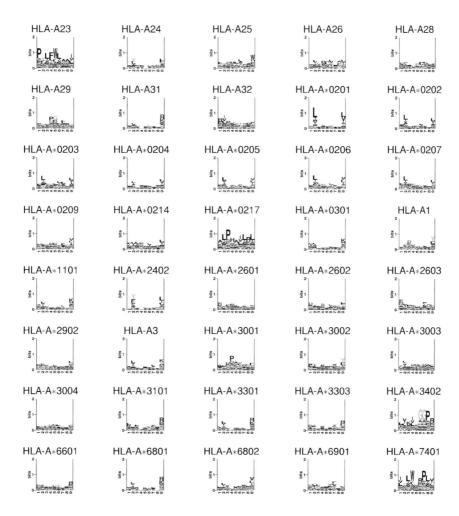

Figure 13.1: Logos displaying the binding motifs for HLA-A molecules. The height of each column of letters is equal to the information content (in bits) at the given positions in the binding motif. The relative height of each letter within each column is proportional to the frequency of the corresponding amino acid at that position. Figure reprinted from Lund et al. [2004]. See plate 22 for color version.

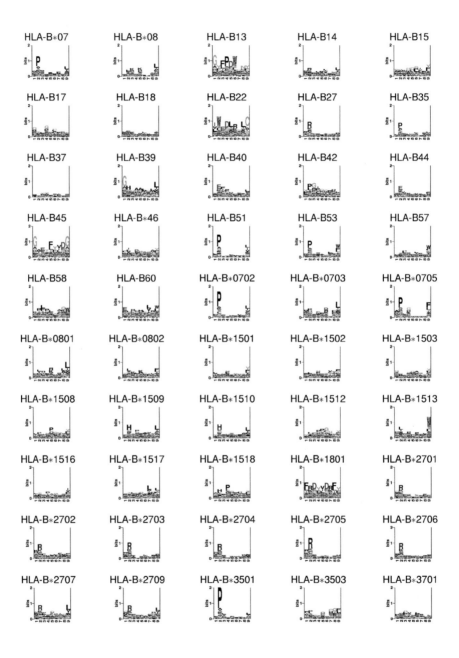

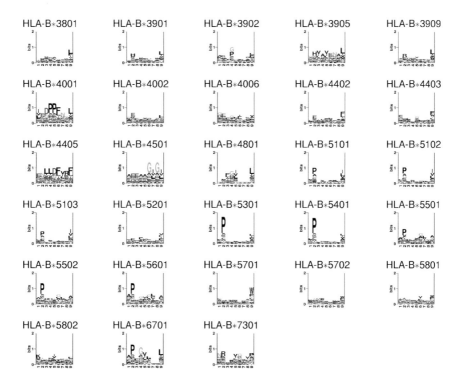

Figure 13.2: Logos displaying the binding motifs for HLA-B molecules. For details on the logo representation, see figure 13.1. Figure reprinted from Lund et al. [2004]. See plates 23 and 24 for color versions.

HLA type	supertype	motif	HLA type	supertype	motif
HLA-A1	A1	.[TS][DE].....Y	HLA-A*0101ª	A1t	.[-]......[-]
HLA-A*0102ª	A1	.[-]......[-]	HLA-A*0201	A2	.[LM]......[VL]
HLA-A*0202	A2	.[AL]......[VL]	HLA-A*0203	A2	.[LV]......[LI]
HLA-A*0204	A2	.[AL]......[VL]	HLA-A*0205	A2	.[LV]......[LS]
HLA-A*0206	A2	.[VQ]......[VS]	HLA-A*0207	A2	.[L-]......[VL]
HLA-A*0209	A2o	.[LA]......[V-]	HLA-A*0214	A2o	.[QV]......[LV]
HLA-A*0217	A2o	.[L-]......[L-]	HLA-A3	A3	K[LY]......[KY]
HLA-A*0301	A3	K[IL]......[K-]	HLA-A*1101	A3	.[YT]......[K-]
HLA-A23	.	.[-]......[-]	HLA-A*2301ª	A24	.[-]......[-]
HLA-A24	A24t	.[YF]......[LF]	HLA-A*2402	A24	.[YF].....[LF]
HLA-A*2403ª	A24t	.[-]......[-]	HLA-A*2404ª	A24t	.[-]......[-]
HLA-A25	A1t	.[-]......[-]	HLA-A*2501ª	A1t	.[-]......[-]
HLA-A26	A1t→A26	.[-]......[-]	HLA-A*2601	A1t→A26	E[TI]......[FY]
HLA-A*2602	A1t→A26	[DE]I......[FY]	HLA-A*2603	A26o	E[VL]......[ML]
HLA-A*2604ª	A1t→A26	.[-]......[-]	HLA-A28	A1→A26	.[-]......[-]
HLA-A29	outlier	.[FN]......[YC]	HLA-A*2902	outlier	K[E-]......[YL]
HLA-A30ª	A24t	.[-]......[-]	HLA-A*3001	A24→A1	K[TF]......[FL]
HLA-A*3002	A24t→A1	R[YV]......[YK]	HLA-A*3003	A24t→A1	R[YL]......[Y-]
HLA-A*3004	A1o	K[YT]......[YL]	HLA-A31	.	.[-]......[-]
HLA-A*3101	A3	[RK]QL.....[R-]	HLA-A32	.	.[-]......[-]
HLA-A*3201ª	A1t	.[-]......[-]	HLA-A*3301	A3	.[LV]......[RK]
HLA-A*3303	A3o	[DE]I......[R-]	HLA-A*3402	A3o	.[V-]......[R-]
HLA-A*3601ª	A1	.[-]......[-]	HLA-A*4301ª	A1	.[-]......[-]
HLA-A*6601	A3o	[ED]T......[R-]	HLA-A*6801	A3	E[VT]......[RK]
HLA-A*6802	A2	D[TV]......[VS]	HLA-A*6901	A2	E[TA]......[R-]
HLA-A*7401	.	.[T-]......[V-]	HLA-A*8001ª	A1	.[-]......[-]
HLA-B07X	B7	.[PV]......[LA]	HLA-B*0702	B7	.[PV]......[LA]
HLA-B*0703	B7	.[DP]......[L-]	HLA-B*0704ª	B7	.[-]......[-]
HLA-B*0705	B7	.[P-]......[FL]	HLA-B08	outlier	.[LP]K.K...[L-]
HLA-B*0801	outlier	.[RK].[RK]....	HLA-B*0802	outlier	.[L-]K.K....[F-]
HLA-B13	.	.[A-]......[-]	HLA-B*1301ª	B62t	.[-]......[-]
HLA-B*1302ª	B62t	.[-]......[-]	HLA-B14	outlier	.[R-]......[LV]
HLA-B*1401ª	B27	.[-]......[-]	HLA-B*1402ª	B27	.[-]......[-]
HLA-B39	B62o	.[FM]......[YF]	HLA-B*1501	B62	.[QL]......[YV]
HLA-B*1502	B62	.[LQ]......[YF]	HLA-B*1503	B27t	.[QK]......[YV]
HLA-B*1508	B7	.[PV]......[YS]	HLA-B*1506ª	B62t	.[-]......[-]
HLA-B*1509	B27→B39	.[H-]......[LF]	HLA-B*1510	B27t→B39	.[H-]......[LF]
HLA-B*1512	B62t	.[QL]......[YS]	HLA-B*1513	B62	.[IL]......[W-]
HLA-B*1514ª	B62t	.[-]......[-]	HLA-B*1516	B58	.[TS]......[IV]
HLA-B*1517	B58	.[-]......[-]	HLA-B*1518	B27t	.[-]......[-]
HLA-B*1519ª	B62t	.[-]......[-]	HLA-B*1521ª	B62t	.[-]......[-]
HLA-B17	.	.[-]......[-]	HLA-B18	B44h	.[E-]......[-]
HLA-B*1801	.	.[-]......[-]	HLA-B22	.	.[-]......[-]
HLA-B27	B27o	.[R-]......[-]	HLA-B*2701	B27t	R[RQ]......[Y-]
HLA-B*2702	B27	K[R-]......[YF]	HLA-B*2703	B27	[RK]R......[LY]
HLA-B*2704	B27	R[R-]......[LF]	HLA-B*2705	B27	R[R-]F......[-]
HLA-B*2706	B27	R[R-]......[LV]	HLA-B*2707	B27	[RK]R......[LV]
HLA-B*2708ª	B27t	.[-]......[-]	HLA-B*2709	B27o	[GR]R......[-]
HLA-B35	B7o	.[P-]......[Y-]	HLA-B*3501X	B7	.[PV]......[LY]
HLA-B*3502ª	B7	.[-]......[-]	HLA-B*3503	B7	.[PM]......[MF]
HLA-B37	.	.[F-]......[T-]	HLA-B*3701	B44	.[DE]......L[I-]
HLA-B*3801	B27→B39	.[HF]D......[LF]	HLA-B*3802ª	B27	.[-]......[-]
HLA-B39	B27o	.[H-]......[L-]	HLA-B*3901	B27→B39	.[HR]......[L-]
HLA-B*3902	B27	.[-]......[MF]	HLA-B*3903ª	B27	.[-]......[-]
HLA-B*3904ª	B27	.[-]......[-]	HLA-B*3905	.	.[-]......[-]
HLA-B*3909	B27o→B39	.[RH]......[L-]	HLA-B40	B44o	E[F-]......[L-]
HLA-B*4001	B44	.[E-]......[L-]	HLA-B*4002	B44o	.[E-]......[L-]
HLA-B*4006	B44	.[E-]......[VA]	HLA-B*4101ª	B44h	.[-]......[-]
HLA-B42	.	.[PL]......[-]	HLA-B*4104	B44	.[E-]......[-]
HLA-B*4402	B44	.[E-]......[FL]	HLA-B*4403	B44	E[E-]......[FW]
HLA-B*4405	B44o	.[E-]......[R-]	HLA-B45	.	.[-]......[-]
HLA-B*4501	B44h	.[E-]......[L-]	HLA-B*4601	B62	.[MI]......[YF]
HLA-B*4801	B27t	.[QK]......[L-]	HLA-B*4802ª	B27t	.[-]......[-]
HLA-B*4901ª	B44h	.[-]......[-]	HLA-B*5001ª	B44h	.[QK]......[-L]
HLA-B51	B7	.[AP]......[IL]	HLA-B*5101	B7	.[AP]......[LY]
HLA-B*5102	B7o	.[PA]......[IV]	HLA-B*5103	.	.[FG]......[YI]
HLA-B*52ª	B62	.[-]......[-]	HLA-B*5201	B62o	.[QF]......[VF]
HLA-B53	B7o	.[P-]......[W-]	HLA-B*5301	B7	.[P-]......[FL]
HLA-B*5401	B7	.[P-]......[A-]	HLA-B*5501	B7	.[P-]......[A-]
HLA-B*5502	B7	.[P-]......[AV]	HLA-B*5601	B7	.[P-]......[AL]
HLA-B*5602ª	B7	.[-]......[-]	HLA-B57	B58	.[AS]......[WT]
HLA-B*5701	B58	.[ST]......[WF]	HLA-B*5702	B58	.[TS]......[WF]
HLA-B58	B58	.[-]......[-]	HLA-B*5801	B58o	.[TS]......[WF]
HLA-B*5802	B58o	.[ST]......[FM]	HLA-B*6701	B7	.[P-]......[L-]
HLA-B*7301	B27	.[R-]......[P-]	HLA-B*7801	B7	.[GP]......[S-]

Table 13.1: HLA type (column 1,4), supertype (column 2,5) and amino acid motif (column 3,6) for all alleles described by Sette and Sidney [1999] and Rammensee et al. [1999]. Letters in square parenthesis correspond to the same position. X: X-ray structure exists. Table adopted from Lund et al. [2004]. ª: Allele is not in SYFPEITHI. h/t: hypothetical/tentative supertype assignment according to Sette and Sidney [1999]. o: the supertype assignment presented here. →: assignment changed by Lund et al. [2004].

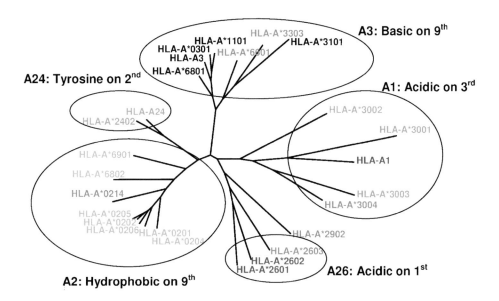

Figure 13.3: Tree showing clustering of HLA-A specificities. The alleles are colored according to the supertype classification by Sette and Sidney [1999]: A1: red, A2: orange, A3: black, A24: green, A29 and nonclassified alleles: gray. Figure reprinted from Lund et al. [2004]. See plate 25 for color version.

Sidney [1999]. We assign six alleles to be outliers and the remaining thirteen we cannot classify.

13.2.3 HLA-A Supertypes

The tree describing the HLA-A alleles is characterized by five clusters: A1, A2, A3, A24, and A26. The corresponding branch bootstrap values are 0.37, 0.39, 0.59, 0.98, and 0.38, respectively.

A2 supertype — hydrophobic amino acids in position 9: The resulting definition of this supertype largely overlaps with the definition by Sette and Sidney [1999]. The unassigned HLA-A*0214 and HLA-A*0217 is added to the A2 supertype.

A3 supertype — basic amino acids in position 9: A*3303 and A*6601 are assigned to the A3 supertype characterized by basic amino acids in position 9. The other alleles in the cluster follow the classification suggested by Sette and Sidney [1999].

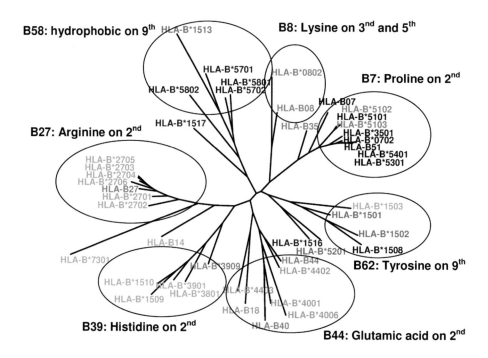

Figure 13.4: Tree showing clustering of HLA-B specificities. The alleles are colored according to the supertype classification by Sette and Sidney [1999]: B7: black, B27: orange, B44: green, B58: blue, B62: violet, and nonclassified alleles and outliers (B8 and B46): gray. Figure reprinted from Lund et al. [2004]. See plate 26 for color version.

A1 supertype — acidic amino acids in position 3: Here the clustering shows a large difference from the A1 supertype defined by Sette and Sidney [1999]. The clustering suggests splitting the A1 supertype into two clusters. One cluster is the A1 cluster that contains the A1 and A*3001-4 alleles based on their common preference for acidic amino acids in position 3, and Y or F at position 9. The other cluster is a proposed new A26 supertype. Sette and Sidney have assigned HLA-A*3001-3 tentatively to an A24 supertype together with the alleles of A*24 and A*2402. The bootstrap branch value for the A24 cluster suggested by Sette and Sidney (A24, A*2402, A*3001, A*3002, and A*3003) is found to be 0.02. Also the bootstrap value for a cluster containing both the A2601, A*2602, and the A1 alleles is below 0.01. These numbers stand in contrast to the bootstrap branch values for the A1 cluster and the new A26 clusters, which are 0.37 and 0.38, respectively.

Proposed new A26 supertype — acidic amino acids in position 1: HLA-A*2601-3 have E/D in position 1 rather than at position 3 in HLA-A1. This difference is consistent with the motif descriptions by Marsh et al. [2000]. These alleles therefore form a new supertype. Including HLA-A*2902 in the A26 supertype leads to a decrease in the branch bootstrap value from 0.38 to 0.12, so this allele is left as an outlier.

A24-supertype — tyrosine or hydrophobic in position 2: A24 and A*2402 is assigned to the A24 supertype. These alleles have a bootstrap value of 0.98.

Based on the background of what is described above, a redefinition of the A1 supertype is made: The HLA-A*2601/2 alleles may form a new separate A26 supertype. The following alleles remain unclassified: A23, A31, A32, A*7401.

13.2.4 HLA-B Supertypes

The HLA-B supertype tree contains many more alleles than the HLA-A tree. In order to make the clustering analysis more feasible and clear, the HLA-B clustering is limited to the alleles where at least 15 peptide sequences are available in either the SYFPEITHI or MHCPEP databases. This limits the analysis to 45 HLA-B alleles out of 99 available.

B7 supertype — proline in position 2: The definition of the B7 supertype by Sette and Sidney [1999] largely corresponds to the B7 cluster in figure 13.4, but with one important exception. Sette and Sidney place the HLA-B*1508 in the B7 supertype. However, the bootstrap branch value for the Sette and Sidney B7 cluster is 0.042, whereas the corresponding value for the B7 cluster, excluding the HLA-B*1508 allele, is 0.66.

New B8 supertype — lysine in position 3 and 5: The B8 alleles were defined as an outlier group by Sette and Sidney [1999] and the specificities of B*08, and B*0802 define a cluster with a corresponding branch bootstrap value of 0.72 in figure 13.4.

B62 supertype — tyrosine in position 9: The B62 cluster shown in figure 13.4 is restricted to contain only the alleles HLA-B*1503, HLA-B*1501, HLA-B*1502, and HLA-B*1508. The bootstrap branch value for the cluster is 0.62. Including the alleles HLA-B*1516 and HLA-B*5201 make the bootstrap value drop to 0.06. These two alleles are thus left out as outliers. The bootstrap branch value for the B62 cluster defined by Sette and Sidney is < 10-3. This low branch value is due to the misplacement of the HLA-B*1513 and HLA-B*5201 alleles in the B62 supertype, and the HLA-B*1508 allele in the B7 supertype.

B27 supertype — basic in position 2: The definition of the B27 supertype by Sette and Sidney has a branch bootstrap value < 10-3, whereas the B27 cluster defined in figure 13.4 has a branch value of 0.22. The low branch value for the Sette and Sidney B27 supertype is due to a misplacement of the HLA-B*1503 allele. As described above, this allele is placed in the B62 cluster. Splitting up the B27 cluster into two subclusters leaving out the HLA-B*7301 and the HLA-B*14 alleles as outliers, leads to a bootstrap branch value for the remaining B27 cluster of 0.62. The other alleles form a new B39 supertype with a bootstrap branch value of 0.41. The B39 cluster contains the alleles of HLA-B3909, HLA-B*3901, HLA-B*3801, HLA-B*1510, and HLA-B*1509. These alleles have similar B and F pocket residues as defined by Sette and Sidney [1999]. The redefined B27 cluster contains the alleles of HLA-B*2705, HLA-B*2703, HLA-B*2704, HLA-B*2706, HLA-B27, HLA-B*2701, and HLA-B*2702.

B44 supertype — glutamic acid in position 2: The definition of the B44 cluster largely corresponds to the supertype definition of Sette and Sidney [1999]. The alleles of HLA-B*40 and HLA-B*44 are included in the supertype, and the bootstrap branch value for the cluster is then 0.36.

B58 supertype — hydrophobic at position 9: The branch bootstrap value for the B58 cluster defined in figure 13.4 is found to be 0.42. Including the HLA-B*1517 allele this value drops to 0.18, thus this allele is left out as an outlier. The bootstrap value for the Sette and Sidney [1999] B58 supertype is 0.156. Leaving out the HLA-B*1516 and HLA-B*1517 alleles as outliers as described above and including the HLA-B*1513 allele lead to the B58 cluster defined in figure 13.4.

There is generally good consistency between the supertypes defined by Sette and Sidney [1999] and the HLA-B tree. In addition, B8 is a novel supertype including the HLA-B*08 and HLA-B0802 alleles as well as splitting the B27 supertype into two, a B39 supertype and a B27 supertype. Further, some of the alleles could be rearranged so as to increase the likelihood of the clustering. The following HLA-B alleles remain unclassified: B17, B*1801, B22, B37, B*3905, B42, B45 (two sequences in SYFPEITHI, both with E in position 2), and B*5301. Only one or two sequences were found in SYFPEITHI for these alleles, except for B17, where five sequences were found.

13.2.5   Do Cross-Loci Supertypes Exist?

The alleles within the supertypes defined by Sette and Sidney [1999] are all encoded by either the A or the B locus. Making a tree of all the HLA-A and HLA-B alleles included in the analysis described above, no mixing of the HLA-A and HLA-B clusters is found. Only the outliers HLA-B*1516 and HLA-A*2902 mix with a cluster defined by the opposite locus. The HLA-B*1516 allele clusters within the A1 supertype consistent with a preference for T and S at position 2, and a preference for Y, F, L, and V at position 9. The HLA-A2902 allele clusters within the B44 supertype consistent with a preference for E at position

2 and a preference for Y in position 9 found in both motifs. The A*2902 molecule used for elution of peptides is often purified from the Ebstein-Barr virus-transformed cell line SWEIG which coexpresses B*4402, and the apparent similarity may be an experimental artifact caused by cross-reactivity of the antibody used for purification from this cell line. This unrelatedness of HLA-A and HLA-B molecules may be a direct result of evolutionary pressure on the immune system to provide optimal protection against infectious diseases. To obtain optimal peptide coverage, it is beneficial for the immune system to have a highly diverse set of HLA specificities. A simple way to achieve this could be to have the HLA-A and HLA-B alleles evolve in an orthogonal manner.

13.2.6 HLA-DR

For most class II molecules relatively few binding peptides are known. To compensate for that the similarities between different alleles are calculated, based on other published specificity matrices. Specificity matrices for HLA class II molecules can be downloaded from, e.g., the ProPred website (http://www.imtech.res.in/raghava/propred/page4.html). The list of alleles is given in table 13.2. These matrices were constructed by Singh and Raghava [2001] using the TEPITOPE (http://www.vaccinome.com) method [Hammer et al., 1994, Sturniolo et al., 1999].

   To test whether the matrices in the ProPred server are similar to those in the TEPITOPE program, test sequences can be submitted to both programs as well as to a program using the matrices from ProPred. The matrix scores are used to estimate the amino acid frequencies at different positions in the motif, assuming that the matrix score is proportional to a log-odds score. The odds score is defined as the probability of observing amino acid a in position p in a binding peptide relative to the probability of observing that amino acid in proteins in general. Thus,

$$p_{pa} = \frac{\exp(s_{pa})q_a}{\sum_i \exp(s_{pi})q_i}, \qquad (13.2)$$

where s_{pa} is the matrix score of amino acid a on position p, and q_a is the background frequency of the amino acid.

   Sequence logos were constructed to visualize the specificities. By visual inspection of different HLA class II molecules (figure 13.5) it is clear that some of these are quite similar. In order to quantify the similarities, the distance between all pairs of matrices was calculated. These distances were then used to construct a tree visualizing the similarities between the peptides that each allele binds (figure 13.6). Based on this tree, the HLA-DR molecules are divided into nine clusters or supertypes. The clusters may be represented by

Allele	Sero type	Pocket profile	Supertype
HLA-DRB1*0101	DR1	[1;1;1;1;1]	1
HLA-DRB1*0102	DR1	[2;1;1;1;1]	1
HLA-DRB1*0301	DR3	[2;3;3;3;2]	3
HLA-DRB1*0305	DR3	[1;3;3;3;3]	3
HLA-DRB1*0306	DR3	[2;3;3;4;3]	3
HLA-DRB1*0307	DR3	[2;3;3;4;3]	3
HLA-DRB1*0308	DR3	[2;3;3;4;3]	3
HLA-DRB1*0309	DR3	[1;3;3;3;2]	3
HLA-DRB1*0311	DR3	[2;3;3;4;3]	3
HLA-DRB1*0401	DR4	[1;4;4;4;3]	4
HLA-DRB1*0402	DR4	[2;5;4;5;3]	4
HLA-DRB1*0404	DR4	[2;6;4;6;3]	4
HLA-DRB1*0405	DR4	[1;6;4;6;5]	4
HLA-DRB1*0408	DR4	[1;6;4;6;3]	4
HLA-DRB1*0410	DR4	[2;6;4;6;5]	4
HLA-DRB1*0421	DR4	[1;4;4;4;2]	4
HLA-DRB1*0423	DR4	[2;6;4;6;3]	4
HLA-DRB1*0426	DR4	[1;4;4;4;3]	4
HLA-DRB1*0701	DR7	[1;8;5;8;4]	7
HLA-DRB1*0703	DR7	[1;8;5;8;4]	7
HLA-DRB1*0801	DR8	[1;9;3;9;5]	8
HLA-DRB1*0802	DR8	[1;9;3;9;3]	8
HLA-DRB1*0804	DR8	[2;9;3;9;3]	8
HLA-DRB1*0806	DR8	[2;9;3;9;5]	8
HLA-DRB1*0813	DR8	[1;9;3;6;3]	8
HLA-DRB1*0817	DR8	[1;9;3;7;5]	8
HLA-DRB1*1101	DR11	[1;7;3;7;3]	11
HLA-DRB1*1102	DR11	[2;11;3;11;3]	13
HLA-DRB1*1104	DR11	[2;7;3;7;3]	11
HLA-DRB1*1106	DR11	[2;7;3;7;3]	11
HLA-DRB1*1107	DR11	[2;3;3;3;3]	3
HLA-DRB1*1114	DR11	[1;11;3;11;3]	13
HLA-DRB1*1120	DR11	[1;11;3;11;2]	13
HLA-DRB1*1121	DR11	[2;11;3;11;3]	13
HLA-DRB1*1128	DR11	[1;7;3;7;2]	11
HLA-DRB1*1301	DR13	[2;11;3;11;2]	13
HLA-DRB1*1302	DR13	[1;11;3;11;2]	13
HLA-DRB1*1304	DR13	[2;11;3;11;5]	13
HLA-DRB1*1305	DR13	[1;7;3;7;2]	11
HLA-DRB1*1307	DR13	[1;7;3;9;3]	11
HLA-DRB1*1311	DR13	[2;7;3;7;3]	11
HLA-DRB1*1321	DR13	[1;7;3;7;5]	11
HLA-DRB1*1322	DR13	[2;11;3;11;3]	13
HLA-DRB1*1323	DR13	[1;11;3;11;3]	13
HLA-DRB1*1327	DR13	[2;11;3;11;2]	13
HLA-DRB1*1328	DR13	[2;11;3;11;2]	13
HLA-DRB1*1501	DR2	[2;2;2;2;1]	15
HLA-DRB1*1502	DR2	[1;2;2;2;1]	15
HLA-DRB1*1506	DR2	[2;2;2;2;1]	15
HLA-DRB5*0101	DR2	[1;10;6;10;6]	51
HLA-DRB5*0105	DR2	[1;10;6;10;6]	51

Table 13.2: A list of the HLA class II alleles used. The list contains the allele, serotype (Type), pocket profile, and our supertype assignment. The pocket profiles used in assembly of virtual DR matrices are from Sturniolo et al. [1999]. For each allele the list of numbers in square parenthesis denotes which pocket specificity has been used to construct the profile for position 1, 4, 6, 7, and 9 (positions 2 and 3 were derived from the DRB1*0401 matrix). The matrix for HLA-DRB1*0421 could not be found at the ProPred website (http://www.imtech.res.in/raghava/propred/page4.html) when the work was done. Table adopted from Lund et al. [2004].

DRB1*0101 (1, 0.92), DRB1*0301 (3, 0.65), DRB1*0401 (4, 0.45), DRB1*0701 (7, 1.0), DRB1*0813 (8, 0.52), DRB1*1101 (11, 0.32), DRB1*1301 (13, 0.39), DRB1*1501 (15, 0.82), and DRB5*0101 (51, 0.95). Here the numbers in parentheses after each allele name correspond to the supertype name assigned to each cluster in figure 13.5, and the cluster bootstrap branch value, respectively. The alleles in figure 13.5 are colored according to the serotype.

The clustering roughly corresponds to the serotype classification, but with some important exceptions. Note, e.g., the mixing of the DR11, and DR13 sequences and that DRB1*1107 clusters with the DR3 sequences. The bootstrap value for the DR11 and DR13 serotype clusters are, e.g., < 0.001 and the bootstrap value for the DR3 serotype cluster, excluding the DRB1*1107 allele, is 0.03. The matrices were constructed under the assumption that the amino acids at different positions contribute independently (by binding to a pocket in the HLA molecule) to the binding of the peptide. Furthermore, it is also assumed that HLA molecules with the same amino acids in a given pocket will have the same specificity profile [Hammer et al., 1997]. Different matrices thus have the same profile at a given position if the corresponding HLA molecules share the amino acids lining the pocket for that position. In table 13.2 it can be seen that DRB1*1107 and DRB1*0305 only differ in one binding pocket. This is hence consistent with placing the DRB1*1107 allele in the DR3 supertype. Similarly, it seems that the alleles placed in the DR11 and DR13 supertypes in most cases share three out of the five pocket specificities.

13.2.7 Experimental Verification of Supertypes

To verify the clustering suggested above, weight matrices for all the class I alleles in this study were constructed as earlier described. These weight matrices can then be used to *predict* the binding affinity for sets of peptides, where the binding affinity to a specific HLA allele had been *measured* experimentally. Alleles for which experimental binding information is available are, e.g., HLA-A*0101 (A1), HLA-A0202 (A2), HLA-A*0301 (A3), HLA-A*1101 (A3), HLA-A*3101 (A3 outlier), HLA-B*2705 (B27), HLA-B*1501 (B62), HLA-B*5801 (B58), and HLA-B*0702 (B7) [Sylvester-Hvid et al., 2004]. Here the name written in parentheses refers to the supertype classification. The linear correlation coefficient, also known as Pearson's r [Press et al., 1992], is calculated between the prediction score and the log of the measured binding affinity. It is now expected that alleles with similar specificity to that of the allele used in the experiments will obtain a positive correlation, and that other alleles will get a correlation close to zero. This calculation actually supports most of the results obtained from the clustering analysis [Lund et al., 2004].

One of the advantages with this kind of clustering is that it can easily be

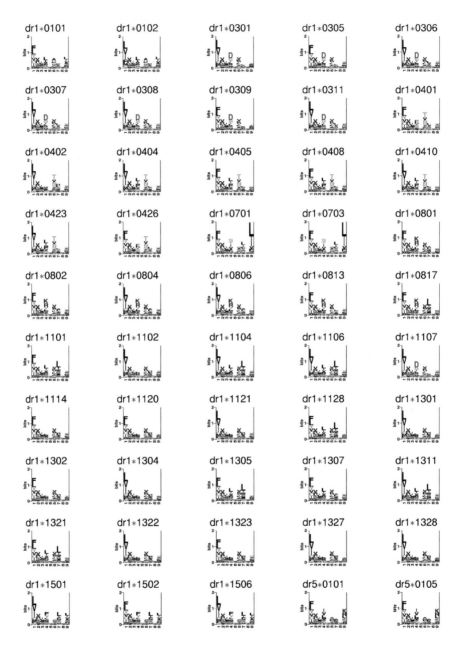

Figure 13.5: Logos displaying the binding motifs for 50 different HLA class II molecules. For details of the logo representation, see figure 13.1. Figure reprinted from Lund et al. [2004]. See plate 27 for color version.

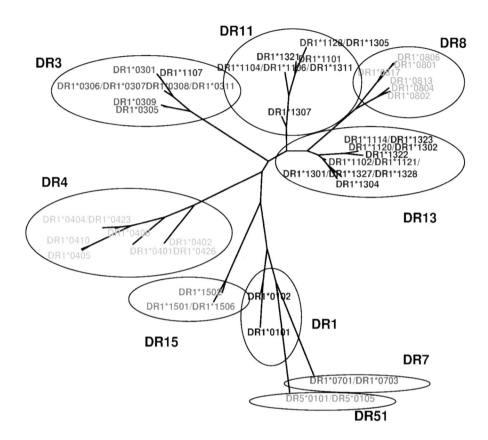

Figure 13.6: Tree showing the clustering of 50 different HLA class II molecules based on their peptide-binding specificity. The proposed clusters are encircled and labeled. Figure reprinted from Lund et al. [2004]. See plate 28 for color version.

recalculated if new data become available in the future. The availability of data is expected to increase as the epitope immune database, and several large-scale epitope discovery projects funded by the NIH have been started. Additional material is available at:

http://www.cbs.dtu.dk/researchgroups/immunology/supertypes.html

and will be updated whenever new data become available.

The clusters define groups of alleles with similar binding specificities. In order to get a broad coverage of the human population with an epitope-based vaccine, it must be ensured that most people from all ethnic groups have an HLA molecule with specificity for at least one of the peptides in the vaccine.

This can in turn be obtained making sure that the specificity defined by each cluster is covered by one peptide in the vaccine.

Chapter 14

Predicting Immunogenicity: An Integrative Approach

The genome era provides opportunities to study the immune system from a systems biology perspective as discussed in chapter 1. We now have not only the sequence information that sheds light on the immunological diversity among individuals in a population but also advanced techniques that allow us to obtain a better estimate of the kinetics and specificity of an immune response. In this chapter we will give an example of such systems biology approaches to immunology: prediction of immunogenic regions for cytotoxic T cells. A very similar study is published by Larsen et al. [2005].

Reliable prediction of immunogenic peptides may be useful for many applications, e.g., for rational vaccine design. Many attempts have been made to predict the outcome of the steps involved in antigen presentation. As we have described earlier in the book, a number of methods have been developed that very reliably predict the binding affinity of peptides to the different MHC-I alleles [Brusic et al., 1994, Buus et al., 2003, Nielsen et al., 2003, 2004]. Likewise, a method has been developed that predicts the efficiency by which peptides of arbitrary length can be transported by TAP [Peters et al., 2003a]. Several methods have also been developed that aim at predicting the proteasomal cleavage pattern of proteins (see chapter 7 for details).

Can predictions of proteasomal cleavage patterns and TAP transport efficiency contribute to an improved identification of epitopes compared to that obtained when using only predictions of MHC-I affinity? Peters et al. [2003a] have shown that combining MHC-I affinity predictions with prediction of TAP transport efficiency leads to improved identification of CTL epitopes. This analysis can be extended to address, for a large set of different HLA alleles, if a combined prediction method mimicking the MHC I pathway can improve prediction of epitopes. The following analysis includes epitopes from close to 70 different MHC alleles from different MHC-I supertypes [Sette and Sidney, 1999, Lund et al., 2004]. The proteasomal cleavage event were modeled by prediction algorithms as described in chapter 7.

To validate the integrative method, a data set (SYF) containing 152 9mer epitopes restricted to more than 70 different HLA alleles extracted from the SYFPEITHI database (http://syfpeithi.bmi-heidelberg.com/) are uesd. The majority of these peptides have successfully passed the steps involved in antigen presentation. The set of negative peptides (peptides that will not be presented by the MHC class I pathway) were defined as all 9mer peptides contained in the protein sequences from which the epitopes originated, except those annotated as epitopes in either the complete SYFPEITHI or Los Alamos HIV databases (www.hiv.lanl.gov/immunology. When using this definition of epitopes/nonepitopes one has to take into account that some 9mers will falsely be classified as nonepitopes because the SYFPEITHI and Los Alamos HIV databases are incomplete. Since the HLA molecules have a very specific peptide binding repertoire, this false-negative proportion will be very small. In a protein of 200 amino acids, one expects to have one binding, and approximately 199 nonbinding peptides [Yewdell and Bennink, 1999]. The potential number of false negatives is hence orders of magnitude smaller than the actual number of negatives.

14.1   Combination of MHC and Proteasome Predictions

To examine whether predictions of proteasomal cleavage can contribute to the classification of peptides into epitopes/nonepitopes independently of the predicted MHC-I binding affinity, one option is to perform a sort/split experiment: two groups of peptides with approximately equal predicted MHC-I affinity, but different predicted proteasomal cleavage, is generated. All 9mer peptides in each protein is individually sorted according to their predicted MHC-I affinity. Looking at two peptides at a time from the top of the sorted list, they are then split into two groups and the peptide with highest predicted proteasomal cleavage value is put in group H, whereas the peptide with the lowest is put in group L. Figure 14.1 shows, for four different methods predicting proteasomal cleavage, how the number of epitopes in the H group deviates from the expected number (50%).

To test if the number of epitopes is significantly different in group H as compared to group L, the binomial distribution is applied. Under the null hypothesis, the epitopes have an equal chance of falling into either group, $\pi_0 = 0.5$. If n is the total number of epitopes, the expected number of epitopes in either group is $\pi_0 \, n$. If r is the observed number of epitopes in one of the groups, the departure from the expected number can be expressed by the z-score [Armitage et al., 2004]:

$$z = \frac{r - n\pi_0}{\sqrt{n\pi(1 - \pi)}}. \tag{14.1}$$

The nullhypothesis is rejected at $p = .05$ if $z > 1.96$, at $p = .01$ if $z > 2.58$, and at $p = .001$ if $z > 3.29$.

All four proteasomal cleavage methods the number of epitopes is significantly higher in group H than in group L. The method with the poorest performance is that of NetChop 20S with a p-value just below .01. The other three methods all separate the H from the L group with p-values below or close to .001. For NetChop 2.0, for example, 34% or 72% more epitopes are found in the H group. Figure 14.1 also shows that the predicted cleavage patterns of the internal amino acids add very little extra information to the predicted MHC-I affinity. When using NetChop 2.0 or NetChop 3.0 to study the predicted cleavage at position 1, only 38% and 39%, respectively, of the epitopes are located in group H. This may indicate that peptides with a high predicted proteasomal cleavage value at this position are rarely epitopes. If, however, the NetChop 20S or NetChop 20S-3.0 network is used, this scenario is reversed.

Applying the bootstrap [Press et al., 1992] method you find that the NetChop 20S method performs significantly worse than the other methods ($p < .05$ in all three comparisons). The difference in predictive performance between the other methods is, however, statistically insignificant ($p > .05$ in all cases). Thus, this analysis demonstrates that only the methods based on *in vivo* cleavage data can improve the identification of epitopes in combination with the predicted MHC-I affinity.

14.2 Independent Contributions from TAP and Proteasome Predictions

To address the question of whether proteasomal cleavage and TAP transport efficiency can contribute independently to the identification of epitopes a sort/split experiment sorting on TAP transport efficiency and splitting on proteasomal cleavage was conducted. When examining if cleavage predictions can contribute to the identification of epitopes independently of the predicted TAP transport efficiency, two groups of peptides with close to equal TAP transport efficiency, but different predicted proteasomal cleavage, were generated using the same method as described in the previous section. In this experiment the two groups H and L thus have similar TAP transport efficiency, but very different predicted proteasomal cleavage values. The result of the analysis is

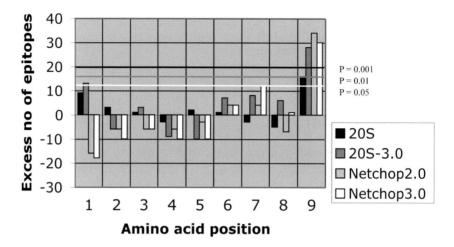

Figure 14.1: Sort/split experiment conducted sorting on predicted MHC-I affinity, splitting on predicted proteasomal cleavage. Two groups with close to equal MHC-I affinity, but with different predicted proteasomal cleavage. In total, the two groups contain 152 epitopes. The figure shows the number of epitopes in group H deviating from the expected number of 76 (50%) L. 1-9: position 1-9 of the peptide (9 is the C-terminal end). Four different methods have been used for predicting proteasomal cleavage: NetChop 20S, NetChop 20S-3.0, NetChop2.0, and NetChop3.0. Also shown are lines indicating levels of significance estimated as described in the text.

shown in figure 14.2, where NetChop 3.0 has been used for the proteasomal cleavage predictions. The figure shows how the number of epitopes in the H group deviates from the expected number (50%). In combination with TAP transport efficiency only, the predicted C-terminal cleavage can contribute significantly to the identification of the epitopes. There is an excess number of 30 epitopes between the H and L groups, corresponding to 70%. This result demonstrates that not all TAP transported peptides are cleaved equally well by the proteasome. Between two groups of peptides with equal TAP transport efficiencies, epitopes are found predominantly in the group with high proteasomal C-terminal cleavage.

Next a sort/split experiment sorting on MHC-I affinity and splitting on TAP transport efficiency is conducted to investigate if TAP transport efficiency and MHC-I binding can contribute independently to the identification of epitopes. In the experiment, most epitopes (66%, $p < .001$) fall into the group with high TAP transport efficiency. Among peptides with similar MHC-I affinity, peptides with high TAP transport efficiency are thus most likely to be epitopes.

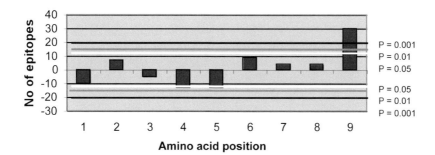

Figure 14.2: Sort/split experiment conducted sorting on predicted TAP transport efficiency, splitting on predicted proteasomal cleavage. Proteasomal cleavage is predicted using the method of NetChop 3.0. Two groups with close to equal predicted TAP transport efficiency, but with different predicted proteasomal cleavage. In total, the two groups contain 152 epitopes. The figure shows the number of epitopes in group H deviating from the expected number of 76 (50%). 1-9: position 1-9 of the peptide (9 is the C-terminal end). Also shown are lines indicating levels of significance.

14.3   Combinations of MHC, TAP, and Proteasome Predictions

A combined prediction score for MHC-I affinity, proteasomal C-terminal cleavage, and TAP transport efficiency can be defined as a weighted sum of the three individual prediction scores. We use an MHC-I affinity rescaled prediction values; TAP prediction method of [Peters et al., 2003a], and the NetChop 2.0 and 3.0 predictors described in chapter 7.

Two nonparametric performance measures are used to evaluate the performance of the combined methods. One measure is the conventional A_{ROC} value (the area under the receiver operator characteristics [ROC] curve) [Swets, 1988]. In this measure, all overlapping 9mer peptides in the SYF data set were sorted according to the prediction score. The epitopes define the positive set, whereas the negative set is made from all other 9mers, excluding 9mers present in the SYFPEITHI or the Los Alamos databases. In a typical calculation, the positive set contains 152 peptides, and the negative set more than 92,000 peptides.

The ROC curve is plotted from the sensitivity and 1-specificity values calculated by varying the cut-off value (separating the predicted positive from the predicted negative) from high to low. The A_{ROC} value is 0.5 for a random prediction method and 1.0 for a perfect method. Even though commonly used, the A_{ROC} measure is not easy to interpret intuitively. A second performance measure with a clear and intuitive interpretation is a rank measure: for each protein in the benchmark, all 9mer peptides are sorted based on the prediction score. A given protein may appear more than once in the benchmark if it contains more than one epitope. The rank value for the protein is calculated as the number of nonepitopes with a score higher than that of the corresponding epitope. From these rank values a rank curve showing the accumulative fraction of proteins with a rank value below a certain value was constructed. From the rank curve one can then extract information on how large a fraction of the proteins will have the epitope within a rank of, e.g., 25. Finally, a single performance measure (A_{RANK}) as the area under the rank curve integrated from rank zero up to rank 100 was defined. A perfect prediction method will have all the epitopes as rank 1, and thus an A_{RANK} value of 1.0, whereas a poor method will have the epitopes well below rank 100 and hence an A_{RANK} value of 0.0. Examples of a ROC and a rank curve are shown in figure 14.3. For both the A_{ROC} and A_{RANK} performance measures, one should be aware that some 9mers will falsely be classified as nonepitopes because the SYFPEITHI and Los Alamos HIV databases are incomplete.

The SYF data set is used to estimate the set of weights where the A_{RANK} and A_{ROC} values are optimal. Next the optimal combined prediction scheme is applied to an HIV data set of 69 epitopes derived from the Los Alamos HIV database to estimate the performance gain on an independent evaluation data set.

The optimal combined method is found to have relative weights on C-terminal cleavage and TAP transport efficiency of 0.15 and 0.115, respectively. In figure 14.3, we show examples of ROC and rank curves for the SYF data set. The figure shows the performance curves for five different prediction scoring schemes: Comb, MHC, TAP, NetChop 2.0, and NetChop 3.0. Here, the Comb method is the combined method with relative weight on TAP and NetChop 3.0 of 0.115 and 0.15, respectively, while others are single predictions. In figure 14.4, we give the details of the performance measures for the different methods and their combinations.

The curves shown in figure 14.3 clearly highlight the problematic aspects of using the A_{ROC} performance measure when dealing with highly unbalanced data sets. The A_{ROC} values for the NetChop 3.0 and TAP prediction methods are close to identical (see figure 14.4). However, looking at the ROC curves for each method, it is clear that the NetChop 3.0 method provides the most useful predictions. The region of the ROC curve where the TAP predictor performs best falls in a highly nonrelevant region of the specificity. The two curves cross at a false-positive ratio of 0.4. This value corresponds to 40% false-positive predictions, and having an improved prediction method only in this specificity range is clearly irrelevant. For the rank curves this problem is not present, and

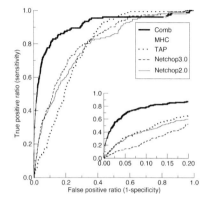 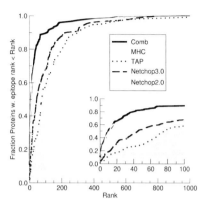

Figure 14.3: ROC and rank performance curves for different prediction methods. Left: the ROC curves. Right: rank curves. A_{RANK} is the area under the rank curve (highlighted as the shaded area under the TAP curve) as described in the text. Predictions are made on the SYF data set. The different prediction methods are; Comb: optimal combined method with relative weight on C-terminal cleavage and TAP transport efficiency of 0.15 and 0.115, respectively; MHC: MHC-I affinity; TAP: TAP transport efficiency; NetChop 3.0: C-terminal cleavage by NetChop; NetChop 2.0: C-terminal cleavage by NetChop 2.0. The inserts to the figures show high specificity/high rank, part of the corresponding curves.

we can directly identify the most relevant method from the integrated A_{RANK} value.

The results shown in figures 14.3 and 14.4 demonstrate that the combined method integrating prediction of proteasomal cleavage, TAP transport, and MHC affinity has the highest performance in terms of both the A_{ROC} and A_{RANK} values. The individual method with the poorest performance is that of NetChop 20S, followed by NetChop 20S-3.0, TAP, the NetChop 2.0 and NetChop 3.0 methods, and MHC-I affinity.

What is also clear from the results shown is that the combined method has a predictive performance superior to that of both MHC-I affinity alone and any method integrating prediction of MHC-I affinity with TAP transport efficiency or C-terminal proteasomal cleavage. The performance values for MHC, MHC+TAP, MHC+NetChop 3.0, and the combined method are 0.88, 0.90, 0.90, 0.91 for A_{ROC} and 0.70, 0.75, 0.73, 0.76 for A_{RANK} respectively. Comparing the performance values for the combined method to that of MHC-I, MHC-I+TAP, and MHC-I+NetChop 3.0, we find the following bootstrap hypothesis test values: <0.01, <0.01, <0.01 and 0.025, <0.01, <0.01 for A_{ROC} and

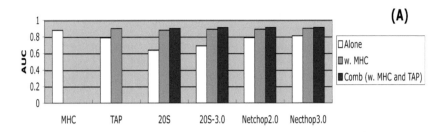

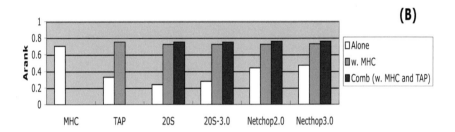

Figure 14.4: Predictive performance for different prediction methods: A_{ROC} (upper panel) and A_{RANK} (lower panel). Predictions are made on the SYF data set. The figure shows for each prediction method the performance measures for each method on its own, the optimal performance in combination with MHC affinity predictions, and the optimal performance in combination with TAP transport efficiency and MHC affinity predictions.

A_{RANK}, respectively. However, we see no significant difference between the combined methods integrating predictions from any of the three proteasomal cleavage prediction methods: NetChop 20S-3.0, NetChop 2.0, or NetChop 3.0. This analysis indeed shows that the combined method performs significantly better than all other methods in the comparison.

It is striking to observe that in combination with MHC-I affinity the TAP predictor provides more additional information useful for epitope identification than any of the NetChop predictors. The MHC-I+TAP predictor has A_{RANK} and A_{ROC} values of 0.75 and 0.90, respectively, whereas the values for MHC-I+NetChop 3.0 are 0.73 and 0.89. Using the bootstrap experiment, we find that these values are significantly different ($p < .05$).

Another interesting finding is that even though the different NetChop predictors, except NetChop 20S, individually have very different predictive performance, they achieve the same predictive performance when combined with MHC-I affinity predictions. In combination with MHC-I affinity predictions, NetChop 20S-3.0, NetChop 2.0, and NetChop 3.0 all have performance values close to 0.90 and 0.73 for A_{ROC} and A_{RANK}, respectively, and the individual performance differences are statistically significant. Finally, we also found that the NetChop 20S-3.0 and TAP predictors can be combined in a constructive manner with a predictive performance significantly higher than that of the individual predictors. This is, however, not the case for the NetChop 3.0 predictor. Here the combination with TAP only leads to a minor and insignificant improvement in the predictive performance (data not shown). This analysis suggests that the NetChop predictor trained on epitope data does indeed predict a combination of MHC-I affinity, TAP transport efficiency, and proteasomal cleavage rather than just proteasomal cleavage. As an individual prediction method for epitope recognition, the NetChop method trained on epitope data clearly outperforms the methods trained on in vitro degradation data. However, when combined with MHC-I affinity and TAP transport efficiency predictions both the epitope and in vitro trained methods achieve similar performance.

A direct measure of the performance gain when comparing the combined method to that of MHC-I affinity prediction alone is the rank number needed in order to identify 75% of the epitopes in the benchmark. For the MHC-I affinity predictions alone this rank number is 55, meaning that in a set of proteins one will have to test 55 peptides from each protein in order to identify 75% of the epitopes. For the combined method this number has dropped to 30. Even though this number is still high, the performance gain is clearly notable.

14.4   Validation on HIV Data Set

The above analysis can be done for indivual pathogens, like HIV. The results of such an analysis are shown in figure 14.5 and confirm the findings from the SYF data set. The combined method has a performance superior to that of all the individual methods. The TAP transport predictor has the poorest performance, followed by that of NetChop 3.0. Estimating the rank number needed in order to identify 75% of the epitopes in the benchmark, we find values of 52 and 30 for the MHC-I predictor alone and the combined method, respectively. These numbers thus confirm the values found when using the SYF data set. A direct implication of this performance gain is a twofold reduction in the experimental efforts needed to identify 75% of the epitopes in a large set of proteins.

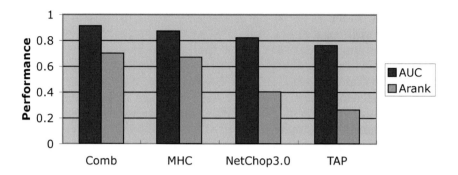

Figure 14.5: Performance for different prediction methods. Predictions are made on the HIV data set. The figure shows the predictive performance for the three individual prediction methods of MHC, C-terminal cleavage (NetChop 3.0), and TAP, as well as the combined method (Comb) with relative weight on C-terminal cleavage and TAP transport efficiency of 0.15 and 0.115, respectively.

14.5   Perspectives on Data Integration

In this chapter, we have demonstrated how an integrative approach combining predictions of the proteasomal cleavage, TAP transport efficiency, and MHC-I affinity can lead to improved CTL epitope recognition.

Other groups have previously combined different prediction methods: Hakenberg et al. [2003] developed a bioinformatical tool for prediction of CTL epitopes by combining prediction of proteasomal cleavage and MHC affinity. On a very small data set of only five epitopes from HIV-1 Nef, Kesmir et al. [2002] showed that combining predictions of proteasomal cleavage with measured TAP and MHC-I binding affinity correlates well with the observed number of MHC-I ligands presented on the cell. In another study, Peters et al. [2003a] improved identification of epitopes by combining predictions of binding affinities to the HLA-A*0201 allele with predictions of TAP transport efficiency. They also combined HLA-A*0201 affinity predictions with predictions of C-terminal cleavages by NetChop 20S, but this led to a less accurate identification of epitopes. What is novel about the analysis given in this chapter is the broad set of MHC-I (70 different alleles) specificities used. This allows us to (1) draw more general and well-founded conclusions about how to integrate the different steps in the class I pathway in an optimal manner, and (2) derive a prediction method that is broadly applicable to the identification of CTL epitopes.

Concern has previously been raised that the NetChop methods, which have been trained on natural MHC-I ligand data, do not only predict proteasomal cleavage but rather a combination of cleavage, TAP transport, and affinity to the average MHC-I allele [Peters et al., 2003a]. We find that when predicting CTL epitopes, the NetChop method trained on epitope data outperforms the methods trained on in vitro degradation data. However, in combination with MHC-I affinity and TAP transport efficiency predictions, both methods trained on *in vitro* digest data and MHC ligands, respectively, show similar performance. This leads to the conclusion that the high performance of the NetChop method trained on epitope data does not come from more accurate prediction of the proteasomal cleavage but rather from indirect integration of TAP transport efficiency and MHC-I affinity. However, this observation also leaves promise for future improvements to CTL epitope predictions, since it should be possible to improve at least the proteasomal cleavage prediction accuracy by developing a method describing the differences between the immuno proteasome and the constitutive proteasome cleavage specificities, and thereby improve the accuracy of the integrative method.

References

H. P. Adams and J. A. Koziol. Prediction of binding to MHC class I molecules. *J. Immunol. Methods*, 185:181–190, 1995.

C. S. Adamson and I. M. Jones. The molecular basis of HIV capsid assembly–five years of progress. *Rev. Med. Virol.*, 14:107–121, 2004.

A. Agrawal, Q. M. Eastman, and D. G. Schatz. Transposition mediated by RAG1 and RAG2 and its implications for the evolution of the immune system. *Nature*, 394: 744–751, 1998.

M. E. Alarcon-Riquelme and L. Prokunina. Finding genes for SLE: complex interactions and complex populations. *J. Autoimmun.*, 21:117–120, 2003.

C. Alexander, A. B. Kay, and M. Larche. Peptide-based vaccines in the treatment of specific allergy. *Curr. Drug. Targets Inflamm. Allergy*, 1:353–361, 2002.

A. J. Alix. Predictive estimation of protein linear epitopes by using the program PEOPLE. *Vaccine*, 18:311–314, 1999.

S. F. Altschul and W. Gish. Local alignment statistics. *Methods Enzymol.*, 266:460–480, 1996.

S. F. Altschul, W. Gish, W. Miller, E.W. Myers, and D.J. Lipman. Basic local alignment search tool. *J. Mol. Biol.*, 215:403–410, 1990.

S. F. Altschul, T. L. Madden, A. A. Schaffer, J. Zhang, Z. Zhang, W. Miller, and D. J. Lipman. Gapped blast and psi-blast: a new generation of protein database search programs. *Nucleic Acids Res.*, 25:3389–3402, 1997.

Y. Altuvia and H. Margalit. Sequence signals for generation of antigenic peptides by the proteasome: implications for proteasomal cleavage mechanism. *J. Mol. Biol.*, 295:879–890, 2000.

Y. Altuvia, O. Schueler, and H. Margalit. Ranking potential binding peptides to MHC molecules by a computational threading approach. *J. Mol. Biol*, 149:244–250, 1995.

255

F. E. André. The future of vaccines, immunisation concepts and practice. *Vaccine*, 19: 2206–2209, 2001.

F. E. André. How the research-based industry approaches vaccine development and establishes priorities. *Dev. Biol (Basel)*, 110:25–29, 2002.

F. E. André. Vaccinology: past achievements, present roadblocks and future promises. *Vaccine*, 21:593–595, 2003.

A. N. Antoniou and C. Watts. Antibody modulation of antigen presentation: positive and negative effects on presentation of the tetanus toxin antigen via the murine B cell isoform of FcgammaRII. *Eur. J. Immunol.*, 32:530–540, 2002.

K. Aoki. A criterion for the establishment of a stable polymorphism of higher order with an application to the evolution of polymorphism. *J. Math. Biol.*, 9:133–146, 1980.

V. Apanius, D. Penn, P. R. Slev, L. R. Ruff, and W. K. Potts. The nature of selection on the major histocompatibility complex. *Crit. Rev. Immunol.*, 17:179–224, 1997.

P. Armitage, G. Berry, and J. N. S. Matthews. *Statistical Methods in Medical research.* Blackwell, Malden, MA, 2004.

S. O. Arndt, A. B. Vogt, S. Markovic-Plese, R. Martin, G. Moldenhauer, A. Wolpl, Y. Sun, D. Schadendorf, G. J. Hammerling, and H. Kropshofer. Functional HLA-DM on the surface of B cells and immature dendritic cells. *EMBO J.*, 19:1241–1251, 2000.

B. Arunachalam, U. T. Phan, H. J. Geuze, and P. Cresswell. Enzymatic reduction of disulfide bonds in lysosomes: characterization of a gamma-interferon-inducible lysosomal thiol reductase (GILT). *Proc. Natl. Acad. Sci. U.S.A.*, 97:745–750, 2000.

S. B. Athauda and K. Takahashi. Distinct cleavage specificity of human cathepsin E at neutral pH with special preference for Arg-Arg bonds. *Protein Pept. Lett.*, 9:15–22, 2002.

A. Bairoch and R. Apweiler. The SWISS-PROT protein sequence database and its supplement TrEMBL in 2000. *Nucleic Acids Res*, 28:45–48, 2000.

P. Baldi and S. Brunak. *Bioinformatics: The Machine Learning Approach.* MIT Press, Cambridge, MA, 2001. 2nd ed.

J. R. Baldridge, T. S. McGraw, A. Paoletti, and M. J. Buchmeier. Antibody prevents the establishment of persistent arenavirus infection in synergy with endogenous T cells. *J. Virol.*, 71:755–758, 1997.

D. J. Barlow, M. S. Edwards, and J. M. Thornton. Continuous and discontinuous protein antigenic determinants. *Nature*, 322:747–718, 1986.

V. Barnaba, A. Franco, A. Alberti, R. Benvenuto, and F. Balsano. Selective killing of hepatitis B envelope antigen-specific B cells by class I-restricted, exogenous antigen-specific T lymphocytes. *Nature*, 345:258–260, 1990.

A. J. Barrett and N. D. Rawlings. Evolutionary lines of cysteine peptidases. *Biol. Chem.*, 382:727–733, 2001.

M. Battegay, D. Moskophidis, H. Waldner, M. A. Brundler, W. P. Fung-Leung, T. W. Mak, H. Hengartner, and R. M. Zinkernagel. Impairment and delay of neutralizing antiviral antibody responses by virus-specific cytotoxic T cells. *J. Immunol.*, 151:5408–5415, 1993.

H. Beck, G. Schwarz, C. J. Schroter, M. Deeg, D. Baier, S. Stevanovic, E. Weber, C. Driessen, and H. Kalbacher. Cathepsin S and an asparagine-specific endoprotease dominate the proteolytic processing of human myelin basic protein in vitro. *Eur. J. Immunol.*, 31:3726–3736, 2001.

N. J. Beekman, P. A. van Veelen, T. van Hall, A. Neisig, A. Sijts, M. Camps, P. M. Kloetzel, J. J. Neefjes, C. J. Melief, and F. Ossendorp. Abrogation of CTL epitope processing by single amino acid substitution flanking the C-terminal proteasome cleavage site. *J. Immunol.*, 164:1898–1905, 2000.

J. B. Beltman, J. A. M. Borghans, and R. J. de Boer. Major histocompatibility complex: Polymorphism from coevolution. In U. Dieckmann, H. Metz, M. Sabelis, and K. Sigmund, editors, *Adaptive Dynamics of Infectious Diseases. In Pursuit of Virulence Management*, volume 2 of *Cambridge Studies in Adaptive Dynamics*, pages 185–197. Cambridge University Press, Cambridge, UK, 2002.

D. A. Benson, I Karsch-Mizrachi, D. J. Lipman, J. Ostell, B. A. Rapp, and D. L. Wheeler. Genbank. *Nucleic Acids Res.*, 30:17–20, 2002.

C. Berek, A. Berger, and M. Apel. Maturation of the immune response in germinal centers. *Cell*, 67:1121–1129, 1991.

C. Berek and C. Milstein. Mutation drift and repertoire shift in the maturation of the immune response. *Immunol. Rev.*, 96:23–41, 1987.

A. Berger and I. Schechter. Mapping the active site of papain with the aid of peptide substrates and inhibitors. *Philos. Trans. R. Soc. Lond. B. Biol. Sci.*, 257:249–264, 1970.

E. A. Berger, B. Moss, and I. Pastan. Reconsidering targeted toxins to eliminate HIV infection: you gotta have HAART. *Proc. Natl. Acad. Sci. U. S. A.*, 95:11511–11513, 1998.

A. G. Betz, M. S. Neuberger, and C. Milstein. Discriminating intrinsic and antigen-selected mutational hotspots in immunoglobulin V genes. *Immunol. Today*, 14:405–411, 1993.

B. Beutler and E. T. Rietschel. Innate immune sensing and its roots: the story of endotoxin. *Nat. Rev. Immunol.*, 3:169-176, 2003.

M. Bhasin and G. P. Raghava. Analysis and prediction of affinity of TAP binding peptides using cascade SVM. *Protein Sci.*, 13:596-607, 2004.

M. Bhasin, H. Singh, and G. P. S. Raghava. MHCBN: A comprehensive database of MHC binding and non-binding peptides. *Bioinformatics*, 19:665-666, 2003.

C. M. Bishop. *Neural Networks for Pattern Recognition.* Clarendon Press, Oxford, 1995.

N. Blom, J. Hansen, D. Blaas, and S. Brunak. Cleavage site analysis in picornaviral polyproteins: discovering cellular targets by neural networks. *Protein Sci*, 5:2203-2216, 1996.

M. J. Blythe, I. A. Doytchinova, and D. R. Flower. JenPep: a database of quantitative functional peptide data for immunology. *Bioinformatics*, 18:434-439, 2002.

M. J. Blythe and D. R. Flower. Benchmarking B cell epitope prediction: underperformance of existing methods. *Protein Sci.*, 14:246-248, 2005.

B. Boeckmann, A. Bairoch, R. Apweiler, M. C. Blatter, A. Estreicher, E. Gasteiger, M. J. Martin, K. Michoud, C. O'Donovan, I. Phan, S. Pilbout, and M. Schneider. The SWISS-PROT protein knowledge base and its supplement TrEMBL in 2003. *Nucleic Acids Res.*, 31:365-370, 2003.

R. J. de Boer, J. A. Borghans, M. van Boven, C. Kesmir, and F. J. Weissing. Heterozygote advantage fails to explain the high degree of polymorphism of the MHC. *Immunogenetics*, 55:725-731, 2004.

J. A. Borghans and R. J. de Boer. Memorizing innate instructions requires a sufficiently specific adaptive immune system. *Int. Immunol.*, 14:525-532, 2002.

J. A. M. Borghans, J. B. Beltman, and R. J. de Boer. MHC polymorphism under host-pathogen coevolution. *Immunogenetics*, 55:732-739, 2004.

P. Bork, L. J. Jensen, C. von Mering, A. K. Ramani, I. Lee, and E. M. Marcotte. Protein interaction networks from yeast to human. *Curr. Opin. Struct. Biol.*, 14:292-299, 2004.

A. J. Bredemeyer, R. M. Lewis, J. P. Malone, A. E. Davis, J. Gross, R. R. Townsend, and T. J. Ley. A proteomic approach for the discovery of protease substrates. *Proc. Natl. Acad. Sci. U.S.A.*, 101:11785-11790, 2004.

P. Brocke, N. Garbi, F. Momburg, and G. J. Hammerling. HLA-DM, HLA-DO and tapasin: functional similarities and differences. *Curr. Opin. Immunol.*, 14:22-29, 2002.

G. F. Brooks, J. S. Butel, and S. A. Morse. *Medical Microbiology.* Lange Medical Books/McGraw-Hill, New York, 2001.

M. A. Brundler, P. Aichele, M. Bachmann, D. Kitamura, K. Rajewsky, and R. M. Zinkernagel. Immunity to viruses in B cell-deficient mice: influence of antibodies on virus persistence and on T cell memory. *Eur. J. Immunol.*, 26:2257–2262, 1996.

V. Brusic, N. Petrovsky, G Zhang, and V. B. Bajic. Prediction of promiscuous peptides that bind HLA class I molecules. *Immunol. Cell Biol.*, 80:280–285, 2002.

V. Brusic, G. Rudy, and L. C. Harrison. Prediction of MHC binding peptides using artificial neural networks. In R. J. Stonier and X. S. Yu, editors, *Complex Systems: Mechanism of Adaptation*, pages 253–260. IOS Press, Amsterdam, 1994.

V. Brusic, G. Rudy, and L. C. Harrison. MHCPEP, a database of MHC-binding peptides: update 1997. *Nucleic Acids Res.*, 26:368–371, 1998a.

V. Brusic, G. Rudy, G. Honeyman, J. Hammer, and L. Harrison. Prediction of MHC class II-binding peptides using an evolutionary algorithm and artificial neural network. *Bioinformatics*, 14:121–130, 1998b.

P. W. Bryant, A. M. Lennon-Dumenil, E. Fiebiger, C. Lagaudriere-Gesbert, and H. L. Ploegh. Proteolysis and antigen presentation by MHC class II molecules. *Adv. Immunol.*, 80:71–114, 2002.

D. R. Burton, E. O. Saphire, and P. W. Parren. A model for neutralization of viruses based on antibody coating of the virion surface. *Curr. Top. Microbiol. Immunol.*, 260:109–143, 2001.

S. Buus, S. L. Lauemoller, P. Worning, C. Kesmir, T. Frimurer, S. Corbet, A. Fomsgaard, J. Hilden, A. Holm, and S. Brunak. Sensitive quantitative predictions of peptide-MHC binding by a 'Query by Committee' artificial neural network approach. *Tissue Antigens*, 62:378–384, 2003.

S. Buus, A. Stryhn, K. Winther, N. Kirkby, and L. O. Pedersen. Receptor-ligand interactions measured by an improved spun column chromatography technique. a high efficiency and high throughput size separation method. *Biochim. Biophys. Acta*, 1243: 453–460, 1995.

J. Y. Byon, T. Ohira, I. Hirono, and T. Aoki. Use of a cDNA microarray to study immunity against viral hemorrhagic septicemia (VHS) in Japanese flounder (*Paralichthys olivaceus*) following DNA vaccination. *Fish Shellfish Immunol.*, 18:135–147, 2005.

H. Cao, P. Kanki, J. L. Sankale, A. Dieng-Sarr, G. P. Mazzara, S. A. Kalams, B. Korber, S. Mboup, and B. D. Walker. Cytotoxic T-lymphocyte cross-reactivity among different human immunodeficiency virus type 1 clades: implications for vaccine development. *J. Virol.*, 71:8615–8623, 1997.

C. Cardozo and R. A. Kohanski. Altered properties of the branched chain amino acid-preferring activity contribute to increased cleavages after branched chain residues by the "immunoproteasome.". *J. Biol. Chem.*, 273:16764–16770, 1998.

M. Carrington and S. J. O'Brien. The influence of HLA genotype on AIDS. *Annu. Rev. Med.*, 54:535–551, 2003.

P. Cascio, C. Hilton, A. F. Kisselev, K. L. Rock, and A. L. Goldberg. 26s proteasomes and immunoproteasomes produce mainly N-extended versions of an antigenic peptide. *EMBO J.*, 20:2357–2366, 2001.

F. A. Castelli, C. Buhot, A. Sanson, H Zarour, S. Pouvelle-Moratille, C. Nonn, H Gahery-Segard, J.-G. Guillet, B. Menez, A.and Georges, and B. Maillere. HLA-DP4, the most frequent HLA II molecule, defines a new supertype of peptide-binding specificity. *J. Immunol*, 169:6928–6934, 2002.

F. Castellino, G. Zhong, and Germain R. N. Antigen presentation by mhc class ii molecules: invariant chain function, protein trafficking, and the molecular basis of diverse determinant capture. *Hum. Immunol.*, 54:159–169, 1997.

CDC   Centers for Disease Control and Prevention, biological agents/diseases, http://www.bt.cdc.gov/agent/agentlist-category.asp, 2003.

M. H. Cezari, L. Puzer, M. A. Juliano, A. K. Carmona, and L. Juliano. Cathepsin B carboxydipeptidase specificity analysis using internally quenched fluorescent peptides. *Biochem. J.*, 368:365–369, 2002.

H. A. Chapman. Endosomal proteolysis and MHC class II function. *Curr. Opin. Immunol.*, 10:93–102, 1998.

H. A. Chapman. Cathepsins as transcriptional activators? *Dev. Cell*, 6:610, 2004.

D. Chassin, M. Andrieu, W. Cohen, B. Culmann-Penciolelli, M. Ostankovitch, D. Hanau, and J. G. Guillet. Dendritic cells transfected with the Nef genes of HIV-1 primary isolates specifically activate cytotoxic T lymphocytes from seropositive subjects. *Eur. J. Immunol.*, 29:196–202, 1999.

W. Chen, C. C. Norbury, Y. Cho, J. W. Yewdell, and J. R. Bennink. Immunoproteasomes shape immunodominance hierarchies of antiviral CD8($^+$) T cells at the levels of T cell repertoire and presentation of viral antigens. *J. Exp. Med.*, 193:1319–1326, 2001.

R. Chenna, H. Sugawara, T. Koike, R. Lopez, T. J. Gibson, D. G. Higgins, and J. D. Thompson. Multiple sequence alignment with the clustal series of programs. *Nucleic Acids Res.*, 31:3497–3500, 2003.

Y. Choi, C-J Ahn, K-M Seong, M-Y Jung, and B-Y Ahn. Inactivated hantaan virus vaccine derived from suspension culture of vero cells. *Vaccine*, 21:1867–73, 2003.

P. Y. Chou and G. D. Fasman. Prediction of the secondary structure of proteins from their amino acid sequence. *Adv. Enzymol. Relat. Areas. Mol. Biol.*, 47:45–148, 1978.

J. K. Christensen, K. Lamberth, M. Nielsen, C. Lundegaard, P. Worning, S. L. Lauemoller, S. Buus, S. Brunak, and O. Lund. Selecting informative data for developing peptide-MHC binding predictors using a query by committee approach. *Neural Comput.*, 15: 2931–2942, 2003.

E. C. Claas and A. D. Osterhaus. New clues to the emergence of flu pandemics. *Nat. Med.*, 4:1122–1123, 1998.

J. Cohen. Public health. AIDS vaccine trial produces disappointment and confusion. *Science*, 299:1290–1291, 2003.

S. Cooper, A.L. Erickson, E.J. Adams, J. Kansopon, A.J. Weiner, D.Y. Chien, M. Houghton, P. Parham, and C.M. Walker. Analysis of a successful immune response against hepatitis C virus. *Immunity*, 10:439–449, 1999.

S. Corbet, H. V. Nielsen, L. Vinner, S. Lauemøller, D. Therrien, S. Tang, G. Kronborg, L. Mathiesen, P. Chaplin, S. Brunak, S. Buus, and A. Fomsgaard. Optimization and immune recognition of multiple novel conserved HLA-A2, human immunodeficiency virus type 1-specific CTL epitopes. *J. Gen. Virol.*, 84:2409–2421, 2003.

J. L. Cornette, K. B. Cease, H. Margalit, J. L. Spouge, J. A. Berzofsky, and C. DeLisi. Hydrophobicity scales and computational techniques for detecting amphipathic structures in proteins. *J. Mol. Biol.*, 195:659–685, 1987.

T. M. Cover and J. A. Thomas. *Elements of Information Theory.* Wiley, Inc., New York, 1991.

M. R. Crittenden, U. Thanarajasingam, R. G. Vile, and M. J. Gough. Intratumoral immunotherapy: using the tumour against itself. *Immunology*, 114:11–22, 2005.

B. C. Cunningham and J. A. Wells. High-resolution epitope mapping of hGH-receptor interactions by alanine-scanning mutagenesis. *Science*, 244:1081–1085, 1989.

B. Dahlmann, T. Ruppert, L. Kuehn, S. Merforth, and P. M. Kloetzel. Different proteasome subtypes in a single tissue exhibit different enzymatic properties. *J. Mol. Biol.*, 303:643–653, 2000.

P. M. Dando, M. Fortunato, L. Smith, C. G. Knight, J. E. McKendrick, and A. J. Barrett. Pig kidney legumain: an asparaginyl endopeptidase with restricted specificity. *Biochem. J.*, 339:743–749, 1999.

S. Daniel, V. Brusic, S. Caillat-Zucman, N. Petrovsky, L. Harrison, D. Riganelli, F. Sinigaglia, F. Gallazzi, J. Hammer, and P. M. van Endert. Relationship between peptide selectivities of human transporters associated with antigen processing and HLA class I molecules. *J. Immunol.*, 161:617–624, 1998.

M. O. Dayhoff, R. M. Schwartz, and B. C. Orcutt. A model of evolutionary change in proteins. In M.O. Dayhoff, editor, *Atlas of Protein Sequence and Structure*, volume 5, pages 345–352, Washington DC, 1978. National biomedical research foundation.

R. Daza-Vamenta, G. Glusman, L. Rowen, B. Guthrie, and D. E. Geraghty. Genetic divergence of the rhesus macaque major histocompatibility complex. *Genome Res.*, 14: 1501–1515, 2004.

L. Debelle, S. M. Wei, M. P. Jacob, W. Hornebeck, and A. J. Alix. Predictions of the secondary structure and antigenicity of human and bovine tropoelastins. *Eur. Biophys. J.*, 21:321–329, 1992.

M. F. Del Guercio, J. Sidney, G. Hermanson, C. Perez, H. M. Grey, R. T. Kubo, and A. Sette. Binding of a peptide antigen to multiple HLA alleles allows definition of an A2-like supertype. *J. Immunol.*, 154:685–693, 1995.

C. Devaux, M. Juin, P. Mansuelle, and C. Granier. Fine molecular analysis of the antigenicity of the *Andr octonus australis* hector scorpion neurotoxin II: a new antigenic epitope disclosed by the pepscan method. *Mol. Immunol.*, 30:1061–1068, 1993.

DMID (division of Microbiology and Infectious Diseases, NIH). Childhood infections, http://www.niaid.nih.gov/dmid/child/, 2004.

T. Doan, K. Herd, I. Ramshaw, S. Thomson, and RW. Tindle. A polytope DNA vaccine elicits multiple effector and memory CTL responses and protects against human papillomavirus 16 E7-expressing tumour. *Cancer Immunol. Immunother*, 54:157–171, 2005.

J. Dodt and J. Reichwein. Human cathepsin H: deletion of the mini-chain switches substrate specificity from aminopeptidase to endopeptidase. *Biol. Chem.*, 384:1327–1332, 2003.

X. Dong, B. An, L. Salvucci Kierstead, W. J. Storkus, A. A. Amoscato, and R. D. Salter. Modification of the amino terminus of a class II epitope confers resistance to degradation by CD13 on dendritic cells and enhances presentation to T cells. *J. Immunol.*, 164:129–135, 2000.

I. A. Doytchinova and D. R. Flower. Toward the quantitative prediction of T-cell epitopes: CoMFA and CoMSIA studies of peptides with affinity for the class I MHC molecule HLA-A*0201. *J. Med. Chem.*, 44:3572–3581, 2001.

C. Driessen, R. A. Bryant, A. M. Lennon-Dumenil, J. A. Villadangos, P. W. Bryant, G. P. Shi, H. A. Chapman, and H. L. Ploegh. Cathepsin S controls the trafficking and maturation of MHC class II molecules in dendritic cells. *J. Cell. Biol.*, 147:775–790, 1999.

R. M. Durbin, S. R. Eddy, A. Krogh, and G. Mitchison. *Biological Sequence Analysis*. Cambridge University Press, Cambridge, UK, 1998.

S. R. Durham, H. J. Gould, C. P. Thienes, M. R. Jacobson, K. Masuyama, S. Rak, O. Lowhagen, E. Schotman, L. Cameron, and Q. A. Hamid. Expression of epsilon germ-line gene transcripts and mRNA for the epsilon heavy chain of IgE in nasal B cells and the effects of topical corticosteroid. *Eur. J. Immunol.*, 27:2899–2906, 1997.

D. H. Ebert, J. Deussing, C. Peters, and T. S. Dermody. Cathepsin L and cathepsin B mediate reovirus disassembly in murine fibroblast cells. *J. Biol. Chem.*, 277:24609–24617, 2002.

S. R. Eddy. Profile hidden Markov models. *Bioinformatics*, 14:755–763, 1998.

W. van Eden, R. R. de Vries, N. K. Mehra, M. C. Vaidya, J. D'Amaro, and J. J. van Rood. HLA segregation of tuberculoid leprosy: confirmation of the DR2 marker. *J. Infect. Dis.*, 141:693–701, 1980.

B. Ehring, T. H. Meyer, C. Eckerskorn, F. Lottspeich, and R. Tampe. Effects of major-histocompatibility-complex–encoded subunits on the peptidase and proteolytic activities of human 20S proteasomes. Cleavage of proteins and antigenic peptides. *Eur. J. Biochem.*, 235:404–415, 1996.

M. van Eijk, T. Defrance, A. Hennino, and C. de Groot. Death-receptor contribution to the germinal-center reaction. *Trends Immunol.*, 22:677–682, 2001.

A. M. Eleuteri, R. A. Kohanski, C. Cardozo, and M. Orlowski. Bovine spleen multicatalytic proteinase complex (proteasome). Replacement of X, Y, and Z subunits by LMP7, LMP2, and MECL1 and changes in properties and specificity. *J. Biol. Chem.*, 272:11824–11831, 1997.

R. W. Ellis. New technologies for making vaccines. *Vaccine*, 17:1596–1604, 1999.

E. A. Emini, J. V. Hughes, D. S. Perlow, and J. Boger. Induction of hepatitis A virus-neutralizing antibody by a virus-specific synthetic peptide. *J. Virol.*, 55:836–839, 1985.

N. P. Emmerich, A. K. Nussbaum, S. Stevanovic, M. Priemer, R. E. Toes, H. G. Rammensee, and H. Schild. The human 26 S and 20 S proteasomes generate overlapping but different sets of peptide fragments from a model protein substrate. *J. Biol. Chem.*, 275:21140–21148, 2000.

P. M. van Endert. Peptide selection for presentation by HLA class I: a role for the human transporter associated with antigen processing? *Immunol. Res.*, 15:265–279, 1996.

P. M. van Endert, R. Tampe, T. H. Meyer, R. Tisch, J. F. Bach, and H. O. McDevitt. A sequential model for peptide binding and transport by the transporters associated with antigen processing. *Immunity*, 1:491–500, 1994.

D. Enshell-Seijffers, D. Denisov, B. Groisman, L. Smelyanski, R. Meyuhas, G. Gross, G. Denisova, and J. M. Gershoni. The mapping and reconstitution of a conformational discontinuous B-cell epitope of HIV-1. *J. Mol. Biol.*, 334:87–101, 2003.

K. Falk, O. Rotzschke, S. Stevanovic, G. Jung, and H. G. Rammensee. Allele-specific motifs revealed by sequencing of self-peptides eluted from MHC molecules. *Nature*, 351:290–296, 1991.

FDA (food and Drug Administration), vaccines licensed for immunization and distributed in the US, http://www.fda.gov/cber/vaccine/licvacc.htm, 2003.

D. T. Fearon and R. M. Locksley. The instructive role of innate immunity in the acquired immune response. *Science*, 272:50–53, 1996.

D. R. Flower, H. McSparron, M. J. Blythe, C. Zygouri, D. Taylor, P. Guan, S. Wan, P. V. Coveney, V. Walshe, P. Borrow, and I. A. Doytchinova. Computational vaccinology: quantitative approaches. *Novartis Found. Symp.*, 254:102–120, 2003.

T. C. Friedrich, E. J. Dodds, L. J. Yant, L. Vojnov, R. Rudersdorf, C. Cullen, D. T. Evans, R. C. Desrosiers, B. R. Mothe, J. Sidney, A. Sette, K. Kunstman, S. Wolinsky, M. Piatak, J. Lifson, A. L. Hughes, N. Wilson, D. H. O'Connor, and D. I. Watkins. Reversion of CTL escape-variant immunodeficiency viruses in vivo. *Nat. Med.*, 10:275–281, 2004.

S. Gabery and M. Sjö. Processing and binding of class II epitopes, bachelor project, Technical University of Denmark, 2004.

T. R. Gamble, S. Yoo, F. F. Vajdos, U. K. von Schwedler, D. K. Worthylake, H. Wang, J. P. McCutcheon, W. I. Sundquist, and C. P. Hill. Structure of the carboxyl-terminal dimerization domain of the HIV-1 capsid protein. *Science*, 278:849–853, 1997.

P. Garside, E. Ingulli, R. R. Merica, J. G. Johnson, R. J. Noelle, and M. K. Jenkins. Visualization of specific B and T lymphocyte interactions in the lymph node. *Science*, 281: 96–99, 1998.

B. Gaschen, J. Taylor, K. Yusim, B. Foley, F. Gao, D. Lang, V. Novitsky, B. Haynes, B. H. Hahn, T. Bhattacharya, and B. Korber. Diversity considerations in HIV-1 vaccine selection. *Science*, 296:2354–2360, 2002.

J. Gaschet, A. Lim, L. Liem, R. Vivien, M. M. Hallet, J. L. Harousseau, J. Even, E. Goulmy, M. Bonneville, N. Milpied, and H. Vie. Acute graft versus host disease due to T lymphocytes recognizing a single HLA-DPB1*0501 mismatch. *J. Clin. Invest.*, 98: 100–107, 1996.

A. Geluk, K. E. van Meijgaarden, N. C. Schloot, J. W. Drijfhout, T. H. Ottenhoff, and B. O. Roep. HLA-DR binding analysis of peptides from islet antigens in IDDM. *Diabetes*, 47:1594–1601, 1998.

J. A. Glazier and F. Graner. Simulation of the differential adhesion driven rearrangment of biological cells. *Phys. Rev. E*, 47:2128–2154, 1993.

A. J. Godkin, M. P. Davenport, A. Willis, D. P. Jewell, and A. V. Hill. Use of complete eluted peptide sequence data from HLA-DR and -DQ molecules to predict T cell epitopes, and the influence of the nonbinding terminal regions of ligands in epitope selection. *J. Immunol.*, 161:850–858, 1998.

G. H. Gonnet, M. A. Cohen, and S. A. Benner. Exhaustive matching of the entire protein sequence database. *Science*, 256:1443–1445, 1992.

O. T. Gorman, W. J. Bean, and R. G. Webster. Evolutionary processes in influenza viruses: divergence, rapid evolution, and stasis. *Curr. Top. Microbiol. Immunol.*, 176:75–97, 1992.

J. Gorodkin, H. H. Staerfeldt, O. Lund, and S. Brunak. Matrixplot: visualizing sequence constraints. *Bioinformatics.*, 15:769–770, 1999.

H. G. Gottlinger. The HIV-1 assembly machine. *AIDS*, 15:S13–S20, 2001.

H. J. Gould, B. J. Sutton, A. J. Beavil, R. L. Beavil, N. McCloskey, H. A. Coker, D. Fear, and L. Smurthwaite. The biology of IGE and the basis of allergic disease. *Annu. Rev. Immunol.*, 21:579–628, 2003.

P. Goulder, D. Price, M. Nowak, S. Rowland-Jones, R. Phillips, and A. McMichael. Co-evolution of human immunodeficiency virus and cytotoxic T-lymphocyte responses. *Immunol. Rev.*, 159:17–29, 1997.

F. Graner and J. A. Glazier. Simulation of biological cell sorting using a two-dimensional extended Potts model. *Phys. Rev. Lett.*, 69:2013–2016, 1992.

D. Gray, P. Dullforce, and S. Jainandunsing. Memory B cell development but not germinal center formation is impaired by in vivo blockade of CD40-CD40 ligand interaction. *J. Exp. Med.*, 180:141–155, 1994.

M. Gréco. The future of vaccines: an industrial perspective. *Vaccine*, 20:S101–103, 2002.

M. Gribskov, A. D. McLachlan, and D. Eisenberg. Profile analysis: detection of distantly related proteins. *Proc. Natl. Acad. Sci. U. S. A.* , 84:4355–4358, 1987.

M. Groettrup, S. Khan, K. Schwarz, and G. Schmidtke. Interferon-gamma inducible exchanges of 20S proteasome active site subunits: why? *Biochimie*, 83:367–372, 2001.

M. Groettrup, A. Soza, U. Kuckelkorn, and P. M. Kloetzel. Peptide antigen production by the proteasome: complexity provides efficiency. *Immunol. Today*, 17:429–435, 1996.

M. Groll, L. Ditzel, J. Lowe, D. Stock, M. Bochtler, H. D. Bartunik, and R. Huber. Structure of 20S proteasome from yeast at 2.4 Å resolution. *Nature*, 386:463–471, 1997.

M. Groll, W. Heinemeyer, S. Jager, T. Ullrich, M. Bochtler, D. H. Wolf, and R. Huber. The catalytic sites of 20S proteasomes and their role in subunit maturation: a mutational and crystallographic study. *Proc. Natl. Acad. Sci. U.S.A.*, 96:10976–10983, 1999.

A. S. de Groot, B. M. Jesdale, E. Szu, J. R. Schafer, R. M. Chicz, and G. Deocampo. An interactive Web site providing major histocompatibility ligand predictions: application to HIV research. *AIDS Res. Hum. Retroviruses*, 13:529–531, 1997.

N. G. de Groot, N. Otting, G. G. Doxiadis, S. S. Balla-Jhagjhoorsingh, J. L. Heeney, J. J. van Rood, P. Gagneux, and R. E. Bontrop. Evidence for an ancient selective sweep in the MHC class I gene repertoire of chimpanzees. *Proc. Natl. Acad. Sci. U.S.A.*, 99: 11748-11753, 2002.

P. Guan, I. A. Doytchinova, C. Zygouri, and D. R. Flower. MHCPred: bringing a quantitative dimension to the online prediction of MHC binding. *Appl. Bioinformatics*, 2: 63-66, 2003.

I. Guggenmoos-Holzmann and H. C. van Houwelingen. The (in)validity of sensitivity and specificity. *Stat. Med.*, 19:1783-1792, 2000.

K. Gulukota and C. DeLisi. HLA allele selection for designing peptide vaccines. *Genet. Anal.*, 13:81-86, 1996.

K. Gulukota, J. Sidney, A. Sette, and C. DeLisi. Two complementary methods for predicting peptides binding major histocompatibility complex molecules. *J. Mol. Biol.*, 267:1258-1267, 1997.

I. Hagel, M. C. Di Prisco, J. Goldblatt, and P. N. Le Souef. The role of parasites in genetic susceptibility to allergy: IgE, helminthic infection and allergy, and the evolution of the human immune system. *Clin. Rev. Allergy Immunol.*, 26:75-83, 2004.

M. Hagmann. Doing immunology on a chip. *Science*, 290:82-83, 2000.

J. Hakenberg, A. K. Nussbaum, H. Schild, H.-G. Rammensee, C. Kuttler, Holzhutter H.-G., P. M. Kloetzel, S. E. H Kaufmann, and H.-J. Mollenkopf. MAPPP: MHC class I antigenic peptide processing prediction. *Appl. Bioinformatics*, 2:155-158, 2003.

T. van Hall, A. Sijts, M. Camps, R. Offringa, C. Melief, P. M. Kloetzel, and F. Ossendorp. Differential influence on cytotoxic T lymphocyte epitope presentation by controlled expression of either proteasome immunosubunits or PA28. *J. Exp. Med.*, 192:483-494, 2000.

J. Hammer. New methods to predict MHC-binding sequences within protein antigens. *Curr. Opin. Immunol.*, 7:263-269, 1995.

J. Hammer, E. Bono, F. Gallazzi, C. Belunis, Z. Nagy, and F. Sinigaglia. Precise prediction of major histocompatibility complex class II-peptide interaction based on peptide side chain scanning. *J. Exp. Med.*, 180:2353-2358, 1994.

J. Hammer, T. Sturniolo, and F. Sinigaglia. HLA class II peptide binding specificity and autoimmunity. *Adv. Immunol.*, 66:67-100, 1997.

J. D. J. Han, N. Bertin, T. Hao, D. S. Goldberg, G. F. Berriz, L. V. Zhang, D. Dupuy, A. M. J. Walhout, M. E. Cusick, Roth F. P., and M. Vidal. Evidence for dynamically organized modularity in the yeast protein-protein interaction network. *Nature*, 430: 88-93, 2004.

S. Han, K. Hathcock, B. Zheng, T. B. Kepler, R. Hodes, and G. Kelsoe. Cellular interaction in germinal centers. Roles of CD40 ligand and B7-2 in established germinal centers. *J. Immunol.*, 155:556–567, 1995.

P. Hansasuta and S. L. Rowland-Jones. HIV-1 transmission and acute HIV-1 infection. *Br. Med. Bull.*, 58:109–127, 2001.

L. J. Harris, S. B. Larson, K. W. Hasel, and A. McPherson. Refined structure of an intact IgG2a monoclonal antibody. *Biochemistry*, 36:1581–1597, 1997.

M. D. Hazenberg, D. Hamann, H. Schuitemaker, and F. Miedema. T cell depletion in HIV-1 infection: how CD4$^+$ T cells go out of stock. *Nat. Immunol.*, 1:285–289, 2000.

S. M. Hebsgaard, P.G. Korning, N. Tolstrup, J. Engelbrecht, P. Rouze, and S. Brunak. Splice site prediction in *Arabidopsis thaliana* pre-mRNA by combining local and global sequence information. *Nucleic Acids Res.*, 24:3439–3452, 1996.

J. Hein and J. Størvlbaek. Genomic alignment. *J. Mol. Evol.*, 38:310–316, 1994.

J. Hein and J. Størvlbaek. Combined DNA and protein alignment. *Methods Enzymol.*, 266:402–418, 1996.

W. Heinemeyer, M. Fischer, T. Krimmer, U. Stachon, and D. H. Wolf. The active sites of the eukaryotic 20 S proteasome and their involvement in subunit precursor processing. *J. Biol. Chem.*, 272:25200–25209, 1997.

S. Henikoff and J. G. Henikoff. Automated assembly of protein blocks for database searching. *Nucleic Acids Res.*, 19:6565–6572, 1991.

S. Henikoff and J. G. Henikoff. Amino acid substitution matrices from protein blocks. *Proc. Natl. Acad. Sci. U. S. A.*, 89:10915–10919, 1992.

S. Henikoff and J. G. Henikoff. Position-based sequence weights. *J. Mol. Biol.*, 243:574–578, 1994.

F. Henningsson, P. Wolters, H. A. Chapman, G. H. Caughey, and G. Pejler. Mast cell cathepsins C and S control levels of carboxypeptidase A and the chymase, mouse mast cell protease 5. *Biol. Chem.*, 384:1527–1531, 2003.

J. Hertz, A. Krogh, and R.G. Palmer. *Introduction to the theory of neural computation.* Addison–Wesley, Redwood City, CA, 1991.

A. V. Hill, C. E. Allsopp, D. Kwiatkowski, N. M. Anstey, P. Twumasi, P. A. Rowe, S. Bennett, D. Brewster, A. J. McMichael, and B. M. Greenwood. Common West African HLA antigens are associated with protection from severe malaria. *Nature*, 352:595–600, 1991.

U. Hobohm, M. Scharf, R. Schneider, and C. Sander. Selection of representative protein data sets. *Protein Sci.*, 1:409–417, 1992.

J. A. Hoffmann, F. C. Kafatos, C. A. Janeway, and R. A. Ezekowitz. Phylogenetic perspectives in innate immunity. *Science*, 284:1313-1318, 1999.

H. G. Holzhutter, C. Frommel, and P. M. Kloetzel. A theoretical approach towards the identification of cleavage-determining amino acid motifs of the 20 S proteasome. *J. Mol. Biol.*, 286:1251-1265, 1999.

H. G. Holzhutter and P. M. Kloetzel. A kinetic model of vertebrate 20S proteasome accounting for the generation of major proteolytic fragments from oligomeric peptide substrates. *Biophys. J.*, 79:1196-1205, 2000.

K. Honey, T. Nakagawa, C. Peters, and A. Rudensky. Cathepsin L regulates CD4+ T cell selection independently of its effect on invariant chain: a role in the generation of positively selecting peptide ligands. *J. Exp. Med.*, 195:1349-1358, 2002.

K. Honey and A. Y. Rudensky. Lysosomal cysteine proteases regulate antigen presentation. *Nat. Rev. Immunol.*, 3:472-482, 2003.

T. P. Hopp. Different views of protein antigenicity. *Pept. Res.*, 7:229-231, 1994.

T. P. Hopp and K. R. Woods. Prediction of protein antigenic determinants from amino acid sequences. *Proc. Natl. Acad. Sci. U. S. A.*, 78:3824-3828, 1981.

T. P. Hopp and K. R. Woods. A computer program for predicting protein antigenic determinants. *Mol. Immunol.*, 20:483-489, 1983.

A. L. Hughes. Evolution of the proteasome components. *Immunogenetics*, 46:82-92, 1997.

A. L. Hughes and M. Nei. Pattern of nucleotide substitution at major histocompatibility complex class I loci reveals overdominant selection. *Nature*, 335:167-170, 1988.

A. L. Hughes and M. Nei. Nucleotide substitution at major histocompatibility complex class II loci: evidence for overdominant selection. *Proc. Natl. Acad. Sci. U.S.A.*, 86: 958-962, 1989.

A. L. Hughes and M. Nei. Models of host-parasite interaction and MHC polymorphism. *Genetics*, 132:863-864, 1992.

A. L. Hughes and M. Yeager. Natural selection at major histocompatibility complex loci of vertebrates. *Annu. Rev. Genet.*, 32:415-435, 1998.

J. Icenogle, H. Shiwen, G. Duke, S. Gilbert, R. Rueckert, and J. Anderegg. Neutralization of poliovirus by a monoclonal antibody: kinetics and stoichiometry. *Virology*, 127: 412-425, 1983.

G. Y. Ishioka, J. Fikes, G. Hermanson, B. Livingston, C. Crimi, M. Qin, M. F. del Guercio, C. Oseroff, C. Dahlberg, J. Alexander, R. W. Chesnut, and A. Sette. Utilization of MHC class I transgenic mice for development of minigene DN utilization of MHC class I transgenic mice for development of minigene DN vaccines encoding multiple HLA-restricted CTL epitopes. *J. Immunol.*, 162:3915-3925, 1999.

J. Jacob, G. Kelsoe, K. Rajewsky, and U. Weiss. Intraclonal generation of antibody mutants in germinal centres. *Nature*, 354:389–392, 1991.

H. Jacobs and L. Bross. Towards an understanding of somatic hypermutation. *Curr. Opin. Immunol.*, 13:208–218, 2001.

B. A. Jameson and H. Wolf. The antigenic index: a novel algorithm for predicting antigenic determinants. *Comput. Appl. Biosci.*, 4:181–186, 1988.

C. A. Janeway, P. Travers, M. Walport, and M. Shlomchik. *Immunobiology. The Immune System in Health and Disease.* Garland Publications, New York, London, 5 edition, 2001.

L. J. Jensen, R. Gupta, N. Blom, D. Devos, J. Tamames, C. Kesmir, H. Nielsen, H. H. Staerfeldt, K. Rapacki, C. Workman, C. A. Andersen, S. Knudsen, A. Krogh, A. Valencia, and S. Brunak. Prediction of human protein function from post-translational modifications and localization features. *J. Mol. Biol.*, 319:1257–1265, 2002.

l. J. Jensen, D. W. Ussery, and S. Brunak. Functionality of system components: conservation of protein function in protein feature space. *Genome Res.*, 13:2444–2449, 2003.

L. Jiang, O. Lund, and T. Jinquan. Selection of proteins for human MHC class II presentation, in press, 2005.

X. Jiang, N. Wilton, W. M. Zhong, T. Farkas, P. W. Huang, E. Barrett, M. Guerrero, G. Ruiz-Palacios, K. Y. Green, J. Green, A. D. Hale, M. K. Estes, L. K. Pickering, and D. O. Matson. Diagnosis of human caliciviruses by use of enzyme immunoassays. *J. Infect. Dis.*, 181:S349–359, 2000.

L. Jin, B. M. Fendly, and J. A. Wells. High resolution functional analysis of antibody-antigen interactions. *J. Mol. Biol.*, 226:851–865, 1992.

E. Joly and G. W. Butcher. Why are there two rat TAPs? *Immunol. Today*, 19:580–585, 1998.

G. Jung, B. Fleckenstein, F. von der Mulbe, J. Wessels, D. Niethammer, and K. H. Wiesmuller. From combinatorial libraries to MHC ligand motifs, T-cell superagonists and antagonists. *Biologicals*, 29:179–781, 2001.

C. M. Kane, L. Cervi, J. Sun, A. S. McKee, K. S. Masek, S. Shapira, C. A Hunter, and E. J. Pearce. Helminth antigens modulate TLR-initiated dendritic cell activation. *J. Immunol.*, 173:7454–7461, 2004.

K. Karplus, C. Barrett, and R. Hughey. Hidden Markov models for detecting remote protein homologies. *Bioinformatics*, 14:846–856, 1998.

Y. Kawakami, T. Fujita, Y. Matsuzaki, T. Sakurai, M. Tsukamoto, M. Toda, and H. Sumimoto. Identification of human tumor antigens and its implications for diagnosis and treatment of cancer. *Cancer Sci.*, 95:784–791, 2004.

S. Kawashima and M. Kanehisa. AAindex: amino acid index database. *Nucleic Acids Res.*, 28:374, 2000.

G. Kelsoe. V(D)J hypermutation and receptor revision: coloring outside the lines. *Curr. Opin. Immunol.*, 11:70–75, 1999.

T. B. Kepler and A. S. Perelson. Cyclic re-entry of germinal center B cells and the efficiency of affinity maturation. *Immunol. Today*, 14:412–415, 1993a.

T. B. Kepler and A. S. Perelson. Somatic hypermutation in B cells: an optimal control treatment. *J. Theor. Biol.*, 164:37–64, 1993b.

C. Keşmir and R. J. de Boer. Can cytopathicity alone explain neutralizing antibody kinetics? *Scand. J. Immunol.*, 48:347–349, 1998.

C. Kesmir and R. J. de Boer. A mathematical model on germinal center kinetics and termination. *J. Immunol.*, 163:2463–2469, 1999.

C. Kesmir and R. J. de Boer. A spatial model of germinal center reactions: cellular adhesion based sorting of B cells results in efficient affinity maturation. *J. Theor. Biol.*, 222:9–22, 2003.

C. Kesmir, A. K. Nussbaum, H. Schild, V. Detours, and S. Brunak. Prediction of proteasome cleavage motifs by neural networks. *Protein Eng.*, 15:287–296, 2002.

C. Kesmir, V. van Noort, R. J. de Boer, and P. Hogeweg. Bioinformatic analysis of functional differences between the immunoproteasome and the constitutive proteasome. *Immunogenetics*, 55:437–449, 2003.

S. Khan, M. van den Broek, K. Schwarz, R. de Giuli, P. A. Diener, and M. Groettrup. Immunoproteasomes largely replace constitutive proteasomes during an antiviral and antibacterial immune response in the liver. *J. Immunol.*, 167:6859–6868, 2001.

L. Kiemer, O. Lund, S. Brunak, and N. Blom. Coronavirus 3CLpro proteinase cleavage sites: possible relevance to SARS virus pathology. *BMC Bioinformatics*, 5:72, 2004.

J. P. Kinet. The high-affinity IgE receptor (Fc epsilon RI): from physiology to pathology. *Annu. Rev. Immunol.*, 17:931–972, 1999.

J. Kipnis and M. Schwartz. Dual action of glatiramer acetate (Cop-1) in the treatment of CNS autoimmune and neurodegenerative disorders. *Trends Mol. Med.*, 8:319–323, 2002.

M. R. Klein, I. P. Keet, J. D'Amaro, R. J. Bende, A. Hekman, B. Mesman, M. Koot, L. P. de Waal, R. A. Coutinho, and F. Miedema. Associations between HLA frequencies and pathogenic features of human immunodeficiency virus type 1 infection in seroconverters from the Amsterdam cohort of homosexual men. *J. Infect. Dis.*, 169: 1244–1249, 1994.

U. Klein, T. Goossens, M. Fischer, H. Kanzler, A. Braeuninger, K. Rajewsky, and R. Kuppers. Somatic hypermutation in normal and transformed human B cells. *Immunol. Rev.*, 162:261–280, 1998.

P. M. Kloetzel. Antigen processing by the proteasome. *Nat. Rev. Mol. Cell. Biol.*, 2: 179–187, 2001.

S. Knudsen. *Guide to Analysis of DNA Microarray Data.* Wiley, New York, 2004.

A. Kondo, J. Sidney, S. Southwood, M. F. del Guercio, E. Appella, H. Sakamoto, H. M. Grey, E. Celis, R. W. Chesnut, R. T. Kubo, and A. Sette. Two distinct HLA-A*0101-specific submotifs illustrate alternative peptide binding modes. *Immunogenetics*, 45:249–258, 1997.

G. Koopman, R. M. Keehnen, E. Lindhout, D. F. Zhou, C. de Groot, and S. T. Pals. Germinal center B cells rescued from apoptosis by CD40 ligation or attachment to follicular dendritic cells, but not by engagement of surface immunoglobulin or adhesion receptors, become resistant to CD95- induced apoptosis. *Eur. J. Immunol.*, 27:1–7, 1997.

B. Korber, M. Muldoon, J. Theiler, F. Gao, R. Gupta, A. Lapedes, B. H. Hahn, S. Wolinsky, and T. Bhattacharya. Timing the ancestor of the HIV-1 pandemic strains. *Science*, 288:1789–1796, 2000.

B. T. M. Korber, C. Brander, B. F. Haynes, R. Koup, C. Kuiken, J. P. Moore, B. D. Walker, and D. I. Watkins. *HIV Molecular Immunology 2001.* Theoretical Biology and Biophysics group, Los Alamos National Laboratoryss, Los Alamos, NM, 2001a.

B. T. M. Korber, B. Gaschen, K. Yusim, R. Thakallapally, C. Kesmir, and V. Detours. Evolutionary and immunological implications of contemporary HIV-1 variation. *Br. Med. Bull.*, 58:19–42, 2001b.

H. Kropshofer, G. J. Hammerling, and A. B. Vogt. The impact of the non-classical MHC proteins HLA-DM and HLA-DO on loading of MHC class II molecules. *Immunol. Rev.*, 172:267–278, 1999.

H. Kropshofer, A. B. Vogt, G. Moldenhauer, J. Hammer, J. S. Blum, and G. J. Hammerling. Editing of the HLA-DR-peptide repertoire by HLA-DM. *EMBO J.*, 15:6144–6154, 1996.

R. T. Kubo, Alessandro Sette, H.M Grey, E Appella, K Sakaguchi, N.Z Zhu, D Arnott, N Sherman, J Shabanowitz, and H Michel. Definition of specific peptide motifs for four major HLA-A alleles. *J. Immunol.*, 152:3913–3924, 1994.

U. Kuckelkorn, S. Frentzel, R. Kraft, S. Kostka, M. Groettrup, and P. M. Kloetzel. Incorporation of major histocompatibility complex–encoded subunits LMP2 and LMP7 changes the quality of the 20S proteasome polypeptide processing products independent of interferon-gamma. *Eur. J. Immunol.*, 25:2605–2611, 1995.

U. Kuckelkorn, T. Ruppert, B. Strehl, P. R. Jungblut, U. Zimny-Arndt, S. Lamer, I. Prinz, I. Drung, P. M. Kloetzel, S. H. Kaufmann, and U. Steinhoff. Link between organ-specific antigen processing by 20S proteasomes and CD8($^+$) T cell-mediated autoimmunity. *J. Exp. Med.*, 195:983–990, 2002.

S. Kullback and R. A. Leibler. On information and sufficiency. *Ann. of Math. Stat.*, 22: 76–86, 1951.

C. Kuttler, A. K. Nussbaum, T. P. Dick, H. G. Rammensee, H. Schild, and K. P. Hadeler. An algorithm for the prediction of proteasomal cleavages. *J. Mol. Biol.*, 298:417–429, 2000.

J. Kyte and R. F. Doolittle. A simple method for displaying the hydropathic character of a protein. *J. Mol. Biol.*, 157:105–132, 1982.

M. V. Larsen, C. Lundegaard, S. Brunak, O. Lund, and M. Nielsen. An integrative approach to CTL epitope prediction. A combined algorithm integrating MHC binding, TAP transport efficiency and proteasomal cleavage predictions. submitted, 2005.

S. L. Larsen, L. O. Pedersen, S. Buus, and A. Stryhn. T cell responses affected by aminopeptidase N (CD13)-mediated trimming of major histocompatibility complex class II-bound peptides. *J. Exp. Med.*, 184:183–189, 1996.

J. Laurence. HAART, side effects, and viral transmission. *AIDS Read.*, 14:210–211, 2004.

S. Laurent, L. Mouthon, E. Longchampt, M. Roudaire, S. Franc, A. Krivitzky, and R. Cohen. Medical cure of plasma cell granuloma of the thyroid associated with Hashimoto's thyroiditis: a case report and review. *J. Clin. Endocrinol. Metab.*, 89: 1534–1537, 2004.

A. Lautwein, M. Kraus, M. Reich, T. Burster, J. Brandenburg, H. S. Overkleeft, G. Schwarz, W. Kammer, E. Weber, H. Kalbacher, A. Nordheim, and C. Driessen. Human B lymphoblastoid cells contain distinct patterns of cathepsin activity in endocytic compartments and regulate MHC class II transport in a cathepsin S-independent manner. *J. Leukoc. Biol.*, 75:844–855, 2004.

C. E. Lawrence, Altschul S. F., M. S. Boguski, J. S. Liu, A. F. Neuwald, and J. C. Wootton. Detecting sutble sequence signals: a Gibbs sampling strategy for multiple alignment. *Science*, 262:208–214, 1993.

T. Leanderson, E. Kallberg, and D. Gray. Expansion, selection and mutation of antigen-specific B cells in germinal centers. *Immunol. Rev.*, 126:47–61, 1992.

A. B. de Leo. p53-based immunotherapy of cancer. Approaches ro reversing unresponsiveness to T lymphocytes and preventing tumor escape. *Adv. Otorhinolaryngol.*, 62:134–150, 2005.

A. J. Leslie, K. J. Pfafferott, P. Chetty, R. Draenert, M. M. Addo, M. Feeney, Y. Tang, E. C. Holmes, T. Allen, J. G. Prado, M. Altfeld, C. Brander, C. Dixon, D. Ramduth, P. Jeena, S. A. Thomas, A. St John, T. A. Roach, B. Kupfer, G. Luzzi, A. Edwards, G. Taylor, H. Lyall, G. Tudor-Williams, V. Novelli, J. Martinez-Picado, P. Kiepiela, B. D. Walker, and P. J. Goulder. HIV evolution: CTL escape mutation and reversion after transmission. *Nat. Med.*, 10:282–289, 2004.

A. M. Lever. HIV RNA packaging and lentivirus-based vectors. *Adv. Pharmacol.*, 48: 1–28, 2000.

M. Levitt. A simplified representation of protein conformations for rapid simulation of protein folding. *J. Mol. Biol.*, 104:59–107, 1976.

M. Levitt. Conformational preferences of amino acids in globular proteins. *Biochemistry*, 17:4277–4285, 1978.

F. Levy, L. Burri, S. Morel, A. L. Peitrequin, N. Levy, A. Bachi, U. Hellman, B. J. Van den Eynde, and C. Servis. The final N-terminal trimming of a subaminoterminal proline-containing HLA class I-restricted antigenic peptide in the cytosol is mediated by two peptidases. *J. Immunol.*, 169:4161–4171, 2002.

S. Levy, E. Mendel, S. Kon, Z. Avnur, and R. Levy. Mutational hot spots in Ig V region genes of human follicular lymphomas. *J. Exp. Med.*, 168:475–489, 1988.

J. J. Lewis. Therapeutic cancer vaccines: using unique antigens. *Proc. Natl. Acad. Sci. U.S.A.*, 101:14653–14656, 2004.

R. C. Lewontin, L. R. Ginzburg, and S. D. Tuljapurkar. Heterosis as an explanation for large amounts of genic polymorphism. *Genetics*, 88:149–170, 1978.

C. Li and W. H. Wong. Model-based analysis of oligonucleotide arrays: expression index computation and outlier detection. *Proc. Natl. Acad. Sci. U. S. A.* , 98:31–36, 2001a.

C. Li and W. H. Wong. Model-based analysis of oligonucleotide arrays: model validation, design issues and standard error application. *Genome Biol.*, 2:RESEARCH0032, 2001b.

M. P. Liang, D. R. Banatao, T. E. Klein, D. L. Brutlag, and R. B. Altman. WebFEATURE: an interactive web tool for identifying and visualizing functional sites on macromolecular structures. *Nucleic Acids Res.*, 31:3324–3327, 2003.

U. de Lichtenberg, L. J. Jensen, A. Fausboll, T. S. Jensen, P. Bork, and S. Brunak. Comparison of computational methods for the identification of cell cycle regulated genes. *Bioinformatics.*, In press, 2004.

U. de Lichtenberg, L.J. Jensen, S. Brunak, and P. Bork. Dynamic complex formation during the yeast cell cycle. *Science*, 307:724–727, 2005.

U. de Lichtenberg, T. S. Jensen, L. J. Jensen, and S. Brunak. Protein feature based identification of cell cycle regulated proteins in yeast. *J. Mol. Biol.*, 329:663–674, 2003.

M. Lichterfeld, X. G. Yu, D. Cohen, M. M. Addo, J. Malenfant, B. Perkins, E. Pae, M. N. Johnston, D. Strick, T. M. Allen, E. S. Rosenberg, B. Korber, B. D. Walker, and M. Altfeld. HIV-1 Nef is preferentially recognized by CD8 T cells in primary HIV-1 infection despite a relatively high degree of genetic diversity. *AIDS*, 18:1383–1392, 2004.

E. Lindhout, G. Koopman, S. T. Pals, and C. de Groot. Triple check for antigen specificity of B cells during germinal centre reactions. *Immunol. Today*, 18:573–577, 1997.

P. S. Linsley, P. M. Wallace, J. Johnson, M. G. Gibson, J. L. Greene, J. A. Ledbetter, C. Singh, and M. A. Tepper. Immunosuppression in vivo by a soluble form of the CTLA-4 T cell activation molecule. *Science*, 257:792–795, 1992.

T. Lohmuller, D. Wenzler, S. Hagemann, W. Kiess, C. Peters, T. Dandekar, and T. Reinheckel. Toward computer-based cleavage site prediction of cysteine endopeptidases. *Biol. Chem.*, 384:899–909, 2003.

O. Lund, M. Nielsen, C. Kesmir, J.K. Christensen, C. Lundegaard, P. Worning, and S. Brunak. Web-based tools for vaccine design. In B.T. Korber, C. Brander, B.F. Haynes, R. Koup, C. Kuiken, J.P. Moore, B.D. Walker, and D. Watkins, editors, *HIV Molecular Immunology*, pages 45–51, Los Alamos, NM, 2002. Theoretical Biology and Biophysics Group, Los Alamos National Laboratory.

O. Lund, M. Nielsen, C. Kesmir, A. G. Petersen, C. Lundegaard, P. Worning, C. Sylvester-Hvid, K. Lamberth, G. Roder, S. Justesen, S. Buus, and S. Brunak. Definition of supertypes for HLA molecules using clustering of specificity matrices. *Immunogenetics*, 55:797–810, 2004.

C. Lundegaard, M. Nielsen, P. Worning, C. Sylvester-Hvid, K. Lamberth, S. Buus, S. Brunak, and O. Lund. MHC class I epitope binding prediction trained on small data sets. In Guiseppe Nicosia, Vincenzo Cutello, Peter J. Bentley, and Jon Timmis, editors, *Proceedings of the Third ICARIS Meeting*, pages 217–225, New York, 2004. Springer.

R. B. Lyngsø, C. N. Pedersen, and H. Nielsen. Metrics and similarity measures for hidden Markov models. *Proc Int Conf Intell Syst Mol Biol*, pages 178–186, 1999.

T. Mabrouk and R. W. Ellis. Influenza vaccine technologies and the use of the cell-culture process (cell-culture influenza vaccine). *Dev. Biol. (Basel)*, 110:125–134, 2002.

I. C. MacLennan. Germinal centers. *Annu. Rev. Immunol.*, 12:117–139, 1994.

I. C. MacLennan, A. Gulbranson-Judge, K. M. Toellner, M. Casamayor-Palleja, E. Chan, D. M. Sze, S. A. Luther, and H. A. Orbea. The changing preference of T and B cells for partners as T-dependent antibody responses develop. *Immunol. Rev.*, 156:53–66, 1997a.

I. C. M. MacLennan, M. Casamayor-Palleja, K. M. Toellner, A. Gulbranson-Judge, and J. Gordon. Memory B-cell clones and the diversity of their members. *Semin. Immunol.*, 9:229-234, 1997b.

J. MacQueen. Some methods for classification and analysis of multivariate observations. In *Proceedings of the Fifth Berkeley Symposium on Mathematical Statistics and Probability, Volume 1*, pages 281-297, Berkeley, 1967. University of California Press.

A. Z. Maksyutov and E. S. Zagrebelnaya. ADEPT: a computer program for prediction of protein antigenic determinants. *Comput. Appl. Biosci.*, 9:291-297, 1993.

H. Mamitsuka. Predicting peptides that bind to MHC molecules using supervised learning of hidden Markov models. *Proteins*, 33:460-474, 1998.

T. Mandrup-Poulsen. Beta cell death and protection. *Ann. N. Y. Acad. Sci.*, 1005:32-42, 2003.

B. Manoury, E. W. Hewitt, N. Morrice, P. M. Dando, A. J. Barrett, and C. Watts. An asparaginyl endopeptidase processes a microbial antigen for class II MHC presentation. *Nature*, 396:695-699, 1998.

B. Manoury, D. Mazzeo, D. N. Li, J. Billson, K. Loak, P. Benaroch, and C. Watts. Asparagine endopeptidase can initiate the removal of the MHC class II invariant chain chaperone. *Immunity*, 18:489-498, 2003.

M. Y. Mapara and M. Sykes. Tolerance and cancer: mechanisms of tumor evasion and strategies for breaking tolerance. *J. Clin. Oncol.*, 22:1136-1151, 2004.

M. Maric, B. Arunachalam, U. T. Phan, C. Dong, W. S. Garrett, K. S. Cannon, C. Alfonso, L. Karlsson, R. A. Flavell, and P. Cresswell. Defective antigen processing in GILT-free mice. *Science*, 294:1361-1365, 2001.

F. M. Marincola, E. Wang, M. Herlyn, B. Seliger, and S. Ferrone. Tumors as elusive targets of T-cell-based active immunotherapy. *Trends Immunol.*, 24:335-342, 2003.

S. G. E. Marsh, P. Parham, and L. D. Barber. *The HLA Facts Book*. Academic Press, San Diego, 2000.

G. S. Marshall, P. H. Dennehy, D. P. Greenberg, P. A. Offit, and T. Q. Tan. *The Vaccine Handbook*. Lippincott Wiliams and Williams, Philadelphia, 2003.

K. W. Marshall, K.J. Wilson, J. Liang, A. Woods, D. Zaller, and J.B. Rothbard. Prediction of peptide affinity to HLA-DRB1*0401. *J. Immunol.*, 154:5927-5933, 1995.

T. Maruyama and M. Nei. Genetic variability maintained by mutation and overdominant selection in finite populations. *Genetics*, 98:441-459, 1981.

L. Mateo, J. Gardner, Q. Chen, C. Schmidt, M. Down, S. L. Elliott, S. J. Pye, H. Firat, F. A. Lemonnier, J. Cebon, and A. Suhrbier. An HLA-A2 polyepitope vaccine for melanoma immunotherapy. *J. Immunol.*, 163:4058-4063, 1999.

M. A. Mathieu, M. Bogyo, C. R. Caffrey, Y. Choe, J. Lee, H. Chapman, M. Sajid, C. S. Craik, and J. H. McKerrow. Substrate specificity of schistosome versus human legumain determined by P1-P3 peptide libraries. *Mol. Biochem. Parasitol.*, 121:99-105, 2002.

B. W. Matthews. Comparison of the predicted and observed secondary structure of T4 phage lysozyme. *Biochim. Biophys. Acta*, 405:442-451, 1975.

H. McDevitt. Specific antigen vaccination to treat autoimmune disease. *Proc. Natl. Acad. Sci. U.S.A.*, 101:14627-14630, 2004.

G. E. Meister, C. G. Roberts, J. A. Berzofsky, and A. S. de Groot. Two novel T cell epitope prediction algorithms based on MHC-binding motifs; comparison of predicted and published epitopes from *Mycobacterium tuberculosis* and HIV protein sequences. *Vaccine*, 13:581-591, 1995.

N. Metropolis, A. W. Rosenbluth, A. H. Teller, and E. Teller. Equation of state calculation by fast computing machines. *J. Chem. Phys.*, 21:1087-1092, 1953.

O. Mirza, A. Henriksen, H. Ipsen, J. N. Larsen, M. Wissenbach, M. D. Spangfort, and M. Gajhede. Dominant epitopes and allergic cross-reactivity: complex formation between a Fab fragment of a monoclonal murine IgG antibody and the major allergen from birch pollen Bet v 1. *J Immunol*, 165:331-338, 2000.

A. X. Mo, S. F. van Lelyveld, A. Craiu, and K. L. Rock. Sequences that flank subdominant and cryptic epitopes influence the proteolytic generation of MHC class I-presented peptides. *J. Immunol.*, 164:4003-4010, 2000.

X. Y. Mo, P. Cascio, K. Lemerise, A. L. Goldberg, and K. Rock. Distinct proteolytic processes generate the C and N termini of MHC class I-binding peptides. *J. Immunol.*, 163:5851-5859, 1999.

S. Mocellin, C. R. Rossi, and D. Nitti. Cancer vaccine development: on the way to break immune tolerance to malignant cells. *Exp. Cell Res.*, 299:267-278, 2004.

J. P. Moore, Y. Cao, D. D. Ho, and R. A. Koup. Development of the anti-gp120 antibody response during seroconversion to human immunodeficiency virus type 1. *J. Virol.*, 68:5142-5155, 1994.

S. Morel, F. Levy, O. Burlet-Schiltz, F. Brasseur, M. Probst-Kepper, A. L. Peitrequin, B. Monsarrat, R. Van Velthoven, J. C. Cerottini, T. Boon, J. E. Gairin, and B. J. Van den Eynde. Processing of some antigens by the standard proteasome but not by the immunoproteasome results in poor presentation by dendritic cells. *Immunity*, 12:107-117, 2000.

Y. Moret and P. Schmid-Hempel. Survival for immunity: the price of immune system activation for bumblebee workers. *Science*, 290:1166-1168, 2000.

B. Morgenstern. DIALIGN 2: improvement of the segment-to-segment approach to multiple sequence alignment. *Bioinformatics*, 15:211-218, 1999.

B. Moss, G. L. Smith, J. L. Gerin, and R. H. Purcell. Live recombinant vaccinia virus protects chimpanzees against hepatitis B. *Nature*, 311:67–69, 1984.

K. Motomura, N. Toyoda, K. Oishi, H. Sato, S. Nagai, S.-i. Hashimoto, S. B. Tugume, R. Enzama, R. Mugewa, C. K. Mutuluuza, P. Mugyeyi, T. Nagatake, and K. Matsushima. Identification of a host gene subset related to disease prognosis of HIV-1 infected individuals. *Int. Immunopharmacol.*, 4:1829–1836, 2004.

M. Muramatsu, K. Kinoshita, S. Fagarasan, S. Yamada, Y. Shinkai, and T. Honjo. Class switch recombination and hypermutation require activation-induced cytidine deaminase (AID), a potential RNA editing enzyme. *Cell*, 102:553–563, 2000.

T. Nakagawa, W. Roth, P. Wong, A. Nelson, A. Farr, J. Deussing, J. A. Villadangos, H. Ploegh, C. Peters, and A. Y. Rudensky. Cathepsin L: critical role in Ii degradation and CD4 T cell selection in the thymus. *Science*, 280:450–453, 1998.

S. B. Needleman and C. D. Wunsch. A general method applicable to the search for similarities in the amino acid sequence of two proteins. *J. Mol. Biol.*, 48:443–453, 1970.

A. F. Neuwald, J. S. Liu, and C. E. Lawrence. Gibbs motif sampling: detection of bacterial oter membrane protein repeats. *Protein Sci.*, 4:1618–1632, 1995.

NIAID (National Institute of Allergy and Infectious Diseases), the Jordan report 2000: accelerated development of vaccines, http://www.niaid.nih.gov/publications/pdf/jordan.pdf, 2000.

NIAID (National Institute of Allergy and Infectious Diseases), NIAID research agenda for CDC category A agents, http://www.niaid.nih.gov/biodefense/research/biotresearchagenda.pdf, 2002a.

NIAID (National Institute of Allergy and Infectious Diseases), the Jordan report, 20th anniversary, accelerated development of vaccines 2002, http://www.niaid.nih.gov/dmid/vaccines/jordan20/jordan20_2002.pdf, 2002b.

NIAID (National Institute of Allergy and Infectious Diseases), biodefense research agenda for CDC category A agents, progress report, August 2003, http://www.niaid.nih.gov/biodefense/research/category_A_Progress_Report.pdf, 2003.

V. Niederberger, F. Horak, S. Vrtala, S. Spitzauer, M. T. Krauth, P. Valent, J. Reisinger, M. Pelzmann, B. Hayek, M. Kronqvist, G. Gafvelin, H. Gronlund, A. Purohit, R. Suck, H. Fiebig, O. Cromwell, G. Pauli, M. van Hage-Hamsten, and R. Valenta. Vaccination with genetically engineered allergens prevents progression of allergic disease. *Proc. Natl. Acad. Sci. U.S.A.*, 101:14677–14682, 2004.

G. Niedermann, E. Geier, M. Lucchiari-Hartz, N. Hitziger, A. Ramsperger, and K. Eichmann. The specificity of proteasomes: impact on MHC class I processing and presentation of antigens. *Immunol. Rev.*, 172:29–48, 1999.

M. Nielsen, C. Lundegaard, O. Lund, and C. Kesmir. The role of the proteasome in generating cytotoxic T cell epitopes: Insights obtained from improved predictions of proteasomal cleavage, 2005.

M. Nielsen, C. Lundegaard, P. Worning, C. S. Hvid, K. Lamberth, S. Buus, S. Brunak, and O. Lund. Improved prediction of MHC class I and class II epitopes using a novel Gibbs sampling approach. *Bioinformatics*, 20:1388–1397, 2004.

M. Nielsen, C. Lundegaard, P. Worning, S. L. Lauemoller, K. Lamberth, S. Buus, S. Brunak, and O. Lund. Reliable prediction of T-cell epitopes using neural networks with novel sequence representations. *Protein Sci.*, 12:1007–1017, 2003.

C. Noda, N. Tanahashi, N. Shimbara, K. B. Hendil, and K. Tanaka. Tissue distribution of constitutive proteasomes, immunoproteasomes, and PA28 in rats. *Biochem. Biophys. Res. Commun.*, 277:348–354, 2000.

C. Notredame, D. G. Higgins, and J. Heringa. T-Coffee: A novel method for fast and accurate multiple sequence alignment. *J. Mol. Biol.*, 302:205–217, 2000.

V. Novitsky, U. R. Smith, P. Gilbert, M. F. McLane, P. Chigwedere, C. Williamson, T. Ndung'u, I. Klein, S. Y. Chang, T. Peter, I. Thior, B. T. Foley, S. Gaolekwe, N. Rybak, S. Gaseitsiwe, F. Vannberg, R. Marlink, T. H. Lee, and M. Essex. Human immunodeficiency virus type 1 subtype C molecular phylogeny: consensus sequence for an AIDS vaccine design? *J. Virol.*, 76:5435–5451, 2002.

J. Novotny, M. Handschumacher, E. Haber, R. E. Bruccoleri, W. B. Carlson, D. W. Fanning, J. A. Smith, and G. D. Rose. Antigenic determinants in proteins coincide with surface regions accessible to large probes (antibody domains). *Proc. Natl. Acad. Sci. U. S. A.*, 83:226–30, 1986.

A. K. Nussbaum, T. P. Dick, W. Keilholz, M. Schirle, S. Stevanovic, K. Dietz, W. Heinemeyer, M. Groll, D. H. Wolf, R. Huber, H. G. Rammensee, and H. Schild. Cleavage motifs of the yeast 20S proteasome β subunits deduced from digests of enolase 1. *Proc. Natl. Acad. Sci. U.S.A.*, 95:12504–12509, 1998.

A. K. Nussbaum, C. Kuttler, K. P. Hadeler, H. G. Rammensee, and H. Schild. PAProC: a prediction algorithm for proteasomal cleavages available on the WWW. *Immunogenetics*, 53:87–94, 2001.

M. Odorico and J.-L. Pellequer. BEPITOPE: predicting the location of continuous epitopes and patterns in proteins. *J. Mol. Recognit.*, 16:20–22, 2003.

M. Oprea and A. S. Perelson. Somatic mutation leads to efficient affinity maturation when centrocytes recycle back to centroblasts. *J. Immunol.*, 158:5155–5162, 1997.

M. Oprea, E. Van Nimwegen, and A. S. Perelson. Dynamics of one-pass germinal center models: implications for affinity maturation. *Bull. Math. Biol.*, 62:121–153, 2000.

F. Ossendorp, M. Eggers, A. Neisig, T. Ruppert, M. Groettrup, A. Sijts, E. Mengede, P. M. Kloetzel, J. Neefjes, U. Koszinowski, and C. Melief. A single residue exchange within a viral CTL epitope alters proteasome-mediated degradation resulting in lack of antigen presentation. *Immunity*, 5:115-124, 1996.

E. G. Pamer, C. E. Davis, and M. So. Expression and deletion analysis of the *Trypanosoma brucei rhodesiense* cysteine protease in *Escherichia coli*. *Infect. Immun.*, 59:1074-1078, 1991.

Z. Pancer, C. T. Amemiya, G. R. Ehrhardt, J. Ceitlin, G. L. Gartland, and M. D. Cooper. Somatic diversification of variable lymphocyte receptors in the agnathan sea lamprey. *Nature*, 430:174-180, 2004.

J. M. Parker, D. Guo, and R. S. Hodges. New hydrophilicity scale derived from high-performance liquid chromatography peptide retention data: correlation of predicted surface residues with antigenicity and X-ray-derived accessible sites. *Biochemistry*, 25:5425-5432, 1986.

K. C. Parker, M. A. Bednarek, and J. E. Coligan. Scheme for ranking potential HLA-A2 binding peptides based on independent binding of individual peptide side-chains. *J. Immunol.*, 152:163-175, 1994.

L. D. Pasquier and M. Flajnik. Origin and evolution of the vertebrate. In W. E. Paul, editor, *Fundamental Immunology*, pages 605-649. Lippincott-Raven, New York, 1999.

W. R. Pearson. Effective protein sequence comparison. *Methods Enzymol.*, 266:227-258, 1996.

W. R. Pearson and D. J. Lipman. Improved tools for biological sequence comparison. *Proc. Natl. Acad. Sci. U. S. A.*, 85:2444-2448, 1988.

A. G. Pedersen, L. J. Jensen, S. Brunak, H. H. Staerfeldt, and D. W. Ussery. A dna structural atlas for Escherichia coli. *J. Mol. Biol.*, 299:907-930, 2000.

C. N. S. Pedersen, R. B. Lyngsø, and J. Hein. Comparison of coding dna. In Martin Farach-Colton, editor, *Proceedings of the 9th Annual Symposium of Combinatorial Pattern Matching (CPM)*, Lecture Notes in Computer Science. Springer, 1998.

J. L. Pellequer, E. Westhof, and Van M. H. Regenmortel. Predicting location of continuous epitopes in proteins from their primary structures. *Methods Enzymol.*, 203: 176-201, 1991.

J. L. Pellequer, E. Westhof, and Van M. H. Regenmortel. Correlation between the location of antigenic sites and the prediction of turns in proteins. *Immunol. Lett.*, 36: 83-99, 1993.

B. Peters, S. Bulik, R. Tampe, P. M. van Endert, and H. G. Holzhutter. Identifying MHC class I epitopes by predicting the TAP transport efficiency of epitope precursors. *J. Immunol.*, 171:1741-1749, 2003a.

B. Peters, K. Janek, U. Kuckelkorn, and H. G. Holzhutter. Assessment of proteasomal cleavage probabilities from kinetic analysis of time-dependent product formation. *J. Mol. Biol.*, 318:847–862, 2002.

B. Peters, W. Tong, J. Sidney, A. Sette, and Z. Weng. Examining the independent binding assumption for binding of peptide epitopes to MHC-I molecules. *Bioinformatics*, 19: 1765–1772, 2003b.

T. C. Pierson and R. W. Doms. HIV-1 entry and its inhibition. *Curr. Top. Microbiol. Immunol.*, 281:1–27, 2003.

D. C. Pimenta, A. Oliveira, M. A. Juliano, and L. Juliano. Substrate specificity of human cathepsin D using internally quenched fluorescent peptides derived from reactive site loop of kallistatin. *Biochim. Biophys. Acta*, 1544:113–122, 2001.

O. Planz, S. Ehl, E. Furrer, E. Horvath, M. A. Brundler, H. Hengartner, and R. M. Zink-ernagel. A critical role for neutralizing-antibody-producing B cells, CD4$^+$ T cells, and interferons in persistent and acute infections of mice with lymphocytic chori-omeningitis virus: implications for adoptive immunotherapy of virus carriers. *Proc. Natl. Acad. Sci. U.S.A.*, 94:6874–6879, 1997.

O. Planz, P. Seiler, H. Hengartner, and R. M. Zinkernagel. Specific cytotoxic T cells elim-inate B cells producing virus-neutralizing antibodies. *Nature*, 382:726–729, 1996.

S. A. Plotkin and W. A. Orenstein. *Vaccines*. W. B. Saunders Company, Philadelphia, 3rd edition, 1999.

W. H. Press, B.P. Flannery, S.A. Teukolsky, and W.T. Vetterling. *Numerical Recipies in C: The Art of Scientific Computing*. Cambridge University Press, Cambridge, UK, 2rd edition, 1992.

J. C. Prinz. Disease mimicry–a pathogenetic concept for T cell-mediated autoimmune disorders triggered by molecular mimicry? *Autoimmun. Rev.*, 3:10–15, 2004.

J. Quackenbush. Computational analysis of microarray data. *Nat. Rev. Genet.*, 2:418–427, 2001.

J. Quackenbush. Microarray data normalization and transformation. *Nat. Genet.*, 32: 496–501, 2002.

John Quackenbush. Genomics. microarrays–guilt by association. *Science*, 302:240–241, 2003.

RAC   (Recombinant   DNA   Advisory   Committee),   appendix   B, http://www4.od.nih.gov/oba/rac/guidelines_02/APPENDIX_b.htm, 2002.

L. Raddrizzani and J. Hammer. Epitope scanning using virtual matrix-based algo-rithms. *Brief Bioinform.*, 1:179–189, 2000.

M. D. Radmacher, G. Kelsoe, and T. B. Kepler. Predicted and inferred waiting times for key mutations in the germinal centre reaction: Evidence for stochasticity in selection. *Immunol. Cell. Biol.*, 76:373–381, 1998.

G. Ragupathi and P. Livingston. The case for polyvalent cancer vaccines that induce antibodies. *Expert Rev. Vaccines*, 1:193–206, 2002.

W. Rahn, R. W. Redline, and T. G. Blanchard. Molecular analysis of *Helicobacter pylori*-associated gastric inflammation in naive versus previously immunized mice. *Vaccine*, 23:807–818, 2004.

H. Rammensee, J. Bachmann, N. P. Emmerich, O. A. Bachor, and S. Stevanovic. SYFPEITHI: database for MHC ligands and peptide motifs. *Immunogenetics*, 50:213–219, 1999.

H. G. Rammensee, J. Bachmann, and S. Stevanovic. *MHC ligands and Peptide Motifs.* Chapman & Hall, New York, 1997.

H. G. Rammensee, T. Friede, and S. Stevanoviic. MHC ligands and peptide motifs: first listing. *Immunogenetics*, 41:178–228, 1995.

D. Raoult, S. Audic, C. Robert, C. Abergel, P. Renesto, H. Ogata, B. La Scola, M. Suzan, and J. M. Claverie. The 1.2-megabase genome sequence of Mimivirus. *Science*, 306: 1344–1350, 2004.

N. D. Rawlings, D. P. Tolle, and A. J. Barrett. MEROPS: the peptidase database. *Nucleic Acids Res.*, 32:D160–D164, 2004.

S. Raychaudhuri, J. M. Stuart, and R. B. Altman. Principal components analysis to summarize microarray experiments: application to sporulation time series. *Pac Symp Biocomput*, pages 455–466, 2000.

P. A. Reche and E. L. Reinhertz. Definition of MHC supertypes through clustering of MHC peptide binding repetoires. In *Proceedings of the Third ICARIS Meeting*, New York, 2004. Springer-Verlag.

M. H. van Regenmortel. Mapping epitope structure and activity: From one-dimensional prediction to four-dimensional description of antigenic specificity. *Methods*, 9:465–472, 1996.

M. H. van Regenmortel and S. Muller. *Synthetic Peptides as Antigens.* Elsevier, Amsterdam, The Netherlands, 1999.

M. H. van Regenmortel and J. L. Pellequer. Predicting antigenic determinants in proteins: looking for unidimensional solutions to a three-dimensional problem? *Pept. Res.*, 7:224–228, 1994.

E. Reits, A. Griekspoor, J. Neijssen, T. Groothuis, K. Jalink, P. van Veelen, H. Janssen, J. Calafat, J. W. Drijfhout, and J. Neefjes. Peptide diffusion, protection, and degradation in nuclear and cytoplasmic compartments before antigen presentation by MHC class I. *Immunity*, 18:97–108, 2003.

E. Reits, J. Neijssen, C. Herberts, W. Benckhuijsen, L. Janssen, J. W. Drijfhout, and J. Neefjes. A major role for TPPII in trimming proteasomal degradation products for MHC class I antigen presentation. *Immunity*, 20:495–506, 2004.

E. A. Reits, A. C. Griekspoor, and J. Neefjes. How does TAP pump peptides? Insights from DNA repair and traffic ATPases. *Immunol. Today*, 21:598–600, 2000.

M. Rewers, J. Norris, and D. Dabelea. Epidemiology of type 1 Diabetes Mellitus. *Adv. Exp. Med. Biol.*, 552:219–246, 2004.

M. Robert-Guroff, M. Brown, and R. C. Gallo. HTLV-III-neutralizing antibodies in patients with AIDS and AIDS-related complex. *Nature*, 316:72–74, 1985.

J. Robinson, M.J. Waller, P. Parham, J.G. Bodmer, and S.G.E. Marsh. IMGT/HLA database - a sequence database for the human major histocompatibility complex. *Nucleic Acids Res.*, 29:210–213, 2001.

K. L. Rock and A. L. Goldberg. Degradation of cell proteins and the generation of MHC class I-presented peptides. *Annu. Rev. Immunol.*, 17:739–779, 1999.

F. Rodriguez, L. L. An, S. Harkins, J. Zhang, M. Yokoyama, G. Widera, J. T. Fuller, C. Kincaid, I. L. Campbell, and J. L. Whitton. DNA immunization with minigenes: low frequency of memory cytotoxic T lymphocytes and inefficient antiviral protection are rectified by ubiquitination. *J. Virol.*, 72:5174–5181, 1998.

D. Rognan, S. L. Lauemøller, A. Holm, S. Buus, and V. Tschinke. Predicting binding affinities of protein ligands from three-dimensional models: application to peptide binding to class I major histocompatibility proteins. *J. Med. Chem.*, 42:4650–4658, 1999.

M. A. Romanos, J. J. Clare, K. M. Beesley, F. B. Rayment, S. P. Ballantine, A. J. Makoff, G. Dougan, N. F. Fairweather, and I. G. Charles. Recombinant *Bordetella pertussis* pertactin (P69) from the yeast *Pichia pastoris*: high-level production and immunological properties. *Vaccine.*, 9:901–906, 1991.

F. Ronchese, B. Hausmann, S. Hubele, and P. Lane. Mice transgenic for a soluble form of murine CTLA-4 show enhanced expansion of antigen-specific CD4+ T cells and defective antibody production in vivo. *J. Exp. Med.*, 179:809–817, 1994.

J. B. Rothbard and W. R. Taylor. A sequence pattern common to T cell epitopes. *EMBO J.*, 7:93–100, 1988.

O. Rotzschke, K. Falk, S. Stevanovic, G. Jung, P. Walden, and H. G. Rammensee. Exact prediction of a natural T cell epitope. *Eur. J. Immunol.*, 21:2891–2894, 1991.

B. Rozman, M. P. Novljan, A. Hocevar, A. Ambrozic, P. Zigon, T. Kveder, and M. Tomsic. Epidemiology and diagnostics of primary Sjogren's syndrome. *Reumatizam.*, 51: 9-12, 2004.

K. H. Rubins, L. E. Hensley, P. B. Jahrling, A. R. Whitney, T. W. Geisbert, J. W. Huggins, A. Owen, J. W. Leduc, P. O. Brown, and D. A. Relman. The host response to smallpox: Analysis of the gene expression program in peripheral blood cells in a nonhuman primate model. *Proc. Natl. Acad. Sci. U. S. A.*, 101:15190–15195, 2004.

D. E. Rumelhart, G. E. Hinton, and R. J. Williams. Learning representations by back-propagating errors. *Nature*, 323:533Ŭ–536, 1991.

N. Saitou and M. Nei. The neighbor-joining method: a new method for reconstructing phylogenetic trees. *Mol. Biol. Evol.*, 4:406–425, 1987.

C. S. Sarandeses, G. Covelo, C. Diaz-Jullien, and M. Freire. Prothymosin α is processed to thymosin α 1 and thymosin α 11 by a lysosomal asparaginyl endopeptidase. *J. Biol. Chem.*, 278:13286–13293, 2003.

T. Saric, S. C. Chang, A. Hattori, I. A. York, S. Markant, K. L. Rock, M. Tsujimoto, and A. L. Goldberg. An IFN-gamma-induced aminopeptidase in the ER, ERAP1, trims precursors to MHC class I-presented peptides. *Nat. Immunol.*, 3:1169–1176, 2002.

M. Sathiamurthy, H. D. Hickman, J. W. Cavett, A. Zahoor, K. Prilliman, S. Metcalf, M. Fernandez Vina, and W. H. Hildebrand. Population of the HLA ligand database. *Tissue Antigens*, 61:12-19, 2003.

P. Saxova, S. Buus, S. Brunak, and C. Kesmir. Predicting proteasomal cleavage sites: a comparison of available methods. *Int. Immunol.*, 15:781-787, 2003.

J. R. Schafer, B. M. Jesdale, J. A. George, N. M. Kouttab, and A. S. de Groot. Prediction of well-conserved HIV-1 ligands using a matrix-based algorithm, EpiMatrix. *Vaccine*, 16:1880-1884, 1998.

A. Scherer, J. Frater, A. Oxenius, J. Agudelo, D. A. Price, H. F. Gunthard, M. Barnardo, L. Perrin, B. Hirschel, R. E. Phillips, A. R. McLean, and Swiss HIV cohort. Quantifiable cytotoxic T lymphocyte responses and HLA-related risk of progression to AIDS. *Proc. Natl. Acad. Sci. U.S.A.*, 101:12266-12270, 2004.

A. Schiott, M. Lindstedt, B. Johansson-Lindbom, E. Roggen, and C. K. A. Borrebaeck. CD27- CD4+ memory T cells define a differentiated memory population at both the functional and transcriptional levels. *Immunology*, 113:363-370, 2004.

M. Schirle, T. Weinschenk, and S. Stevanovic. Combining computer algorithms with experimental approaches permits the rapid and accurate identification of T cell epitopes from defined antigens. *J. Immunol. Methods*, 257:1-16, 2001.

T. D. Schneider and R. M. Stephens. Sequence logos: a new way to display consensus sequences. *Nucleic Acids Res.*, 18:6097-6100, 1990.

K. Schønning, O. Lund, O. S. Lund, and J. E. Hansen. Stoichiometry of monoclonal antibody neutralization of T-cell line-adapted human immunodeficiency virus type 1. *J. Virol.*, 73:8364–8370, 1999.

O. Schueler-Furman, Y. Altuvia, A. Sette, and H. Margalit. Structure-based prediction of binding peptides to MHC class I molecules: application to a broad range of MHC alleles. *Protein Sci.*, 9:1838–1846, 2000.

E. S. Schultz, J. Chapiro, C. Lurquin, S. Claverol, O. Burlet-Schiltz, G. Warnier, V. Russo, S. Morel, F. Levy, T. Boon, B. J. van den Eynde, and P. van der Bruggen. The production of a new MAGE-3 peptide presented to cytolytic T lymphocytes by HLA-B40 requires the immunoproteasome. *J. Exp. Med.*, 195:391–399, 2002.

U. K. von Schwedler, K. M. Stray, J. E. Garrus, and W. I. Sundquist. Functional surfaces of the human immunodeficiency virus type 1 capsid protein. *J. Virol.*, 77:5439–5450, 2003.

M. Sela and E. Mozes. Therapeutic vaccines in autoimmunity. *Proc. Natl. Acad. Sci. U.S.A.*, 101:14586–14592, 2004.

T. Serwold, F. Gonzalez, J. Kim, R. Jacob, and N. Shastri. ERAAP customizes peptides for MHC class I molecules in the endoplasmic reticulum. *Nature*, 419:480–483, 2002.

A. Sette, L. Adorini, E. Appella, S. M. Colon, C. Miles, S. Tanaka, C. Ehrhardt, G. Doria, Z. A. Nagy, and S. Buus. Structural requirements for the interaction between peptide antigens and I-Ed molecules. *J. Immunol.*, 143:3289–3294, 1989a.

A. Sette, S. Buus, E. Appella, J. A. Smith, R. Chesnut, C. Miles, S. M. Colon, and H. M. Grey. Prediction of major histocompatibility complex binding regions of protein antigens by sequence pattern analysis. *Proc. Natl. Acad. Sci. U .S .A .*, 86:3296–2300, 1989b.

A. Sette and J. Fikes. Epitope-based vaccines: an update on epitope identification, vaccine design and delivery. *Curr. Opin. Immunol.*, 15:461–470, 2003.

A. Sette and J. Sidney. Nine major HLA class I supertypes account for the vast preponderance of HLA-A and -B polymorphism. *Immunogenetics*, 50:201–212, 1999.

C. E. Shannon. A mathematical theory of communication. *Bell System Tech. J.*, 27: 379–423, 623–656, 1948.

N. Shimbara, K. Ogawa, Y. Hidaka, H. Nakajima, N. Yamasaki, S. Niwa, N. Tanahashi, and K. Tanaka. Contribution of proline residue for efficient production of MHC class I ligands by proteasomes. *J. Biol. Chem.*, 273:23062–23071, 1998.

K. Shirahama-Noda, A. Yamamoto, K. Sugihara, N. Hashimoto, M. Asano, M. Nishimura, and I. Hara-Nishimura. Biosynthetic processing of cathepsins and lysosomal degradation are abolished in asparaginyl endopeptidase-deficient mice. *J. Biol. Chem.*, 278:33194–33199, 2003.

J. W. Shiver, T. M. Fu, L. Chen, D. R. Casimiro, M. E. Davies, R. K. Evans, Z. Q. Zhang, A. J. Simon, W. L. Trigona, S. A. Dubey, L. Huang, V. A. Harris, R. S. Long, X. Liang, L. Handt, W. A. Schleif, L. Zhu, D. C. Freed, N. V. Persaud, L. Guan, K. S. Punt, A. Tang, M. Chen, K. A. Wilson, K. B. Collins, G. J. Heidecker, V. R. Fernandez, H. C. Perry, J. G. Joyce, K. M. Grimm, J. C. Cook, P. M. Keller, D. S. Kresock, H. Mach, R. D. Troutman, L. A. Isopi, D. M. Williams, Z. Xu, K. E. Bohannon, D. B. Volkin, D. C. Montefiori, A. Miura, G. R. Krivulka, M. A. Lifton, M. J. Kuroda, J. E. Schmitz, N. L. Letvin, M. J. Caulfield, A. J. Bett, R. Youil, D. C. Kaslow, and E. A. Emini. Replication-incompetent adenoviral vaccine vector elicits effective anti-immunodeficiency-virus immunity. *Nature*, 415: 331–335, 2002.

J. Sidney, M. F. del Guercio', S. Southwood, V. H. Engelhard, E. Appella, H. G. Rammensee, K. Falk, O. Rotzschke, M. Takiguchi, and R. T. Kubo. Several HLA alleles share overlapping peptide specificities. *J. Immunol.*, 154:247–259, 1995.

J. Sidney, H. M. Grey, S. Southwood, E. Celis, P. A. Wentworth, M. F. del Guercio, R. T. Kubo, R. W. Chesnut, and A. Sette. Definition of an HLA-A3-like supermotif demonstrates the overlapping peptide-binding repertoires of common HLA molecules. *Hum. Immunol.*, 45:79–93, 1996.

A. J. Sijts, S. Standera, R. E. Toes, T. Ruppert, N. J. Beekman, P. A. van Veelen, F. A. Ossendorp, C. J. Melief, and P. M. Kloetzel. MHC class I antigen processing of an adenovirus CTL epitope is linked to the levels of immunoproteasomes in infected cells. *J. Immunol.*, 164:4500–4506, 2000.

H. Singh and G. P. Raghava. ProPred: prediction of HLA-DR binding sites. *Bioinformatics*, 17:1236–1237, 2001.

D. J. Smith, A. S. Lapedes, J. C. De Jong, T. M. Bestebroer, G. F. Rimmelzwaan, A. D. Osterhaus, and R. A. Fouchier. Mapping the antigenic and genetic evolution of influenza virus. *Science*, 305:371–376, 2004.

T. F. Smith and M. S. Waterman. Identification of common molecular subsequences. *J. Mol. Biol.*, 147:195–197, 1981.

J. T. Snyder, I. M. Belyakov, A. Dzutsev, F. Lemonnier, and J. A. Berzofsky. Protection against lethal vaccinia virus challenge in HLA-A2 transgenic mice by immunization with a single CD8+ T-cell peptide epitope of vaccinia and variola viruses. *J. Virol.*, 78:7052–7060, 2004.

R.R. Sokal and C.D. Michener. A statistical method for evaluating systematic relationships. *Univ. Kansas Bull.*, 28:1409–1438, 1958.

E. L. Sonnhammer, S. R. Eddy, and R. Durbin. Pfam: a comprehensive database of protein domain families based on seed alignments. *Proteins*, 28:405–420, 1997.

S. Southwood, J. Sidney, A. Kondo, del M. F. Guercio, E. Appella, S. Hoffman, R. T. Kubo, R. W. Chesnut, H. M. Grey, and A. Sette. Several common HLA-DR types share largely overlapping peptide binding repertoires. *J. Immunol.*, 160:3363–3373, 1998.

P. C. Jr Spiegel, M. Jacquemin, J. M. Saint-Remy, B. L. Stoddard, and K. P. Pratt. Structure of a factor VIII C2 domain-immunoglobulin G4kappa fab complex: identification of an inhibitory antibody epitope on the surface of factor VIII. *Blood*, 98:13-9, 2001.

J. Stokes and T. B. Casale. Rationale for new treatments aimed at IgE immunomodulation. *Ann. Allergy Asthma Immunol.*, 93:212-217, 2004.

L. Stoltze, A. K. Nussbaum, A. Sijts, N. P. Emmerich, P. M. Kloetzel, and H. Schild. The function of the proteasome system in MHC class I antigen processing. *Immunol. Today*, 21:317-319, 2000a.

L. Stoltze, M. Schirle, G. Schwarz, C. Schroter, M. W. Thompson, L. B. Hersh, H. Kalbacher, S. Stevanovic, H. G. Rammensee, and H. Schild. Two new proteases in the MHC class I processing pathway. *Nat. Immunol.*, 1:413-418, 2000b.

A. Stryhn, L.O. Pedersen, T. Romme, C. B. Holm, A. Holm, and S. Buus. Peptide binding specificity of major histocompatibility complex class I resolved into an array of apparently independent subspecificities: quantitation by peptide libraries and improved prediction of binding. *Eur. J. Immunol.*, 26:1911-1918, 1996.

J. M. Stuart, E. Segal, D. Koller, and S. K. Kim. A gene-coexpression network for global discovery of conserved genetic modules. *Science*, 302:249-255, 2003.

J. A. Studier and K. J. Keppler. A note on the neighbor-joining algorithm of Saitou and Nei. *Mol. Biol. Evol.*, 5:729-731, 1988.

T. Sturniolo, E. Bono, J. Ding, L. Raddrizzani, O. Tuereci, U. Sahin, M. Braxenthaler, F. Gallazzi, M. P. Protti, F. Sinigaglia, and J. Hammer. Generation of tissue-specific and promiscuous HLA ligand databases using DNA microarrays and virtual HLA class II matrices. *Nat. Biotechnol.*, 17:555-561, 1999.

A. Suhrbier. Multi-epitope DNA vaccines. *Immunol. Cell Biol.*, 75:402-408, 1997.

A. Suhrbier. Polytope vaccines for the codelivery of multiple CD8 T-cell epitopes. *Expert Rev. Vaccines*, 1:207-213, 2002.

T. J. Suscovich, M. Paulose-Murphy, J. D. Harlow, Y. Chen, S. Y. Thomas, T. J. Mellott, B. D. Walker, D. T. Scadden, S. Zeichner, and C. Brander. Defective immune function of primary effusion lymphoma cells is associated with distinct KSHV gene expression profiles. *Leuk. Lymphoma*, 45:1223-1238, 2004.

J. A. Swets. Measuring the accuracy of diagnostic systems. *Science*, 240:1285-1293, 1988.

C. Sylvester-Hvid, N. Kristensen, T. Blicher, H. Ferr, S.L. Lauemøller, X.A. Wolf, K. Lamberth, M.H. Nissen, L.. Pedersen, and S. Buus. Establishment of a quantitative ELISA capable of determining peptide-MHC class I interaction. *Tissue Antigens*, 59:251-258, 2002.

C. Sylvester-Hvid, M. Nielsen, K. Lamberth, G. Roder, S. Justesen, C. Lundegaard, P. Worning, H. Thomadsen, O. Lund, S. Brunak, and S. Buus. SARS CTL vaccine candidates; HLA supertype-, genome-wide scanning and biochemical validation. *Tissue Antigens*, 63:395–400, 2004.

N. Takahata and M. Nei. Allelic genealogy under overdominant and frequency-dependent selection and polymorphism of major histocompatibility complex loci. *Genetics*, 124:967–978, 1990.

K. Tanaka and M. Kasahara. The MHC class I ligand–generating system: roles of immunoproteasomes and the interferon-gamma-inducible proteasome activator PA28. *Immunol. Rev.*, 163:161–176, 1998.

T. Tanaka and M. Nei. Positive Darwinian selection observed at the variable-region genes of immunoglobulins. *Mol. Biol. Evol.*, 6:447–459, 1989.

C. B. Thompson. New insights into V(D)J recombination and its role in the evolution of the immune system. *Immunity*, 3:531–539, 1995.

J. D. Thompson, D. G. Higgins, and T. J. Gibson. CLUSTAL W: improving the sensitivity of progressive multiple sequence alignment through sequence weighting, position-specific gap penalties and weight matrix choice. *Nucleic Acids Res.*, 22: 4673–4680, 1994.

W. Thompson, E. C. Rouchka, and C. E. Lawrence. Gibbs recursive sampler: finding transcription factor binding sites. *Nucleic Acids Res.*, 31:3580–3585, 2003.

A. R. Thomsen, J. Johansen, O. Marker, and J. P. Christensen. Exhaustion of CTL memory and recrudescence of viremia in lymphocytic choriomeningitis virus-infected MHC class II-deficient mice and B cell- deficient mice. *J. Immunol.*, 157:3074–3080, 1996.

S. A. Thomson, M. A. Sherritt, J. Medveczky, S. L. Elliott, D. J. Moss, G. J. Fernando, L. E. Brown, and A. Suhrbier. Delivery of multiple CD8 cytotoxic T cell epitopes by DNA vaccination. *J. Immunol.*, 160:1717–1723, 1998.

J. M. Thornton, M. S. Edwards, W. R. Taylor, and D. J. Barlow. Location of "continuous" antigenic determinants in the protruding regions of proteins. *EMBO J.*, 5:409–413, 1986.

R. E. Toes, A. K. Nussbaum, S. Degermann, M. Schirle, N. P. Emmerich, M. Kraft, C. Laplace, A. Zwinderman, T. P. Dick, J. Muller, B. Schonfisch, C. Schmid, H. J. Fehling, S. Stevanovic, H. G. Rammensee, and H. Schild. Discrete cleavage motifs of constitutive and immunoproteasomes revealed by quantitative analysis of cleavage products. *J. Exp. Med.*, 194:1–12, 2001.

H. H. Tong, J. P. Long, D. Li, and T. F. DeMaria. Alteration of gene expression in human middle ear epithelial cells induce d by influenza A virus and its implication for the pathogenesis of otitis media. *Microb. Pathog.*, 37:193–204, 2004.

E. Trachtenberg, B. Korber, C. Sollars, T. B. Kepler, P. T. Hraber, E. Hayes, R. Funkhouser, M. Fugate, J. Theiler, Y. S. Hsu, K. Kunstman, S. Wu, J. Phair, H. Erlich, and S. Wolinsky. Advantage of rare HLA supertype in HIV disease progression. *Nat. Med.*, 9:928-935, 2003.

D. Turk, V. Janjic, I. Stern, M. Podobnik, D. Lamba, S. W. Dahl, C. Lauritzen, J. Pedersen, V. Turk, and B. Turk. Structure of human dipeptidyl peptidase I (cathepsin C): exclusion domain added to an endopeptidase framework creates the machine for activation of granular serine proteases. *EMBO J.*, 20:6570-6582, 2001.

S. Uebel, W. Kraas, S. Kienle, K. H. Wiesmuller, G. Jung, and R. Tampe. Recognition principle of the TAP transporter disclosed by combinatorial peptide libraries. *Proc. Natl. Acad. Sci. U.S.A.*, 94:8976-8981, 1997.

S. Uebel and R. Tampe. Specificity of the proteasome and the tap transporter. *Curr. Opin. Immunol.*, 11:203-208, 1999.

T. S. Uinuk-Ool, N. Takezaki, N. Kuroda, F. Figueroa, A. Sato, I. E. Samonte, W. E. Mayer, and J. Klein. Phylogeny of antigen-processing enzymes: cathepsins of a cephalochordate, an agnathan and a bony fish. *Scand. J. Immunol.*, 58:436-448, 2003.

L van Valen. A new evolutionary law. *Evol. Theory*, 1:1-30, 1973.

C. Videla, G. Carballal, A. Misirlian, and M. Aguilar. Acute lower respiratory infections due to respiratory syncytial virus and adenovirus among hospitalized children from argentina. *Clin. Diagn. Virol.*, 10:17-23, 1998.

M. Vingron and M. S. Waterman. Sequence alignment and penalty choice. review of concepts, case studies and implications. *J. Mol. Biol.*, 235:1-12, 1994.

M. T. Vossen, E. M. Westerhout, C. Soderberg-Naucler, and E. J. Wiertz. Viral immune evasion: a masterpiece of evolution. *Immunogenetics*, 54:527-542, 2002.

M. Wabl, M. Cascalho, and C. Steinberg. Hypermutation in antibody affinity maturation. *Curr. Opin. Immunol.*, 11:186-189, 1999.

C. Watts. The exogenous pathway for antigen presentation on major histocompatibility complex class II and CD1 molecules. *Nat. Immunol.*, 5:685-692, 2004.

A. P. Weetman. Autoimmune thyroid disease: propagation and progression. *Eur. J. Endocrinol.*, 148:1-9, 2003.

R. A. Weiss, P. R. Clapham, R. Cheingsong-Popov, A. G. Dalgleish, C. A. Carne, I. V. Weller, and R. S. Tedder. Neutralization of human T-lymphotropic virus type III by sera of AIDS and AIDS-risk patients. *Nature*, 316:69-72, 1985.

G. W. Welling, W. J. Weijer, R. van der Zee, and S. Welling-Wester. Prediction of sequential antigenic regions in proteins. *FEBS Lett.*, 188:215-218, 1985.

R Wernersson and A. G. Pedersen. RevTrans: multiple alignment of coding DNA from aligned amino acid sequences. *Nucleic Acids Res.*, 31:3537-3539, 2003.

WHO (World Health Organization), the World Health Report 2004, annex table 2, http://www.who.int/entity/whr/2004/annex/topic/en/annex_2_en.pdf, 2004a.

WHO (World Health Organization), the World health report 2004, changing history, http://www.who.int/entity/whr/2004/en/01_contents_en.pdf, 2004b.

G. D. Wiens, V. A. Roberts, E. A. Whitcomb, T. O'Hare, M. P. Stenzel-Poore, and M. B. Rittenberg. Harmful somatic mutations: lessons from the dark side. *Immunol. Rev.*, 162:197-209, 1998.

K. Wollenberg and J. C. Swaffield. Evolution of proteasomal ATPases. *Mol. Biol. Evol.*, 18:962-974, 2001.

T. Woodberry, J. Gardner, L. Mateo, D. Eisen, J. Medveczky, I. A. Ramshaw, S. A. Thomson, R. A. Ffrench, S. L. Elliott, H. Firat, F. A. Lemonnier, and A. Suhrbier. Immunogenicity of a human immunodeficiency virus (HIV) polytope vaccine containing multiple HLA-A2 HIV CD8(+) cytotoxic T-cell epitopes. *J. Virol.*, 73:5320-5325, 1999.

D. C. Wraith, H. O. McDevitt, L. Steinman, and H. Acha-Orbea. T cell recognition as the target for immune intervention in autoimmune disease. *Cell*, 57:709-715, 1989.

J. Wu and L. L. Lanier. Natural killer cells and cancer. *Adv. Cancer. Res.*, 90:127-156, 2003.

W. Xiang, O. Windl, G. Wunsch, M. Dugas, A. Kohlmann, N. Dierkes, I. M. Westner, and H. A. Kretzschmar. Identification of differentially expressed genes in scrapie-infected mouse brains by using global gene expression technology. *J. Virol.*, 78: 11051-11060, 2004.

Z. Yang and R. Nielsen. Estimating synonymous and nonsynonymous substitution rates under realistic evolutionary models. *Mol. Biol. Evol.*, 17:32-43, 2000.

J. Yelamos, N. Klix, B. Goyenechea, F. Lozano, Y. L. Chui, A. Gonzalez Fernandez, R. Pannell, M. S. Neuberger, and C. Milstein. Targeting of non-Ig sequences in place of the V segment by somatic hypermutation. *Nature*, 376:225-229, 1995.

J. Yewdell, L. C. Anton, I. Bacik, U. Schubert, H. L. Snyder, and J. R. Bennink. Generating MHC class I ligands from viral gene products. *Immunol. Rev.*, 172:97-108, 1999.

J. W. Yewdell and J. R. Bennink. Immunodominance in major histocompatibility complex class I-restricted T lymphocyte responses. *Annu. Rev. Immunol.*, 17:51-88, 1999.

J. W. Yewdell and J. R. Bennink. Cut and trim: generating MHC class I peptide ligands. *Curr. Opin. Immunol.*, 13:13-18, 2001.

S.-H. Yook, Z. N. Oltvai, and A. L. Barabasi. Functional and topological characterization of protein interaction networks. *Proteomics*, 4:928–942, 2004.

I. A. York, S. C. Chang, T. Saric, J. A. Keys, J. M. Favreau, A. L. Goldberg, and K. L. Rock. The ER aminopeptidase ERAP1 enhances or limits antigen presentation by trimming epitopes to 8-9 residues. *Nat. Immunol.*, 3:1177–1184, 2002.

K. Yu, N. Petrovsky, C. Schonbach, J. Y. Koh, and V. Brusic. Methods for prediction of peptide binding to MHC molecules: a comparative study. *Mol. Med.*, 8:137–148, 2002.

K. Yusim, C. Kesmir, B. Gaschen, M. M. Addo, M. Altfeld, S. Brunak, A. Chigaev, V. Detours, and B. T. Korber. Clustering patterns of cytotoxic T-lymphocyte epitopes in human immunodeficiency virus type 1 (HIV-1) proteins reveal imprints of immune evasion on HIV-1 global variation. *J. Virol.*, 76:8757–8768, 2002.

M. Y. Zhang, X. Xiao, I. A. Sidorov, V. Choudhry, F. Cham, P. F. Zhang, P. Bouma, M. Zwick, A. Choudhary, D. C. Montefiori, C. C. Broder, D. R. Burton, G. V. Jr. Quinnan, and D. S. Dimitrov. Identification and characterization of a new cross-reactive human immunodeficiency virus type 1-neutralizing human monoclonal antibody. *J. Virol.*, 78:9233–9242, 2004.

R. M. Zinkernagel. Immunology taught by viruses. *Science*, 271:173–178, 1996.

Index

Acquired immunodeficiency syndrome, 18
Adaptive immunity, 9
AEP, 179
Affinity maturation, 188
AIDS, 17
Alanyl aminopeptidase N, 178
Alignment, 36
  DNA, 54
  global, 47
  local, 47
  ungapped, 36
Allele, 111
Allergy, 31
Anchor positions, 112
  auxiliary, 112
ANN, 92, 112
  backpropagation, 95
  feedforward, 93
  sequence encoding, 98
ANOVA, 105
Anthrax, 24
Antibodies, 187
  neutralizing, 201
Antigen
  complex with antibody, 192
  presentation, 11
  processing, 11, 135
  tumor specific, 211
Antiretroviral therapy, 18
APN, 178
Arenavirus, 29
Artificial Neural Network, see also ANN, 92
ASHI, 221

Asparaginyl Endopeptidase, 179
Autoimmune disease, 3, 32

B cell
  Selection in GC, 189
Bacille Calmette-Guérin, 19
Background
  distribution, 72
  frequency, 71
  model, 71
Backpropagation, 95
BCG, 19
BIMAS, 112, 217
Binding motif, 112
Biodefense, 24
BLAST, 49
BLOCKS database, 40
BLOSUM, 37, 40
Bootstrap, 147
Botulism, 29
Bunyavirus, 29

Cancer, 30
Cathepsins, 177
CD4, 18
cDNA, 103
Chickenpox, 21
Childhood diseases, 21
CLIP, 179
ClustalW, 56
Clustering, 54, 102, 106
  MHC binding specificities, 226
Combination
  of MHC and proteasome predictions, 244

of MHC, TAP and proteasome predic-
  tions, 247
Constitutive proteasome, 137
Cross-loci supertypes, 236
CTL, 111

Database search, 47
Databases
  ASHI, 221
  BLOCKS, 40
  Dodo, 22, 205
  EPIMHC, 216
  HIV molecular immunology database,
    216
  IEDB, 216
  IMGT, 221
  JenPep, 216
  MHC Ligands, 215
  MHC ligands, 215
  MHC sequences, 220
  MHCBN, 216
  MHCPEP, 215
  SYFPEITHI, 215
Diarrheal diseases, 21
Diphtheria, 21
Distance matrix, 54
DNA microarray, 103
Dodo, 22, 205
Dynamic programming, 41

E-value, 50
Ebola, 30
ELISA, 118
Emerging pathogen, 17
Endoplasmic reticulum, see also ER,
  111
Entropy, 72
Enzyme-linked immunosorbent assay,
  118
EpiMatrix, 218
EPIMHC, 216
Epipredict, 218
ER, 111, 153
Escape, 57
  from Proteasomal Cleavage, 149
Evolution

proteasome, 154
TAP, 154
Expectation value, 49

Fab, 187
FASTA, 50
Fc, 187
Feedforward, 93
Filovirus, 29
follicles, 188
Forward-backward algorithm, 86
FragPredict, 147
Free energy calculations, 114

Gap penalty, 41
Genome atlas, 5
Germinal centers, 188
Gibbs sampling, 80, 159
GILT, 178
Global alignment, 47

HAART, 18
helper T lymphocytes, 157
Hemorrhagic flavivirus, 29
Henikoff sequence weighting, 77
Heterozygote advantage, 223
Hidden Markov model, 84
Highly active antiretroviral therapy, 18
HIV, 17, 56, 150
  polytope vaccine, 208
  Prediction of immunogenicity, 251
  variability, 213
HIV molecular immunology database,
  216
HLA, 111
  supertypes, 233
HLA Ligand/Motif Database, 216
HLA-A supertypes, 228
HLA-B Supertypes, 235
HLA-B supertypes, 228
HLA-DM, 179
HLA-DR, 158
HLA-DR supertypes, 237
HMM, 113
  forward-backward algorithm, 86
  Higher order models, 88

posterior decoding, 86
profile, 90
Hobohm algorithm, 77
Host-pathogen coevolution, 223, 224
HTL, 157
Human immunodeficiency virus, 18
Human leukocyte antigens, see also
    HLA, 111

IEDB, 216
Image processing, 104
IMGT, 221
Immune system, 1
    evolution of, 3
Immunity
    adaptive, 9
    innate, 9
Immunization
    passive, 207
Immunoglobulins, 187
Immunoproteasome, 137
Immunosubunits, 137
Innate immunity, 9
Integrative biology, 2
Interferon–Gamma Reducible Lysoso-
    mal Thiol Protease, 178
Invariant chain, 179

JenPep, 216

K-means, 107

Lentivirus, 18
Local alignment, 47
locus, 111
Log-odds ratio, 71
Logo, 73
LpPep, 218
Lymphocyte
    B, 9
    T, 9
        Cytotoxic, 111
Lysosomal Proteases
    Phylogeny, 180

Malaria, 17, 19

MAPPP, 219
Marburg virus, 30
Mathematical models
    MHC polymorphism, 224
Matthews correlation coefficient, 100
Measles, 21
MHC, 111
    clusters of binding specificities, 226
    functional difference, 225
    linkage disequilibrium, 225
    Polymorphism, 223
    population coverage, 226
    supertypes, 225
MHC class I
    pathway, 135
    presentation, 135
    structure of, 113
MHC class II, 13, 157
    binding prediction, 158
    structure of, 158
MHCPEP, 215
MHCpep, 161
MHCPred, 218
Microarray, 103
Mimivirus, 4
Monte Carlo
    move, 82
Multiple alignment, 52
Mumps, 21
Mutual information, 73, 121
Mycobacterium tuberculosis, 19

N-glycosylation, 184
Needleman-Wunsch, 41, 47
Neighbor-joining, 107
NetChop, 143, 147, 219
NetMHC, 218
Neural Network, see also ANN, 92
Neutralizing antibodies, 201
NN, see also ANN, 92
Nonself, 3
Null model, 71

Odds ratio, 71
Oligonucleotide chip, 104
Overdominance, 223

P. malariae, 19
PAM, 37
PAN, 38
PAProC, 147, 219
Pathogen, 4
PCA, 105
peptidase
    Asparaginyl Endopeptidase, 179
peptide
    promiscuous, 111
Percent identity, 37
Plague, 24
Polio, 21
Polymorphic, 111
Polymorphism
    MHC, 223
Population bottlenecks, 224
Position-specific scoring matrix, 52
Post-proteasomal processing, 150
Post-translational modification, 62
Posterior decoding, 86
PREDEPP, 218
Prediction
    B cell epitopes
            continuous, 192
            discontinuous, 199
    functional features, 61
    Immunogeneticity, 243
    integrative approach, 243
    MHC binding, 217
    neutralizing antibody binding site,
        201
    Proteasomal cleavage site, 218
    proteasome specificity, 143
    servers, 217
    specificity of AEP, 184
    specificity of cysteine endopepti-
        dases, 183
    specificity of lysosomal enzymes,
        182
    TAP specificity, 153
Prediction algorithm
    data-driven, 69
Prediction methods, 112
Prediction servers

BIMAS, 217
    Epipredict, 218
    LpPep, 218
    MAPPP, 219
    NetChop, 219
    NetMHC, 218
    PAProC, 219
    PREDEPP, 218
    ProPred, 218
    ProtFun, 62
    SYFPEITHI, 217
    Tappred, 220
Predictions
    Integrated, 220
    TAP Specificity, 220
Principal Component Analysis, 105
Probability matrix, 72
Probe, 104
Profile method, 54
ProPred, 218
Proteases
    Alanyl aminopeptidase N, 178
Proteasome, 135
    constitutive, 137
    evolution, 154
    immuno, 137
    specificity, 139
Proteasome specificity prediction, 143
Protein-protein interaction, 6
ProtFun, 62
Pseudocount, 160
Pseudocount correction, 77
PSI-BLAST, 51
PSSM, 52
PTM, 62

RAC, 22
Receiver operator characteristics, 100
Recombinant DNA
    advisory committee, 22
Relative entropy, 72
Repertoire
    antigen receptor, 11
Representative sets, 102
Respiratory infections, 21

Response
   cytotoxic T cell, 18
Retrovirus, 18
RG, 22
Risk group, 22
ROC curves, 100
Rubella, 21

Scoring matrix, 38
Self, 3
Sequence
   alignment, 37
   analysis, 35
   encoding, 98
   families, 35
   motifs, 69
   variation, 57
   weighting, 75
Sequence weighting, 161
Shannon entropy, 72
SIV, 225
Smallpox, 21, 24
Smith-Waterman, 47
Substitution
   nonsynonymous, 137
   synonymous, 137
Supertype, 111
   clustering method, 227
   Cross-loci, 236
   HLA-A, 228
   HLA-B, 228
Supertypes
   experimental verification, 239
   HLA, 233
   HLA-B, 235
   HLA-DR, 237
   MHC class I, 233, 235
   MHC class II, 237
SYFPEITHI, 112, 161
   database, 215
   prediction server, 217
Systems analysis, 6

T cells
   in germinal center reactions, 191
T-Coffee, 54

TAP, 89, 153
   evolution, 154
TAP specificity prediction, 153
Tapasin, 180
TB, 19
TEPITOPE, 218
Tetanus, 21
Theraphy
   cancer, 211
Threading, 114
Thymus, 12
TLR, 9, 36
Toll-like receptor, see also TLR, 9
Transition, 190
Transversion, 190
Tree, 57
   rooted, 57
   unrooted, 57
Tuberculosis, 17, 19
Tularemia, 29

UPGMA, 54, 106

Vaccination, 203
   history, 203
Vaccine, 24
Vaccines
   allergy, 211
   available, 205
   cancer, 211
   design, 207
   genetic, 206
   live, 204
   polytpe, 207
   subunit, 205
   therapeutic, 209
      for autoimmune diseases, 213
      for HIV, 212
      for persistent infections, 212
Vertebrate, 4
VHF, 29
Viral evolution, 57
Viral hemorrhagic fever, 29
Viterbi algorithm, 85

Web tools, see also prediction servers,
    215
Weight-matrix, 112, 160
  Training, 115
West Nile virus, 30
WHO, 17
Whooping cough, 21

Yellow fever, 29